EVOLUTIONARY INTELLIGENCE

EVOLUTIONARY INTELLIGENCE

The Anatomy of Human Survival

Rolf W. Frohlich

Copyright © 2004 by Rolf W. Frohlich

Library of Congress Number: 2005900248
ISBN : Hardcover 1-4134-0955-5
Softcover 1-4134-0954-7

All rights reserved. No part of this book may be reproduced or transmitted in any form or by any means, electronic or mechanical, including photocopying, recording, or by any information storage and retrieval system, without permission in writing from the copyright owner.

This book was printed in the United States of America.

To order additional copies of this book, contact:
Xlibris Corporation
1-888-795-4274
www.Xlibris.com
Orders@Xlibris.com
19096

My Family and Friends

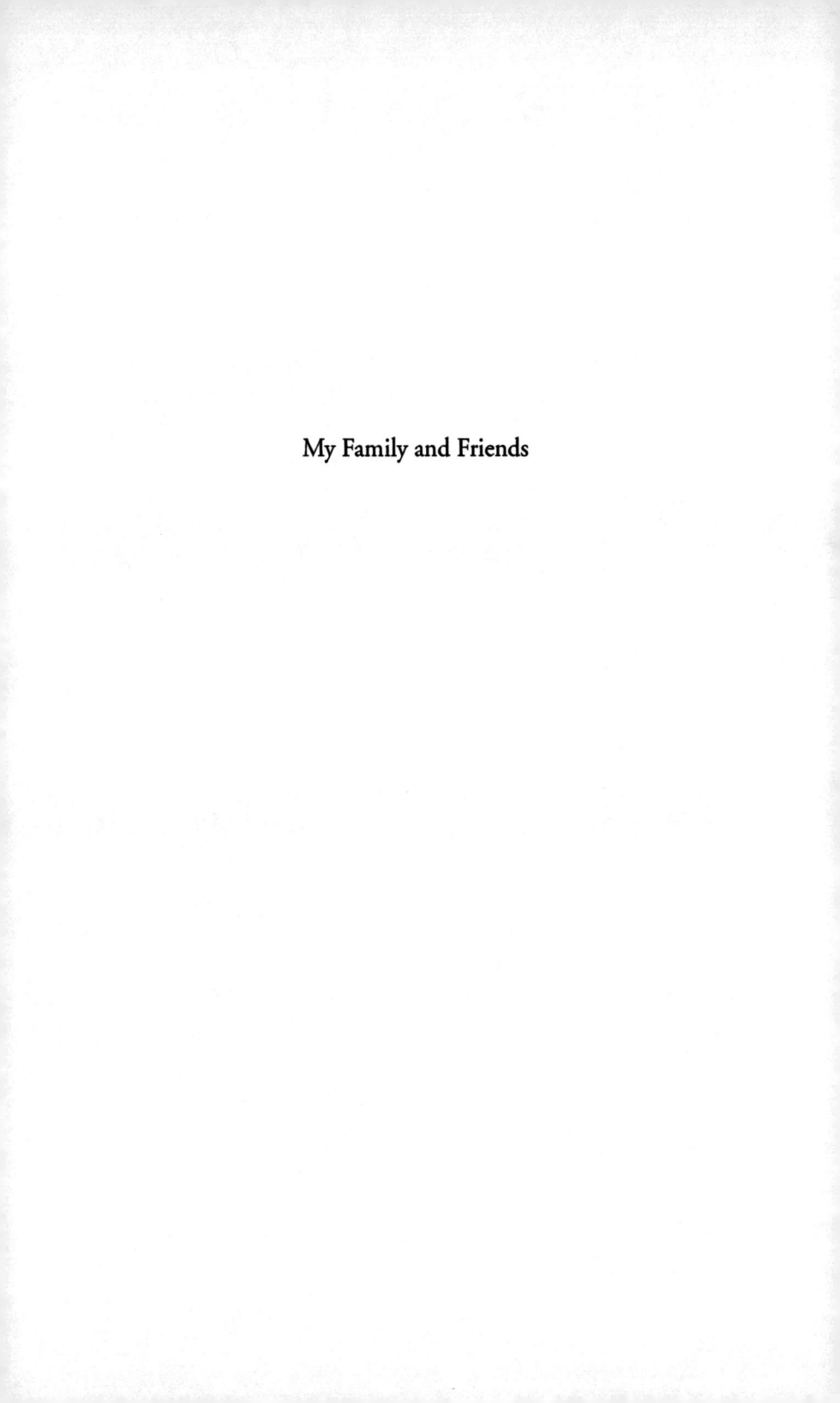

CONTENTS

Acknowledgements 11
Introduction 15
Note To The Reader 19

PART I

Chapter One
Discovering Human Nature 27
    The Essence of Human Nature 28
    Our Natural Psychology 29
    Worlds Apart 33
    The Natural History of Our Species 36
    The Natural Foundations of Human Life 39
    The Effects of Human Civilization 43
    The Ethics of Biology 46
    The Biological Reality of Life 48

Chapter Two
Evolutionary Functioning 54
    Ethological Behavior 58
    Biological Imperatives and Attitudes 69
    Biological Values 71
    Primary Sensations and Emotions 74
    Psychic Function 80

Chapter Three
Advanced Adaptive Functioning 88
    The Evolution of Higher Consciousness 90
    The Evolution of Advanced Morality 97

PART II

Chapter Four
Behavioral Adaptation 107
   Operating Life As a Business 109
   Family and Child-Rearing 116

Chapter Five
Mental Adaptation 123
   Marriage As a Biological and Spiritual Union 126
   Religious Attitude and Survival 133

Chapter Six
Personal Adaptation 142
   Survivor Personality 146
   Personal Evolution and Mythology 153

PART III

Chapter Seven
The Parameters Of Human Survival 170
   Survival Environment 170
   Survival Strategies 180
   Survival Skills 197
   Survival Scenarios 211
   Survival Frontiers 217

Chapter Eight
Recovering Human Nature 220
   The Survival Value of Human Nature 220
   Ten Steps to Recover Human Nature 227

Chapter Nine
The Way Of The Hunter 231
   Becoming a Hunter: The Journey into Life 232
   Being a Hunter: Mastery of Two Worlds 240
   The Hunter Within: The Essence of Power 242

EPILOG

Issues And Conclusions 259
    Evolutionary Intelligence 259
    Survival in The Modern World 277
    Discussion 285

APPENDIX

Notations For The Professional 299
    Scientific Epistemology 299
    The Neurology of Human Survival 301
    Adaptive Therapy 307
    Depression As a Case in Point 341
    The Normative Foundations of Biological Behavior ... 347
Glossary Of Terms 353
Notebook Of Evolutionary Functioning 355
Notes 359
Selected Bibliography 420

Acknowledgements

As young boys we used to camp near the site where Konrad Lorenz, the founder of modern ethology, did his research work on animal behavior in the natural world. There was a vivid curiosity about his work with geese and the man who 'talked to the animals'. His more popular books were common reading. Years later, I attended public lectures by Irenaeus Eibl-Eibesfeldt, his student, who continued the ethological research program at the Max-Planck-Institut near Starnberg outside of Munich and who transformed Lorenz's work with animals to establish the field of human ethology. The work of Carl G. Jung, the Swiss psychiatrist, has always been important to my outlook on life, both personally and professionally. His are among the most significant contributions to the fields of psychology and psychiatry in the 20th century. Influential also were the writings of Laurens van der Post on his African experience and his friendship with Jung. I had the good fortune to meet Joseph Campbell, the great mythologist and interpreter of the human experience, on several occasions during his Seattle lectures. His insights have significantly shaped my perception of life. I also want to acknowledge my indebtedness to the remarkable book by British psychiatrist Anthony Stevens, "Archetype: A Natural History of the Self", which has aided me to expand my understanding of Jungian psychology and its relationship to other disciplines. Last but not least, I want to thank my friends Morrene and Jonathan Nesvig, Jeri Kirkegaard, Judy Johnson, Courtney Adkins, Marianne Macdonald, Mary Ellen Lewis, and Jennifer Virant for copyediting the manuscript and their helpful suggestions in this process. My appreciation, too, goes to Judy Reynolds and Claudia McCormick for editorial contributions to earlier versions of the book material. Special thanks, also, to my friend Eric Haugen for providing art direction for the book.

If, starting from the condition of modern science, we try to find out where the bases have started to shift, we get the impression that it would not be too crude an oversimplification to say that for the first time in the course of history modern man on this earth now confronts himself alone, and that he no longer has partners or opponents . . . . In previous times man felt that he confronted nature alone. Nature populated by creatures of all kinds was a domain existing according to its own laws, to which he had somehow to adapt himself. In our age, however, we live in a world which man has changed so completely that in every sphere—whether we deal with the tools of daily life, whether we eat food which has been prepared by machines, or whether we travel in a countryside radically changed by man—we are always meeting man-made creations, so that in a sense we meet only ourselves. . . . It is obviously the task of our age to come to terms with this new situation in every sphere of life, for only when we have been able to do so will we recover that 'certainty in the strivings of the soul' of which the Chinese sage has spoken. The road to this goal will be long and painful, and we do not know what Stations of the Cross we have yet to encounter on it.

Werner Heisenberg

INTRODUCTION

According to ancient legend, the gods once pondered where to hide the true treasures of life to protect them from discovery and theft. They argued against ocean floors and mountaintops as hiding places. They even considered the center of the Earth and rejected it too. Finally, they decided to bury these treasures deep inside the human being, so that nobody would know and suspect where to look for them. We all carry within ourselves gifts beyond imagination—though they are mostly dormant and unknown.

The verification of these inner treasures and their existence came to me from a rather unexpected source. Through my work with suicide cases, I discovered that humans have innate powers and resources that sustain life and survival from within.

Our mental health clinic was across the street from the major city hospital. We received frequent referrals for people who had survived suicidal episodes and were now discharged from medical care. In therapy people related their feelings of guilt, anxiety, sadness and depression. They also revealed the inner dialogue that corroborated their mental status and the decision to end their lives.

I began to notice the socialized aspects of their personality and to understand how much these acquired instructions and injunctions constricted their psychological functioning, at times, with crippling effects. After that, therapy turned into a process of removing layer upon layer of social learning and cultural conditioning—not unlike peeling off the skins of an onion. Until one day, one moment, something remarkable happened, totally unexpected.

There was the emergence, first of energy, then power and vitality, paired with decisiveness and an intent for action—and with it, the will to live. At first, I did not realize what had happened.

Yet from patient to patient the same thing seemed to repeat itself. Finally, I began to understand that there is something strong and vital inside the person—much stronger and more vital than the psychology that had failed them before. Gradually, I began to suspect that there are innate forces that sustain the survival of the individual. Once this power and wisdom began to emerge, people changed. They started to trust themselves and develop confidence in the newly found strength inside.

My own psychological training had made me aware of the influence of socialization on personality formation and of the difference between natural, authentic expression and social adjustment and conformity. Interestingly, socialization seems to take the fight out of us—the strength we need to survive.

The discovery of innate features and capabilities brought back what I had read about human instincts and human survival behavior in the works of the European ethologists. This information coupled with Freud's concept of the life instinct began to shape a notion about the existence of an innate life force and survival capability we possess as a biological creature. The step from there to an interest in biological evolution and the evolutionary history of our species was short. My understanding of the origin and evolution of our species was deepened from travels to Kenya and Tanzania, and from my interest in anthropologist Louis Leakey's human fossil research and in Swiss psychiatrist Carl Jung's work on the human archetypes. My personal interest has been to distill this information into a useful behavioral and mental concept that can help people live stronger and more effective lives.

It is usually the human intellect that is given the limelight to take center stage. There is no language grand enough to overstate the achievements of the human mind. However, this book puts the spotlight on the innate biological intelligence of human nature. This is the unschooled wisdom of our instincts and intuition. Throughout the book, the intellect remains mainly backstage, and there will be occasional critical comments when it overreaches and becomes counterproductive. Yet, the issue of reviewing our internal faculties is not to take sides and to prefer one over the other. It is rather a matter of balance and of aligning the various sources of our inner strength to best advantage. However, the book itself is about becoming acquainted with the lesser known evolutionary side of ourselves and its value for our lives.

I am aware of the historical controversy surrounding human nature and human instincts. But I have also felt that there is room for new understanding. Most people still fear they will unleash a demon when they uncover their innate human nature. Consequently, they never get close to appreciating the gifts nature has embedded in the human psyche.

There is, however, a caveat. Originally, the instincts came with constraints to curb their vital forces. Since modern civilization has mostly overruled these natural inhibitions, we now need a further evolution—the evolution of higher consciousness and morality to provide the controls for the instincts that nature had originally installed. *This is both the opportunity and the challenge of human survival, both individually and as a species.*

Note To The Reader

I want this book to be relevant and readable. Because of the nature of the material, some sections needed to include theory and background information. These are mainly the Chapters 2, 3, 7. The reader who looks for quick information may want to skip those. A good fast track would most likely include Chapters 1, 8, 9. Chapters 4, 5, 6 provide practical applications; and the first section in the Epilog summarizes the chief ideas of the book. The leisurely reader will possibly enjoy additional information. The Chapters 2, 3 and the second section in the Notations for the Professional detail modern understanding of human nature, containing further research.

I have also included a glossary of the key terms used in the book as a reference for the reader. The notes for each chapter are located at the back of the book.

'Survival' affects us all, and what is said in the book applies both to men and women. To simplify understanding and language I have, for the most part, chosen to use the masculine personal pronoun in the generic sense to mean both genders.

PART I

Traveling with friends to Nairobi, Jung awoke as his train 'was just making a turn round a steep red cliff. On a jagged rock above us a slim, brownish-black figure stood motionless, leaning on a long spear, looking down at the train. Beside him towered a gigantic candelabrum cactus.

I was enchanted by this sight—it was a picture of something utterly alien and outside my experience, but on the other hand a most intense *sentiment du déjà vu*. I had the feeling that I had already experienced this moment and had always known this world which was separated from me only by distance in time. It was as if I were this moment returning to the land of my youth, and as if I knew that dark-skinned man who had been waiting for me for five thousand years.

The feeling-tone of this curious experience accompanied me throughout my whole journey through savage Africa . . . I could not guess what string within myself was plucked at the sight of that solitary dark hunter. I knew only that his world had been mine for countless millennia'.

Carl G. Jung

The history of the human species divides into two distinct sections. First, there was the long period of biological evolution. It ended about 35,000 years ago. This was followed by the relatively short period of the cultural evolution, which is still in progress. Natural and cultural history dovetail but stand separate. Anthropology and paleontology place the origin of our species at more than two million years ago. During its natural evolution, our species developed important physical, anatomical and behavioral features which shaped the biological constitution of the human being. Cultural evolution brought the intellectual, social, technological and artistic developments that would eventually form human civilization.

This book looks at the biological evolution of our species and what happened there. It also looks at the carry-over—the elements of this part of our history that are still relevant today. After all, the biological evolution of our species occupies more than 99% of human history. Cultural evolution, that is human civilization, only began approximately 10,000-12,000 years ago.

Modern science tells us that the lasting effects of natural evolution are not limited to the anatomy and physiology of the body. Human ethology and sociobiology have established that survival behaviors of early man have remained part of our genetic make-up and are still evident today. Jung and others have suggested that the entire survival experience of our species of over two million years had shaped a psychic constitution that remains active in the human mind to this day. In fact, C. G. Jung speaks of the "2 million year-old man that lives in all of us"[1].

Western civilization has had an ambivalent relationship to the natural evolution of our species and to nature in general. In fact,

23

the cultural evolution in the Western hemisphere was essentially designed to improve on nature rather than to complement it. Moreover, unlike Oriental cultures, Western civilization developed at the expense of nature.

Our appreciation of nature has been decidedly selective. We treasure nature in the outdoors, we like it in animals and we admire its miracles in our bodies. While we appreciate flowers and landscapes, and we marvel at the intricate workings of the human body, we stop short when it comes to our own nature. Here we suddenly find things wrong. We are conditioned to do so. Since the beginning of human civilization people were told to ignore their evolutionary origins. The assumption of man's likely descent from the animal loomed large over most of civilized history. The ascent of man was burdened by doubts about his past. Doubt was met with denial. During certain periods, human nature was demonized as evil and stigmatized with taboos. Western civilization forged the distinction between culture and nature to create distance between human creation and biological heritage. Culture was to take the place of nature.

Human culture has affected man's relationship to the natural world. Science took it upon itself to decode Nature's mysteries and technology to control her powers. Yet man has retained a humble respect for the awesome forces of Nature and a sense of wonder for her beauty. Nature continues to be a source of inspiration for many of us. By analogy, she gives us a sense of our own life. By comparison, she puts our life in perspective. As an experience, she connects us with our own nature. As an image of creation, she lifts our eyes to the realm of the universe and lets us sense the transcendent.

Human mythology has given Nature the attributes of 'mother' and 'teacher', making us 'children' and 'students' of her mysteries and powers. Ancient cultures considered the Earth as sacred—a place of events and memories. Everything was precious to them: the freshness of the air, the taste of the wind, the mist in the forest, every sandy beach, each animal and plant, the sky, the mountains and the sea[2]. The basic principle of archaic ritual and myth was to put man in accord with nature. Ancient peoples sought to confirm that all things were connected: that man was part of the earth and the earth part of him; that the harmony of Nature was the harmony of his own nature.

Before the advent of the scientific, technological age, nature was considered the measure of all things. Goethe maintained that 'nature is always right'. In days of the past, nature was credited with harmony, goodness and ultimate wisdom. It was revered as the cornucopia of plenty, the source of supply, the giver of life. Laudations of nature abounded, all concurring with Juvenal's observation—'never does nature say one thing and wisdom another'. The Stoic philosopher Xeno saw the goal of life as 'living in agreement with nature'. We have since veered from the reliance on nature. It is no longer the reference point as it was in the past. Now we give credence and approval to man-made creations. For instance, we are now at a point where we eat and drink synthetically, chemically produced foods, and where organically grown food needs to be certified for human consumption[3]. We have gone in the opposite direction. Compared to the past, we live in a world where things are reversed. We now need to certify what's natural.

Human nature is the product of the biological evolution of our species. It developed alongside the anatomy and physiology of the body. Human nature consists of behaviors, attitudes, abilities and values. It came into being during those millions of years when the species evolved and our ancestors survived as hunters and gatherers. The behaviors, attitudes, and abilities that comprise human nature are, therefore, relevant to survival. Like all other creatures on this planet, nature gave us the biological intelligence of life. It has prepared us for life, more than we think and more than we give it credit. Nature has given us an innate psychology that is meant for survival. We all have it. It is part of a shared biological and psychological history.

Somehow, we have deprived ourselves. By rejecting our own nature, we have rejected a large part of ourselves. The most essential features of our being are prehistoric, recorded in the DNA of our species. More than 99% of human history is etched into the psychic constitution of human nature. The poet Robert Bly and so many others have mourned the disappearance of 'the wild man', the silencing of the wilderness in us. But nature did not go away. The stirrings remain. All of us feel vestiges of that when we return from a weekend in the country to the rush and complexity of city life. Something in us rebels and mourns and pulls back. Facing survival in the modern world is stressful and hard. It is, therefore, no surprise that most deaths in our culture occur around 9 am on Monday mornings. It is at that juncture in time when both worlds come together each week for most of us.

Human nature should not need any introduction. It should be familiar to us. We owe it to ourselves to know our own nature. Understanding its make-up, functioning and usefulness is important to our lives. Knowing how human nature works provides grounding and strengthens our footing in life. Once we come to view human nature as a reliable resource that is there when we need it, we derive a sense of confidence and calm. To understand human nature is to understand one of the secrets of life.

Appreciation of nature does not mean rejection of culture. The objective is not to replace culture with nature, even though the reverse had been attempted in the past. The issue is to combine the two and complete the human evolution, integrating biology and consciousness. We want to add nature, while we keep culture. Culture consists of the uniquely human ability to invent new behaviors and to pass them along to succeeding generations. However, we certainly do not want to be a species that holds a taboo about its past—as if it were ashamed of itself.

Chapter One

Here—let there be no mistake—lies the great divide.

If the first men had been brutish, murderous, cannibalistic, if their rapacity had driven them to acts of extermination and conquest, then any State, by providing an umbrella of force, will have saved men from themselves and must, inevitably, be considered beneficial. Such a State must, however frightful for the individual, be counted a blessing. And any action by individuals to disrupt, weaken or threaten the State will be a step in the direction of primaeval chaos.

If, on the other hand, the first men themselves were humbled, harried, besieged, their communities few and fragmented, forever gazing at the horizon whence help might come, clinging to life and one another through the horrors of the night—might not all the specific attributes we call 'human'—language, song-making, food-sharing, gift-giving, intermarriage—this is to say, all the voluntary graces which bring equipoise to society, which suppress the use of force among its members; and which can only function smoothly if equivalence is the rule—might not all these have evolved as stratagems for survival, hammered out against tremendous odds, to avert the threat of extinction? Would they, therefore, be any less instinctual or directionless? Would not a general theory of defence explain more readily why offensive wars are, in the long run, unfightable? Why the bullies never win? . . . the idea that murder made man made no evolutionary sense.

Bruce Chatwin
Conversations with Konrad Lorenz

Discovering Human Nature

This book is about survival. It is about the ability of the individual to live in a complex, constantly changing world. Survival is the governing principle of life and determines most of what we do. Ultimately, life is about survival. Survival is defined as effective adaptation to life[1]. In essence, survival is about need fulfillment and the best means to achieve it. Our nature, as both physical and mental beings, determines our most fundamental needs, which are essentially material and spiritual in nature. Human survival is inextricably tied to the gratification of these needs.

Survival is an evolutionary response to life and its changing conditions[2]. At its hardest, survival is a reaction to crisis or catastrophe and, at its highest, it is the best and smartest way to live. The capacity to create maximum fit between individual and environment together with the ability to employ relevant strategies and skills to affect desired outcomes determine the survival capability of a person.

The Essence of Human Nature

Human nature is a biological entity designed for survival—a product of evolution. It was shaped during more than two million years of human history and contains the survival experience of our species[1]. Evolution has equipped humans, like any other species, with the necessary capability to survive. The evolutionary development of human nature involved the body as well as the psyche. The human brain, mainly the older midbrain, contains certain adaptive responses and life patterns which are specifically designed for survival.

Our history goes back to the time when our ancestors survived as hunters and gatherers. They confronted the forces of nature in search of shelter and food, and survival was the order of the day. It was then that our basic anatomy, behavior and psychology were formed. These features and abilities entered our genetic make-up and have stayed with us ever since. Like that of all other living organisms, our nature was formed by the adaptive forces of evolution. For that, we possess the same natural powers to adapt and survive that we admire in animals. Formed by evolutionary process, our nature holds the biological intelligence of life. Evolution shapes the organism for survival—by making sure that the organism is matched to its environment and its needs are met.

Evolution secured our survival and we made out rather well. Nature gave us a unique brain. Other species are bigger, stronger or faster. We, on the other hand, are smarter. Rather than developing the physical advantages of size, strength or speed, we started out with a larger, more capable brain. This added other advantages. All other forms of life are fixed to a particular environment or specific routine; we are not. In fact, the enlarged brain makes it possible to manipulate and change the environment. The evolution of other species concentrated primarily on the formation of body and anatomy. The demands on our survival were different. Relative size and lack of relevant physical features required additional capabilities. This made our evolution different from that of other species. Human survival depended foremost on the evolution of the brain rather than that of the body. Our specific survival advantage as a species lies, therefore, in our behavior and psychology—the human psyche.

Our Natural Psychology

Part One

Nature went to great lengths to perfect the human body. The same is true for the human psyche—that other less tangible aspect of our being. Both our body and our psyche are products of evolution. The psyche was molded and shaped much the same way as were our physical features. As it turns out, the human psyche is the sum total of our collective survival experience as a species.

While nature fitted other species with extra strength, size, or speed to survive, we were given a unique brain. Our survival advantage as a species stands on the abilities of a special brain and its psychology. Over two million years of evolutionary history have shaped this brain and this psychology to secure our survival.

What is this psychology made of that nature has designed for us? There are two sides to it. One enables us to secure our practical and material needs; the other makes it possible to meet our mental and spiritual needs. One is there for us to survive in the world; the other to survive life itself—as it comes without instruction, leverage or guarantee. The first we have in common with other mammals. We need the second because we are conscious of our existence and the universe around us.

Observing our pets or animals at the zoo, we often find that we are like them in many ways. Animals are concerned about territory—so are we. Like us, they tend to live in hierarchically organized groups; family and community are important to them. They use aggression to get what they need, yet the aggression has definite limitations set by the interests of the group and the perpetuation of the species. Animals, like humans, shrink from strangers and from danger. The behaviors we have in common with lions, bears, chimps and other mammals involve territory, hierarchy, sexuality, aggression and xenophobia. They are survival behaviors shaped by evolution to respond to these kinds of circumstances and conditions. These behaviors exist to ensure our survival. They enable us to get what we need and survive in the environment we live in. These behaviors form the biological part of our survival psychology. They provide for the practical needs of life as survival is always about "territory, resources and succession"[1].

What is so special about this psychology, which is very strong and useful, is the fact that it is *innate*. It's always there and always available when we need it. It is part of our genetic equipment. Our biological survival psychology, the behaviors and attitudes we need to make it in this world, originates in the older section of our brain—the midbrain. The genes bear the long survival history of our species. They reflect the fight against the environment and the struggle for food, shelter and family.

Now all of this is, of course, remote and forgotten history. Most of us are not even aware that those behaviors exist inside of us. And even though dormant and mostly unconscious, they are genetically present. The vestiges of our evolutionary past stir in us constantly:

- When somebody takes your seat or cuts into your lane of traffic—you sense it, the invasion of your territory.
- When somebody orders you around and tells you what to do—you sense it, the dominance forcing submission.
- When you meet a stranger, are out in the dark, or are threatened in any way—you sense it, the fear for fight or flight.
- When you see a woman or a man you want and desire— you sense it, the sexuality set to pursue.
- When you are hungry, hurt or desperate—you sense it, the aggression to change and improve your condition.

These are evolutionary behaviors—territorial, hierarchical, xenophobic, sexual and aggressive—wired into our brain. These biological behaviors evolved to provide humans with livelihood, shelter, family, community and territorial defense. Their biological purpose was to secure material survival. This purpose has remained unchanged and is still there today. Whenever our life and survival are at stake, this ancient psychology goes to work.

Part Two

Then there is this other side of us and of life where things are quite different. Here we are alone. No other creature goes there. This is the realm of consciousness, cosmos and universe. Here we are forced into the major leagues. Here we are exposed to circumstances, forces and laws that are not of our making and beyond our control. Here we are dealing with higher dimensions and the inexorable facts of destiny, disease, disaster and death. Human life is as much a mental as it is a physical event.

We are housed in a three-dimensional world measured by our senses, yet we live on the boundary of a larger universe that sets the laws for our existence. In the end, human life is an event that comes without instruction, leverage or guarantee.

Given these odds, it seems as if we don't have much to work with. This is where the psyche comes in. Our psyche, this depository of the human survival experience from the beginning, has developed capabilities to bring down this handicap. It has given us the ability to face the unknown, preserve our sanity, and cope with the flux and the fear of life.

Here again, nature has come through for us. It has given us, what Jung called, the ability to maintain psychic balance and coherence of our world. Mental survival depends upon our ability to keep on living and functioning when things are difficult, overwhelming, even incomprehensible. Evolution has shaped the human psyche in such a way that allows us to adapt to the circumstances and demands of life.

Mental adaptation is an inborn, genetic ability and originates in the midbrain. It also involves other parts of the brain that provide concepts, vision and memory. Together, innate ability and mental concept make up our survival consciousness. We use it much like a picture frame to look at our life and all that's happening, trying to make sense of it all. When events and experiences go beyond what we can handle, this conceptual frame—often fashioned by religion, science, philosophy or a personal spirituality—breaks, and we have to develop a new one. The ability for psychic adaptation allows us to address the mental, emotional and spiritual repercussions of life. It helps us to overcome difficult events and recover from crisis and disaster. And, on a wider scale, it enables us to function within the context of a larger macrocosm, to cope with laws, forces and events we do not control, and to go on living in the face of unpredictable and incomprehensible circumstances. Here, too, we have a genetic psychology that kicks in whenever we need it. Without it, we would not even be able to get out of bed and live our lives.

We are all genetically programmed to survive. We are born with a biological intelligence that contains the full adaptive and therapeutic powers of nature. If our innate survival behavior, geared to secure our material needs, represents the level of the instinct, then the psychic ability to maintain a sense of balance and coherence operates on a spiritual level. Nature has provided us with a psychology, an evolutionary intelligence, that reaches from instinct to spirit superbly matched to the duality of the human existence between a physical world and a metaphysical cosmos.

Worlds Apart

What all the human brain is capable of is often rather elusive. We use it to speak, think, sense, feel and remember, to execute movement and to perform similar functions. Beyond that things can become quite fuzzy. Even comparing the brain to a computer does not help much unless we know the software and what it can do.

Intellect and instinct are two of the major players of the human brain. They belong to separate parts of the brain and operate different psychologies. The instinct and the intellect provide separate sets of behaviors and ways of operating. They are both useful; each in its own way.

We owe our brain to our ancestors. Their experiences and endeavors shaped the brain we have today. Our instincts developed during the hunting period of our species when man was exposed to the forces of nature and the threat of the animal. The instincts formed in response to the living conditions our ancestors faced while securing food and shelter and coping with the unpredictable forces and events of their lives. The instincts were honed in the long history of biological adaptation to the environment and have since become part of our genetic make-up. The psychology of the instincts consists of a set of survival behaviors, along with an ability for mental adaptation. Our inborn psychology is lodged permanently in the older brain. Hunting, as the essential goal-oriented activity, remains the 'master behavior pattern' of the species and our most fundamental psychology. Its purpose is adaptation and survival.

The intellect is a later development. It is part of the newer brain that made it possible to develop language, social organization, artifacts and weapons, and most importantly to manipulate the environment. The refinement of the intellect parallels the history of human civilization. Its mainstay is the capacity for rational knowledge and innovation. In contrast to the instinct, the psychology of the intellect is not innate. It needs to be acquired and learned. The learning occurs during the process of socialization. It conditions us to function in society. It transforms the individual into a member of the group. The psychology of the intellect consists of a set of rational behaviors and responses that are socially compatible. We learn how to act, think, feel and get along with each other from society. Socialized or culturally conditioned psychology is a medium to facilitate social conduct and to reinforce the integrity of the community. Its purpose is adjustment and conformity.

The innate psychology of the instincts has biological origins and is lodged in the midsection of the older brain. It enables adaptation and evolutionary functioning. The acquired psychology of the intellect reflects the influence of the social and cultural environment. It operates from the newer brain, primarily the left brain hemisphere, and facilitates adjustment and cognitive functioning.

Why is this important and how can understanding how the brain works improve our lives? The answer to these questions refers to the fact that instinct and intellect connect us with different realities.

Our natural psychology relates us to our own nature as the source that contains the evolutionary experience of our species and the universal elements of human life. The ancient hunter lives on in us as our natural self. In that, our innate psychology connects us with the biology of survival. Our world may have shifted from the savannah to the skyscraper but survival is still essentially biological. Human society itself is based on the biological model found in nature. We mark power and rank with symbols of position and status. We protect our territory and resources with fences and laws. As a survival environment society has a definite biological quality. Our inborn psychology also resonates with the phases and events of the natural life cycle between birth and death which human life is subject to. Here it connects us with needs, values and experiences essential to the completion of a meaningful life.

The intellect is the driving force behind human civilization. Culture began approximately 10,000 years ago and after the biological evolution of our species was concluded. It started as the attempt to make survival more predictable by growing crops and domesticating animals. While the instinct responds to an existing environment, the intellect is capable of creating its own. It is safe to say that our world of urban existence is an extension of the rational mind. The psychology of the intellect matches the fabric of modern life, a world firmly grounded in science and technology. This psychology enables us to function within the rational, instrumental environment of society. The cultural standards promoted by the intellect emphasize the social and functional value of the individual. Human life is redefined by an *industrial life cycle* that starts with school and ends with retirement. Social conditioning provides us with the necessary psychology to interface and cope with the conditions of our man-made environment.

The bases have shifted. For most of its existence, about two million years or 99% of its history, our species lived as hunters and gatherers. Since then we have invented a new reality. Civilization replaced the wilderness. We no longer confront nature and adapt to its laws. Culture is a human creation—an environment separate from nature. Ours is a world within a world, disconnected from the larger realities of nature and cosmos which surround it. Civilization replaced the values of nature with values of its own based on rationality and innovation. We now live in a world, which we have 'changed so completely' that we are dissociated from nature and all other species.

In the larger scheme of things, human survival happens on two frontiers: biology and metaphysics. If we include intuition as the mental and spiritual extension of the instincts, we can say, that our innate psychology relates us to the world of nature and cosmos. Instinct connects us to biology and the gratification of our material needs, intuition to metaphysics and the spiritual mastery of life. For instrumental survival, within the context of modern society, we depend on the intellect to function in the social and occupational aspects of our lives. Instinct, intuition and intellect together give us the means and necessary psychology to meet all the demands of life. Modern neurology now speaks of four brains in one—old and new, left and right—each with its own intelligence. Optimal survival depends on utilizing the entire brain. Surprisingly, this is less an issue of accessing millions and millions of cells than a matter of using all parts of our brain.

The Natural History of Our Species

Nature puts a definite emphasis on reality. It only allows what works in the real world. Survival is the governing principle determining the structure and functioning of all living organisms[1]. Adaptation equips the organism with a repertoire of behaviors to respond to its particular environment. It optimizes the survival capacity, the need gratification, the life expectancy and successive procreation of the organism and its progeny. Adaptation aims to establish maximum fit between the organism and its environment. Evolution screens strategy and fit for survival. It validates the effectiveness and survival value of the adaptation. Evolution is the most rigorous test of reality. What passes that inspection can survive in the real world.,

For 99% of his history, man lived as a hunter[2]. It was during this period, when man confronted the forces of nature and the cunning of the animal, that our survival experience was founded and our basic anatomy, behavior and psychology were formed. Man's biological evolution was concluded before civilization began. Culture is the creation of mankind during the last 10,000 years of its history. Originally introduced as agriculture, it was designed to regulate human survival by settling, growing crops and domesticating animals. From there began the meteoric ascent of civilization that took mankind from a nomadic past to the technological achievements of modern day. All this happened in a comparatively short time, totaling less then 1% of human history.

For most of his history, man survived as a hunter. The human survival instinct manifests in the hunting way of life. *"Hunting is the master behavior pattern of the human species. It is the organizing activity which integrated the morphological, physiological, genetic, and intellectual aspects of the individual human organism and of the population who compose our single species. Hunting is a way of life, not simply a 'subsistence technique', which importantly involves commitments, correlates, and consequences spanning the entire biobehavioral continuum of the individual and of the entire species of which he is a member . . . Hunting is an active process which puts motion and direction into the diagram of man's morphology, technology, social organization, and ecological relations. Hunting involves goals and motivations for which intricate inhibition systems have been developed. Hunting has placed a premium upon inventiveness, upon problem solving, and has imposed a real penalty for failure to solve the problem. Therefore it has contributed as much to advancing the human species as to holding it together within the confines of a single variable species."*[3]

Hunting is a deliberately strategic approach to life and survival. Over the millions of years during which man evolved as a hunter, this behavioral system remained universal and stable. Hunting belongs to the category of inborn, instinctive behaviors that do not have to be learned. As an inherited behavioral pattern, it is a genetic program contained in the genome structure of the species and located in the older section of the human brain. As part of the organic structure, it is contained in our biology and permanently available for our survival.

The hunting way of life consists of five particular adaptations:

- The behavior pattern is governed by a genetic program causing goal-directed behavior;
- it is based on a conscious behavior strategy supported by generalized skills to facilitate goal achievement;
- it is field-independent and makes selective use of the environment, retaining control of opposite external conditions;
- it constitutes social organization through language, communal activity, food sharing, inhibition of aggression, mating, child-rearing and screening contacts with the outside;

- and it incorporates a pragmatic view of life with a close eye on reality and results.

Human nature is a product of evolution. The basic nature of our species developed during that period of our history when man was a hunter. It is a nature geared for survival. Body and mind were shaped by evolution. This basic biology of anatomy, behavior and psyche differentiates us from other creatures and gives us our unique survival advantage. "Evolution builds a relation between biology, psychology and behavior, and, therefore, the evolutionary success of hunting exerted a profound effect on human psychology."[4] The distinct survival advantage of the human being rests on the evolutionary psychology and behavior achieved by our species.

Survival involves biologically relevant behavior. Survival aims at need gratification and is always about "territory, resources and succession"[5]. It is about our fundamental needs for security, food and shelter, family and community. Man's basic adaptive pattern evolved to secure satisfaction of these needs. At the core, human behavior is, thus, about property and boundary, competition and aggression, dominance and submission, sexuality and succession, friend and foe. The natural history of the human species consistently shows "that we are innately territorial, inclined to mate for life, potentially cooperative with allies and hostile to foes, prone to congregate in hierarchically organized communities and so on, much in the same way as many other mammalian and primate species"[6]. This core of instinctive, biological behavior is central to human survival. To ensure our survival and to have what we need, nature has equipped us to be territorial, hierarchical, aggressive, sexual and xenophobic—providing a set of innate behaviors to respond to the environment. All are adaptive responses of the evolutionary psyche, relevant to human survival and the preservation of the species.

Survival further includes the biologically relevant occurrences of life. They extend evolutionary adaptation to the human life cycle and amplify the genetic program which secures our survival. The primal events and experiences of life—"being born, forming attachments, gaining initiation into the adult state, courting, mating and rearing children, collective bonding by males for the purposes of hunting and interspecific conflict, and dying"[7]—are all subject to control by the human psyche. These events and experiences unfold the progression of human life, structure individual development, and provide the basis for the satisfaction of human needs throughout the course of life.

Survival is the conditioning event of human nature. Anything relevant to our survival is preformed in the human psyche. Biologically relevant behaviors and occurrences form the rudimentary psychology of our species. This evolutionary psyche is at the core of human nature.

The Natural Foundations of Human Life

The human psyche contains the collective survival experience of our species: "Endless repetition has engraved these experiences into our psychic constitution"[1]. The evolution of the human species is not only reflected in the sequential formation of the human brain[2] but also in the genetic manifestations of a common biological and psychological history. The basic psyche is a collective psyche, common to all of us, not a personal acquisition. We all inherit the same psyche[3]. It is in this sense that, says Jung, "every individual life is at the same time the eternal life of the species"[4]. Like the human anatomy, the psyche is a biological entity and subject to the laws of evolution. Tempered by the experience of survival, it evolved through natural selection. This inborn psychic structure forms the essential nature of the human being. It also provides the basic blueprint for human life.

Referring to the universal, genetic elements of the human psyche, Jung introduced the term 'archetype'. This is an important concept to understand. Jung viewed archetypes as genetic predispositions of behavior and consciousness—as the common ground of the human experience. Human ethology and sociobiology have long since confirmed the existence of archetypal structures as the basis of human life.

Archetypes refer to universal elements of human life, common to all people everywhere throughout history. The archetypes are genetic structures encoded in the midsection of the brain. They contain the innate bio-program that instigates and determines the biologically important experiences and events in a person's life[5]. Jung defined the archetype as "an inherited mode of functioning, corresponding to the inborn way in which the chick emerges from the egg"[6]. Archetypes determine the fabric of human existence, prompting the significant stages and needs of human life. The archetypal structure of the evolutionary psyche is the genetic blueprint according to which human life unfolds. As in the living stuff of the plant, there is something in man "that represents the natural configuration of the whole, as a norm to which its growth conforms"[7]. The primal events and experiences of life—"being parented, exploring the environment, distinguishing familiar figures from strange, learning the language or dialect of one's community, acquiring knowledge of its values, rules, and beliefs, playing in the peer group, meeting the challenges of puberty and adolescence, being initiated into the adult group, accomplishing courtship and marriage, and child-rearing, contributing to the economy through gathering and hunting, participating in religious rituals and ceremonials, assuming the responsibilities of advanced maturity, old age, and preparation for death"[8]—are all coordinated and controlled by the human archetypes. The archetypal blueprint contains the complete scenario of the human life cycle. The archetypes are our tie to biology, nature and life.

The archetypes "evolved in adaptation to outer reality"[9], shaping not only the behavioral response but also the subjective experience. The archetypes of the collective human psyche furnish the innate capabilities for successful adaptation to the world around us. The archetypes, according to Jung, provide the innate bio-program "to meet all the exigent demands of life"[10]. The adaptation provided by the archetypes is twofold: behavioral and mental. Jung noted the dual nature of the archetypes, underscoring that human events involve behavioral responses as well as the psychological experiences associated with them. He understood the archetype as "the common origin of both behavioural and psychic events"[11]. Jung saw the archetypes as genetic predispositions of universal human events and experiences operating from the deepest biological recesses of the adaptive psyche as *systems of readiness for action* and equally as symbolic systems of experiences and emotions[12]. He maintained that archetypes manifest in the fundamental duality of instinct and spirit[13]. The instinctive component of the archetype activates as objective behavior. The psychic or 'spiritual' aspect "finds symbolic expression in consciousness"[14].

The behavioral manifestations of the archetypes circumscribe all the biologically and psychologically relevant activities related to livelihood and physical well-being, family, space, security, community, myth and religion, economics and defense, mating and procreation. The symbolic expressions of the human archetypes are to be found in our fantasies, images, and dreams and, on a larger scale, in the myths and symbols of mankind. As part of the collective human psyche, the archetypes are expressed in the universal themes of folklore, literature, and art of both primitive and modern cultures[15]. These symbolic representations reflect "the inner, unconscious drama of the human psyche"[16]—the story of Everyman. They record the ordeals, travails, and triumphs of the hero symbolizing the life of the individual.

The archetypes are biological entities and constitute a genetic survival program. Archetypes are both "conscious and unconscious"[17] but not under the control of reason or will. They are activated by significant stimuli that prescribe survival behavior. Each archetype is released by a specific stimulus. The territorial archetype, for instance, asserts dominance related to property and procreation; the mother archetype creates attachment between mother and the newborn child; and the contra-sexual archetype mediates sexual relationships when people fall in love. Activated, the archetypes take over and we come under the force of their influence. The power of this experience will release the biobehavioral program contained in the archetype. The organic relevance of these inborn mechanisms is to promote life and survival. Our conscious efforts to live and survive rest on a powerful natural foundation.

Our rudimentary nature is set up and wired for survival. The archetypes cover all aspects of life. Jung believed that there are as many archetypes as there are human situations.

The archetypes provide the basis for behavioral and mental adaptation. They form the biological foundation of the human experience. The different aspects of the archetype, instinct and spirit, relate us to different domains of our existence—the domain of biology and nature and the realm of consciousness and cosmos. From these connections emerges the larger configuration of human life, spanning biology and metaphysics. The archetypes of the human psyche correspond to outer realities, perfectly matched to the context within which it exists.

This leaves the intellect and the world we have created. As part of the newer brain, the intellect lacks the biological base of adaptive capability provided by the evolutionary psyche. The manmade world itself, where we spend so much of our time unaware of the larger context of natural and cosmic realities that surrounds it, is an extension of the human intellect. It originated in relatively recent history and after the conclusion of the natural evolution of our species. The world of culture and society is an invented reality, essentially a world within a world, yet unable to shield against the laws and forces that penetrate it from outside and affect our existence in absolute terms. Within this world we invent our own survival scenarios[18]—giving them descriptions such as 'war zone', 'battlefield', 'jungle', 'supermarket', or 'pastures of milk and honey'—forgetting that the reality of survival is essentially determined by biology, and that individual destiny is inextricably interwoven with extramundane influences beyond human control.

The ultimate objective for the invention of an additional world was to increase the level of existential control. As it turns out, however, even in our own man-made world we do have little control over things after all: material survival is still controlled by biology and human destiny is still affected by cosmic law. In fact, our ability to understand and determine the events of our lives is limited in time and space to a small range of decisions and activities. Many of these do not go beyond the next day or the people around us.

Instinct and spirit, the two aspects of the primary psyche, carry with them the evolutionary history of human survival. They provide the biological foundation for human adaptation and relate us to the archetypal reality of life. The intellect is a later addition to the human experience providing the instrumental capacity to shape the environment. Instinct and spirit are the two basic poles of human existence, with the conscious mind as a powerful third party and ally.

We often mistake the intellect for our foremost strength, but it is not embedded in the process of life and without the same backing by biological evolution as are instinct and spirit. There is a generic, universal reality to life (*bios*), woven into it like an invisible tapestry, which is replicated in the archetypes of the human psyche[19] as a result of evolutionary process. This correspondence of outer and inner life ordains the archetypes as the principal agents of human adaptation. As genetic predispositions of behavior and consciousness, the archetypes are something we are born with and already have.

The human psyche is the result of evolutionary adaptation. The archetypes of the evolutionary psyche provide the essential adaptation for human life. However, "since the archetypes evolved to equip us for the hunter/gatherer existence in which our species has lived out 99 per cent of its existence, the archetypal programme equips us for a life which is not always in tune with the life of contemporary urban society"[20]. The adaptation to the contemporary environment with regard to personality, behavior and skills is mainly social and instrumental. This adaptation, which enables the interface with modern society, is driven by the 'social' or 'conformity' archetype[21]. This process begins in childhood. It is motivated by the necessity to function in the modern world. Children are taught early on how to behave, how to relate, what they need to know, and what they must be able to do.

The Effects of Human Civilization

Culture is the creation of mankind during the last 10,000 to 12,000 years. Originally introduced as agriculture, it was designed to optimize human survival by settling, growing crops and domesticating animals. From there began the meteoric ascent, which took mankind from a nomadic past to the urban existence of today.

Modern civilization has dramatically altered the human condition. Unlike other civilizations, Western culture developed at the expense of nature. Cultural evolution was designed to improve on nature. Civilization rejected man's evolutionary nature just as it set out to control and dominate the natural world. We have come "to view nature as something to be 'mastered'"[1], shaped, and controlled. Likewise, cultural conditioning aimed to repress and replace human nature with a psychology of its own. Culture has tamed and domesticated the human being like the animal before him. As a culture we have systematically attempted to distance ourselves from our biological past. In rejecting our inherent nature, we also refuted its biological wisdom. Thus we have come to exchange evolutionary functioning for conditioned behavior, archetypal for societal values. On an even larger scale, we have replaced the natural environment with a man-made world in which 'we meet only ourselves' and our own creations. In essence, we instigated our own evolution, trying to outdo nature and to undo whatever it had developed in us.

Civilization, however, did not come without a price. The cultural rejection of our biological nature has inflicted an *instinctual wound* in the human psyche, which has affected our basic trust in the process of life and our overall ability to function in the world. As a result we have lost the instinctive confidence in our ability to fulfill our needs. The *instinctual wound* has severed us from our biological origins and from the forces nature provides for life and survival. Additionally, Western religious and scientific traditions have established a concept of reality and life, which sets us apart from the rest of organic and inorganic life separate from the universe and any higher cosmic order. We have taken ourselves out of the loop of nature and cosmos. We feel separate and we feel afraid. The loss of unity with all creation has forced a *spiritual wound* and driven a deep rift into human existence. It has broken the coherence of our world and the relationship to a larger context of being. The *spiritual wound* has destroyed the trust in the universe to provide for our needs—as it does for all other forms of life.

What had taken our species several million years to develop was quickly overturned. The evolutionary psyche and its innate survival capacity would be replaced by a culturally conditioned psychology, suppressing instinct and spirit and simultaneously overriding the archetypal foundations of human life. The rejection of biological evolution and of our natural self has inadvertently extended the domestication of the animal to the human being itself, setting off a neurobehavioral trauma whose repercussions reverberate deeply in our psyche. On an even more profound level, we have lost the instinctive 'certainty in the strivings of the soul' and the sense of belonging to life. Its instincts assure the animal that there will always be prey and the necessary food to survive. We, however, fret about tomorrow (Matthew, 6:25-34). Despite the abundance of the universe, as a species we remain weak, worried and wanting.

These wounds have profoundly shaped the human experience. They incite both a sense of vulnerability and agitation, which so deeply characterize our daily lives as well as the fabric of modern civilization in its insatiable quest for answers and a restlessness that can never be satisfied. In all this there is a need for healing and therapy. Healing the *instinctual wound* restores the innate capability and confidence to fulfill our needs. Healing the *spiritual wound* restores the sense of connection and belonging to a larger order as the source of supply for our needs.

Through civilization man has sought to reinvent himself. And in many ways he has done so, often, however, at the expense of nature. The harmony between culture and nature has never been found. The fact of this imbalance has profoundly affected human psychology and functioning. Like it did for the animal, evolution has given us the means to fend for ourselves. Culture has refuted nature and its powers, staging an evolution of its own. The process has compromised and weakened our survival position because biological behavior is always stronger than learned behavior, and biological values are always more durable than social ones.

All this, in face of the fact that survival has remained unchanged. It is no less intense, rigorous and, at times, fierce in today's world than it was when man fought the forces of nature and the threat of the animal. In this context it needs to be remembered that survival is always structured by biology—in nature as in society, whether in our political, financial and communal institutions or in the events of our daily lives. Evolution is rigorous and unforgiving.

The Ethics of Biology

Western civilization has been critical of human nature since its inception. The human instincts, especially, have had a rough going throughout civilized history. References to the evil and bestiality of human nature were common. Human aggression and sexuality were usually singled out as the most deviant aspects of our instinctual nature. We hear the same accusations in today's language. The daily media reports about violence in our streets, schools, and society everywhere link this violence to something deep inside of us. The blame for any excesses of human behavior usually goes to our inherent nature. Violence and cruelty are considered to be inborn traits. Somehow we are made to assume that there is a brute beast within us that needs to be tamed and exorcised. This demonization of human nature has a long history mainly under the direction of political and religious thought. It has convinced us that we need civilization to protect us from ourselves.

The facts, however, don't bear this out. There is an ethic in biology. It safeguards community, territory, property, and, foremost, it protects life and the continuation of the species. Human nature is a biological entity designed for survival, honed by successive adaptation. Survival required effective responses to the environment. This is how we acquired our instincts. The instincts are survival behaviors and as such life-enhancing and life-preserving. They are designed to promote the existence of the individual and that of the group in which he lives, calibrated to mediate between individual and collective interests. The biology of behavior is regulated. Since the instincts evolved to support the life of individual and community, they are vested with rules and inhibitions. These serve to curb and control non-adaptive deviations of instinctual behavior. The intent of biological norms is the preservation of the species.

Biological norms relate to specific aspects of existence and prescribe conduct. The ethics of biology center primarily on the protection of life, property and community. Foremost are (1) the inhibition against killing, (2) the norms controlling the possession of objects and (3) norms sanctioning the possession of the partner[1]. These biological norms further imply a desire for peace, respect for the property of others, and a regard for honesty, loyalty and obedience. All these human behaviors and attitudes have biological origins[2]. In its biological state, human nature is neither violent, cruel nor brute. Like the animal, it is bound to the biological imperative to further life and survival.

The change came with civilization. It affected the balance of human nature. Most significant was the invention of gunpowder and firearms. It removed the natural inhibition to kill, which depends on close physical proximity and certain body language like smile and displays of deference. The use of firearms, which allows killing over great distance, eliminates these biological inhibitors and turns killing into an anonymous act. But there was an even more insidious and far-reaching invasion of human nature by man. It set up the infamous pairing between intellect and aggression. Ever since, man has used his innate aggression as a destructive force. As a species we have spent more ingenuity on designing methods of torture and destruction than on those of love and compassion. In fact, most of civilized human history is a seamless succession of wars, torture, devastation, cruelties and destruction instigated by the intellect. All this is the work of the left brain—the human neocortex. It has nothing to do with the natural aggression of the instinct needed to survive. Cruelty and violence come from the mind not from the instincts. The instinct has been diverted from its original purpose and enlisted for our left-brain inventions to harm, torture and kill. A. Koestler has called the combination of intellect and instinct the fateful invention of our species. As a result of this 'inadequate co-ordination' between "the 'rational' neocortex and the 'instinctual' hypothalamus", we have somehow acquired a 'unique, murderous, delusional streak'[3]. Culture has corrupted the human instincts, overturned their normative foundations and joined them with the intellect. It has brutalized human nature[4].

Violence is not biological in origin. Its roots are in society and culture. The medieval torture chamber remains a vivid symbol of the ingenuity of human cruelty. Violence is acquired and learned. Today, the media, the music, the video and film industries, not to mention a mighty military with its massive machinery of war and destruction, incubate us with new versions of human violence and devastation. Our children receive violence training on a daily basis. It commonly comes in the form of wanton, frivolous violence without consequence and moral reference.

Cultural evolution in the West was persistently motivated by the ambition to improve on nature—nature on the outside as well as on the inside. This is also how we tended to lose our bearings. By corrupting the balance and biological intent, nature ordains on life, we forfeited our own sense of relevance and proportion. The sin of modern man is against nature. Man's rejection and violation of nature is the hubris of the modern age. It haunts us in the divorce and bankruptcy courts, psychiatric offices and confession booths, in the crime rates, poverty statistics, military budgets, ecological disasters, and political conflicts, which make up the symptomatology of a world out of sync with itself. We have succeeded in putting great distance between our life and our past—not always to our advantage.

The Biological Reality of Life

Hungry wolf cubs feeding at their mother's breast claw and scramble all over each other to get what they need. Naturally aggressive, they fight to survive. The ones that get to the top get the most. Once that first surge of satisfaction is felt, they are lost in the euphoric swirl of life, drinking in all those sweet milky juices. Satiated and content, they curl up with their siblings and sleep.

The runt cub stepped over, nipped and snarled at is left behind. Instead of applying its inborn rooting instinct, it weakens and denies its own needs. It gives up, displays defeat and goes hungry. Submission is signaled by a whimpering cry and deferential gesture, cowering in a depressed almost fetal position. Withdrawal is demonstrated by moving away from the center of action to the periphery of life.

It has now become an onlooker. Waiting. Watching. It foretells its own death.

The gripping elements of this scenario carry significant implications for survival behavior in humans. Survival can be a reaction to crisis and catastrophe or an effective response to the needs and demands of life. We survive the way we live. Need fulfillment stands at the core of survival. Success or failure in these efforts depends on our survival capability.

Observing animals opens up the biological reality of life. When we watch animals as they feed, drink, hunt or mate, comparisons to our own survival experience emerge. Biology shifts the perception to things that are important to our survival.

Usually, we refer to animals as objects of curiosity, forgetting that there is an analogous reality that determines our own lives. Cultural conditioning, however, has taken us in a different direction. It has closed off this realization. Instead, we are taught a psychology based on social behavior and cultural norms. It is designed to replace the innate survival psychology provided by nature. The learning process begins at birth. The new psychology, which uses the understanding of the intellect, sits in the left brain and is cognitive. It is a culturally conditioned psychology. It ignores biology and denies human instinct and intuition. This socialized psychology does two things: It screens out the biological aspect of our experiences and needs, and it blunts our innate survival capabilities. Through it we understand our life and our world in social and cultural terms, no longer biologically. Through it we are cut off from our evolution and biology. Cultural attitudes lead us away from the importance of human nature and its demands on our life. Socialization conceals the biological aspect of our existence. This leads us to underestimate the biological implications of human situations, and we fall short in getting what we need.

However, we actually do live in a biological world as part of the larger design of nature and evolution. In it things happen that are crucial to our survival. All the significant occurrences of life—being parented, "exploring the environment, playing in the peer group, adolescence, being initiated, establishing a place in the social hierarchy, courting, marrying, child-rearing, hunting, gathering, fighting, participating in religious rituals, assuming the social responsibilities of advanced maturity, and preparation for death"[1]—are biologically determined and carry survival value. These occurrences involve archetypal needs, universal to our species and essential to our survival: the physical need for food, warmth and shelter; the need for family, parents and peers; the need for community, initiation and identification; the need for language and communication; the need for home and belonging; the need for myth, religion, rituals, codes, values and rules; the economic need for hunting, gathering, and defense against warfare; and the need for a mate, children and a family of our own. Therefore, when it comes to making money, selecting a mate, child-rearing, providing for family and community, we are engaged in matters of biology.

Konrad Lorenz, known as the father of modern ethology, first referred to the biobehavioral adaptation involved in survival as ethological behavior[2]. Ethology is the study of biological behavior in animals and humans in relation to the environment[3]. This is also an important concept to understand. Ethology draws our attention to innate traits but also to external conditions. All occurrences related to survival are ethological events. The wolf cub, along with its other siblings, is feeding. Hunger is the physical need, feeding is the ethological event. The biology of human behavior involves how we adapt and respond to the environment and how effectively we secure the satisfaction of our needs. We learn from human ethology several important things. First, that the success of our survival efforts to satisfy our needs is contingent on our ability to respond to significant life situations behaviorally. Second, that our behavioral response needs to be biologically based.

Finally, that this response, in turn, depends on our ability to perceive the relevant biological reality of our circumstances and needs. This is where animal observation and analogy come in.

Most of us treat work, marriage and family as social events. Discarding their biological significance, they lose their ethological, adaptive potency, and we tend to fail in them. Discounting what should be meaningful ethological events in our lives, we treat them with ignorance or indifference. Anymore, we only react to life-threatening situations in biological fashion. Being attacked with a gun jolts the ethological response. Once we view the occurrences of life biologically rather than socially, we begin to access innate powers and responses that support our survival. Once we treat life's essential realities as ethological events, our inborn ethological behavior goes to work. Then, need gratification, positioning for resources, territorial defense and other ethological behaviors and responses begin to determine our approach.

Often we are blind to the reality we require to meet our needs. Reality exists through the perception, definition and interpretation we put on events and experiences. Such issues and events as work, marriage, family, property, territory, and resources are not primarily social matters and affairs. They are biological in nature. Within the ethological context things do not proceed in social, culturally prescribed ways. Instead, behavior is determined by the biological parameters of dominance and submission, aggression, sexuality, xenophobia and territory. As soon as we understand this version of reality, we can start acting in turn.

This brings us back to the wolf cubs. Most of the cubs get what they need. They perceive the feeding situation as an ethological event, and they put their ethological survival behavior to work. They end up nourished and satisfied. A few cubs do not succeed. They fail to utilize their instincts. They fail to meet their needs. They stay hungry and dissatisfied.

The analogy to human survival is startling. People who operate ethologically live strong, fulfilled lives. They have a profound biological orientation to life. They respect human nature and treat it as the baseline of their survival activity. They understand the biological reality of life and act accordingly, relying on instinct and intuition. These people are astute to reality, sharp in their actions and biologically grounded in the way they live. Then there are people who fail to relate to the ethological reality of life. They depend on intellect and rationality. They see the world in social and cultural terms. They favor a culturally conditioned psychology using what they have learned rather than what is innate. To them, nature and biology are a nuisance. For them, life takes place in a social world. Faced with the biological reality of making a living, engaging in relationships or procuring assets, they act in socially and culturally prescribed ways. Typically, they fail in these kinds of situations. They end up dissatisfied and depressed.

Depression is an ethological issue—the result of a failure to respond to ethological events successfully, leaving primary needs unfulfilled. Conventionally, depression is seen as an intra-psychic affliction. It first appears cognitively as an absence of a desired state or condition. Consequently, it is experienced as an emotional state of dejection and despondency. Meanwhile, it may affect metabolic, motor and mental processes. In essence, however, depression is the consequence of a failed response to life. It is directly related to a failure in need gratification as the result of a stunted survival capability usually caused by oversocialization and incessant cultural conditioning. Depression is the existential opposite of aggression, the failure to respond to life occurrences biologically. Like the response of the runt cub, depression in humans ends in withdrawal, apathy, detachment and surrender, and in an existence at the periphery of life.

Ethological responsiveness requires a cortical shift—a change in brain functioning. Ethological behavior originates in the midbrain. The biological view of life exists in the evolutionary psyche. To be able to address the survival issues we face effectively, we need to retract from the intellect and neutralize its dominance on the way we conduct our lives. The culturally conditioned psychology we have learned is not equipped to deal with survival. To the contrary, it overrides our innate adaptive abilities with layers of learned, socially acquired forms of behavior.

There is the case of a woman who has been having problems for many years. She worries a great deal and has problems sleeping. She thinks she is destitute and feels lonely even though she has considerable assets and many good friends. She has been receiving a plethora of treatments for her condition—medical, chemical, nutritional, educational, etc. Yet, after all this care, nothing has changed. Her problems are still there, and she feels just as bad as before—if not worse. The predicament is quite common and is the direct result of viewing depression as an intra-psychic conflict instead of addressing it as an ethological issue. If she or her doctors were to change perspective and look at things differently, she would immediately begin to take an active role in her own survival and a real solution might be in sight.

The story of the woman is reminiscent of the wolf cub. More prescriptions won't help. The challenge is clear and simple: the way to be healthy is to learn how to live. An increase in self-care, but especially an increase in adaptive capability would turn things around for her. Like the runt cub, she needs to cross the threshold and apply her biologically innate survival ability. In order for the runt cub to get food and survive, it needs to engage its natural instincts. The woman needs to transition from trained psychology to evolutionary functioning. Recovery from depression requires aggression and active pursuit and fulfillment of our needs.

Effective adaptation to life is contingent on a biological perception of our needs and circumstances and on the use of our innate adaptive capabilities.

Chapter Two

A world shorn of instinct would be a far more deadly and dangerous place . . . The fact is that, at a date some time after 2.5 million, there appears in eastern Africa a small, agile creature with a very startling development to his frontal lobes.

Bruce Chatwin
Conversations with Konrad Lorenz

Evolutionary Functioning

Early human history takes the lion share of the evolutionary development of our species. In fact, the most essential features of our being are prehistoric, recorded in the DNA of our species. Most experts agree that human history began on the plains of Africa. The transition from forest to savannah separated man from the ape. It marked the beginning of our species. Changes in the body reflected the changes in the new way of life. Comparatively "small, defenseless and slow"[1], early man was no match for the animals who preyed on him—lions, hunting dogs, hyenas. Living on the plains forced an upright position of the human body, "advance warning of the approach of enemies must have been of the greatest importance and the ability to stand upright and look around might make the difference between life and death"[2]. With the upright position and changes in pelvis and torso came bipedalism, the ability to walk on two legs. This was followed by other physical changes. "The jaw bones became smaller and the forehead more domed."[3] The brain doubled in size. Physically, Upright Man, Homo erectus, gained in stance and height. "So the bodies of men responded to the impress of the world they lived in and made the most recent major physical changes to be incorporated in their genes"—fixed by natural selection[4].

Fossil research shows that early humans lived as hunting people. The ability to make tools and weapons, premeditate and organize communal hunts made early man "a very formidable hunter"[5]. He was "dexterous of hand and inventive of mind"[6]. Upright Man became more and more successful and numerous and began to spread to many parts of the world. Migration led to the dissemination of genetically established human traits and abilities everywhere. The deep-seated universal characteristics of human anatomy, behavior and consciousness became "the common inheritance of humanity"[7]. Early man lived "in harmony with the natural world around them, altering it not at all and making do with what it immediately provides. Nowhere are they overwhelmingly numerous. Their expectation of life is short, their birthrate and the survival of their children are curbed by the scarcity of food and the hazards of their lives. Such was the condition of man for almost all his existence"[8].

Homo erectus, our earliest ancestor, was followed by Homo sapiens, the Wise Man. This was about 35,000 years ago. Homo sapiens led an existence much like his ancestor, "hunting animals and gathering fruits, seeds and roots everywhere in the world for many thousands of years. Such a life is hazardous and rough. Men, women and children are exposed to the pitiless sifting of an impersonal environment. The slow and the careless are likely to be killed by predators; the weak may starve; the old may fail to survive the torment of a drought. Those whose bodies were, by the chance of genetic variation, better suited to the conditions, had an advantage. They survived and reproduced, handing on that advantage to their children"[9]. Homo sapiens is our closest human ancestor. Physically, Homo sapiens was the same as us. Biological evolution had ended. "The difference between the life of a skin-clad hunter leaving a cave with a spear over his shoulder to hunt mammoth, and a smartly dressed executive driving along a motorway in New York, London or Tokyo, to consult his computer print-out, is not due to any further physical development of body or brain during the long period that separates them"[10]—what separates them is "the revolution caused by the sharing of experience and the spread of knowledge"[11] through communication.

Even though "ingenious, communicative and resourceful" and comparatively successful in securing a livelihood, as a species early humans seemed "to be subject to the same laws and restrictions which govern the numbers of other animals"[12]. This changed dramatically about eight thousand years ago with the discovery of grain and its harvest in regular cycles. Human evolution was about to change directions. Agriculture provided the foundation for a new development: man "could settle down beside his plots and wait for the grain to sprout, stop being a gatherer and become a farmer, build himself permanent huts and live in villages. So he founded his first towns"[13]. Human population growth has since, albeit disproportional to natural law, accelerated and increased significantly, establishing us as the dominant species on the planet.

The evolution of human nature makes for an impressive story. It established us as a viable species with the biological capacity to survive, giving us the same natural powers of adaptation and survival as animals. It also constituted the duality of human nature between biology and consciousness, separating us from the animal by a different destiny.

The evolutionary experience of our species shaped the nature all of us carry inside. The experience is lastingly etched into the human psyche. More than two million years of collective survival experience are genetically encoded in the human brain. During this process, we went from a nomadic past to the urban existence of today. The brain holds a genetic record of the evolutionary achievements of our species.

The human brain consists of several parts; all linked to different stages of evolution. The reptilian brain, which we share with all vertebrates, belongs to the oldest section of the human brain. Located in the brain stem, it regulates basic vital processes. It controls the cardiovascular and respiratory systems, and it maintains consciousness. The operations of this part of the brain are largely automatic and deeply anchored in the organic processes of life. The mammalian brain represents a further evolutionary stage. It makes up the midsection of the human brain. This part of the brain provides balancing mechanisms and as such regulates hormone levels, the sensations of hunger and thirst, sexual drive and sleep. In addition, it controls the emotions of anger and fear along with the related behaviors of fight and flight. The midbrain is the province of instinctive and affective behavior. In that, it controls in all mammals as well as in humans important responses to the environment. It is responsible for such inborn and biologically relevant behaviors as "maternal attachment, courting and erotic behaviour, dominance and submission, and territorial defence"[14]. These are genetically inherited behavior patterns and species-specific. The midbrain is the center of ethological behavior and the neurological foundation of man's archetypal nature.

The neocortex, which makes up the outer layer of the human brain, is the most recent formation in the development of the brain. This new portion of the brain is common to all higher mammals, including humans, and responsible for cognition and perception on a more sophisticated level. Unique to man and to the evolution of the human brain, finally, is the division of the neocortex into the left and right brain hemispheres. This lateralization of the new part of the brain is the result of man's particular adaptation to the environment, which differentiates him from the animal. The development of weapons, tools, social organization, language and speech led to a specialization of the left brain hemisphere in humans, setting the two halves of the neocortex apart. The left cerebral hemisphere is closely associated with the cultural evolution of our species, which it initiated. The right brain carried on the natural evolution of our species. It took on sophisticated adaptations, refining our abilities to relate to the environment. The right hemisphere is the center of intuition, sensation and perception.

Human evolution formed body and psyche simultaneously. The physical, behavioral and mental characteristics were shaped by evolutionary process, creating the basic biology of anatomy, behavior and consciousness, which sets us apart from other species.

Our distinct survival advantage as a species lies in this innate psychology. This psychology reflects the duality of our being and of our needs.

Ultimately, human beings have two essential needs. One is the need to have what we require to live. The other is the need to seek a connection with the supernatural. At the most fundamental level, human needs have to do with food, shelter, family, and community and with a sense of belonging to a higher order of things. Human life hinges on the combination of physical and metaphysical needs and on the ability of the individual to fulfill them both.

Nature has equipped us to have both. Evolution has provided the behavioral and mental capabilities to meet these needs. More than two million years of survival history have formed innate adaptive structures to deal with the fundamental requirements of our existence. We have the innate capacity for behavioral and mental adaptation. The capacity originates in the midbrain.

Ethological Behavior

Each species is uniquely fitted to its environment, equipped with a set of behaviors adapted to the world in which it originates and evolves. Even given greater environmental variability and adaptability, we are no exception. These biological behaviors, also called ethological behaviors, enable each species to meet the circumstances and demands of its environment. This adaptive repertoire of "'species-specific patterns of behavior '"[1] is genetic in nature. Ethology and sociobiology teach us that human behavior is highly circumscribed by the genetic consequences of evolutionary adaptation[2]. And here again, we are no exception. The genetic evolution of these adaptive behavior patterns in humans was prompted by changes in environment and living conditions faced by our early ancestors after leaving the forests to live on the plains.

Survival is always about "territory, resources and succession"[3]— our fundamental needs for security, food, shelter, family, and community. The environmental conditions, on the other hand, are always structured by the ethological parameters of dominance and submission, property and defense, competition and aggression, sexuality and succession, friend and foe. Survival and need gratification are primarily structured by access to resources, defense of property and boundary, assertion of rank and power, as well as, intra- and inter-group competition. The survival reality of human life, like that of animal life, is essentially determined by the ethological parameters of territory, hierarchy, aggression, sexuality and xenophobia. Survival is thus inextricably related to biology. The biology of human needs and environmental conditions has not changed, even though survival has moved from the savannah to life in the modern city. Survival requires and activates biological behavior. This is just as true today as in prehistoric time.

Our distant ancestors forged the brain we have today. The exposure to a harsh, unforgiving world in an unrelenting struggle for survival set the stage for the unique evolution our species would undertake. The competition for 'territory, resources and succession' required effective responses to the environment. This is how we acquired our instincts—behaviors based on biology. They developed to secure the gratification of basic needs. The instincts are ethological behaviors and respond to specific survival situations. Human ethology stresses five primary instinctual survival behaviors established through evolutionary adaptation[4]. Each individual ethological behavior satisfies particular survival needs and serves a particular adaptive function:

- *Hierarchical* behavior, which involves issues of dominance and submission, establishes position and access to resources;
- *territorial* behavior, which relates to issues of space and boundaries, claims property and defends it against outsiders;
- *sexual* behavior, which relates to family and child-rearing, secures attachment, community and succession;

- *xenophobic* behavior, which responds to safety needs, protects against danger from people and environment; and
- *aggressive* behavior, which responds to threat, injury and deprivation, prompts self-protection, recovery and need fulfillment.

We normally observe these behaviors in animals as they pursue their needs for food, territory and mating. However, if we take a closer look at our own behavior or its symbols—such as fences, rank, status, power, and politics—then we notice the same kind of behaviors among people. The major instincts cover significant behavioral aspects of our relationship to the environment. The territorial instinct is aimed at the protection of property and boundary; the hierarchical instinct establishes access to resources cast in terms of dominance and submission; the aggressive instinct fuels the impetus towards need gratification and provides the necessary energy and forcefulness to assure success; the xenophobic instinct, finally, addresses safety issues in our relationship to the world around us. The instincts are neither good nor bad. They are an evolutionary reality of the human psyche and the result of our collective survival experiences as a species over a period of more than two million years.

Instinctive behavior helps us to adapt to external conditions. The instincts evolved to address the biological issues of life—everything related to livelihood and physical well-being, family, space, security, community, economics and defense, mating and procreation, religion and ritual. The evolutionary background of ethological behavior in humans is the hunting history of early man. Hunting constitutes "the master behavior pattern of the human species"[5]. The objective of hunting is the fulfillment of practical needs. The hunter is the archetypal survivor. This inner hunter or hunter within is still with us today. Evolutionary history makes it evident that these behaviors are crucial to the survival and adaptation of the individual.

Ethology affects human survival in two ways: it determines

both the adaptive capability of the individual and the adaptive conditions of the environment. Nature has equipped humans to be hierarchical, territorial, sexual, aggressive and xenophobic to get what we need and to deal with the environment we face. The underlying reason for the formation of these patterns of adaptive behavior lies in the fact that survival is always structured by biology. The evolutionary qualities of human behavior are reflected in the organization and functioning of the political, economic, and communal institutions of society. These qualities are present in the structure of our political and bureaucratic institutions, the organizations and operations of the business world, the running of our political and economic affairs, in the distribution of status, power and wealth, the fabric of urban existence, and even in the events of daily life. Evolutionary conditions are the ultimate reality that determines and shapes the events of human existence.

People are territorial when they fence their gardens, protect their jobs against competitors, or defend their relationships through sexual jealousy. They express their hierarchical nature through professional titles, military rank and insignia, supervisory and subordinate behavior, issuing and following orders. Evolutionary behavior related to sexuality appears in dating and mating, family and child-rearing. People exhibit xenophobic behavior when they face unfamiliar situations, encounter strangers, fear for their safety, or when confronted with other circumstances that cause self-protective responses. Aggressive behavior related to survival is present when people pursue resources, strive for position, seek selective advantage, restore deficits due to loss or deprivation, overcome barriers.

Ethological behavior is always present when people meet for the first time. There is a sizing-up phase. People check each other out for physical prowess, intellectual superiority, wit, sexual potency or any other selective advantage relevant to a given circumstance. People tend to act and react in evolutionary ways when situations involve survival issues. Such situations relate to archetypal needs and conditions. Protection of family and property, the performance of work roles, and relationships in courtship, marriage, and child-rearing call up evolutionary responses. Evolutionary behavior is present when a person competes for a job, the boss dominates his subordinates, two contenders fight over the same partner, a man and a woman engage in a relationship or a mother protects her children. Evolutionary principles determine and assist human adaptation.

Hierarchical behavior relates to rank order and status, which, in turn, are typically associated with the access to resources. "The dominance-submission archetype is evidently a crucial determinant of masculine behaviour in all social mammals, not only in the way in which males seek to dominate each other, but also in the manner that males dominate their mates and their offspring"[6]. Dominance reveals the position of the individual in the social rank order. The hierarchical dominance patterns among males are biologically motivated and have survival value. They exist "for the purposes of mating, hunting, and defence"[7]: that is, for the purposes of marriage and family, the organization of work and production, the receipt of income and rewards, and the protection of home and community. Hierarchical behavior and displays of authority and deference keep fighting over status to a minimum. The primary "function of the dominance hierarchy is to control aggressive competition in the interest of social cohesion"[8].

We can observe human dominance behavior in many instances of life—in the politician who challenges his opponent, in the police officer who controls traffic, in the manager who conducts a meeting, in the lover who outranks his competitor. Hierarchical behavior is common to male pursuits; women find themselves exposed to it as soon as they enter the public domain of business and institutions.

Dominance behavior among males is sex-related. The male expresses dominance either toward other males over territory and power, or towards females in issues of "courtship and mating"[9]. Both patterns are familiar themes in every day life as well as in mythology and art—the man who competes in the corporate world and dates the beautiful woman; the knight who defeats the black prince in battle and in the bedroom; or the sidekick of the star who does not have a chance to get the only female in the movie.

Territoriality involves issues of space, property and boundary along with the claim for possession. The ethological basis of territorial behavior lies in the defense and protection of community and property. Generally, it operates on the 'first come, first served' principle[10]. We find examples of territorial behavior in daily life: the worker who protects his job against the newcomer, the passenger who reserves her seat with a suitcase, the wife who defends her marriage against the mistress, the inventor who protects his ideas with a patent, the homeowner who surrounds her house with a fence, the prospector who stakes his claim with the recording office, the tenant who claims her parking spot against unauthorized occupants, and so forth.

Both hierarchical and territorial behaviors, the submission of competitors and the defense against outsiders, involve aggression[11]. Aggression, usually, involves fear of the situation or the opponent. When circumstances call for hierarchical or territorial responses, the conflict between aggression and fear often causes approach-avoidance behavior, a fight or flight response. Attack or appeasement settles the matter.

Human sexuality and sexual behavior relate to primary archetypal needs of individual and group. Sexuality establishes family and marriage, secures procreation and succession, provides bonding and attachment between intimates, and preserves community and continuation of the species. Evolution attached ethological significance to sexual behavior. Sexuality is adapted to the biological requirements of the species. Mate selection, courting, and mating are optimized by natural selection. Choosing a partner for marriage and family is directed by biological, evolutionary principles. The man looks for certain features in the woman and vice versa[12].

Aggression also plays an important role in courtship and mating. Here, aggression conflicts with the fear of the partner. Sexual aggression in the male has to do with maintaining potency, in the female with selecting a mate. The conflict between aggression and fear plays out differently for males and females. If the male is afraid of the female and feels anxious and intimidated by her, he becomes sexually ineffective. Anxiety collapses potency in the male, his erection turns flaccid and he has to withdraw. Erectile dysfunction often results from emotional distress, anxiety and depression. The parasympathetic nervous system, which is under the control of emotions rather than will, regulates sexual functioning. On the other hand, when the man feels strong and is unafraid of the woman, his sexuality functions. Natural aggression sustains sexual potency in the male. In other words, the male can be aggressive and sexual, but not anxious and sexual at the same time. The opposite is true for the female. She may be afraid and feel intimidated by the male and still be sexually motivated towards him. Anxiety does not affect sexual functioning in the female. However, if she senses that the man is not strong enough for her and she could prevail over him, she loses interest and ceases to be sexually attracted to him. Weakness in the male turns her off and excites her aggression. Natural aggression curbs sexuality in the female. In short, the female cannot be aggressive and sexual at the same time. Evolution has programmed the female to look for the male who is invincible (to her) and who can give her healthy children, ample food supply, and reliable protection.

Dating, courtship and mating have definite evolutionary undercurrents. The social situation is in many cases the cover for the ethological event. Sexuality is an omnipresent aspect of human life. It even affects the non-sexualized world of work. Frequently it is of archetypal importance as in courtship and mating. Ethological events stimulate the evolutionary dimension of human nature, setting off aggression and fear, appetite and avoidance—all behind the sensation of romance and excitement[13].

Human aggression is a response to threat, injury and deprivation or similar life circumstances that require active intervention. Aggression typically responds to situations and conditions in the environment that need to be improved, altered or rectified, and it provides the impetus to act on these issues. Aggression is a specific form of survival behavior, characteristic only of higher mammals and of man, directed at members of the same species[14]. As with higher mammals, aggression in humans is a vital factor of survival.

It promotes survival in all biologically relevant aspects of life. It plays a role in territorial, hierarchical, sexual and xenophobic behavior. Aggression secures individual survival, but not at the expense of the community. It is counter-balanced by inborn constraints that protect the social order[15]. Biologically, aggression is bound by a code of ethics and the archetypal instruction to learn and follow the rules[16]. "If aggression is to promote the welfare of the group, and not its destruction, there have to be collectively recognized constraints to its use."[17] The interrelatedness of individual and group survival is the foundation for the ethics found in nature and biology. Aggression is evil and destructive only if it overturns the ethical limitations biology has placed on it.

Because of the cultural stigma attached to aggression and aggressive behavior, it is important to distinguish between survival-related, adaptive and destructive aggression. Aggression related to survival is regulated by biological rules, "governing the circumstances in which aggression may be employed, how much of it can be appropriately expressed and when it should be inhibited"[18]. Destructive aggression is controlled by the intellect, which, while using the force of the instinct, overrides the instinct's natural inhibitions. There is good aggression and there is bad aggression. Innate aggression designed to further adaptation carries survival value. It deserves reverence and respect. The contemporary admonition to be assertive rather than aggressive is ill-advised. Assertion is the culturally conditioned response. It is cognitive and mental and as such lacks the genetic, biological backing and inherent strength of ethological behavior. The body of rules constraining aggression, evolved by natural adaptation, is more appropriate, "which, while encouraging the aggressive, discourages the violent"[19]. Aggression is a necessary part of the adaptation to life and environment. In order to be adaptive, it needs to be guided and monitored by the instinct. The violence we see in society today is instinctive aggression corrupted and contaminated by the intellect. Destructive aggression, abusive of instinctual intent and inhibitions, has no place in human survival. As R. Ardrey observes, "the problem of man is not that we are aggressive but that we break the rules"[20]. This means, "in man aggression becomes a moral problem"[21].

Like sexuality, aggression contributes to the survival of individual and species. From an ethological point of view, aggression is essential to adaptation and one of survival's most significant tools. Aggression "performs vital biological functions": "(1) it promotes defence; (2) it permits access to valued resources (e.g. territory, food, water and females in oestrus); (3) it ensures good use of the available habitat by spreading the population out as widely as possible; (4) it affords an effective means of settling disputes within the group; (5) it provides leadership for the group—a factor which can prove critical for survival at times of danger; and (6) it promotes differential reproduction—i.e. the 'fittest' (more aggressive and dominant) males are more likely to sire the next generation and so pass on selectively advantageous genes"[22]. Ethologically, aggression is the driving force that makes successful adaptation possible. It provides us with the power and energy to compete for resources, protect our territory, and select a suitable mate.

"Aggression, like sexuality, is an ineradicable feature of human nature, and its manifestations in battle with outsiders for territory and resources and in struggle with insiders for power and prestige are everywhere characteristic of the life of mankind."[23] Although innate inhibitions temper and ethical codes constrain it, aggression is a fundamental fact of human nature and human life.

There is still another aspect of human life with ethological significance to our survival. It has to do with our need and ability to protect ourselves against danger and harm. Xenophobic behavior responds to needs of personal safety and protection against threat and danger from people or in the environment. Just as civilization has tried to "remove us from the lethal, unfettered competition of the jungle"[24], it has likewise brought about changes and conditions that can brutalize human nature[25]. In the end, it does not matter "that we *are* aggressive, xenophobic, sexual, hierarchical and territorial" as much as the "*attitude* we adopt to these *a priori* aspects of our nature"—"what matters" is "how we live them, and how we mediate them to the group. It is the ethical orientation that counts"[26].

Not all people think that way; not all people follow the rules. While some people deny the existence of ethological behavior, others misuse it to attack and prey on other people. They are human predators, different in degree, but not in kind. There are those who like to play the role of the 'alpha male'. They desire to dominate and control other people, monopolizing work situations and social gatherings by resorting to manipulation and/or intimidation. Next are people with severe disorders. They are parasitic. These people abuse others for their material and emotional gain unmindful of the destruction and pain they leave behind. Then there is the sociopath—people who totally dismiss ethological and social restraints imposed on human aggression, and who violate the boundaries and lives of others. They view people as victims and prey. After unscrupulous study of a person's vulnerabilities, they move in for the attack.

Human biology has equipped us with the ability to perceive danger[27]. The recognition of threatening objects and situations is part of our archetypal and instinctive nature[28]. Ethologically, perception is tied to survival. It is not the reality out there, rather our innate perceptual program that determines what we perceive. Our perception is controlled from the inside. It anticipates and takes note of outside events that are biologically relevant. That is, we rediscover and recognize those signs and stimuli in the external world that are pertinent to our survival.

Evolutionary adaptation has formed our perceptual system, forcing it to develop selective advantage. Its program is "immune to change" and "the foundation of all experience"[29]. With it, we can recognize cues and conditions signaling alarm and retreat. Like the chick that shrinks from the hawk, we are able to detect signs of danger and threat in the environment. This is possible through an innate archetypal alarm system, activated by threatening stimuli from the outside. The most common of these inherited warning systems among many animal species is the predator archetype.

Our equivalent to this 'innate releasing mechanism'[30] is an archetypal prefiguration that warns us against strangers.

We first encounter this archetype in early childhood. During the initial attachment phase to the mother, the infant "learns to trust the continuity of existence"[31]. Later, the child begins to explore the world beyond the mother. The exploration, at first tentative and with constant reference to her presence, takes the child outside the haven of safety and puts him/her in contact with the unknown. At that time, this archetype awakens. The inherited alarm system goes off each time the child meets a situation or person that is strange or unfamiliar to him/her. Encountering strangeness distresses the child, who usually responds by crying, screaming, and turning away. Unfamiliarity or threat cause fear-avoidance behavior, most likely "an evolutionary vestige of the flight response in lower mammals"[32].

By perceiving danger and responding to potential threat, we safeguard our survival. We generally associate strange and unfamiliar situations with natural cues for danger. The "early establishment of the familiar-unfamiliar dichotomy has evident survival value for all mammals: it results in behaviour which maintains proximity to conspecifics who are friendly and places which are safe, and withdrawal from subjects which are potentially hostile and situations which could be dangerous"[33]. In humans, this predisposes us for the in-group/out-group polarities, which label people as friend or foe. The fear of strangers, or xenophobia, is crucial to human adaptation and as such part of the instinctive behavior of our evolutionary nature.

The archetypes "are of obvious survival value, as instances of instinctive behaviour"[34]. They are the imprint of nature on the human psyche. As an aspect of the archetypes, instinctive ethological behavior is part of the genetic make-up of the human psyche. Archetypes, including the human instincts, evolved through adaptation to external conditions to support the survival of individual and group.

Most genetic capabilities and characteristics of our biological nature are a potentiality called upon in time of need. The functional structures of the archetypal psyche, both behavioral and mental, operate much like 'innate releasing mechanisms', instantly activated when environmental circumstances necessitate a response. Yet, we do not inherit specific instinctive behavior patterns as such rather the potential to develop them. While the human instincts are innate, instinctive behavior itself "is not inherited", only "the potential to develop . . . behavioural systems"[35].

Instinctive behavior assists us to adapt to the external environment. An additional advantage is its genetic, adaptive capacity as an 'open programme'[36]. This enables the organism to adapt appropriately, by 'trial and success', as K. Lorenz puts it, to changes in the environment[37]. This means that our instinctive system can adjust itself to the survival conditions of modern life as long as it is independent from left-hemispheric control[38] and given the practice it requires to develop. As an 'open programme', instinctive behavior needs to have some kind of cognitive information to select the response which best fits the circumstances. Its capacity to make choices proves that instinctive behavior is flexible and adaptable and not merely an automatic reflex.

Even though the genetic structures of the human psyche are mostly dormant, it is possible, however, to activate the archetypes and to integrate them into behavior and conscious action. This moves survival activity from reflex to strategy. Thus, survival becomes a decidedly strategic undertaking and the best and smartest way to live—rather than being a reaction to crisis or catastrophe.

The instincts are survival responses of the evolutionary psyche. Instincts present the behavioral aspect of the archetypes and are a crucial part of evolutionary functioning. The ethological reality, which determines survival behavior and survival environment, supersedes cultural conditioning and individual psychology.

Biological Imperatives and Attitudes

Ethological behavior is paired with biological imperatives that reinforce its survival value and fortify its contribution to the successful adaptation of the individual. Nature puts a premium on reality and responsibility. Biological behavior corresponds to the order found in nature and quite explicitly to the demands nature puts on adaptation and maturity. The significance of ethological behavior is underscored by a set of evolutionary principles, which are imposed on the functioning and survival of the organism—species and individual alike. Nature sets the example. The instruction it puts to its creatures is always quite simple, clear and concise. The primary command is that the organism is responsible for its survival. After a brief period of attachment and protected growth, survival becomes the task of the organism. This is true for all living organisms and we are no exception[1]. Nature drives for self-reliance and self-sufficiency of the organism. It demands personal initiative and responsibility for the life it gives.

Survival depends on self-reliance. Alongside the biology of behaviors to assist human need gratification, nature has placed a set of attitudes to reinforce the viability of ethological survival behavior and to match the demands of existential adaptation. These attitudes stress individuality, initiative and responsibility to achieve self-reliance and self-sufficiency. Individuality, personal initiative and responsibility are evolutionary traits of human nature supportive of successful adaptation. These attitudes form the motivational core structure of individual functioning. At the center of individual survival, therefore, is an attitudinal structure, driving both need gratification and effective adaptation. This internal structure provides motivation and direction; it also generates the necessary field-independence of action and goal-achievement to render individual survival resistant to environmental changes and conditions. The function of attitudinal adaptation is thus threefold: (1) to motivate need satisfaction, (2) to reinforce ethological behavior, and (3) to create field-independence.

Two factors complicate the achievement of self-reliance and autonomous functioning. There are biological as well as sociological reasons. Compared to most other species, we require a longer rearing period. Care and upbringing of the human child extend over many years. Protracted rearing prolongs the period of attachment and dependency between offspring and parents, postponing maturation towards self-sufficiency. Moreover, society has further added an extended period of intellectual growth, psychosocial development, and instrumental skill training before the young enter adult life. Adolescence, as a transitional phase between childhood and adulthood, is a creation of modern society. While it is intended to prepare the young person through schooling and higher education for the ever-increasing intellectual, occupational, social, and financial demands of the modern world, it simultaneously reinforces the very dependency it is designed to overcome. Tribal societies practice direct transition from childhood to adulthood. They do not have the protracted dependency of the offspring. Rituals of initiation and transition establish clear roles and responsibilities at an early age, specifying adult status. Industrialized societies deviate from the natural rule. The sociology of dependency stands in contrast to the requirements of survival set forth by nature. While society tends to foster conformity and dependency, biology demands autonomy and self-reliance[2]. Reviewing these alternatives, it is important to remember that survival itself is always structured by biology.

Biological Values

Human survival incorporates biological values. The biologically relevant events and experiences of life constitute the archetypal value system of human life. Values define what is important in life. These occurrences involved in the archetypal program include "being parented, exploring the environment, distinguishing familiar figures from strange, learning the language or dialect of one's community, acquiring a knowledge of its values, rules, and beliefs, playing in the peer group, meeting the challenges of puberty and adolescence, being initiated into the adult group, accomplishing courtship and marriage, and child-rearing, contributing to the economy through gathering and hunting, participating in religious rituals and ceremonials, assuming the responsibilities of advanced maturity, old age, and preparation for death"[1]. The significant events of human life are arranged along the natural life cycle of our species and ordained with biological purpose—which is the realization of the universal human blueprint contained in the archetypal psyche.

Because of the common elements present in the archetypes of the human psyche, all people all over the world live essentially the same life, replicating the universal life of the species. Typically, people go through childhood with its usual experiences, then come the adolescent years followed by adulthood, which commonly includes work, marriage and family, before human life enters old age and subsequent death. Then the same cycle of events and experiences begins again, and is repeated by the next generation. The same is true for people everywhere, in all cultures and at all times.

The human being is a biosocial system with a built-in 'biological clock': its structure is based on the human life cycle and predetermined by the evolutionary history of its genes. But what you and I experience as the whole process is only the end result. We are aware only of the personal aspects of our own maturation, being largely unconscious of the universal, species-specific blueprint on whose basis it proceeds. There exist in human beings certain psychic and behavioral forms that are universally present in all members of our species. Each individual life is, thus, "at the same time the eternal life of the species"[2]. The essential role of personal experience is to develop what is already there, encoded in the genetic make-up of the individual[3].

Our genetic endowment presupposes the natural life cycle of our species. The common ground of the human experience exists preformed in the evolutionary psyche. As in the 'living stuff' of the plant, there is something in man "that represents the natural configuration of the whole, as a norm to which its growth conforms"[4]. This genetic blueprint provides the foundation for biological values, specifying the important experiences of human life and the relevant needs of the individual.

Jung speaks of a "transpersonal, instinctive, biologically grounded"[5] collective psyche as the common source of the human experience. The contents of this evolutionary psyche are not a personal acquisition but "owe their existence exclusively to heredity"[6]. The content of the collective psyche consists, according to Jung, essentially of archetypes—genetic determinants of human nature. Archetypes are universal structures within the human mind. Like the instinct, the archetype is a species-specific structure, a genetic potentiality of expression and manifestation.

The archetypes are basic to all essential phenomena of human life and refer to universal behavioral and psychic elements, common to all people everywhere at all times. Archetypes, much like instinctive or ethological behavior, are central to human survival. They are genetic structures biologically encoded in the midsection of the human brain. They function at a level of cerebral activity mainly below the reach of consciousness. Archetypes contain the innate bio-program that forms the neurobehavioral and neuropsychic centers which control human adaptation. They "are responsible for co-ordinating the behavioural and psychic repertoires of our species in response to whatever environmental circumstances we may encounter"[7]. The archetypal intent is to promote life and survival.

That is to say, our biology sets the occurrences and the sequence of the natural life cycle, the stages of human development and maturation, the experiences and events that are universally human and existentially relevant—eliciting a set of values and an organizing principle to direct our lives.

Biological values refer to universal human experiences. They spell out what is important in life. Biological values such as family, property, and succession are endowed with archetypal intent to secure the preservation of the species. These values are, in turn, protected by the ethics of biology. Modern society has redefined human values, often in ignorance or defiance of natural law and biological intent. The ensuing confusion and value conflict affect both culture and individual with deep-seated pathology. The widening gap between culture and nature, human functioning and natural design, has intensified the *instinctual* and *spiritual wounds* and their repercussions on human life. Nature is, of course, always right; any errors or mistakes are always committed by people. Any failure to achieve the archetypal intent of life is punished by pathology, disease, or even death.

Primary Sensations and Emotions

Feelings are like children; they require attention—*your* attention. If left unattended, feelings create problems. Feelings are a crucial part of our make-up. They provide energy. Typically, when we feel good, we feel energized; when we feel bad, we are slow, weak, and have little energy. We are either animated or listless depending on how we feel. Feelings are a primary source of energy. Electrical devices run on power from the outlet in the wall. Aside from the food we eat, we depend on our feelings for energy.

Our feelings have evolutionary origins. They support our survival as we relate to the environment. They help us define internal and external experiences. Our feelings tell us which situations to approach and which to avoid. Feelings are based on neurochemical processes and originate in the midsection of the brain, mainly the limbic system.

The evolutionary design of our feelings is rather straightforward and simple. On the biological level of human psychology there are only four kinds of feelings. These are the sensations of pleasure and pain, and the emotions of fear and anger. The sensations of pleasure and pain inform us whether physical or mental stimuli and experiences involve comfort or discomfort. The emotions of fear and anger inform us about the quality of environmental stimuli and they regulate our responses to them.

- *Pleasure* involves everything that advances our survival. Experiences of pleasure promote well-being and effective adaptation. Ultimately, procreation and thus the preservation of the species are tied to the pleasure principle.

- Experiences of *pain*, on the other hand, indicate discomfort and notify us of the presence of harmful and hurtful conditions. They force us to change our response to the environment and to look elsewhere to get our needs met.
- *Fear* alerts us to danger and life-threatening situations. It also tells us what to do, either fight or flight.
- *Anger*, finally, is a secondary emotion; it results from either pain or fear. Anger provides emotional backup; it either supports fear or heals pain.

These biological sensations and emotions constitute physiological information and energy systems developed by evolutionary process and designed to advance the survival of the organism. The biological sensations and emotions are structured as biphasic mechanisms of approach and avoidance. This biphasic adjustment mode applies to the entire spectrum of environmental survival conditions, encompassing the objects, events, and people of our world.

All survival depends on the ability to move towards what we need and away from what is harmful[1]. The newborn infant provides a vivid demonstration of the range of human sensations and emotions, and confirmation of the fact that they are inborn and inherited. From the child's reactions we can usually tell if it experiences comfort or discomfort. We also know when the child is afraid or angry. Pleasure and pain record our physical and mental experiences. Fear alerts us to the presence of acute or potential danger and requires an instant response. We either withdraw and run or we stay and fight. Anger, which is a close cousin of human aggression, is not a stand-alone. It is activated by experiences of either pain or fear and provides the physiological and psychological response to reduce the pain or to react to the fear effectively. The biology of human feelings is basic and simple. It limits affective responses to the environment to enable a focused approach to survival events. Just as there are only three primary colors, there are only four natural feelings.

What most people call 'feelings' are, properly speaking, self-induced physiological and neurochemical reactions stimulated by internal thought process. Many of our emotions result from thoughts rather than experience and are in reality ways of thinking rather than feeling. Real feelings are related to events. They usually last as long as the experience. Depression, anxiety or guilt, for example, are not direct physiological reactions to events. They result from cognitive interpretations of our experiences. As we begin to think about particular events and experiences, we create certain emotions. In cases like these, it is useful to rephrase the statement "I *feel* depressed, anxious or guilty" to "I *think* depressed, anxious or guilty". The verbal shift furthers the understanding of how we cause our own mood states. Using the term "I feel" rather than "I think" tends to mislead the person as to the origin of her affective experiences, assuming that outside, if not supernatural forces, are causing her to 'feel' a certain way. Rephrasing helps us realize that many of our feelings result from our thinking. We make them up.

Even though they may appear real and may be experienced as true emotions, 'feelings' of anxiety, depression or guilt are nonetheless pseudo-emotions. They are not immediate physiological reactions to reality, but rather cognitive productions representing or interpreting personal experience. Furthermore, they lack authenticity still in another sense. Not infrequently, they stand for other internal processes and mask or camouflage emotions like anger, fear, or sexuality that may not be culturally acceptable. These so-called 'feelings' are a major portion of a person's culturally conditioned psychology and are in the main the treatment focus of contemporary psychiatry and psychotherapy. They are not, however, part of the original make-up of human nature and, thus, do not constitute the basic and essential psychology of the individual.

The biological sensations and emotions evolved to support need gratification and to provide protection in our transactions with the environment. By contrast, self-induced feelings such as depression, anxiety or guilt are essentially unproductive affective states and, generally, stand in the way of life. Pseudo-emotions lack survival value. To state the obvious, depression and anxiety do not support our adaptation to life. Depression results from the experience that we don't have what we need. Anxiety is based on the anticipation that we won't have what we need. Unless we understand depression and anxiety as indications of ineffective survival behavior and a breakdown of personal responsibility, these emotions remain useless, unproductive feelings. Self-induced feelings can produce survival advantage only when transformed into action in order to change the underlying condition. Ultimately, the individual must look at his/her needs and at his/her life.

Our needs give us clear and strong messages. Unless we assume responsibility to meet those needs and get back into life, we continue to experience the underlying deprivation and suffer ongoing depression, anxiety or guilt. Here is where human aggression comes in. It responds to experiences of threat, injury, loss or lack, and provides the necessary ethological behavior to resolve the issue at hand. In the long run it is, generally, more productive to address the issues of our lives than to resort to pills or drugs which tend to mask the real problems. There are, however, conditions and circumstances when appropriate medication is an essential and necessary step to reclaiming our lives. As long as we resist life and refuse to improve our condition and fulfill our needs, there will be no change to the emotional pain. In order to take this quite often difficult step into life, people require increased adaptive competence and the confidence to do so. But once you start working on your needs, other powers take over and assist you—the forces of self-preservation and biological adaptation.

Just as the color green is a mixture of yellow and blue, many of the feelings we experience are combinations of two or more of the four primary sensations and emotions. Sadness, for instance, combines pain and anger. The loss of a person, object or opportunity causes both emotions. We feel hurt over the deprivation we suffered and we feel angry that it happened. Shame is a profound emotional experience for people who go through it. It involves fear, pain and anger. It is fear of the perpetrator who insults us, pain from the injury to our integrity, and anger about the assault and violation we incur. In essence, all feelings trace back to one or more basic sensations and emotions on the biological level. And it is on this level where, in the final analysis, all feelings have to be dealt with and resolved.

There is a great deal of confusion about feelings and emotions in our culture. Some feelings seem acceptable, others not. Some feelings, although very real, are not talked about; other feelings are easily admitted. Why is that? We all have two psychologies. One we are born with, the other is learned and acquired. Each outlines different behaviors and responses. One psychology is innate and evolved through *adaptation* to life; the other results from ongoing *adjustment* to society. Our natural psychology refers to the four primary sensations and emotions of pleasure, pain, fear and anger. These are natural emotions generated by the human body; they are real feelings in that they result from actual experiences and responses to the environment. Our learned psychology involves socially and culturally acceptable feelings. These are conditioned emotions and more often than not ways of thinking rather than feeling. Socially acceptable emotions are the product of socialization. We learn them as acceptable expressions of emotional experiences. Alongside, we also learn to conceal or deny what we really feel. When we incur loss, for example, we are allowed to be sad. Sadness is an acceptable feeling; anger is not. It's okay, in other words, to be sad but not to be angry. Anger is a controversial emotion in our culture; most find it unacceptable. A similar taboo extends to sexuality and sexual feelings. The emotion of fear is particularly unacceptable to men: although a natural response to danger, it is seen as a sign of male weakness. Society has developed intricate labels and maneuvers to mask our true feelings.

Managing our feelings is an important responsibility. The state of our feelings is not only important for our overall health and well-being, but it is also a vital energy source and a large part of our outlook on life. We need to attend to our feelings the same way we take care of our children. They inform us of distress, they let us know when things are going well and when they are not, and, most importantly, they tell us about our needs and what we must do about them. Survival is about need fulfillment.

- First, we have to keep our emotional life current. Unresolved feelings fester like weed. Often they turn against us—in our health, in our relationships and in our appreciation of life.
- Secondly, we need to assess what we really feel—being mindful of the thinking process that is often involved in making up certain emotions. A good rule of thumb is to trace all emotions back to the basic natural feelings and to resolve them in that form: deal with the pain, face the fear, and express the anger.
- Thirdly, understand what our emotions are telling us. Feelings, like dreams, often contain messages. The messages are meant to have us take a look at our lives and to make the necessary changes.

We can only experience the full power of our life force if we keep our natural feelings free of clutter. Culturally conditioned feelings clog the pathways of this energy flow like cholesterol affects the blood vessels and the body's circulation. Reverting back to our natural sensations and emotions keeps things real and clear. They provide the potency we need to live strong and effective lives. All behavioral and emotional reality reveals its essence or purpose only on the level of biology.

Ethological behavior together with our basic sensations and emotions constitute our natural life force. This biobehavioral system, seated in the midsection of the brain and crucial to human survival, presents the relevant reality of the organism. It is at this level of functioning that body and mind connect, and we connect with the world. Here is where health, human survival and well-being take their origin.

Psychic Function

Our mental faculties add a whole other world to our experience and existence. This world beyond biology and nature extends to the inner and outer reaches of non-material reality. Consciousness opens the door to the awareness of our own existence and to a realization of a higher order and cosmic universe.

The extension of our world, likewise, stretches the requirements of human survival into the realm of the mental and metaphysical. Human life is a biological as well as a mental event. The metaphysical aspect of the human condition adds additional adaptive demands.

Our ability to understand and determine the events of our lives is effectively limited, in time and space, to a small range of decisions and activities. Within this microcosm of daily and domestic events, we can plan and act with reasonable certainty and success. But there is a boundary where other powers and phenomena seem to take over and influence our lives. Moreover, the events and effects that lie beyond the threshold of our control are those most consequential to our lives: catastrophe, accident, illness, disaster, and death. Unsustained, any such experience would be devastating. Catastrophic experiences encountered by early humans like disaster, death and disease were overwhelming and annihilating at first. The exposure to the unpredictable and uncontrollable occurrences of life required the ability to cope with the mental and spiritual repercussions of their existence. Here, too, evolution matched abilities to the demands of event and environment. The instincts, responding to outer conditions, forced the brain to extend its evolution to the human mind. The need for both behavioral and mental adaptation spawned our dual nature as biological and spiritual beings.

We function in a three-dimensional world measured by our senses, yet we live on the boundary to a larger universe that sets the laws for our existence. We are equipped to comprehend our world of causality and time but nothing beyond that. Our intelligence and our senses are designed for this factual kind of reality. They permit us to operate within a three-dimensional world and to understand the principles governing it. Then comes a point where everything is veiled by 'an interesting and puzzling mystery'. Our intelligence fails to understand whatever lies beyond that boundary.

But the things that really affect us come from there—influencing us with forces and laws we do not control and exposing us to the inexorable facts of destiny, disease, disaster, and death. We are not privy to the higher order realities that determine our lives. This means there is a player on the other side—a player we do not know and cannot control[1]. Human existence is pivoted on the organic paradox of life and death, growth and decay, permanence and change. In turn, the human condition is torn by the existential ambivalence between salvation or despair, creation or chaos, meaning or futility.

The awareness of our own being and of the predicament surrounding our existence requires adaptive capabilities that can address the mental, emotional and spiritual repercussions of life—an event that comes without instruction, leverage or guarantee. We require the means to accommodate the ambivalence that beleaguers the human existence. We need a concept or construct that provides structure and support for the day-to-day experience of living—we need something that holds our world together; something that provides the motivation to do the daily chores, make a living, and go on with our lives despite all that happens; and, finally, we need something that fends off the hardness and horrors of life[2].

We have the ability to fashion such a consciousness. The human psyche contains the capacity for mental and psychological adaptation. The capability is instinctual and innate. Jung referred to it as the 'religious function' or archetype[3]. Specifically the instigator of religious experience and manifest in religion, this archetype, in the most general sense of its function, is the source of human survival consciousness. It has the adaptive capability "to maintain the psychic balance"[4] of the individual in the face of unpredictable and uncontrollable circumstances. It furnishes a reference system to allow orientation and a sense of coherence and security. The capacity for psychic adaptation enables us to function within the larger context of a macrocosm, which exposes us to realities and influences we do not understand or control.

Human survival is to a large extent mental. Mental adaptation depends on the psychological ability to maintain coherence and stability amid difficult, complex and often incomprehensible experiences and events. Survival consciousness involves a mental concept that we use to comprehend and master the demands and experiences of life. This mental concept is a system of thoughts, assumptions, and convictions reflective of our beliefs and attitudes about life. We use it as a reference or guidance system to interpret the events and experiences of daily life and to integrate the long-term implications of our existence. The concept is much like a picture frame. We use it to look at life and define our experiences.

Evolutionary development has equipped the human psyche with the ability for mental adaptation. This capacity enables us to adapt to the circumstances and demands of life in a constructive, self-sustaining manner. Survival consciousness is part archetypal function, part cognitive construct. It is a dynamic mental concept impelled by the religious archetype to maintain psychic balance. The genetic, archetypal capacity for mental adaptation is paired with the assumptions and explanations we use to cope with troubling conditions, situations or experiences we face. Survival consciousness has an innate, instinctive and a conscious, conceptual component. The human psyche provides the genetic function; we provide the concepts. The conceptual content is our contribution to the survival consciousness that we use to deal with the difficulties that affect our lives. Survival consciousness combines innate capacity with personal perspective. The psychic function is inborn and constant; the conceptual content is added and variable.

The adaptation to difficult, contrary, and changing conditions and experiences sets off a sequence of several steps. The archetype instigates the recovery from the initial event (setback, misfortune, loss, etc.) and subsequently involves other parts of the brain to come to terms with the experience. The process is as follows:

- First, the *impact* of the external event,
- followed by the internal *reaction* to the event;
- once the experience has bottomed out, the archetype (instinctive function) activates the genetic ability to maintain psychic balance, thus, initiating a *reversal* in the response;
- the reversal leads to *recovery* from the initial impact of the event, and, finally,
- to a coming to terms with the given situation and achieving *resolution* through problem solving, decision making, and cognitive expansion.

The actual process, usually, involves a period ranging from several hours to several days of internal processing. During this time, psychic and cognitive processes combine to fashion an effective response and to restore mental equilibrium and well-being.

Mental survival is an adaptive capacity of the psyche—a genetic predisposition of the human organism. It is as much a genetic feature as ethological survival behavior. Mental survival is based on organic, adaptive processes and operates largely independent of the conscious content we add to it. Like any archetypal predisposition, it is a functional potentiality dormant in the ground of our being ready to emerge and go into action. When evoked, it fashions an adaptive conceptual response able to accommodate the situation at hand.

We know that ancient peoples worshipped sun and moon and animated the forces of nature to appease them. This tells us about their hardships and fears as well as their attempts to mediate the effects of powers and circumstances they could not control. Over time, the human psyche furnished the ability to adapt not only behaviorally but also mentally to the conditions of the environment. This innate capacity to maintain psychic balance in the face of unforeseen, catastrophic events makes it possible for us to function within the context of a larger macrocosm beyond our control.

Mental adaptation is an archetypal function of the human organism. It enables us to function effectively within a world that is not under our control. While the adaptive function of the psyche is permanent and constant, the content of human survival consciousness differs from person to person. The content sources may vary. Commonly, religion, science, philosophy, mysticism or a personal spirituality provide the particular concepts that comprise a person's survival consciousness. It is the explanation we put on events and experiences that enables us to come to terms with them and to go on with our lives.

Psychic adaptation starts at the archetypal level in the midbrain. It moves from there through a person's psychology and eventually manifests in a specific conceptual content. Survival consciousness is thus an adaptive capacity, which involves genetic and acquired factors as well as different sections of the human brain.

The religious archetype of the human psyche provides an essential adaptive function. This capability exists independent of conscious will and irrespective of the survival concept the individual uses to function in the world. Psychological adaptation is as important to human life as physical, anatomical or environmental adaptation. It allows us to maintain mental balance and stability in our daily lives, even when we experience crisis, catastrophe or change. The archetypal function engenders a psychic process that takes the experiential impact sustained by the person and transposes it into a mental context, making the actual experience tolerable and acceptable. By shifting the experience to the conceptual level it is being transformed and integrated into the individual's existing psychological make-up, restoring coherence and stability. During this process a person's survival concept is often adjusted or enlarged at the same time. The mental concept needs to be renewed or rebuilt when it no longer provides satisfactory explanations for the experiences we face. Then it breaks like a picture frame and needs to be repaired or replaced altogether.

A person's survival consciousness is not static, set, and fixed for life. It is in fact a working concept, essentially based on our hypotheses about life at any given point in time. On occasion, our beliefs and assumptions about life fail us and we have to let them go. We tend to hold on to them as long as they work for us. Our survival concept is continuously being put to the test by the occurrences of our lives, which either confirm or contradict the validity of our theories and explanations. At times, this adaptive concept may be challenged and may need to be revised.

The conceptual content of survival consciousness corresponds to a person's psychological development. The level of psychological development determines a person's relationship to the world as well as her perception of the events in it. The developmental psychology of the individual, therefore, provides the foundation for the interpretation of experiences as well as the filter for the selection of particular conceptual contents. Just as a child sees the world differently from grownups, so do adults, depending on their developmental level, differ in the way they perceive and interpret the experiences and events of their lives.

Survival consciousness is, therefore, based on an archetypal function and a psychological variable. The mental concept typically addresses the various dimensions where adaptation is sought: relationship to self, environment, and universe.

The survival concept varies on a developmental continuum. Usually, the content of survival consciousness is remarkably consistent with the person's level of psychological maturity. A survival concept formed on the basis of psychological dependency involves low self-esteem and self-deprecation, feelings of anxiety and insecurity, deficiency and scarcity thinking, the belief that human events are determined by external or supernatural factors, the notion that life is a struggle and that the odds are against the individual. The person perceives herself as the object of outside powers and the victim of circumstance; the universe is seen as hostile and adverse; there is the belief in an anthropomorphic deity based on psychological projection, a cosmology of good and evil, and a basic dissociation of individual and universe.

By contrast, a survival concept based on autonomy includes positive self-worth and self-referral. Human consciousness, at that level, emanates from a psychology of confidence, responsibility, and self-reliance. Life is seen in the wider context of nature and universe, and the individual perceives himself/herself as part of an evolutionary and cosmic process. Human events are viewed as the result of mental attitudes and an interdependence with the higher order of a cosmic universe. The underlying scientific and metaphysical concept is a notion of unity. The main features of this syndrome are maturity and mastery. The individual has learned how to live and to be in alignment with the universe.

The actual survival concept for the majority of people lies somewhere in-between. The content of a person's survival consciousness tends to change in accordance with the degree of his/her psychological development. This change of content usually occurs gradually. On occasion, experiences of crisis and disaster force the reconstruction of a person's survival concept. With each revision, survival consciousness expands and grows—the world looks different and life changes.

A state of dependency usually limits effective adaptation to the challenges and changes of life, setting up a vicious cycle of insecurity and deprivation. Associated experiences of anxiety and depression stifle effective adaptive responses. A survival concept based on dependency tends to be rigid, fragile, and quite often ineffective. Limited psychological resources minimize the person's adaptive capacity. The resilience of the survival consciousness correlates directly with the level of psychological development. Mature people are usually strong. Their survival concept is supported by personal growth. Maturity and autonomy promote effective adaptation. When faced with identical life circumstances, mature and dependent people respond and operate differently. Independent people exhibit the flexibility and expansiveness of the survivor personality. Their actions are usually enhanced by feelings of serenity and accompanied by a sense of purpose. Their survival consciousness is reliable and robust.

Survival consciousness has a genetic and a developmental component. On the most basic level, the human psyche provides the adaptive response. Higher levels of survival consciousness are evidenced by a reverse correlation between fear and faith. Trust in one's ability to come to terms with the unpredictable, uncontrollable events and experiences of life and trust in the intelligence and functioning of the larger order of life, nature, and universe are the hallmark of advanced survival consciousness. Total trust means absence of fear. Ultimately, trust in life heals the *spiritual wound*, dissolving the separation of mind and body, biology and nature, psyche and cosmos.

Psychological adaptation is a product of genetic evolution and a primary function of the human psyche. The adaptive capability to adapt to life circumstances and to 'maintain psychic balance' is innate. Psychic adaptation is part of the natural healing process of the human organism.

The human psyche, formed by evolutionary process, enables behavioral and mental adaptation. The bipolarity of the archetypes between instinct and spirit sets the stage for the adaptation we have to achieve. Ethological behavior and psychic function manifest the two poles of the human archetypes—the organic ground of life. Here is where we connect with the physical reality of our lives and with the metaphysical dimension of human existence.

Evolutionary functioning goes back to the innate, archetypal structure of the human psyche. It brings to bear the collective wisdom and survival experience of our species, which shaped the human psyche through evolutionary adaptation. Because of its genetic foundation, evolutionary functioning is a metapsychology that is common to our species and supersedes all individual psychologies.

Chapter Three

> A hunter uses his world sparingly and with tenderness, regardless of whether the world might be things, or plants, or animals, or people, or power.
>
> Carlos Castaneda
> Lessons

Advanced Adaptive Functioning

Ours is an evolution from biology to consciousness. When our ancestors left the forest for life on the savannah, the instinct provided the adaptation to the environment. Faced with new living conditions in the open plains without the protection of the forest, things had to change. Relative body size and limited physical abilities, combined with a new way of life, pushed the evolution of our species in a different direction from that of the animal. To compensate for lack of size, strength or speed compared to the animals around them, early man began to develop tools and weapons. Another phase of adaptation had begun.

The development of tools, weapons and rudimentary communication for hunting, feeding and group activity forced the evolution of the human brain. As the brain evolved and eventually doubled in size, adaptation began to expand beyond the instinct. The exposure to nomadic life, the constant threat from predators and the vicissitudes of nature posed events and experiences that had to be dealt with. The brain carried the evolution to accommodate the adaptation to ever changing conditions and requirements of life. Early man began to develop elaborate strategies for hunting, he began to develop organization and language to engage in communal activities, and he began to animate nature to come to terms with its forces. This journey from instinct to consciousness and spirit, which transformed the species, is replicated in the human brain. The evolutionary formation in layers of functional capabilities, from the reptilian and mammalian to a uniquely human brain, reflects the various phases of human adaptation to the outer and inner realities of life.

Human nature is a product of evolutionary adaptation. The basic nature of our species developed during a period of our history when the primordial ancestor survived as a hunter and gatherer: both body and mind were shaped by evolutionary process. This unique formation of anatomy, behavior, and psyche sets us apart from other creatures and gives us our distinct survival advantage. Evolution did not fit the human being to any particular environment or specific routine like all other forms of life. And, rather than developing particular physical features such as strength, size or speed that favor the animal, nature gave us the advantage of a unique brain. Human survival depended on the evolution of the brain rather than that of the body.

Neurological research during the last few decades has significantly contributed to our understanding of brain functioning and human behavior. It has revealed the intricate anatomy of the brain—old and new, right and left—and the delicate interaction of its neurology. It has also established structure and functioning of the brain as the manifestation of the evolutionary history of our species.

The human brain consists of several components, all linked to various stages of evolutionary development[1]. The reptilian brain, located in the brain stem, belongs to the oldest section of the human brain: it regulates the vital functions of the body. The younger mammalian brain in the midsection provides essential balancing mechanisms. It controls important physiological and biochemical processes such as metabolism, sleep, hormonal and sexual functioning. Additionally, it regulates basic emotions and behavioral responses to the environment. The midbrain is the center of instinctive, ethological behavior and the neurological foundation of man's archetypal nature. The new brain, neocortex, is responsible for cognition and perception. Unique to the evolution of the human brain is the development of two separate halves, located in the left and the right hemispheres. This lateralization of the neocortex is the result of man's particular adaptation to the environment—through the development of weapons, tools, social organization, language and speech, on the one side, and through the development of perceptual, sensory, intuitive, synthetic abilities, as well as, the formation of higher consciousness, on the other.

Each part of the brain performs critical survival functions. The older sections of the brain (brain stem and midbrain) are responsible for biological survival, essentially controlling physiology, consciousness and behavior. These parts of the brain involve the organic and archetypal structures, basic to the process of life. The midbrain in conjunction with the new brain is responsible for mental adaptation and survival, sustaining psychic equilibrium by fashioning cognitive and emotional coherence in response to human events and experiences. The new brain (right and left brain hemispheres) facilitates instrumental survival by providing such advanced functions as perception, orientation and language and by controlling essential processes such as learning, movement and memory. The left brain, in particular, confers competence to interface and interact with the survival environment of the modern world, which is its own creation. The right brain, carrying on the natural evolution of our species, engenders connection to a larger context of being through higher consciousness and spirituality.

The Evolution of Higher Consciousness

The archetypes of the human psyche, described by Jung, have been identified as part of the older brain. The archetypal system is located primarily in the limbic system and the brain stem. Survival behavior such as courting, sexuality, dominance and submission, territorial defense and maternal attachment originate from the neuronal systems in the midbrain. Survival consciousness involves both the old and the new brains. The instinctive pole of the archetypes is associated with the limbic system and the brain stem; the spiritual pole involves limbic system and both cerebral hemispheres, especially the right. Advanced adaptive functioning involves coordinated neurological functioning between all parts of the brain.

The survival value of the new brain results from its separation into two halves. The right brain has intuitive, creative and visual-spatial properties; its visionary and synthetic qualities make it "the strategic side of the brain"[1]. It lets us see the 'whole picture' and enables us to incorporate change. Right-sidedness provides the notion of the coherence of life, a deeper sense of meaning, and a vision and plan for human existence. The left brain provides the basis for rational knowledge. It is the locus of cognitive, linguistic and manipulatory skills; given its empirical, analytical and rational abilities it is action-oriented. Left-sidedness provides instrumental adaptation. Its instrumentality teaches technical skills and operational know-how; its principle of cause and effect motivates growth. The survival contributions of both cerebral hemispheres are important for effective adaptation.

Since the beginning of the scientific and industrial revolutions, cultural conditioning in the West has favored the development and use of the left brain. This was at the expense of right-brain functioning. This left-sided dominance[2], however, goes beyond cultural influence. The neurological inhibition executed by the left brain can intercept interaction between right and left brain, as well as, transmission of adaptive processes between the old and the new brain[3]. The intellect can silence the remainder of the brain. It happens often. People do it constantly. It is common in our culture. The survival value of the left human brain, the domain of the intellect, has traditionally been overrated at the expense of evolutionary functioning. The consequences of this development are far-reaching, both individually and collectively.

Dominance of the left brain, even though culturally favored, produces a significant survival disadvantage: it suppresses vital adaptive processes of human nature—instinctual, ethological, archetypal, intuitive, strategic, holistic, affective. It excludes other parts of the brain, which are essential to human survival. It diminishes our abilities for successful adaptation. Left-sided dominance severs us from our evolutionary past and from the powers nature provides for survival.

The anatomical complexity of the human brain shows the imprint of evolutionary adaptation. Modern neurology speaks of three, even four, brains in one—each with its own special intelligence, memory, sense of time and space, and its own motor functions[4]. The survival value of the new brain exists in conjunction with the adaptive systems of the older brain. Optimization of survival advantage and survival ability depends on the functioning of the brain as a total entity. Full utilization of the brain is less a matter of using infinite amounts of brain cells as it is an issue of employing the various parts of it. Effective survival and adaptation—material, environmental and spiritual—are dependent upon the psyche functioning as a balanced totality. The neurology of human survival rests indispensably on the horizontal integration between left and right hemispheres and the vertical integration of old and new brains[5].

Survival comes from within. It originates and operates from within the brain. Three major faculties are involved in our survival: instinct, intuition and intellect. They support us in a sundry of ways. Each faculty relates to different aspects of our life. The instincts refer to the biological aspect of survival. They position us to pursue our practical needs and to address the environmental conditions we face. Intuition, a function of the right brain, the seat of higher consciousness, enables mental and metaphysical survival. It provides the perception of life in time and space and alignment with a larger context or higher order of being. The intellect enables instrumental survival. It furnishes the ability for rational thought, inquiry and manipulatory action along with the cognitive, social and occupational skills to function in society.

These internal faculties relate to external realities. Each faculty stands for a unique reality. The instincts connect us with nature and biology, intuition relates us to the realm of spirit and the cosmic universe. Furthermore, the intellect takes us into the man-made world of society and culture. Each of these realities is important to our survival. We can access each of these faculties, enter each of these worlds, at will, as we would shift gears in a car.

The survival demands posed by a specific domain call for the corresponding faculty. We require the instincts, our ethological behavior, to pursue our practical needs within a given environment. We need our intuition, as part of the psychic function, to address the spiritual issues of life and to maintain psychic balance. And, finally, we enlist the intellect to accommodate the rational conventions of society (with regard to language, time and techniques) and to function within the social and occupational context of our lives. In short, biological, material needs require the use of the instincts; mental or spiritual issues require the use of our intuition; and last but not least, social and cultural interaction requires the use of the intellect.

The different domains of our lives are not physical locations, rather, separate realities, composing the external conditions of our survival. At the same time, they are extensions of our internal faculties: they are reflective of our organic constitution as biological, spiritual and cognitive beings. The reciprocity of outer and inner worlds, both as an outside condition and as an extension of ourselves, defines the parameters of human survival.

In each domain, we are part of a larger context, and the key events in each are subject to outside rule. Whether controlled by the laws of biology, the principles of metaphysics and cosmic law, or by the conditions of society, we find ourselves in a situation where external facts and forces set the terms of our existence. The magnitude of these issues and their implications for the human

Internal Faculties and Survival Activity

	Instinct	Intuition	Intellect
Origin	innate	innate	developed
Brain Region	midbrain, brain stem	right cerebral hemisphere	left cerebral hemisphere
Adaptive Feature	survival behavior(*)	survival consciousness(**)	survival skills
Adaptive Function	biological/material survival	mental/spiritual survival	instrumental survival
Adaptive Domain	biology and nature	spirit and universe	society and culture

(*) Ethological behavior plus primary sensations and emotions.
(**) Instinctive function (midbrain, brain stem) combined with conceptual content (predominantly, right cerebral hemisphere; some left-brain collaboration).

Table 1

condition are enormous. Man's existential position forces the paradoxical issue: how to be in charge without having control?

Effective adaptation to life favors instinct and intuition, with the intellect on standby. The intellect does not have the reinforcement of biological intelligence that fortifies evolutionary functioning. It is not embedded in the archetypal process of life. The important things in life, the long-term issues, call for instinct and spirit. Our relationship to life exists on the inside, preformed in the archetypes. From there, comes the 'know-why' of life. The intellect supplies instrumental skills and information for the interface with the world of society and culture. It provides the necessary 'know-how' for life.

Human survival in the modern age requires a paradigm shift to a world of different dimensions, placing life into the larger context of natural and cosmic realities and lessening our dependence on the intellect. It requires a perspective on things that stays close to biology and metaphysics—the ultimate frontiers of human survival. Life needs to be brought in line with the timeless, universal issues of the human experience. There needs to be the realization that human destiny transcends the transitory appeal of culture and society.

Left and right brains, both parts of the new brain, have assumed different functions. The left brain is primarily cognitive, analytical and operates on the principle of cause and effect, establishing a world of intellectual distinctions and relationships. The right brain with its intuitive, holistic, synthetic qualities lets us see the 'whole picture' and transforms experiences and thoughts into concepts and decisions[6]. Words are the language of the left brain, pictures are the language of the right brain. One is the center of speech, the other the hub of our visions and dreams. The left brain enables rational thought; the right brain creates symbolic expression. We need both parts of the new brain to operate effectively in the world: the right brain is strategic, the left brain action-oriented. Both evolved from the older midbrain, the seat of the evolutionary psyche.

Because of related qualities, evolutionary psyche and right brain make a natural match. There is no relationship between left brain and midbrain; the intellect inhibits evolutionary functioning[7]. Formation and functioning of the human brain symbolize the history of our species. While the left brain was driving cultural evolution towards human civilization, the right brain was carrying on the natural evolution of our species towards higher consciousness and morality. The left brain initialized our cultural evolution separate from our biological past, whereas, the evolution of the human psyche extended to the right brain. Natural adaptation consistently followed the biological line. This evolution was carried by the archetypes, expanding from instinct to spirit. Human survival was to include biology and metaphysics, behavior and mind.

Basic consciousness emanates from the organic ability of the brain stem to maintain alertness and animation; higher consciousness results from the expansion of the evolutionary psyche to the new brain. Higher consciousness involves the awareness of our being and existence. Mental adaptation reaches its highest level in advanced consciousness and spirituality. Higher consciousness resonates with the myths and symbols reflecting the universal life of the species, echoing the human archetypes. It also connects us to the larger realities of the cosmic universe. Modern physics and metaphysics tell us that "cosmos and man . . . obey the same law; that man is a microcosm and is not separated from the macrocosm by any fixed barriers. The very same laws rule for the one as for the other, and from the one a way leads into the other. The psyche and the cosmos are to each other like the inner world and the outer world. Therefore man participates by nature in all cosmic events, and is inwardly as well as outwardly interwoven with them"[8]. Higher consciousness enables us to maintain psychic balance and to function within the larger context of a macrocosm that is beyond our comprehension and control. Spanning from instinct to spirit, the evolutionary psyche relates us both to the biology of life and nature and to the metaphysics of the cosmic order that surrounds us: it integrates worlds.

The Evolution of Advanced Morality

The expansion of biology to higher consciousness includes the evolution of advanced morality. The ethics of biology are based on the preservation of the species. The instincts are life-enforcing and designed to promote the existence of the individual and that of the group, calibrated to mediate between individual and collective interests. Because the instincts are meant to support the life of individual and community, they are vested with rules and inhibitions. The ethics of biology center primarily on the protection of life, property and community[1]. Basic norms of biological behavior—regulating (a) the inhibition to kill, (b) the possession of property, and (c) the possession of the partner—imply that, by nature, we seek peace and we respect property, honesty, loyalty and obedience[2]. The human intellect broke with the laws of nature, obviating the intent of the instinct. It has subverted the biological inhibition against killing, and it has employed our innate aggression for destructive designs. While the pairing of left brain and instincts suggests destructive consequences, the combination of midbrain and right brain furthers the moral evolution of human conduct.

Higher consciousness engenders a spiritual ethic, which places human life in the context of the natural and cosmic order. Its hallmark is a moral sense to protect and not to harm, which not only extends to our fellowman but to all living things that share our world. Moral evolution expands the ethics of biology. Not only are we charged with the responsibility for our own survival, we are also given the responsibility for the impact of our lives and our actions on the world. This is not the kind of socialized morality that constantly needs to be enforced by either priest or police, where violence or abuse are an option, where opportunity provides the alibi, and where the prospect of absolution reinforces immaturity. It is, instead, a morality that has archetypal roots and comes from within, where aggression is constrained by natural inhibition and not subject to the designs of the intellect. It is a morality that is there when nobody is watching and where public face and private face are one and the same. It is a morality based on an innate moral sense that promotes personal responsibility and integrity, and that seeks harmony with people and environment in the pursuit of individual and collective survival.

Moral integrity is the sign of advanced personal evolution and maturity and it starts at home. It combines compassion with respect and reaffirms our common bond with all other forms of life on the planet. Spiritual ethics present the pinnacle of human evolution. If we, as a species, were to advance human consciousness by following the evolutionary path laid out by the right brain hemisphere, humanity would truly have a chance to survive—curbing the imperialism of the intellect[3], which potentially has the ability to take us to the brink of our own destruction.

The paradigm of human evolution is the journey from the biology of the instincts to the higher consciousness of the human spirit. From its biological beginnings, the human psyche extended to the realm of rational thought and spiritual awareness expanding from the old brain to the new. The evolution is reflected in the polarity of the archetypes. They reach from the behavior of the instincts to the symbolic expressions of human consciousness. The instincts evolved to address the biological issues of life—everything related to livelihood, physical well-being, family, space, security, community, economics and defense, mating and procreation, religion and ritual. Rationality and spirituality evolved to address the mental, emotional and spiritual repercussions of life, which result from the awareness of our own being and existence.

The evolutionary journey from biology to consciousness is the subject of mythologies and artistic expression of all peoples. The symbolic representations of this journey, which is genetically laid out in the archetypes of the human psyche, appear in the myths and symbols of mankind[4]. We find them in the universal themes of folklore, literature and art. They portray the human journey, the universal drama of the human psyche. The story is the story of Everyman, the individual, cast as a universal story—the evolutionary story of the species. The hero's journey is the evolutionary journey. Human evolution is not only replicated in the formation of the brain but also in our genes, that is, in the archetypes of the collective human psyche, which impel human life to unfold in accordance with the eternal life of the species[5]. Myths represent this journey of the human psyche and symbolically tell the common story of all of us.

The archetypal polarity between instinct and spirit is the pathway of human evolution for the species and for the individual. The expansion from instinct to spirit, from biology to metaphysics, is invariably the paradigm for personal evolution and mythology, that journey we all must take, the advancement we all must seek, to achieve higher consciousness and adaptive functioning—the hero's journey of mythology.

PART II

Where the moralist would be filled with indignation and the tragic poet with pity and terror, mythology breaks the whole of life into a vast, horrendous Divine Comedy. Its Olympian laugh is not escapist in the least, but hard, with the hardness of life itself—which, we may take it, is the hardness of God, the Creator. Mythology, in this respect, makes the tragic attitude seem somewhat hysterical, and the merely moral judgment shortsighted. Yet the hardness is balanced by an assurance that all that we see is but the reflex of a power that endures, untouched by the pain. Thus the tales are both pitiless and terrorless—suffused with the joy of a transcendent anonymity regarding itself in all of the self-centered, battling egos that are born and die in time.

Joseph Campbell

Evolutionary functioning involves genetic features and abilities. It utilizes behaviors, feelings, values and psychic functions preformed in human nature to enable our survival. Evolutionary functioning relies on innate capabilities particularly designed for the adaptive requirements imposed on human life. As a genetically preexistent capacity of human nature, evolutionary functioning is part of our natural make-up, readily and permanently available for our survival. It depends on inherent, human qualities that hold the wisdom of nature and have withstood the test of time. The fact that we live in a modern, different world does not dispute their value and validity. The fact is that even the modern world, although man-made, is still biological in nature. The biology of human evolution did not stop when man decided to take over and to determine his own fate. Evolutionary functioning is as relevant today as in other times of human history in addressing the biological and metaphysical needs of the individual.

The culturally conditioned psychology, that society teaches us and that most of us rely on to live our lives, is not related to evolution and survival. It originates in the left brain hemisphere and it is operated by the intellect. The new brain is a latecomer, missing out on a large portion of human history. Culturally conditioned psychology itself is a creation of human civilization and lacks the survival experience of our species. Its purpose is consistent with the priorities and expectations of the environment, not the survival needs of the individual. The main focus of socialized psychology is adjustment to society, not adaptation to life. Socialized psychology is based on social learning and enables cognitive functioning. It provides understanding through the intellect rather than "understanding through life"[1]. Culturally conditioned psychology is not qualified to deal with the adaptive issues of life. Evolutionary functioning, on the other hand, contains the biological intelligence of life. It is firmly grounded in the behavioral and psychological history of our species to provide the adaptive capability for us to survive in the modern complex, constantly changing world.

Evolutionary adaptation forged the duality of our nature as both physical and mental beings. Our dual nature spells out special needs for body and mind. The needs of the body, biological in nature, are practical and material. The needs of the mind are metaphysical, that is, mental and spiritual. Human survival is always about biology and metaphysics making them the ultimate frontiers of our survival.

Survival is about the business of living. Life is a large assignment. Most of its tasks involve lifelong commitments. We need food for nourishment and a home for shelter. For that we need to secure a livelihood, go to work and maintain our health. Alongside, we lead a marriage, raise children, relate to people, go to church, obey laws and follow customs. During all these events we need to form attachments, grow into maturity, take our place in the world, assume adult responsibilities, make decisions, deal with change, success and misfortune, and, finally, prepare for dying. And in the end and all along, we need to make sense of it all.

Unlike the animal, human beings are conscious of the experience of life. This condition is both the peculiar dilemma and the challenge of human existence. We look for reasons, consider outcomes, enjoy love, feel sorrow, remember yesterday and know about tomorrow. We do, think, and feel all at the same time. Action and awareness fall together.

Human life is fixed at the juncture of opposites. It is constantly suspended between the practical demands of living and the psychological necessities of personal growth, the biological imperatives of human nature and the cultural influences of society, the physical reality and the spiritual significance of human events. On one side, we are subject to the organic paradox of growth and decay, life and death. On the other side, we are faced with the existential ambivalence of meaning or futility, salvation or despair.

We all live two lives—a practical and a spiritual one. Neither is a totality of itself. Each is the counterpart of the other. It is the interplay between them, the practical-spiritual realization of the two as one, that constitutes life. Such a life spans a mind which is both conscious and unconscious, a being which is both primordial and civilized, a condition which is both biological and cultural, an existence which is both physical and metaphysical, a history which is both contemporary and timeless, and a destiny which is both personal and universal.

The application and use of evolutionary functioning in modern life requires a reality switch. It requires sorting out realities. It is a switch that brings the important dimensions of life to the foreground and moves the lesser important to the background—much like the figure-ground switch in the picture when, while watching it, the 'old hag' suddenly turns into the 'pretty young woman'. Whatever we focus on and pay attention to becomes figure and foreground. We need to recognize the biological dimension of life and separate it out from the social reality of values, norms and rituals. We need to do the same with regard to the metaphysical reality of life. Once we understand money-making, family, community, or territorial defense as ethological issues and events, we respond to them with biological intent and effectiveness. Once we understand the metaphysical dimension of life as our connection and relationship with a larger context of being, we can discard the unimportant and unnecessary. The archetypes of the human psyche bring us closer to life. They involve us in biology and metaphysics—the frontiers of our primary needs. Society, on the other hand, is only an instrumentality, a contemporary manifestation of human culture.

By sorting out the different dimensions and realities of life, we are reconstituting our world. What was important once, no longer seems important now. What was unconscious, ignored or only vaguely felt and imagined, has now assumed vital importance. Here, a word of caution about avoiding extremes and doing one thing at the expense of the other. Too much of the biological leads to materialism. Too much of the metaphysical engenders mysticism. Mere practicality overcomes a person with blindness, excessive spirituality with weakness. Either extreme ends in a life devoid of substance and stability. There needs to be a balance, a bipolar orientation to life, to have a clear sense of direction and meaning. Behavioral and mental adaptation are the two sides of the same coin. Practicality and spirituality are complementary aspects of human nature and human events. Crossing the divide unifies the two aspects of our being and, in that, joins outer and inner worlds.

Behavioral and mental adaptation embody the biological and metaphysical sides of our being and follow the archetypal principles "governing the organic and psychic processes of life"[2]. The practical and spiritual realities of life begin in us. The archetypes are the imprint of nature on the human psyche. The duality of our being and the duality of human life are preexistent in the archetypes of our nature.

Chapter Four

> Every one, whether consciously or unconsciously, is trying to recover the luxurious, effortless sense of security which he knew in the womb. Those who are able to realize themselves do actually achieve this state; not by a blind, unconscious yearning for the uterine condition, but by transforming the world in which they live into a veritable womb.
>
> Henry Miller
> Essays

Behavioral Adaptation

Behavioral adaptation rests on the biological orientation that views life as an organic process subject to biological intent. The universal blueprint of human life exists in the archetypes of the collective psyche common to all of us. It defines the basic stages, events and needs characteristic of human life. These patterns reflect the fundamental biological requirements of human nature and have distinct survival quality. Like any other form of life, we too need to follow the design of our nature to find completion and fulfillment. Behavioral adaptation addresses the material requirements of life—such as economic, familial, communal and territorial needs.

The practical side of human life relates to biology, the organic level of the archetypes. Whether we know it or not, we live not only our own lives but also the universal life of our species. Our lives draw from the generic blueprint of human life genetically engraved in the archetypes. Like the 'living stuff' that makes the seedling grow into a mature fruit-bearing plant, the archetypal life cycle of our species—from birth, bonding with mother and initiation by father, to sexual and social maturity, and then on to adult membership in society, old age and death—already exists preformed in our nature.

Preexistent also is a pattern of human needs, which, to a large extent, determines what is important in life. These are the archetypal needs, universal to our species and essential to human survival. They include the need for food, shelter, family and children; the need for community and belonging, for language and communication; the need for values, customs, religion and rituals; the economic need for hunting, gathering; the need for security and territorial defense.

All of our lives are intimately tied to these needs and the universal cycle of events they reflect. Most of human life revolves around them. These primal needs and occurrences are the result of a long history of evolutionary adaptation, establishing the requirements of human life. We need to match life's design with nature's demands. Consciously or unconsciously, we are always in pursuit of those needs, often in disguised or symbolic ways—such as when we go to work, fall in love, establish residence, acquire insurance, make friends, get married, join clubs, protect the neighborhood, pray in church, or celebrate holidays.

Nature holds us to these needs. It holds us accountable for any perpetration against its ways. It retaliates with restlessness, despair or disease. The relevance of this adaptation is such that few substitutes will do. Nature requires life to be on its terms. A survival scenario that accommodates the requirements of human nature results in a life of health and inner peace.

There is, of course, nothing new about the nature of human needs; what changes are the cultural circumstances that surround the gratification of those needs. Political and social trends along with economic conditions tend to influence the sentiments toward work, property, marriage, sexuality, family, religion, community, roles, rules, and so forth. Often, this revision of cultural attitudes leads us away from the importance of human nature and its demands on our lives. Cultural and social values often compete or conflict with the realization of our basic human nature.

As a result of modern industrial and technological events, many institutions have undergone changes including a revision of the human life cycle altogether. The family, for instance, has been cut dramatically in size and functions; religious life has been extensively secularized; marriage has become extremely fragile and tenuous; and human life has been centered exclusively on the duration of a person's work life. These changes are externally induced and have not developed organically as extensions of human nature. The needs society creates—consumption, prestige, status symbols and many others—rarely correspond to our basic human needs.

A life that disregards all of its biological imperatives and that is totally absorbed in external values remains incomplete and unfulfilled. Any default against human nature will eventually come back to haunt us. Nature retains the ultimate authority to set the pace and purpose of life. Using human nature as the baseline for life and survival gives a clear and linear direction.

Human fulfillment, ultimately, refers to a life that achieves alignment with its nature. Compliance with the biological intent of life, doing what we are supposed to do, yields a twofold fulfillment: we satisfy our most basic needs, getting what we need; and we complete the psychic development outlined by our destiny, becoming what we are meant to be.

Operating Life As a Business

Material survival has undergone drastic changes throughout the course of human history. Our species went from a nomadic hunting society to a self-sufficient rural society, and from there to the complex urban society of today. Also changed have the means by which we secure food, shelter and all the other material necessities of life. What was the bow to the early hunter, the plough to the pre-industrial farmer, is the bank note or credit card to the modern consumer—all instruments used to provide a living. We no longer hunt the animal, work the fields or grow our own food. Material survival now requires only one thing: money. It has been reduced to a single issue: the ability to buy, with money as the means of exchange. The attainment of money, the principal token of survival, involves still another transaction: the exchange of work, products or services for wage or salary, payment, or fee.

The changes in the economics of the human condition brought about far-reaching consequences for the survival of the individual. Industrialization and urbanization moved people from the land to the city, yet on a deeper level caused a shift from self-sufficiency to economic dependence. Large-scale industrial production introduced employment as a new form of economic activity. Employment, the exchange of work and time for pay, is primarily controlled by external interests—the employer, the industry, and the marketplace in general. Employment requires certain behaviors and attitudes. It changes the conditions of material survival. Employment asks people to assume company values, pursue company goals, and perform company roles. It causes people to assume functional identities, specialize their skills, attach their financial fortunes to that of the company, keep or lose their jobs at the discretion of the employer. In essence, employment subjects the individual to the control and conditioning of the *industrial life cycle*[1]. This process unfolds in typical sequence: after learning a trade or profession, a person finds a job, works in an office or factory, and receives money in exchange for time and labor. Work life lasts an average of forty years. It starts at age 20 to 25 and ends at age 62 or 65 with schooling on one side and retirement on the other. Often, school lasts longer than retirement.

The industrial life cycle, which overrides the natural life cycle, isolates adulthood as the single most important phase in life based on its economic potential. Targeted are people's productive and commercial value as a labor and consumer force. Western industrial society defines human life in strictly economic terms. In essence, most people are faced with survival conditions where the purpose and sequence of life are defined for them, where the demands are large and control is minimal, and where the benefits come with a high price. Industrial employment carries with it the risks and vulnerabilities of the marketplace. The growing complexity of the global economy only adds to the financial and existential vulnerabilities in people's lives. All these factors exacerbate the economic dependence and undermine the successful survival of the individual.

The economic conditions of the modern age require new adaptations to secure the material survival of the individual. The objective of environmental adaptation is to gain and retain selective survival advantage. Effective adaptation to the industrial and post-industrial environment builds on the reversal of key elements of economic activity that restrict individual survival. Adaptive strategies are aimed at reversing economic dependence, skill specialization, diminished autonomy and control, and the personality factors of externalized values and identities. The goal of effective adaptation is to establish the foundation for autonomous functioning as the basis for individual survival activity. The primary objective of adaptation is to maintain control of need gratification. Essential elements of adaptive functioning include strategic positioning, field-independence and generality of skills. These adaptive principles allow people to maintain control in determining their economic activities, pursuing revenue opportunities, deploying their skills and talents. These principles also provide the platform for controlling personal and family finances, managing change and transitions, responding to changes in external, macroeconomic conditions. Reversing the elements of contemporary survival, adverse to independent functioning, transfers all components of the survival activity to the individual. This transfer of control and responsibility, which consolidates the survival position of the individual, is the critical economic adaptation in modern life.

Taking charge of all components of the material survival activity compares to managing and operating a business. The business is survival. This coincides with the biological imperative that makes survival the person's responsibility and business. Survival today is structured in an unprecedented way. It requires adaptation to an environment where material survival depends on a symbolic token—money—in exchange for labor, products or services. Conducting life as a business provides an economic concept designed to adapt to the industrial conditions of modern life. The whole of life with all its financial matters is turned into a business. This adaptation puts life directly at the survival frontier of modern existence. It enlarges the financial effort into a comprehensive venture with an opening towards the future, able to accommodate various revenue options and opportunities over time consistent with an existing business plan and fiscal schedule.

As with any business, its aim is profitability and overall asset growth. Conducting life as a business requires versatile and transferable skills. The strategy for the deployment of professional and financial resources is set on a wide, diversified scope. It may involve the production and/or distribution of goods, professional services of any kind, contract work, retail, real estate, financial investments, and other income-producing options, individually or in combination. The notion of pursuing a lifelong career, usually, is too narrow and limiting to fit the business plan, unless additional economic activities provide revenue and security. The business strategy typically includes low-risk investments and insurance schemes to create the necessary immunity against changes and economic downturns, and to control for worst-case scenarios.

Accountability and measurement of progress are as much part of routine business practice as are promotion and marketing. The business format can be employment or self-employment—as long as it provides the flexibility of an open system and a shield against external threats. In the case of employment, it is always advantageous to choose trades or professions that lend themselves naturally to transfer or eventual self-employment, unless a second career or line of business is envisioned before retirement. On the expenditure side, the venture carries the usual items of a household and family budget.

Economic behavior is the most immediate and direct manifestation of the human survival instinct. It is designed to furnish the material provisions and necessities of life. Economic skills are crucial to material survival. They provide the combined ability to generate income, develop assets, establish financial, economic well-being and security. Important skills include financial planning, budgeting, investing, marketing and product development. It is important to understand the dynamics of money and asset building, investment principles, tax codes, basic economic science; as it is important to accumulate the necessary practical experience[2].

Economic behavior activates ethological processes. It brings the survival value of human aggression into play. Aggression facilitates survival. It evolved to support need gratification. Adaptive aggression is designed to fortify our transactions with the environment and to provide the necessary energy and forcefulness to carry through. Aggression enables us to face the world, transact with the environment, compete for resources, achieve economic gain. Aggression is the propelling force that provides drive and confidence. It tends to bring out the best in people—strength and performance. Economic behavior is today's equivalent of the hunting behavior of the early ancestor. Pioneering the economic frontier of human existence follows the evolutionary impulse of the species.

Need gratification proceeds through transaction with the environment. It depends on how successful we are in approaching the world, in promoting our skills and achievements, and in gaining financial returns on our products and services. These transactions frequently hinge on personality factors that determine how we position and present ourselves. A secondary function of aggression lies in alleviating limiting psychological issues[3]. Aggression can be used to overcome the inhibiting effects of socialization on adaptive functioning[4]. Adaptive aggression, thus, supports material survival both externally and internally: as a driving force for accessing environmental resources and as an antidote to anxiety.

The responsibility for survival goes to the individual. The concept of operating life as a business manifests the notion that we are totally responsible for ourselves and that survival is entirely our business. Once we adopt this perspective on life, matters of time, money, assets and opportunities take on a new, significant meaning. This economic concept, which converts the activities of material survival in a person's life into a business venture, is in line with evolutionary principles. Operating one's life as a business is consistent with the fact that individuality, personal initiative and responsibility are evolutionary traits of human nature and, as such, supportive of successful adaptation[5]. Overall management remains in the hands of the individual as owner and executive. Management is concerned with securing material survival and steering clear of the pitfalls of the industrial life cycle. This concept has an entrepreneurial aspect that seeks to develop the business and maximize its returns. Like any other business, it is operated on the principle of perpetual existence as the individual retains responsibility for survival until the very end. This, in itself, is a life-enhancing posture. The emotional and existential goals that motivate this concept are a sense of basic comfort, security and peacefulness, a life that moves in harmony with the natural life cycle, and a condition where money and financial matters—the key elements of modern survival—are no concern.

'Life as a business' can be operated at various risk levels, depending on the strength of financial assets and on whether employment or self-employment is involved. These adaptive principles work for employment, in that they provide the necessary perspective; they work best for self-employment, where they can be put to full use. In essence, however, operating life as a business is less a matter of employment, self-employment or financial independence than that of a total approach and commitment to survival. Conducting life as a business is a conscious and strategic adaptation to and in a world where survival largely depends on financial assets and buying power.

Like a business firm, this approach to material survival is devised to manage for maximum results. It is organized to increase growth and return on assets. The underlying strategy treats revenues, expenditures, capabilities, resources, market factors, and economic conditions with the intent to gain competitive advantage. The business focus provides the strategic framework "to guide those choices that determine the nature and direction"[6] of the venture. Strategic management is just as essential for individual as it is for corporate survival. It enables superior performance and prosperity.

Running life as a business is the opposite of the preoccupation with a job that takes over a person's life. It is the difference between 'doing the right things' and 'doing things right'[7]. The person who is overidentified with a job often has succumbed to the values and demands of society—blinded by status and prestige, caught in appearances and expectations, and often trapped in a specialized and narrow career track. Conformity and compliance may be 'doing things right' on one side, yet, may not be 'doing the right thing' when it comes to survival.

In contrast, operating life as a business provides a format for material survival that uses the marketplace to its own advantage. In this model you hire your own employer, devise your own business plan, and never retire because nobody had hired you in the first place. This model turns things around: you no longer hold a job but run a business, you no longer work for someone but for yourself. You are no longer an employee, subordinate, and dependent on a company to provide for you. Instead, you are the boss who calls the shots and runs the show.

Strategic decision-making and control are retained by the individual who assumes final responsibility for his/her survival. The business mission is aimed at financial health and longevity. It involves doing whatever is necessary to make the venture successful. Thus, abilities to solve problems, make decisions, take action, and manage time are at a premium. Assuming absolute accountability works with the premise: to take nothing for granted and to accept that nobody owes you a living. Running your life as a business makes you at all times the responsible executive who makes the decisions, deploys the resources, takes the risks, controls the operation, and enjoys the rewards.

Material survival, however, is not an isolated activity separate from the rest of life. The economic concept of operating life as a business has still another side, one that deepens and empowers the process of attaining material well-being and security. In composing vision and content of the business venture, there are choices between different activities, inclinations and intentions. We can choose what suits us. As a rule of thumb, a person's talents and interests are the mission. This is also where the energy is. Doing what we like and what we are meant to do enhances the endeavor. It makes what we do meaningful. At its best, this approach to survival brings both material abundance and spiritual vitality. Operating life as a business is a multi-dimensional undertaking. In addition to the material, biological, behavioral aspects, there are personal, existential and spiritual elements.

Aside from its financial goals and benefits, the idea of conducting life in this fashion offers a more general format for fulfillment. On one level, it creates an umbrella to exercise one's full range of professional capabilities within a multitude of income-producing options. On another level, it stimulates psychic growth by positioning oneself face-to-face with the survival frontier. And still on a third level, this way of life may combine the fulfillment of an individual destiny with a contribution to mankind.

The pursuit of material survival provides the reality base for personal growth and development. Material security and welfare are coupled with personal, professional and humanitarian interests. Practical and spiritual aspects interact and invigorate each other. The organic task turns into a psychic venture. That way, survival and personal evolution come together. This is the pivotal point of operating life as a business, where the purely economic, material endeavor merges with the existential pursuit of a personal destiny, integrating instinct and spirit, behavior and consciousness. The frontier is, thus, not only on the outside but on the inside as well. The pioneering venture is not only concerned with discovering external opportunities but also with developing internal resources. It is this kind of practical and spiritual involvement in survival—the mastery of two worlds—that gives direction, intensity and meaning to life.

Family and Child-Rearing

The family usually is the arena from where the individual makes his stand for survival. At the same time, the family is in itself a major survival environment. It satisfies many very basic human needs and is, therefore, central to most people's lives. Likewise, it brings up a series of practical issues such as providing food and shelter, managing a household, and protection against danger from the outside. The significance of the family to human survival is fundamental. This is why the family has existed in all cultures at all times.

The family serves many uses and needs. It is unique in its composition, combining members of both sexes and different ages in a socially and spatially enclosed unit. The overall purpose of the family is the continuation of the species. Its most essential features parallel those of higher primate cultures: the bonding behavior between mother and child, parental care and investment, protection against strangers, pair formation and bonding, feeding behavior, hierarchical organization and rank order between the old and the young, intimacy, cooperation and familiarity in relationships, friendship and play behavior, mutual support and territorial defense.

The particular make-up of the family has evolved to provide a prolonged rearing environment for the human offspring whose upbringing and transition into maturity involves an extended period of time. Marriage is in itself an evolutionary follow-on to secure continuity of parenthood. It guarantees an ordered partnership over time with bonding on the basis of sexual gratification.

The family is the workshop of nature. It has universally evolved to create and perpetuate life. Through the family we participate in the mystery of nature. The family is the vehicle of procreation, charged with biological purpose. It is here where much of the archetypal scenario and activity of human life unfolds—between the genders and the generations. The events of the family are biologically and psychically significant to all its members. It is here where our sense of belonging to life and time and nature originates.

The need to form a family rests in our evolutionary nature. It is, like the family itself, an expression of archetypal intent and essentially immune to cultural influence. Each family repeats the same universal and timeless process of generating life and continuing the species as all the generations before and everywhere throughout human history. The family presents us with a reality that goes beyond the intentions and circumstances of the individual. It presents us with the mystery of life. As such, as parents and children, we partake in the endless process of creation. Everything that happens in the family is, therefore, both personal and universal, biological and psychic, practical and spiritual.

The family exists for mating and rearing—to create new life and to unlock the archetypal nature in the child. This process engages both woman and man, as mother and father, in an archetypally determined way. Beginning with the act of conception, the bonding process between mother and child is set in motion. After birth, the infant begins to reestablish the feeling of unity it felt in the womb by forming attachment with the mother. The child's behavior, in turn, activates the mother archetype in the woman. She responds with love, nurturance and protection. Mother and child begin to mutually release inherent biological and psychic patterns of behavior and emotion in each other. This process eventually leads the child to maturity and the mother to the full realization of her female nature.

Through the attachment to its mother, the child develops a sense of trust in the continuity of existence. It comes to feel that it can depend on life, people, and the world. The child's natural growth is assured as long as the continuous and reliable care of its mother is available. The essential requirement of the mother regarding the child is *being there*—and that over time.

The role of the father is minimal and indirect during this period of intense involvement between mother and child. Generally, the father gets more involved with child-rearing as the child grows older. The mother's involvement with the child peaks at the beginning of the infant's life and then gradually decreases. In each case, archetypal necessity guides parental involvement, because it is designed to serve the survival needs of the child. By bonding with the mother, the child feels trust and belonging to the world. Involvement with the father opens the door to adulthood and responsibility.

The first significant contribution of the father to the child's psychosocial development has to do with the formation of sexual identification. It confirms the female identity of the girl and establishes the male identity of the boy. By identifying with its biological gender, which is the bedrock of a sense of personal identity, the child begins to express sex-specific patterns and behaviors inherent in its nature. Examples would be nurturance, devotion to relationships and assumption of personal responsibility in girls, and physical activity, aggression and independence in boys.

The other essential involvement of the father in the rearing process relates to the transition of the mature child, particularly the boy, into adulthood and the larger society of the public. This, in turn, brings out the father archetype in the man—authority, order, responsibility and discipline—which allows him to develop the male aspects of his nature more fully.

At puberty, the maternal bond has outlived its survival value and usefulness. It is essentially replaced by the father principle that gains importance at that time. The boy matures by confirming the masculine principle in opposing and leaving the mother. The girl becomes a young woman by reaffirming her original identification with the feminine principle represented by the mother. "Whereas nature turns girls into women, society has to make boys into men."[1] The relationship with the mother helps the child to develop the basic trust and emotional strength to deal with the demands of life. The relationship with the father establishes the personal identity and social initiation, which serve as a bridge between childhood and adulthood, between family and society.

The universal purpose of the family, among both humans and animals, is to prepare the youngster for his own survival. This not only requires the necessary physical maturity of the child, but also the activation of those adaptive capabilities that are genetically inherent in its nature. The role of the parents, therefore, is always twofold: on one level, they are ordinary people with their normal strengths and weaknesses, handling the practical affairs of family life; on another level, they function as archetypal figures, endowed with symbolic significance and the power to activate the innate survival capacity of the child. The mother represents nature, permanence and eternity, the mystery of creation and life, the realm of feelings and instincts, in essence, the things that don't change.

The father is connected to society, history and change, the principles of rationality and achievement, and to the world as a place to be shaped by action and events. The mother symbolizes love and belonging, the father the principles of logic and penetration. Maternal love is accepting and unconditional, welcoming the child into the world. Paternal love is discriminating and conditional, demanding performance, testing the readiness of the growing child for his or her entrance into the adult world.

As a rearing environment, the family has at least one adult female and one adult male. The parent may not always be the actual mother or father. But the maternal and paternal principles represented by a mother and a father figure are indispensable to the foundation of the child's life. This way, the eternal archetypal drama of the family with all its symbolic and mythological implications can unfold in order to release the psychic development of the child.

Commonly, the practical and transpersonal roles of the parents are closely aligned. The preoccupation with the infant child, who needs constant nurturing and care, tends to draw the mother naturally to the domestic sphere of household and home. Child-rearing makes more demands on the personal resources of the woman. As she fulfills her biological purpose, she has a more expressive and centripetal role than the father. This leaves the father with the task of protecting and providing for the family. His family role, therefore, tends to be essentially more instrumental and centrifugal. This is possible because most of the time the rearing requirements of the child demand less of his involvement.

The more public role of the father, moreover, exactly fits his function in the child's life as the representative of the outside world. This intense involvement with the wider world also satisfies a deep psychological need of the male at that time, since the strong bond between mother and child tends to replace him in his primary relationship with the female. This way, he can compensate for his seeming lack of importance by contributing to the family in a meaningful way.

Child-rearing requires a biologically designed division of labor between the female and the male: each parent has a specific practical and archetypal role according to her or his contribution to the raising of the child. In each case, both roles of each parent support the survival and growth of the child. One role provides for its physical well-being, the other contributes to its mental, social and ethical development.

The family events that involve the generations in an intense drama of growth and survival are, of course, no less important to the parents as they are to the children. It is part of their psychic development as well. The experience of being a mother or father brings forth maternal and paternal aspects of an archetypal quality and magnitude. Archetypes, those universal patterns of human functioning contained in our genes, are "systems of readiness for action"[2] which manifest themselves simultaneously in outer behavior and inner experience.

Constellating the parental archetype with the child and the gender archetype between each other as spouses sets off a profound psychic process in the individual. Each person is fulfilling the biological intent of their individual nature: the woman as the female and the man as the male. And while they are involved with the growth of the child, from conception to maturity, their lives are in line with what they are meant to be. They are engaged in the dynamic interplay between the polar opposites of nature, the archetypal principles of yin and yang: the female being receptive, containing, life-giving, introverted and passive, concerned with gestation and nurturance; and the male being creative, penetrating, energetic, extroverted and active, involved with consciousness and combat.

Jung suggested that it is essential to follow one's basic nature as a woman or as a man during the first half of life, out to realize one's biological purpose. Contra-sexual ambitions and endeavors are best left to the second half of life[3]. At that point, a natural reversal between femininity and masculinity takes place. This is when the woman replaces 'feminine' things like love, caregiving and motherhood with 'masculine' pursuits like work and leadership; and when the man pulls back from purely 'masculine' ambitions and takes up 'feminine' activities and attributes such as housekeeping, hobbies and art.

Neglect of the archetypal intent of one's gender results in stunted growth—as in the effeminate man or the masculine woman, the eternal boy or girl—often irreversible in its character and consequences. Entrenched in our personal convictions and social positions, we tend to ignore the demands nature makes on our growth and survival, forgetting "that the achievements which society rewards are won at the cost of a diminution of personality"[4].

When a man or a woman fails to fully take on the role of the parent, as in the absent father or mother, both child and adult will suffer. Ignoring, belittling or rushing through those archetypal experiences of family life, as so often happens today, leaves unfinished business and deficits behind. The archetypal patterns of sexual, social, moral and cognitive development that remain dormant in child or adult will be lost and unavailable for future life. In addition, "repressed archetypal components tend to erupt in primitive destructive ways"[5].

It is important to understand the archetypal implications of family life, of being a mother or a father. Understanding the issues of family and child-rearing helps to sort out their timeless essence from the trivia of social trends. This understanding also engenders the awareness that the tasks and events flowing from human nature are the actual content of human life. They spur mature commitment and hold ultimate fulfillment. Understanding helps in realizing that marriage and family are not casual pastimes to fill the space between other excitements.

The archetypal reality of human experience puts us in touch with the joys and wonders of life. It opens the gate to the eternal mysteries of nature. In the final analysis, it is these basic, beautiful, timeless things that animate our daily lives and get us through the hardships along the way. This holds true for all areas of life—work, marriage, family, home, community, and so forth—where survival and commitment come together, and where we have to do things whether we like them or not. The practical life receives its value and vitality from the spiritual fiber it contains.

Chapter Five

> Though nothing can bring back the hour
> Of splendour in the grass, of glory in the flower;
> We will grieve not, rather find
> Strength in what remains behind;
> In the primal sympathy
> Which having been must ever be;
> In the soothing thoughts that spring
> Out of human suffering;
> In the faith that looks through death
> In the years that bring the philosophic mind.
>
> William Wordsworth
Odes

Mental Adaptation

Mental adaptation addresses the psychological and metaphysical needs of the individual. Steeped in the psychic processes of life, it is beholden to the archetypal biology and intelligence of the human psyche. Mental adaptation accommodates the needs for psychic balance, coherence and transcendence.

For better or worse, man like no other creature is aware of his own existence and, at least as a matter of faith, is conscious of a higher cosmic order and universe. Consciousness impels us to look at the experience of life in time and space. We are confronted with who we are and where we are going.

Consciousness makes us realize the gap between what is and what should be, between what was and what could have been. It creates tensions, because "our psychic processes are made up to a large extent of reflections, doubts and experiments"[1]. This generates uncertainty, turmoil and fear.

All this is "almost completely foreign to the unconscious, instinctive mind of primitive man"[2] who trusts the guidance of nature. The unconscious is free of tensions; problems do not exist. Guided by instinct, the unconscious mind works on automatic pilot, oblivious to doubt and indecision.

Civilization has caused a split between the conscious and the unconscious by pitting culture against nature. The emergence of rational consciousness in man replaced the security of the instinct with the uncertainty of the questioning mind. This threw life open to experiment and doubt and caused "the existence of problems"[3]. There are no problems without consciousness; "they are the dubious gift of civilization"[4].

However, once man had lit the fire of consciousness and had picked the fruit from the Tree of Knowledge, the process became irreversible despite "an all-to-human fear that consciousness—our Promethean conquest—may in the end not be able to serve us in the place of nature"[5]. Left without return, man called upon the conscious mind of rationality and intellect "to do that which nature has always done"[6] before: to provide unquestionable guidance and certainty—but to no avail.

Early man was attuned to his nature and its archetypal demands. Civilization broke this connection, disrupting the security of the instinctive state and concealing our archetypal nature. Humanity forfeited the natural state of innocence and stepped into the conscious world of experience.

Dissociation from the archetypes causes problems of living. Unable to return to the natural state of the instincts, survival now depends upon our reconnection with the archetypes, the biological determinants of human life. Personal growth and maturation hinge on bringing the archetypes to the attention of the conscious mind.

Having lost the 'certainty in the strivings of the soul', we now need to reach beyond rational consciousness to "a wider and higher consciousness . . . to give us the certainty and clarity we need"[7]. Higher consciousness results from the natural evolution of instinct to spirit, the expansion of the older midbrain to the new brain, especially the right hemisphere.

Higher consciousness brings back the security of the instinct. It restores the wisdom of nature. The development of advanced consciousness is based on a process of retrieving psychic content from the realm of the unconscious, much like claiming land from the sea. This way, we reestablish connection with our own nature and the biological foundations of life. Modern man, says Jung, needs to reconcile himself with the "2 million year-old man that is in all of us"[8].

The "origin and nature of human behavior"[9] is founded in man as the hunter. The rejection of human nature by civilization calls for a new and different adaptation. It requires the transformation of the original hunter into an inner hunter—the man of higher consciousness, indebted to his archetypal heritage. Culture has a role in this process.

The archetypes are responsible for universal forms and features of human life everywhere. They are genetically inherited predispositions of our species and the result of our evolutionary experience. Their symbolic expressions in artistic and mythological form shape the culture of a community or a people. The archetypal world of the human psyche appears in the universal themes of art, folklore, fairly tales and mythology. They depict the universal life of our species inherent in the archetypes of the collective human psyche. The cultural expression of human archetypes like marriage, family, community life, myth or religion varies in time and place. The archetypes are universal, but their manifestations and symbolic expressions show local differences[10]. The study of comparative mythology makes it evident that the local expressions of the universal themes of human life vary from place to place and throughout history.

It is in this sense that 'culture' is essential to the spiritual growth and development of the individual. Culture as the manifestation of a collective psychic history provides a specific world of ideas and experiences as a foundation of individual life. Culture alone makes higher consciousness possible—not so much, however, as an extension of the left brain and its cognitive, scientific rationality, but as a symbolic manifestation of the archetypal world of the universal human psyche in the cultural idiom of art, folklore, fairy tales and myths. "Our potential for culture resides in our biology as a species: we live in societies because we are social animals. As babies each one of us is born unfinished, with an evolutionary past and a social future: we need culture to complete us."[11] Always remembering, however, that psychic expansion originates in biological roots, "just as trees never grow from the sky downward, but upward from the earth, however true it is that their seeds have fallen from above"[12]. Spirituality is the enhancement of our biology.

Higher consciousness or spirituality is essential to our survival. It does for us what the instinct did for our ancestors. Without spirituality we cannot survive. Without it, the conscious mind becomes paralyzed by problems and cannot cope with the demands of life. Fall from power, loss of wealth, failed marriages and provisional lives usually are the consequence of arrested psychic development. Spiritual growth and personal maturity, however, do not come cheaply or easily. Higher consciousness is an achievement. Matters like "money-making, social existence, family and posterity are nothing but plain nature—not culture"[13]. 'Culture' has to do with consciousness, with the meaning and purpose of life. The spiritual aspect of life relates to the psychic elements of the archetypes. Spirituality, in effect, has two parts. One helps us to work out the biological mandate of human nature—such as marriage and family. The other looks to man's relationship with a higher order—with fate, the universe or God.

Marriage As a Biological and Spiritual Union

Marriage is the girder of the human family. In the not so distant past of rural life and handicraft, before the arrival of the industrial machine age, the family was basically a group of people who worked together in the workshop or on the farm. The communal effort of providing livelihood and shelter for each other was directed at the survival of the group. Marriage, then, was based on property, religion and tradition and recognized as part of the family production unit and survival effort. Mutual sentiments of romance, love and affection did not enter the picture and were considered 'the frosting on the cake'[1]. Conventional marriages were highly functional and thus relatively impersonal.

Things have changed since then. Most of the reasons behind traditional marriage and family have disappeared. The family no longer is the collaborative production group in and around the home. The survival environment has shifted to office and factory. Conventional values, rituals, and customs have been lost to the modern way of life.

The modern family rests on a marriage that stresses the importance of individuality, unrestricted mate selection and romance in the relationship. Compared to the past, contemporary marriage is much less practical and much more personal. The religious and traditional values of marriage have mostly disappeared. The family's production-related survival activity has ceased. Marriage in the past was formed for the physical survival and well-being of two people and their offspring. Modern marriage is primarily based on the feelings of attraction and affection between the partners. These, at one time, were merely 'the frosting on the cake'. This development has increased the vulnerability of marriage and family.

Before, it was the need to work and produce together as a family that helped to hold the marriage together. Now, it is love between the spouses that needs to hold the family together. The fact that the contemporary marriage has to rely largely on subjective rather than objective factors to secure the continuity of marital and family life poses a new and unique survival condition. It puts the individual on the spot. Aside from a vague, intangible and often fragile state of emotions, today's marriage has very little to stand on. Increasing divorce rates attest to the difficulty facing the survival of modern marriage relationships. These rates make it obvious that its biological and practical functions are not sufficient to keep the modern marriage together.

Faced with pressing survival issues, marriage today requires a particular kind of adaptation: the development of the marriage as a physical and psychological relationship. There must be an expansion of consciousness to enhance the biological facts of married life—money-making, household, sexuality and family—which by themselves are not enough to sustain the marriage. The objective matters of the household as well as the subjective issues of the relationship must both be managed if the marriage is to survive. They are interrelated. Because of their obvious nature, most people are aware of the physical necessities involved in marriage. They make sure they have enough money and food to live on, a house to live in and a bed to sleep on. Entertainment and hobbies fill their leisure time. Their sexual desires and physical attraction to each other are used to bond the relationship.

The psychic and spiritual issues involved in the marital relationship, however, are commonly less understood and practiced. And it is here where marriages usually fail. Marriage has lost its traditional props, and partners are left to their own devices. The spouses must fully appreciate the survival challenge to modern marriage. Today, marriage hinges on the individuals themselves and their relationship to each other.

The marital relationship consists of the interaction between the spouses and the different factors that determine their behavior. On one side are the sexual, social, financial and legal aspects of marriage. On the other side are the psychic processes inside and between the people that tend to influence the relationship in more intangible but no less powerful ways. These psychic processes are partly conscious. That is, they are known and understood in their origin and effect. They are also partly unconscious and unknown and, therefore, unpredictable and likely to control the relationship from behind the scenes.

The relationship between man and woman is mediated by adaptive, genetically inherited forces and dispositions, which lead the sexes to each other. These preexistent patterns are archetypal drives and images. They cause the physical and mental attraction between males and females. The man "carries within him the eternal image of woman"[2], as the woman holds inside her the eternal image of man. These are definite images of the opposite sex[3]. These primordial imprints are later fused with images of actual people: the experiences with mother and other females in the case of the man, and the encounter with father and other males in the woman's life.

These images and experiences are unconscious powers. Unknown to us, they determine whom we are attracted to and fall in love with. They control our adjustment to a partner of the opposite sex and our feelings and expectations toward the other person. They guide our motives and needs in the relationship. To adapt in a marriage today, both partners must become conscious of their contra-sexual archetypes. Each needs to understand his/her unconscious image of the opposite sex and how it affects his/her behavior in the relationship. Left in the unconscious, the contra-sexual archetypes influence the relationship in uncontrollable ways. They can severely disrupt the marriage. As long as the partners are unaware of these archetypes, the relationship between them stays arrested at an instinctive and impersonal level. The marriage will remain unconsummated psychologically. In this state, the partners are in love with an image, not with the individuals they are.

Making the archetypes conscious individualizes the marriage[4]. It removes it from the primordial and impersonal. The relationship takes on a personal and spiritual quality. This way, the partners come to understand themselves and each other, their psychic world and history. This understanding is essential for the growth and consolidation of the marriage. It forms the basis for marital trust and spiritual bonding. And it opens the door to true love and affection.

On this level, the individuality of the partners and the unity between them come into full play. Here, the relationship has reached the adaptation it needs to survive, while setting in motion a development in and between the partners that continuously adds strength to their bonding. The relationship has reached a higher adaptation or consciousness: the marriage has been consummated and consolidated not only physically but also spiritually and psychologically. It has evolved into a spiritual union, immune to surprise invasions and attacks by the unconscious in the form of deception, resentment, violence, rejection, abandonment or betrayal. The expansion of consciousness clears out the ghosts and demons of the unconscious mind. The partner is no longer mistaken for a mother or a father image or the memory of a past lover, burdened with the expectations to match the ideal. The spouse is no longer rejected for the phantom lover or a future fantasy and thus inflicted with pain and despair. Husband and wife no longer treat each other as impersonal objects of basic desires, violating each other in body and soul. Instead, both have emerged as individuals and partners in the dance and dialogue of life. Together they acknowledge their primordial ancestry. Together they rediscover the relationship between male and female. And together they transform the meaning of their lives.

Once the marriage has achieved this individual and spiritual quality, the biological and psychological aspects of the relationship are integrated in a new way. Lust is unified with love, sensuality with spirituality. At this level, the marriage relationship shows a deep appreciation of the masculinity and the femininity of the partners: the man's nature to be aggressive and potent, the woman's to be receptive and yielding. It brings out the male in the man and the female in the woman, allowing each to develop their basic nature and destiny. It unifies them in the archetypal yang and yin of natural opposites and it lets them play out the eternal symphony of nature and life.

The spiritual attitude frees them from the limitation and imprisonment of a narrow biological standpoint and allows them to recognize the person in the partner. Their relationship turns into a compassionate pedagogy, each helping the other to develop as an individual. In short, at this stage, the marriage becomes a universe all of its own.

The psychic growth and transformation of the marriage puts high demands on each individual. It requires the willingness to resolve and withdraw the projections that come from the unconscious mind. Both partners must be ready to abandon the self-promoting interests and needs of the ego in order to put the 'we' in front of the 'I'. A vital marriage relationship, fortified by physical and spiritual bonding between the partners, is the result of the psychic evolution of each: 'the higher the players, the higher the marriage'. Both become a tool in the realization of the relationship and of their own individuation as people.

A vital marriage is part of a rich life—a reenactment of the male-female mystery, a world of personal discovery, a drama of mythological proportion, a sanctuary of interpersonal unity, and a microcosm of the wonders and beauty of life. The approach to marriage needs to go beyond the opportunistic notion of 'what's in it for me'. The spiritual attitude dissolves this type of *quid pro quo*, which is constantly on the lookout for leverage and advantage.

In a marriage founded on a spiritual union, people are transformed and priorities are reversed. The partners are motivated by what they may give to the relationship rather than by what they expect to get from it. The most meaningful things each partner can give to the relationship are trust, compassion and kindness. These are gifts of love from the spirit. They create an environment of security, affection and respect for each other. Through these gifts to each other, husband and wife create their own world where they can rely on each other, love and care for each other, appreciate, support and help each other, and where together they can grow, enjoy and shape a life of their own.

Security in marriage comes from trust in oneself and from belief in the maturity of the partner. And as any relationship is based on the interplay of forces, both partners are aware of how their behavior and attitudes affect each other. The spiritual attitude—committed to personal growth, maturity and responsibility, mutual union, dependability, love and support, to giving rather than receiving—takes the pressure off the relationship and defuses any manipulation related to issues of power, sex and dependency. Each is secure in the other's motives and intentions, knowing of the mutual commitment and bonding they share. This certitude gives freedom. It opens up the relationship to wider involvement. The spouse is no longer only husband or wife but also friend, partner and confidant. When the spouses unite in a common effort and the relationship is fueled by the contributions they volunteer to each other, the rewards of marriage come naturally. It is as if they had stepped into a world of plenty, where one gets by giving. The union they have forged between them becomes a rich source of fulfillment. It provides a feeling of belonging and a sense of being grounded in life, a place for growth and creativity. It heightens their experience of sexuality and intimacy, enriches their lives with common activities inside and outside the home, and invigorates the energy and vitality between them.

While these rewards benefit the personal and mutual fulfillment and happiness of both, they consolidate the relationship even more. In other words, the marriage has entered a stage where it functions as a positive loop in which input and output add to the value of the product. This level of marital development is the appropriate adaptation of marriage in our time when it has little support from external values and is totally dependent on the relationship between the spouses. For the marriage to survive, the spouses need to complement their physical attraction and bonding, instigated by the instincts, with a spiritual attraction and bonding, initiated by each person's psyche. Adapting to today's marriage requires drawing the contra-sexual archetype beyond its biological ground. Being in love or wanting to be married is not enough.

Marriage demands a large personal investment. It is a process involving the lives of two people over a long period of time. It covers the better portion of the life cycle and mental development each person goes through over the years. Marital adaptation requires a continuous and successful adjustment to the interpersonal dynamics of the relationship. The spouses must attend to the practical issues of living, the external reality of the marriage, the stages of individual growth of the partner, the presence and rearing of children, and so forth.

Marriage calls on the spouses for a great deal of commitment, compassion and support for each other as people, partners and parents. In turn, the marriage greatly contributes to the survival of the individual, satisfying important archetypal needs. However, the survival value of marital life hinges on the quality of the relationship. Successful adaptation requires linearity of purpose and action.

A strong marriage is both an achievement and an art, because it means relating oneself and one's essence lastingly to another person. In that, it is a most distinguished accomplishment and as such an unmistakable sign of personal maturity and human greatness.

Religious Attitude and Survival

The need of the human being to relate to a higher order or being is universal. At all times and in all places, man has been consumed by the attempt to establish a connection with the world of the supernatural and find explanations for the inexplicable. The "history of man's attempt to relate to the eternal is enshrined in his myths and religions"[1]. This timeless, archetypal endeavor arises from the need to come to terms with forces and events, which transcend his life and his ability to grasp and control them. It stems from a need for security and for a "metaphysical foundation of his existence"[2].

Here, we enter the realm of those perennial questions that have preoccupied human imagination from the beginning: 'How do things happen in life?', 'What causes them to occur?', 'Do we have a part in what happens to us?', 'Is there a grand design or do we live in a random universe?'. Despite man's incessant search for reliable explanations, the answers to these questions remain unknown. The workings of the world stay concealed in the mystery of life. Short of any conclusive evidence to the contrary, man's orientation towards the universe, therefore, continues to be a matter of personal belief, scientific conviction, biological necessity, philosophical assumptions, religious faith, and so forth. Each position lists a different theory on how things happen. Each accounts for the events of human life in a different way—as the result of either magic, individual effort, chance or fate, luck or circumstance, cause and effect, meaningful coincidences, preordained destiny, or Divine Providence. Each interpretation contains its own bias and is only able to detect and explain those facts and phenomena that it claims to exist. None of these explanations is fully substantiated or able to validate everything that happens in a person's life. The seam to show the connection between life and the universe is missing.

In fact, our ability to understand and determine the events of our lives is effectively limited, in time and space, to a small range of decisions and activities. Many of these do not extend beyond the next day or the people around us. Within this microcosm of daily and domestic events, we can plan and act with reasonable certainty and success. But even this immediate environment of our experiences and actions, where we attempt to exert control and influence outcomes, can be invaded by unforeseen events at any given time without notice.

We live on the boundary of realities we are unable to comprehend whether through our senses or through the intellect. The human condition is rather simple and straightforward: we do not control the important, most consequential events and experiences of our lives—such as disease, disaster or death. They are subject to forces and laws beyond the threshold of our control. We are left to deal with the effects these events have on our lives.

The human psyche has developed abilities to cope with this aspect of human life. Man's effort to cope with the unpredictability and magnitude of such experiences is the basis of religious attitude and experience. Myths and religions are archetypal adaptations of the human psyche to respond to the unforeseeable and uncontrollable events of life. Archaic man balanced the extraordinary events of his world by animating nature and creating myths. Civilized man has formed religions to explain and accommodate the realm of the supernatural. The religious experience is a significant way to adapt to the world. It takes over where our ability to determine our lives leaves off. Ultimately, it is the adaptation provided by the human psyche that enables us to come to terms with the "submission to the irrational facts of experience"[3] and to relinquish the need for control. The religious function lets us see order and purpose in the universe. It provides belief in a transcendent meaning and in the purpose of life. The creation of myths and symbols is the psychic adaptation that makes the encounter with the unknown possible. All goes back to the religious archetype, the instinctive function genetically preformed in the human psyche.

Evolutionary adaptation has fashioned the capacity to deal with the mental, emotional and spiritual repercussions of life. It has given us the most remarkable ability to function within a macrocosm we do not understand or control. The adaptive capability to adapt to life circumstances and to 'maintain psychic balance' is innate. Psychological and spiritual adaptation is a product of genetic evolution and a primary function of the human psyche.

Mental adaptation combines innate capability with conscious concepts. It joins the midbrain with the left and right hemispheres, adding mental contributions to the archetypal function. The instinctive ability for maintaining psychic balance and coherence is matched with our interpretations of events and experiences. Human survival consciousness pairs psychic function and personal content. While the adaptive function of the human psyche is permanent and constant, the content of human survival consciousness differs from person to person. The content used for mental adaptation generally reflects our beliefs and assumptions about life and the world we live in. Content is our own creation. Commonly, religion, science, philosophy, mysticism or a personal form of spirituality provide the particular concepts of a person's survival consciousness. Content is the explanation we put on events and experiences to cope with the impact they have on our lives.

The view of life and universe held by archaic man "assumes that everything is brought about by invisible, arbitrary powers—in other words, that everything is chance. Only he does not call it chance, but intention"[4]. To early man, "the real explanation is always magic"[5]. At one with nature and adapted to its laws, he is less concerned about natural causes. As long as things are normal, he does not worry. Having animated nature with his own projections of fear and power, he is also totally accustomed to things that we would deem supernatural. Mysterious events "belong to his world of experience"[6]. What are invisible, mysterious powers to him are perceptible, natural causes to us. Primitive man explains the same phenomena with different assumptions. He is fine as long as everything stays within the usual. Natural and supernatural events are ordinary events for him. His security is assured by the common occurrences of his world. What disturbs and frightens him is anything out of the ordinary. Chance occurrences cause a "rift in his well-ordered world"[7]. He needs to accommodate the extraordinary event. He does so by magic—"the science of the jungle"[8].

Religion constitutes the most common effort to provide a conceptual scheme that facilitates psychological adaptation. It addresses the need to come to terms with forces and events that transcend our lives and our inability to comprehend and control them. The need of the human being to relate to the extramundane and supernatural is universal. It comes from a need for existential security and from a desire for a metaphysical foundation of life. In strictly biological terms, the key function of religion and religious experience is adaptive. Myth and religion fortify "against the obvious and inevitable force of circumstances"[9]. The effort to cope with the "uncontrollable happenings"[10] of life and the desire to establish a connection with the supernatural are the basis of the religious attitude. Myths and religions help people to balance the existence of unpredictable and uncontrollable events with their exposure to the macrocosm of an unknown universe. Religious belief gives people the symbolism to restore a sense of meaning and personal assurance in face of the supernatural[11]. Managing the microcosm of life demands accountability and discipline. Facing the macrocosm, affecting human existence, requires an attitude of trust and abandon. Eventually, all attempts to come to terms with the eternal are adaptations and measures of a religious nature.

Commonly, religion offers its believers the symbolic system of a creed along with rituals and moral values for a special way of life with which to conduct their relationship with the supernatural. The belief system gives a complete mythological account of the supernatural. It describes how the universe began and how man along with other creatures came into this world. It explains about the gods, often divided in the eternal struggle between the powers of good and evil over the rule of heaven and earth. The belief system speaks to the ultimate purpose of human life and the end of all things. Religious rituals are a means of common worship and collective confirmation of the belief system. In affirming the existence of a higher order or being that governs the destiny of man, religion assures us of a transcendent meaning of life. In that, it enables the psychic balance necessary to deal with the extraordinary factors of our existence. Yet religion itself is, as history has shown, a 'working concept', constantly changing. Historically, this is also true for man's image of God[12]. The religious function, however, as the ability to maintain psychic balance by relating to the eternal "is an instinctive attitude peculiar to man"[13]. The religious archetype in us creates the necessary mythology[14] to balance the gravity of extramundane factors in our lives.

Our interest in science is also fueled by the need for psychic adaptation. The history of science, not unlike the origin of religion, exhibits man's effort to come to terms with a basic sense of existential insecurity. Historically, science emerged as a response to the irrationality, capriciousness and existential chaos characteristic of medieval life. The scientific view introduces the notion of regularity and causal connections as the foundation of cosmic and human events. Based on the principles of rationality and causality, it has erected a three-dimensional universe of space, time and matter—essentially in analogy to the scientific laboratory where "a definite cause . . . (gives) rise to a definite effect"[15]. The scientific view assumes order and purpose in the universe. Driven by a rigorous determinism, scientific theory erases the psychic qualities of the primal world by withdrawing all the archaic projections that original man had placed there. In this way, it introduced the polarity between "the I and the world"[16]. It has established a division between subjective and objective reality, between psychic and physical events. This concept of reality is the common model for our understanding of human life. We use it to conduct our business and to coordinate our affairs. Scientific theory paints a neatly composed picture of a world where things are ordered, events follow a strict causal pattern, and outcomes are predictable.

The notion of chance and non-causal events is offensive to the mind that has constructed "a picture of the cosmos worthy of rational consciousness"[17]. The view of life and universe held by archaic man "assumes that everything is brought about by invisible, arbitrary powers—in other words, that everything is chance"[18]. Still untouched by rationality and science, to him "the real explanation is always magic"[19]. We, on the other hand, are repelled by chance occurrences because they upset our calculations and threaten our undertakings. And they stir up memories of "that frightening world of dreams and superstitions"[20], which belong so much to our history—the chaos that science helped to dispel. In the final analysis, therefore, science, in both its theories and applications, is an adaptive effort—the endeavor to understand and then to control the world around us. Both science and religion are means to comprehend a world beyond the reach of human control.

Philosophy, too, has its roots in man's effort to adapt to the world of his environment and the larger cosmos, attempting to make sense of the events and experiences that shape human destiny. Philosophy aims to provide a sense of coherence and tranquility throughout a person's life. Despite its literal meaning as the love of knowledge, the main drive of philosophy has been the adaptive nature of this knowledge. Philosophical knowledge and wisdom attempt to understand the world around us and human life in it. Philosophy's intent is to advise the individual, particularly when faced with difficult and devastating experiences. Philosophers from Seneca to Emerson have come forth with a plethora of insights and information, providing a foundation for the psychological adaptation of the individual. Their wisdom is available to the user in the form of treatises, fables, aphorisms, etc., intended to help people with their lives.

Finally, a personal spirituality fills in for many people when things are difficult and the chips are down. Spirituality or higher consciousness involves the individual in an extended process of inner growth aimed at developing the psychic, spiritual aspect of his archetypal nature. The process of discovering the power of the spirit within is not unlike a journey. In the mythological idiom, it is the hero's quest of the Holy Grail—the mysticism of the warrior who is fearless of death and follows his destiny. This adaptation aims to establish a relationship with the higher self or God within. Its essence is the belief in life's meaningfulness, in an order and intelligence of something—nature, the universe or God—that knows what it is doing. It is the faith in a purposeful existence that comes from tolerating the pain and keeping the vision.

Spirituality, as the attempt of achieving psychic balance opposite the uncontrollable factors and events of life, combines psychic growth with religious process. The parallel between religion and human nature needs to begin with the observation that the God of theology exists as "the archetype of the Sacred and Holy"[21] in the psyche of man. Religion exists and spirituality is possible because "the pattern of God exists in every man"[22]. The psychic energy invested in all forms of religion reflects the fact that "all religions are true expressions of the biological reality"[23] of the human psyche and its need to grow. The theological God of religion reappears in the higher self of the person—both the archetype of advanced consciousness. On the archetypal level, religious belief and psychic growth are no longer contradictory. The dual notion of God as a reflection of the self and of the self as an image of God energizes the relationship man seeks with his Creator.

This personal spirituality may take on many forms, ranging from concepts of randomness to the notion of synchronicity—all in the attempt to explain to ourselves how the universe works and why things happen the way they do. Randomness maintains that there is no connection between cosmic processes and human events. Its premise is very succinct and direct: "This is it! There are no hidden meanings. You can't get there from here, and besides there's no place to go. We are already dying, and we will be dead for a long time. Nothing lasts. The world is not necessarily just. Being good often does not pay off and there is no compensation for misfortune"[24]. Randomness denies any purpose or order in the cosmos or any influence on human affairs. This way, all occurrences in human life are purely accidental. There is no rhyme or reason as to why and how things happen; nor is there any sign that anybody cares. This is not a very popular view, because it offends our pride and obliterates our hope, suggesting that the universe looks at us and our concerns with total indifference. The notion of a random universe arouses a metaphysical and existential loneliness which only few are willing to face. This view collapses all our desires, dreams and illusions together with our need for understanding and psychological projection. The notion that we live in a random universe forges a particular adaptation. It confronts a person with the necessity to generate her own meaning of life and to bring meaning to the universe.

The concept of synchronicity perceives human life as part of a larger cosmic order. In contrast to the scientific model, it maintains that chance plays a part in human life and that it can affect us in major ways, but it also says that unforeseen events have natural causes and are not out of the ordinary. Emphasizing non-causal connections, it understands human events as the result of "meaningful coincidences"[25]. It sidesteps the notion of physical objectivity and allows for things to be as they are in themselves, set against the background of "a cosmic order independent of our choices and distinct from the world of phenomena"[26]. While science views the world as bound by physical evidence and differentiates between objective and subjective events, this concept perceives "an ultimate unity of all existence"[27]. It maintains "that not two or more fundamentally different worlds exist side by side or are mingled with one another"[28]. According to synchronicity, everything that exists "belongs to one and the same world"[29] and follows the laws of nature—physical and psychic events alike. The cosmological and psychological premises here are "that the cosmos and man, in the last analysis, obey the same law; that man is a microcosm and is not separated from the macrocosm by any fixed barriers. The very same laws rule for the one as for the other, and from the one a way leads into the other. The psyche and the cosmos are to each other like the inner world and the outer world. Therefore man participates by nature in all cosmic events, and is inwardly as well as outwardly interwoven with them"[30].

The cosmos is seen "as one inseparable reality—forever in motion, alive, organic; spiritual and material at the same time"[31]. Synchronicity says that "empirical reality has a transcendent background"[32]—that beyond the realm of strict causality there exists the inherent unity and dynamism of a 'neutral cause', which governs cosmic and human events. Modern physics—relativity and quantum physics—confirms this view of the universe "as a dynamic, inseparable whole"[33] reflective of nature's inherent harmony. Synchronicity explains that what happens in our lives stems from a juncture of physical events and psychic states. Outer happenings correspond to inner experiences. Jung defined synchronicity as an "acausal connecting principle"[34]. Here, the events of human life are no longer caused by chance or happenstance, but are the result of 'meaningful coincidences'. Their occurrence is not determined by the laws of physical causality: a meaningful coincidence involves the interaction of psychic and physical events. The principle implies an innate design giving meaning and order to a person's experiences. Jung believed that synchronous events "(rested) on an archetypal foundation"[35]. He believed that the human psyche has a peculiar synchronistic capacity—the propensity to arrange and attract circumstances that fit into a person's life in a meaningful way. To the unconscious, the psychic and the physical worlds are connected; time and space are relative. Synchronous events give us a "feeling of fatedness"[36]. It is as though the inner and outer worlds belonged and acted together, as if something 'had its hands' in both realms of mind and matter[37]. Synchronicity goes beyond causality in explaining the occurrences of human events. What on the surface may appear as accident or chance is really a meaningful coincidence. Synchronicity ties human life into the web and the flow of cosmic events. It connects the individual to a higher order—that of a preordained destiny or Divine Providence. Such events happen whenever the psyche is ready to express itself physically and the life of the individual intersects with the patterns and events of the universe on its path towards wholeness. Personal spirituality aims to accomplish psychic adaptation and balance through self-development and psychological growth.

Chapter Six

> If one isn't crucified, like Christ, if one manages to survive, to go on living above and beyond the sense of desperation and futility, then another curious thing happens. It's as though one had actually died and actually been resurrected again; one lives a super-normal life, like the Chinese. That is to say, one is unnaturally gay, unnaturally healthy, unnaturally indifferent. The tragic sense is gone.
>
> Henry Miller
> Novels

Personal Adaptation

Evolutionary functioning redefines the reality of human life. It prompts a reorientation—a different way of looking at things. This adaptive perspective subjects the common template of life, conditioned by society and cultural influence, to review and revision. Modern society has superimposed an arbitrary life cycle, based on industrial and economic factors, on the natural biological cycle of human life[1]. The *industrial life cycle* functionalizes people into specific roles and performances, exerting pressure to conform. Our perception of life is framed by the industrial life cycle, which, in essence, spells out the expectations and demands of the environment on the biography of modern man. This external organizing principle of human affairs defines our goals, activities and identities. It creates a one-dimensional world of values and norms, aimed at social conformity and adjustment without attention to the survival requirements of the individual.

Evolutionary functioning takes a different view of life and environment. It puts a premium on the survival of the individual. Evolutionary functioning reconstellates the world. It shifts priorities and attachments. It collapses the world as it is and puts a different one in its place, where survival and evolutionary adaptation are the ultimate and binding reality. It lessens the influence of society on life and resurrects the significance of universal principles and values inherent in the archetypal world of human nature. Evolutionary functioning constellates the world from within, drawing on the archetypal blueprint of the natural life cycle and the biological intent it contains.

The world is the realm outside and beyond the womb, that place of no return where security ends and reality begins. Womb and world are the cornerstones of the human experience, symbolic of the journey of life and the task of survival. Evolutionary functioning projects a larger world, which reflects the totality of our being and where the individual is in charge of his destiny. It envisions a world of greater dimensions, which corresponds to our organic constitution as biological, spiritual and cognitive beings and where our relationships to the natural and cosmic realities of biology and metaphysics play a prominent role.

Left brain dominance[2] in Western culture, supported by science, technological and industrial development, has established a pervasive, uniform concept of reality excluding vital aspects of human life. Evolutionary functioning challenges the suppression of relevant human realities instigated by the intellect. Personal adaptation to survival in the modern world incorporates a larger, total view of life. It bears in mind, that our man-made world of culture and society is a creation of the intellect and its limited concept of human life. The left cerebral hemisphere is the architect of the survival environment we face. As an invention of the left brain, it is essentially a 'left-sided' reality of social and scientific properties—not organically evolved as an extension of human nature and its archetypal needs. Left-sidedness comes with a prescription. It holds people hostage to the notion that there is only one kind of world and only one way of life, subjecting personal destiny to cultural definition.

Changing our perception of the world and redefining the scope of relevant realities is a significant adaptation to modern life. The intellect has a tendency to dominate our perception and to encourage exclusivity of cognitive functioning. Typically, this happens at the expense of our survival capacity. By suppressing the functioning of other parts of the brain, it limits our adaptive capabilities and it shuts down awareness of important realities that belong to human life. Personal adaptation redefines the reality of human existence. It puts human life on a wider footing.

Our nature as biological, mental and spiritual beings exposes us to multiple realities. These external realities, in turn, correspond to internal survival capabilities. We have three principal faculties related to survival: instinct, intuition and intellect. Each faculty refers to a separate reality, a different world. Each world puts different demands on our survival and, correspondingly, each faculty serves a distinct survival function. We can enter each of these worlds by accessing the various internal faculties.

Each faculty furthers our adaptation to the environment. Each faculty is both informational and transactional and relates us to different aspects of our lives. The instincts, biological behavior originating in the midbrain, connect us with the realm of nature and biology. Intuition, the mental and spiritual function of the right brain, relates us to the world of spirit and the cosmic universe. Finally, the intellect, the cognitive function of the left brain, takes us into the man-made world of society and culture.

These internal faculties relate to external conditions and demands. Behind each faculty stands a different world. Each world is important to our survival and has its own laws requiring a specific response:

- The instincts refer to the biological aspect of survival. They involve the biological demands of livelihood and need gratification. The instincts position us in the realm of practical needs and environmental conditions and

furnish a repertoire of ethological behaviors, attitudes and values to address them. They assist our transactions with the outside world and gratification of our material needs.
- Intuition enables mental and metaphysical survival. It provides the consciousness that allows the perception of human life in time and space and the alignment with a larger context or higher order of being. In conjunction with the instinctive function to maintain psychic balance, intuition makes it possible to address the emotional, mental and spiritual repercussions of life. Engaging our mental and spiritual faculties, intuition provides the psychological equivalents to cope with difficulties and to function within the context of a larger macrocosm that is beyond human comprehension and control.
- The intellect refers to instrumental survival. It enables the interface with society through the social and occupational aspects of our lives. The intellect furnishes the ability for rational thought and inquiry along with the instrumental skills to operate in accordance with the rational conventions of language, norms and techniques. It supplies the cognitive and social capabilities to function in the cultural, social and occupational environment of modern society.

We are equipped to function in all aspects of the environment. We enter these domains and respond to these demands by engaging the respective faculties. Particular survival demands stipulate the use of specific faculties. We need the instincts to pursue our practical needs within a given environment; we need our intuition, the unschooled wisdom of the soul, to address the mental and metaphysical issues of life; and we need the intellect to function within the cognitive, instrumental context of society. We can access each of these three faculties, enter each of these three worlds, at will, as we would shift gears in a car with 'three on the floor'.

These different domains of human life are not physical locations compartmentalized into divisions and covered with distinct landscapes, even though they may coincide with geographic spaces in our world. These domains are, in essence, separate realities configuring the external conditions of our survival. And they are, at the same time, extensions of our internal faculties reflective of our organic constitution as biological, spiritual and cognitive beings. The interplay of outer and inner worlds—as an outside condition and as an extension of human psychology—defines the parameters of our survival.

Personal adaptation turns the survival experience into an evolutionary process. It makes us responsible for the transaction with the world and for the gratification of our needs. Personalizing survival as evolution creates distinct adaptive advantage. It adds meaning to the daily experience and it brings purpose to life.

Survivor Personality

Survival is a biological imperative. Nature has provided the genetic endowment to ensure it. We are no exception. The biological equipment and neurological software are there and available as long as culture, society and individual do not interfere. Survival is the governing principle determining the structure and functioning of all living organisms[1]. The survival of the human being, like that of all other species and living organisms, is arranged and preformed on the level of biology. The human psyche is the biological entity that contains the genetic bio-program for our survival.

Human survival activity first found expression in the hunting behavior of our primordial ancestor. The hunter is the prototype of the human survivor, the embodiment of the human survival instinct. Hunting is "the master behavior pattern of the human species"[2]. The original hunter faced the wilderness, people today live and survive in a different world. Yet, even though the survival environment has shifted from forest and savannah to office and factory, making personality more important than the body, our innate survival capability has remained unchanged and survival itself is still determined by biology. Survival is essentially an inner game. The environment provides the external conditions. Biology sets the parameters. The essential survivor is the inner hunter, genetically capable of optimal adaptation. This inner hunter is present in everyone. Our natural self is the hunter in us. It is the evolutionary behavior and psychology that form our archetypal nature. Through it we are still connected with the collective history of mankind, our roots, and a part of nature. This natural self served the survival of our species for most of its history. The ancient hunter lives on in us—in the archetypal world of the evolutionary psyche.

The hunter within is the archetypal survivor. The organic relevance of the archetypes is to promote life and survival. The survivor personality is founded on the reconnection with our own nature and the biological foundations of life. It resurrects the natural self in us and adapts it to modern life. Every age needs to review the changes and conditions of life and reaffirm the coherence of its world[3]. Modern man has changed the world so completely that it requires new adaptations from the individual. Modern man is at a turning point where he has to reconsider his survival. This time the challenge is put to him in an unprecedented way: he is forced to transcend the very condition he himself has created. Evolution has put us on the spot[4]. Survival always depends on creating a viable adaptation that enables satisfaction of relevant needs within a given environment. Again, the survival of our species depends on the evolution of the human brain—this time, on the evolution of higher consciousness.

The inner hunter is a contemporary figure. The evolutionary experience is transformed into an existential metaphor. It is the metaphor of the hunter within, the man of higher consciousness, who has realigned himself with the evolutionary impulse of his species. The evolution of higher consciousness is the forward adaptation that brings the innate capability of evolutionary functioning to bear on the modern world. Like his ancestor, the modern hunter is grounded in biology and, in contrast to his contemporaries, has a spiritual rather than a scientific understanding of life, world and universe. He transcends the limitations of the cognitive, analytical concepts of the intellect and returns the experience of human life to the universal, timeless context of the archetypal idiom. Man as the archetypal hunter provides the "transcendent context for our brief existence here on earth"[5].

The survivor personality builds on a strong inner connection with the natural self and on a viable alignment with the instinctual world of nature and the spiritual realm of a cosmic universe. Instinct and spirit, the dual poles of the archetype, form the inner world of personality and relate to the outer realities of life. Psyche, nature and cosmos are not separated from each other "by any fixed barriers"[6]. Survivors retain the primordial quality of the creature and seek a relationship with the unchanging context of a larger order in nature and universe unobstructed by human intention. Adaptation, including need gratification, is directed toward biology and spirituality aimed at having what we need to live and making a connection with the extramundane.

Human life, not unlike that of all other living organisms, is determined by a genetic bio-program. This program is imprinted in the archetypes of the human psyche and controls the biologically relevant behaviors and occurrences of the natural life cycle. Like in animals and plants, there exists in us a genetic code of human maturation as a norm toward which individual development is invariably directed. This code reflects the "archetypal intent"[7] of human life.

Survivors pursue the archetypal intent of life. Their lives resonate with the natural life cycle and manifest the genetic blueprint of biologically relevant experiences and events. Their survival efforts emulate the archetypal paradigm of instinct and spirit as the template for effective adaptation. Human life is essentially biological and spiritual: everything that matters to our lives occurs in one or both of these dimensions. Survival involves sorting out these realities. Biology satisfies the practical needs of life; spirituality enables the necessary psychic adaptation. Failure to realize the archetypal purpose of life causes distress and disease.

Survivors perceive their world as a survival environment. Survivors do not conform and adjust to the world the way they find it. Instead, they create their own adaptation fitting the environment to their needs. They constellate their own world from within. In his life, the survivor combines history and eternity. His world is a stage with a dual purpose and a double plot, where he satisfies both his personal needs and his transpersonal mission. The involvement in daily life is guided by a timeless purpose. His world of people, actions, and events is the time and place for the fulfillment of his basic nature as well as the transcendent context, which finds expression in his destiny. He lives in separate worlds, constantly changing between inner and outer realities. Reality and mythology come together. The survivor is both practical and spiritual, his life is both personal and universal, and his world both contemporary and timeless. In combining these polarities, the survivor achieves mastery of two worlds—a way of being in the world at the juncture of opposites, where the different realities turn into one. He has turned the world into a womb. And although not elitist in nature, this is not an ordinary position. But once a person becomes a hunter, he "is no longer ordinary"[8].

Survivors treat the environment as a means not as a condition of their survival. The survivor has learned "how to live to best advantage"[9]. While he interacts with the world, he is never lastingly identified with it. Involved and detached at will, he is in the world yet not of this world. He has turned the world "into his hunting ground"[10]. Survivors also reverse the effects of cultural conditioning on their psychological development and personal lives, undoing the cultural repression of our innate nature—correcting what we have done to ourselves as a species. Moreover, they revert to the biological intelligence of life contained in the archetypal nature of our being. Evolutionary functioning is the stronger of the two psychologies we have. Cognitive functioning, the result of socialization and cultural conditioning, relies on the rationality of the intellect. Its system of behaviors and emotions is subject to left-brain cognition. It is a learned process, an acquired psychology, that lacks the backing of evolutionary process and the adaptive capacity essential for personal survival. Evolutionary intelligence reflects the wisdom of nature. Survivors depend on the survival value of their innate psychology. When evolutionary functioning is intact, people tend to live strong, healthy lives. Both psychologies differ in purpose and usefulness: cognitive psychology furthers adjustment to society; evolutionary psychology provides adaptation to life.

Survivors differentiate between the relevant realities of life. The man-made environment of our daily lives is a human invention and as such a secondary reality, concealing much of the biological and metaphysical essence of human existence. The intellect inhibits multiple brain functioning, especially limiting right brain and midbrain, much the same way as the socio-cultural context of our lives masks the biological and metaphysical dimensions of life. Cultural and neurological suppression tend to go hand in hand. In and of itself, this invented reality is a chimera, a transitory manifestation without existential substance of its own. Social values and cultural practices, unless reflective of the biological and metaphysical realities of life, are existentially irrelevant.

Our man-made world is, however, a means to satisfy our practical needs. As such, it is important to master its instrumentality. Instrumental skills are like a language that enables us to operate within the cognitive-technical system of the modern, man-made environment. Survivors do not, however, ignore the reality reversal and the relativity of an invented reality when they interact with the social world of society. The cultural view of life tends to misinterpret the survival issues of the modern world—not infrequently to the detriment of the individual. As a result of the cultural distortion of the meaning of life, the individual is often unable to fasten his life to solid ground and to keep it from falling apart—like Biff in A. Miller's *Death of a Salesman*.

The survivor personality manifests vertical and horizontal integration of the brain—the coming together of right and left, old and new brains. Full integration of brain functioning aims at utilizing the entire adaptive capacity of the human brain, both innate and acquired. In contrast to cultural practice, however, survivors emphasize natural inherited faculties, our organic source of strength. Adaptive strategy and positioning target biological and metaphysical involvement to secure successful survival. The survivor inhabits a world primarily composed of nature and cosmos; society is recognized as an environmental means and condition of survival. Correspondingly, principal reference is made to instinct and intuition with the intellect on standby.

Effective adaptation is a deliberate approach to life. It involves strategy and responsibility. This expands the Darwinian adage of *the survival of the fittest* to a higher version: the survival of the strongest is surpassed by the survival of the wisest. Successful adaptation requires some of both. Survival is an evolutionary response to life and its changing conditions. At its hardest, survival is a reaction to crisis and disaster; at its highest, it is the best and smartest way to live. At the highest level, survival is forward adaptation where survival unfolds on the terms of the survivor.

Survival strategy aims to implement the archetypal intent of life and the full continuum of the human experience. It pursues an existence firmly embedded in the natural processes of life, taking its standards and inspiration from the larger designs of nature and universe. Ultimately, survival is about need fulfillment, both practical and spiritual. Adaptive strategy matches need fulfillment with the archetypal intent, engaging the individual in the relevant realities to satisfy those needs. Biology demands having and doing and is about action and experience. Metaphysics involve being and having, the spiritual demands of philosophy and reflection.

The responsibility for survival goes to the individual. Survival requires involvement and commitment and demands linearity of purpose and action to meet both practical and spiritual needs. The survivor personality pursues a resilient action-philosophy that continuously integrates event and experience, reality and meaning, biography and archetype, the demands of human nature and the demands of the world. Effective adaptation is supported by the instrumental qualities of the left brain and by the complementary features of the right hemisphere.

Biological survival does not have to be learned, only remembered and executed. The ability is a gift of nature. Spiritual survival, however, although genetically preformed, is a matter of personal effort and responsibility—the achievement of personality. The evolution of higher consciousness is at the core of the survivor personality. Limited consciousness projects survival scenarios of scarcity and fear; advanced consciousness operates with scenarios of abundance and availability. Survival consciousness is determined by our attitude toward life and toward the larger context that surrounds it. This is either an attitude of trust or doubt. Higher consciousness entails trust in life and its process. Trust operates on both ends of the archetypal spectrum:

- Instinctive trust is trust in our biology and the tools it provides for our survival. It bears out in the validity of our innate survival behavior and in the confidence we have to fulfill our needs. Instinctive trust is the trust of the animal, sure in its ability to catch prey. At its highest, it is *total confidence* in our inborn, biological ability to survive. It is a confidence that "dares to *be*, like a tiger in the jungle"[11].
- Spiritual trust is trust in the make-up of the universe. It is trust in the support of a 'friendly universe' and the availability of supply and opportunity for what we need in life. It is trust in the constancy of natural and cosmic law and in the reliable functioning of a higher order or intelligence. Spiritual trust rests on the validity of our survival consciousness in sustaining psychic balance and the will to live. At its highest, it engenders *total abandon* in face of the unknown. It is trust that engenders life and "looks through death"[12].

Total confidence restores trust in our ability to survive. It heals the *instinctual wound*. Total abandon brings back trust in our world and heals the *spiritual wound*. Higher consciousness overcomes the loss of 'certainty in the strivings of the soul' and redeems the damage to our natural self as a result of the cultural repression of human nature.

The existential attitude predicates our positioning for survival. Fear and doubt project limitation and failure. Total confidence and total abandon widen our perception of resources and their availability and create the vision of a larger, more abundant life. Total confidence and total abandon form a trust in life, which is essential for survival. It is a trust that accepts the paradoxical predicament of human life as an event that comes without instruction, leverage or guarantee. This type of trust remains in charge but relinquishes control. It does not attempt to force the universe or the outcomes of our efforts. Instead, it moves forward, giving us the opportunity to reinvent ourselves as the archetypal survivor fortified by advanced consciousness. Trust in the biology of our nature and in the make-up of the universe comes with the highest form of wisdom, which Jung saw in an 'understanding through life' rather than through the intellect—knowing that which is unteachable and forging a true adaptation to life.

Personal Evolution and Mythology

The animal exists in non-historic time. Its life unfolds in a timeless, automatic fashion, guided entirely by instinct. The animal does not even know about tomorrow. Human life is more complex. It is set in historic time on the boundary between separate realities. Human survival rests on the successful effort of the individual to establish a lifelong continuity of integrating the cultural and biological aspects of his life. This endeavor creates his history. The modern world is the contemporary arena where the age-old process of human survival takes place.

The evolutionary aspect of human life has all but disappeared in the contemporary idiom. However, the fact remains that our biology sets the time frame and the essential content of human life. It prescribes the terms of human fulfillment and ultimately the mold into which the experiences and events of our lives must fit. Because in the end, each "individual life is at the same time the eternal life of the species"[1]. Each person's life repeats the universal pattern of the human life cycle: being born, forming attachments, exploring the environment, playing in the peer group, youth, gaining initiation into adult status, establishing a place in the social hierarchy, courting, marrying, child-rearing, hunting, gathering, fighting, participating in religious rituals, assuming the social responsibilities of advanced maturity, preparation for death and dying[2]. The personal version of this archetypal story makes up the history of the individual.

The evolution of our species is the journey from instinct to higher consciousness, from biology to metaphysics. The process is replicated in our own lives. The genetic bio-program of the archetypes sets the course. The journey along the archetypal axis spans the entire human experience. It begins with the biology of childhood. Directed by the archetypes, we follow the evolutionary path. The path takes us through the biologically and psychologically relevant experiences of life, the "stages of childhood, coming to sexual maturity, transformation of the dependency of childhood into the responsibility of manhood or womanhood, marriage, then failure of the body, gradual loss of its powers, and death"[3]. The polarity of the archetypes between instinct and spirit is the paradigm of human evolution for species and individual alike. Our own individual process refers to the universal pattern of human evolution.

Alongside the evolutionary blueprint of our species, we need to create our own story and fulfill our own destiny. Personal adaptation converts survival into an evolutionary process of maturation. It combines the biological imperative to survive with the spiritual quest for advanced consciousness, turning survival into a personal evolution. The survival experience becomes the conditioning event for personal maturation.

Mythology gives a symbolic account of the story of human life and the process of individual maturation. It depicts the process as the hero's journey of 'departure', 'initiation' and 'return'. The metaphor of the myth presents the steps of human development, the sequence of outer and inner events, towards maturity and mastery: separation from parents and home, initiation into adulthood, courtship, marriage, and the assumption of the responsibilities of family, work and home. On the psychological level, this corresponds to the resolution of dependency, the acceptance of autonomy and adult responsibility, the successful transition into the public sphere of achievement and social commitment, and the final breaking of the psychic bond with the parents to allow individual investment in a marriage and family of one's own. Myths provide "spiritual instruction"[4] and essentially deal with the "transformation of consciousness"[5]—"the human quest", the "stages of realization", "the trials of the transition from childhood to maturity"[6]. Myths present the inner drama of the human psyche.

Even though the archetypal bio-program is innate, we need to initiate it. We activate it by engaging in the relevant events and experiences of life prescribed and prompted by the archetypes. The hero's journey is the evolutionary journey. There are many ways to do this—the hero has 'a thousand faces'. Evolution is always biologically driven. Its purpose is invariably the adaptation and survival of the organism.

Personalizing the evolutionary process fortifies and elevates our adaptation to life. It creates a personal mythology. Central to this venture is a sense of personal destiny founded on an enduring commitment to personal survival and growth, turning evolution into a personal story. But the myth is not only a story. In another, more profound sense, it contains a plan, intent and strategy. It spells out a map and a teleology for human existence. Individual survival needs a personal mythology. Such a mythology makes it possible to address the existential questions of 'Who am I and where am I going?', 'How do I get there and what is it all about?'. A personal mythology strengthens a person's ability to survive, providing an inner framework to sustain the experience of life over time. It creates a sense of direction, coherence and continuing identity. The inner story and mythology provides "the golden thread of personal identity"[7] which endures throughout life.

A personal mythology is born from within, authored by a sense of personal destiny—that part in us that is unchangeable and eternal. It is founded on an understanding of human life in its relation to the cosmic order of the universe and enshrines a person's ultimate destiny and reason for being. As a dynamic master plan, it contains a general notion of purpose and mission and a bare outline of essential events and experiences—leaving the choices and circumstances of life to fill in the detail over time. Nevertheless, it contains the essence of a person's being and a concept of the expression it seeks in actions, relationships and commitments. It views life with a sense of history, in terms of evolution and biography. Being an archetypal vision of life, a personal mythology commonly takes on a philosophical or symbolic form recurrent with certain universal images, metaphors and themes. Inner and outer events combine in a resilient action-philosophy relating experience to meaning, biography to archetype, continuously creating the generative force to expand the story.

Because of its very nature as a mythic concept of life, it is, like the archetypes themselves, partly conscious and partly unconscious, animated by the inner and outer events that circumscribe a person's destiny. Such a personal mythology is not a detailed, rationally derived life plan spelling out concrete objectives, activities and dates. Rather it is a spiritual understanding of oneself, people, events and things set against the larger background of life's meaning and purpose. It is not a creation of the left brain and its instrumentality but rather the manifestation of the intuitive and instinctive wisdom of human nature. And although it presents only an outline not specific in detail, a personal myth gives a clear sense of direction and a framework for choices and decisions. Ultimately, it instills a linearity of purpose and action.

A personal mythology develops gradually with increased understanding of life and oneself. Archetypal encounters with people and events or exposure to mythic landscapes, usually, move the awareness along. Sometimes it may take shape rapidly through the experience of crisis or catastrophe.

The survivor has a story and that story changes his world. As his personal mythology unfolds, it takes on shape in the outer world. It is really an inner story that manifests on the outside. The story seeks expression and reveals itself in the activities, actions and events of the outer life. The story is directed from within, as if by an inner producer-director, who, given the outline, is charged with giving it reality and form. The mythology inverts the person's world: what happens on the outside becomes an expression of the inner story. The events, people and things in the individual's life—education, work, marriage, home, family, friendships, possessions, travel, interests, hobbies, and so on—are outer manifestations of his story, but not the story itself.

The story is a person's identity, not the various roles he performs. Role and identity are not the same. Roles are only manifestations of the story. Being a husband or mother, a welder or engineer, is just an external expression of the individual's reason for being inherent in the personal myth. Identification with particular roles risks unnecessary vulnerability. Taking on a *functional identity* involves outside definition of personality, values and attitudes—a process encouraged by an emphasis on specialization and externalization. Modern society suggests that we define ourselves in terms of what we do. There is a danger in adopting a culturally imposed identity. To do so involves defining oneself in terms of usefulness, attractiveness, etc. This becomes an issue particularly in crisis and old age with the loss of spouse, family, work, or any other loss affecting major aspects of a person's identity. Elderly in our culture tend to suffer from a ruptured identity. After retirement or the departure of the children, they often feel unproductive, not useful and important anymore. Not uncommonly, retirement marks the premature death of the spirit. The spirit dies, when the story ends.

Modern mass society tends to urge people to adopt an outer-directed identity, either affixed to the functional sphere of work and profession or to the private sphere of lifestyle and recreation. The survival value of an assumed identity is limited and questionable. The conformity it sets up creates a false sense of belonging in defense against the anonymity and alienation of modern life. Outer-directedness distracts from reality. It results in vicarious living and inauthentic lives, living through something other than one's own experience and reality. As a survival strategy, outer-directedness lacks sufficient validity to sustain a meaningful life. It creates vulnerability instead of security, confusion instead of stability, and dependency rather than self-reliance.

The survival value of a personal mythology is significant. Individual mythology bestows a personal identity that persists through time. It also provides a sense of the coherence of life. We live in a world of enormous complexity and ongoing change. Nothing stays around for long. The old erodes constantly and the new is similarly fated. The life span of technological innovations, economic conditions, social and religious trends, values, beliefs, and lifestyles shortens as the pace of cultural change quickens. The result is a kaleidoscopic reality that changes at every turn—a broken world of unrelated, conflicting, overlapping conditions. The modern world presents a picture of complexity, change, chaos and confusion—a reality in which the parameters of human survival are constantly shifting.

Personal mythology dissolves the polarity and ambiguity of the world. Its inner coherence makes up for the lack of balance and harmony in the world. It holds things together. It seeks "the biological ground"[8], the reference to the organic imperative of survival. Individual mythology sets up a linearity of purpose and action and dispels the paralyzing push and pull of modern life. It makes it possible to steer a true course in life—unrestrained by the Scylla and Charybdis of modern existence—and to follow the 'path of bliss'[9] that proceeds with inner certainty and opens the door to human fulfillment.

Individual mythology is built around life's purpose and meaning. Drafted from the archetypal world of human nature and patterned after the universal life of the species, it reflects the transpersonal, eternal themes of life, as well as, the aspirations, desires and needs that determine human fulfillment. A sense of meaning and purpose is vital to human survival. It contains the motivation and intent, the teleology, of human life. Without it, life drifts aimlessly towards despair and destruction. Man's "need to perceive meaning and seek explanations"[10] is deeply rooted in our nature. Meaning and purpose spring from an inner intent, that strives to manifest in a person's life.

Not everything designated as value has meaning. In fact, much of modern life comes in the shape of substitute or second-hand reality pretending to be important and meaningful. The commercial persuasion to adopt extroverted lifestyles is pervasive and the social push towards conformity is strong. The result is an externalized value system dissociated from our psychological and existential needs. The by-product is a profound crisis of meaning and spirituality that afflicts modern life.

Human nature contains "the collective wisdom of our species, the basic programme enabling us to meet all the exigent demands of life"[11]. This archetypal heritage of inborn behavioral and psychic patterns is the basis of the human story. This heritage enters into the life of the individual through his personal mythology. Having a lasting program, anchored deeply within, creates certitude and confidence. Its sense of personal stability dispels fear and insecurity. It is the companion inside that helps us endure and absorb the shocks and changes of life.

The personal myth is only a story outline, drafted from the archetypal blueprint of human life. The individual fills in its content over the period of his lifetime. The story is the gate whereby reality enters his life. It looks at the options and possibilities of life in terms of self-realization. In pursuing his story, the survivor lives an intense life of experiences, commitments and accomplishments. As the myth unlocks the flow of life, the richness of reality begins to flesh out his biography. And like the larger myths of mankind, his own myth "is the secret opening through which the inexhaustible energies of the cosmos pour into"[12] his life.

The survivor knows that his story spans the length of an entire lifetime. The lifelong progression of the personal mythology parallels the unfolding of the biological life cycle. The story, in essence, is his evolution as a human being. The survivor is conscious of his growth and development, formal learning as well as spiritual development. They, more than anything, give him the wherewithal to complete his story. As a story of human evolution, his own myth joins up with the realm of cultural mythology, which reflects on a larger scale the universal life of mankind in the figure and journey of the hero. The ultimate purpose of his story, of becoming a hunter—the archetypal survivor, is the quest for wholeness. Thus, his story reflects the universal myth of the destiny of Everyman, "the dynamic transfigurative theme" of "man in action on his quest for wholeness symbolized by the Holy Grail"[13]. It is a process of illumination and transformation. This striving for wholeness—becoming what one is destined to become from the beginning[14]—enshrines the fundamental meaning of life.

The path to wholeness is an organic progression of events, experiences and actions. As the path unfolds, the archetypal blueprint of human nature determines and directs the evolution of the story. The archetype gives the cues for transformation, releases the life stages, spells out the tasks of human development, and provides the impulse to move. The journey itself is driven by the archetypal intent of life. Personal mythology is founded in the archetypal story of the human species. Its evolution follows the universal pattern of human development and maturation, symbolically expressed in the mythologies of mankind. The Odyssey probably is the supreme example of the cultural myth symbolizing man's journey towards wholeness. Since a person's story is the individual version of the drama of Everyman, a replica of 'the eternal life of the species', it is both unique and generic in that the most personal experiences are always truly universal.

The mythological journey of the hero is the transpersonal version of individual growth and development: "The hero sets out from his commonplace home and receives the call to adventure. He usually crosses some kind of threshold and is then subjected to a series of tests and ordeals. Eventually, he undergoes the 'supreme ordeal'—the fight with the dragon or encounter with the sea monster is a common example—and his triumph is rewarded with 'the treasure hard to obtain'; e.g. the throne of a kingdom and a beautiful princess for his bride"[15].

The cultural myth represents in symbolic form the biologically and psychologically relevant events and achievements of human maturation: leaving home and separating from parents, growing up, transition into adulthood, assuming responsibility for family, home and livelihood, establishing a personal place of social involvement and belonging. These stages of 'departure', 'initiation' and 'return' make up and conclude the first half of life; and this is where the mythological account of the hero journey normally ends. But life and the story of the survivor go on. The second portion of the human life cycle—middle and old age—is no less significant than the first half which sets up the stage for life. These issues tend to be neglected not only in folklore and literature but quite typically in modern society, which favors youth and denies death. The second half of life is as critical as the first, because it is then when "the normal symbols of our desires and fears become converted, in this afternoon of the biography, into their opposites; for it is then no longer life but death that is the challenge"[16].

The survivor embraces all of life and regards his story with affection. Deep involvement in his story gives him a profound sense of history. As the story begins to refer to the archetypal story of human life and his own development represents a personal completion of the universal human story, it becomes a mythology of its own: his personal mythology. And although such an inner story is formed by the archetype, universal and impersonal, its circumstance, individuality and richness provide the variations to make it, in the end, a personal version of the archetypal story.

Modern society tends to interfere with the archetypal development of the individual and to impede the process of growing up. Because of its emphasis on youth and outer-directedness, Western society has caused a backward slide towards the front-end of the human life cycle, creating the syndrome of a "fixated and collective adolescence"[17]. Psychic and spiritual development toward autonomy and self-sufficiency tend to be arrested at the adolescent stage. The result is a severe survival disadvantage. It sets up a life of permanent puerility, a 'provisional life', which fails to penetrate the threshold into adulthood, incapable of the responsibility and commitment of a mature course. The toll on survival is high: existential failure, frequent breakup of relationships or divorce, financial loss, mental breakdown, and suicide are the common price of such a life.

By imposing its own purpose and timing on the process of individual development, as reflected in the *industrial life cycle*, modern society interferes with the natural evolution of personality prescribed by the archetypal pattern of life. Society encourages a biography centered on 'having' and 'doing' at the expense of 'being' and 'becoming'. Growing up in this kind of world is difficult and confusing. Cultural conditions work against the achievement of personal wholeness and prevent the individual from developing a mature and satisfactory destiny. It leaves a person unfinished and incomplete, because the hero needs to come back with wisdom[18]. There is a sadness in this, for not having a story is like not having a life of your own.

To the survivor, his inner story is the primordial guide that leads him on his path of destiny. It serves him as an inner compass, a 'homing device'[19], giving him a sense of direction in life and helping him chart his course in the world. The story is a reflection of his soul which "is the living thing in man, that which lives of itself and causes life"[20]. It links him to a higher order—of advanced human consciousness, the universe, or God—and becomes the inner source of his trust and faith in life. The story is the survivor's "most precious possession"[21] and a secret for his personal keeping.

The story is really an inner story, just as the survivor is ultimately an 'inner hunter'. It is born from the masculine principle, the "Promethean instinct to have a fire of his own"[22], and it is conceived by the soul—that loving, caring, wise and eternally feminine part in all of us. The soul is the protective keeper of the story, its caretaker and guard—engendering the "feeling of belonging to an endless process of birth, death and rebirth"[23].

A personal mythology, having a story, is not the privilege of a few—the hero has many faces. It is a way of being in the world available to everyone. It comes, however, with a price. A life of personal evolution and mythology demands courage, discipline and persistence. And it needs a good portion of steadfastness and autonomy, for "society is jealous of those who remain away from it, and it will come knocking on the door"[24]. Yet the rewards are equally high: discovering one's own mythology vitalizes the meaning of life as it holds the seed and essence of personal history. But not everyone will take on the challenge to discover his story, "not everyone has a destiny: only the hero who has plunged to touch it, and has come up again—with a ring"[25]. The price for failing to fulfill one's archetypal destiny is severe. The survivor has a story. He has a mythological understanding of himself and of the events of his life. He lives a mythic life conscious of completing his archetypal history—and knowing that he will survive.

PART III

At the end of his book, *Life on Earth*, D. Attenborough writes: This last chapter has been devoted to only one species, ourselves. This may have given the impression that somehow man is the ultimate triumph of evolution, that all these millions of years of development have had no purpose other than to put him on earth. There is no scientific evidence whatever to support such a view and no reason to suppose that our stay here will be any more permanent than that of the dinosaur. The processes of evolution are still going on among plants and birds, insects and mammals. So it is more than likely that if men were to disappear from the face of the earth, for whatever reason, there is a modest, unobtrusive creature somewhere that would develop into a new form and take our place.

But although denying that we have a special position in the natural world might seem becomingly modest in the eye of eternity, it might also be used as an excuse for evading our responsibilities. The fact is that no species has ever had such wholesale control over everything on earth, living or dead, as we now have. That lays upon us, whether we like it or not, an awesome responsibility. In our hands now lies not only our own future, but that of all other living creatures with whom we share the earth.

David Attenborough

Compared to the time when our adaptive capabilities evolved, human survival today has not become that much easier. In fact, it may be just as uncertain, relentless and hard as it was then. Our prehistoric ancestors faced the threat of the animal and the vicissitudes of nature. Threats to survival have since taken on different forms—work layoffs, job loss, bankruptcy, divorce, family dissolution, stress-related disease, drug abuse, prolonged illness, poverty in the elderly, to mention just a few. Seen in the evolutionary context, life is a conditioning force that continuously requires the ability to adapt to changing circumstances and conditions.

The demands on survival are always high. That has never changed. Yet nature has ensured our survival through natural selection and by outfitting us with the necessary survival capacity to cope with the adaptive challenges and tasks of our existence. It has given us the basic adaptive equipment to secure our survival. In return, nature has put demands on us. It requires us to contribute to our survival. It demands responsibility for the life it gives. Nature insists on self-reliance and self-sufficiency. It does not tolerate failure to meet the demands of life. We are held to support our own survival. Nature rewards self-sufficiency with a strong, healthy life. Attitudes of self-reliance, personal initiative and responsibility are compatible with effective adaptation and in support of it.

Nature has fortified human survival by giving us the necessary adaptive abilities "to meet all the exigent demands of life"[1]. Yet, culture turned against human nature. Western civilization took it upon itself to suppress and reverse the effects of the evolutionary process in humans. It has, in fact, tamed and domesticated man just like the animal before him. Ours is the only culture that has developed at the expense of nature. It is also the only civilization to disparage and deny the natural history of our species. By suppressing human nature and conditioning a 'civilized human being', culture has also punctured the inherent vitality of our natural self—depriving us of the natural innate survival capacity we possess like all other forms of life.

This doesn't make survival any easier, especially since modern society has not succeeded in making life easier and survival more predictable. Modern culture itself has in many respects turned into a Trojan horse, confronting us with the downside of modern life without providing the proper tools to deal with it. Becoming 'civilized' at the expense of our inherent survival psychology has not been a bargain for people in the modern world. Cultural conditioning jeopardizes effective adaptive functioning in today's society. When it comes to life and living, socialized psychology and cognitive functioning prove remarkably ineffectual and unproductive. Their survival value is fractional and minimal. Evolutionary functioning is nature's way to sustain survival. It makes people strong and wise. Culturally conditioned psychology is society's means to induce people to social conformity and adjustment. It renders a person weak and worried.

Yet despite cultural inhibition and practice, nature, nevertheless, insists on its own ways. Survival is to be on its terms. Whether we like it or not, nature forever has us in its grip. The biology of nature always prevails.

Hunting is "the master behavior pattern"[2] of our species. Hunting is a deliberately strategic approach to survival. It involves a genetic program causing goal-directed behavior to sustain survival and welfare of the hunter, a conscious behavioral strategy as well as generalized skills to assure goal attainment, field independence and selective use of the environment. The hunting behavior pattern further includes social organization through language, communal activity, inhibition of aggression and a *Weltanschauung* fixed on empiricism and teleology, reality and results. Instead of further domestication of the human being through socialization and cultural conditioning, survival in today's world requires the adaptation of evolutionary functioning to modern life.

The contemporary adaptation of the hunting behavior system to modern conditions happens on two levels:

- On the practical level, adaptation utilizes 'hunting' as a strategic system to manage and execute individual survival as it relates to the modern environment. Today's survival conditions are harsh; the survival environment is vast, complex and impossible to master without a strategic focus and framework.
- On the spiritual level, the adaptation takes 'hunting' as a symbolic image, thereby transforming the evolutionary experience of the archetypal survivor into an existential metaphor. The spiritual adaptation of the survivor as the man of higher consciousness aligns individual survival with the evolutionary impulse of the species.

The adaptation of the hunting way of life to contemporary conditions fortifies our survival efforts in the environment of modern society. The original hunter had to be smarter than the animal; the 'modern hunter' needs to be smarter than society.

Nature requires us to participate in our own survival. It provides evolutionary functioning; our contribution is through awareness, attitude and commitment. We augment nature's gift by adapting innate capability to the context of the modern world and by contributing personal initiative and responsibility. Effective adaptation requires knowledge of the environment, reality assessment, strategic approach, preparation and skill development, positioning for resources and need gratification. The hunter understands his world and knows about his prey. He scans the environment for opportunity and danger to prepare himself for the hunt. He moves deliberately and with precision. His skills match the environment and the prey he is after.

Chapter Seven

If you haven't the strength to impose your own terms upon life, you must accept the terms it offers you.

T. S. Eliot
Plays

The Parameters Of Human Survival

Modern survival is a complex issue. Understanding the various aspects and forces that affect it renders survival sufficiently transparent, making effective adaptation possible. Faced with the growing complexity of modern life, individual survival benefits from a deliberately strategic approach that works from the big picture and knows what must be done.

Survival Environment

Modern civilization, with its fabric firmly grounded in science and technology, has no precedent. We live in modern cities, attend schools, hold jobs and shop in supermarkets. Cars, computers, television, microwaves and washing machines are the insignia of urban existence. Politics and economics regulate our environment. Banks, factories, stores, hospitals and churches make up our neighborhoods. Schedules and mortgages control our lives. In the face of these conditions, it is very difficult to imagine that man at one time, in a distant and forgotten past, had staked his life against the forces of Nature and the immensity of the universe. Modern man no longer is a hunter. He left the wilderness: jungle and savannah are behind him. He became civilized, and the world is different now.

Every living organism must adapt to its environment to survive. Adaptation aims at attaining selective advantage in the transaction with the environment to secure need gratification. Unlike other organisms, whose adaptation is controlled by their respective environments, man can change not only his adaptive responses but his environment altogether. The modern survival environment presents a complex, intriguing composition with seemingly conflicting features. Two different realities come together. In effect, two distinct worlds coexist side by side.

First, there is the world of modern society and culture. This is the reality of public institutions, cultural values, norms, folkways, technical knowledge, social roles and conduct—the environment of work, education, economics, politics and religion. This part of our world is of fairly recent history and has close ties to modern civilization. Since the beginning of the scientific and industrial revolutions over two hundred years ago, human culture in the West has been driven by the left cerebral hemisphere. In this process, two important things have occurred. The preoccupation with science and technology has established a dominance of the intellect and left-brain functioning and, in turn, has created a 'left-sided' world[1]. Since then our perception of the world has been slanted in favor of rational, scientific factors at the expense of the biological and spiritual realities of life. This has resulted in the creation of a functional, rationally designed environment of our own making. This invented reality is a direct extension of the left human brain with all its characteristic traits—an instrumental world founded on rational knowledge and innovation and based on the laws of causality and time.

Civilized man was shaping his world, fully exploiting the innate ability to change and manipulate the environment like no other creature can. The outside world formed as an exact replica of the world within, geared to scientific, political and economic concepts and values. This was quite different from our early ancestor who would make do with what the environment immediately provided[2]. In the process of setting up a man-made world other aspects of human life were put aside. The modern, functionally conceived world has superimposed an arbitrary life cycle of industrial and economic factors on the natural, biological cycle of human life. This *industrial life cycle* recruits and releases people based on economic demands and conditions, invariably shaping people's lives and lastingly defining their identities. It has also shifted and redefined the context of human activity and fulfillment.

Society exerts influence in many areas of life. Socialization and cultural conditioning configure a world, which defines and determines our lives from the outside and reinforces compliance through conscience from the inside. It defines values of what people want and need. It shapes people to its way of life by streamlining education, patterning career paths, or by enticing consumer behavior at an early age. Most of us have taken on this way of life. People see and define themselves in terms of society. The scope of cultural conditioning is relatively large, so is the impact of socialization on social adjustment and conformity. Cultural left-sidedness has rewritten the human biography, redesigned our life space, and redefined human values. The man-made reality has taken on a pervasive role in our lives. It is the face of modern urban existence; it has replaced the natural world; and, it has deeply shaped our personality and our way of life.

But foremost, modern civilization has radically altered the survival conditions of human life. The outside world has been made to fit the values of the left brain: it is almost exclusively built around material values and technological progress. The fact that our world is man-made does not necessarily mean, however, that it is created in the best interest of individual survival. The left-sidedness of the modern world has obviously not grown as an extension of human nature and its biological intent. In all this, we need to remember that we inhabit a certain version of reality and that it is important not to confuse the map with the territory. Because what we are made to believe may not be there, and what is there may not be what we need.

The preponderance of left-brain involvement in the creation of our man-made world has led to shortcomings in other areas. Left-brain dominance, encouraged by modern society, has created a cultural bias against right-sided elements of human existence. The left-sidedness of the intellect has omitted the entire notion of the existential meaning of human life: our man-made world lacks the transcendent context for spiritual development and transformation[3].

Left-sidedness creates a world of things, events and activities, the materialism of power, prestige and possessions, which in itself does not capture the meaning and purpose of life. It spurs rather a restlessness that races from substitute to substitute in search of a gratification it never finds. Advertising, which commercializes the left-sided concept of life, understands the gap between the obsession with material possessions and the need for meaning. Advertising references to unfulfillment: it sells products by appealing to people's deeper psychological needs for self-worth, security and belonging. In general, the dominance of left-sided values, inherent in our culture, has discriminated against right-sidedness by favoring rational knowledge over intuitive wisdom, materialism over spirituality, reason over emotion, science over religion, competition over cooperation[4].

It is difficult to detect, let alone escape, this type of societal conditioning, because how we see what we see correspond so closely. The left side of the brain can only perceive and understand a certain kind of reality—one based on rational properties and bound by empirical evidence. Even more so, we are looking at a world that is an exact mirror image of our inside world.

In order to understand the modern world, we need to correct our vision. We need to overcome the blindness of a purely left-sided perception, which looks at the world and finds only what it expects to be there—somewhat like a Ptolemaist conviction, which deemed the earth to be the center of the universe. Moreover, modern formal education does not make us immune against this one-sided view of the world. On the contrary, it grooms us for it. Western culture approves of only one kind of understanding—left-sided understanding through the intellect. There is, however, "another, broader, more profound, and higher understanding" which only the right brain can provide—"understanding through life"[5].

Side by side with the sociological reality of modern life, stands the biological reality of human survival. Despite modern man's desire to create a separate reality, a scientifically conceived world founded on reason and logic alone, he has not succeeded in exorcising his biological ancestry. Man's efforts to replace nature with culture have failed. The rational design of our modern world has not erased the principles and effects of evolution in human life. The cultural suppression of human nature wanted to ensure that all the tracks, which could trace civilized man to the biological lineage of his animal ancestry, were concealed. Ever since the beginning of modern civilization, man has insisted on denying his evolutionary heritage. This was to no avail as the evidence is weighted on the opposite side: "Every human action goes back in some part to our animal origins"[6].

The evolutionary qualities of human behavior are reflected in the structure of our political and bureaucratic institutions, the organization and functioning of the business world, the running of our political and economic affairs, in the distribution of status, power and wealth, the fabric of urban existence, family life, and even in the events of daily life. Much of human life and behavior makes it clear "that we are innately territorial, inclined to mate for life, potentially cooperative with allies and hostile to foes, prone to congregate in hierarchically organized communities, and so on, much in the same way as many other mammalian and primate species"[7]. Human survival is always about "territory, resources and succession"[8]. This is no less true today than it was for early man.

Like other mammalian species, we tend to live in vertically structured groups and communities, establish families to secure succession, protect territory and resources with rules and boundaries, affix access to resources to positions of social status and rank, and defend our security and property against outsiders. Neither a unique brain nor civilization with its efforts to eliminate human nature can alter the fact that biology remains the ultimate reality of human life. The biological parameters of dominance and submission, property and boundary, sexuality and succession, aggression and competition, friend and foe are the determining parameters of human survival.

The invention of a world separate from nature, distant from our evolutionary past, had no effect on the relevance of the ethological reality of life. The shift of the survival environment from savannah to skyscraper, from life in the wilderness to the urban existence of today, has not removed the biological dimension from our lives and from our survival. Despite its functional, rationally designed world, fashioned by the intellect, human society remains forever based on the biological model found in nature. Nothing that modern civilization has done to remove human nature from the equation, even creating our own world, has ever changed the fact of our biology. The ethological reality of life stands. We mark rank with symbols of power and status; we regulate access to resources by position and influence; we protect territory and property with fences and laws; we establish family for child-rearing and belonging—not unlike other species. The popular cliché of movies, cartoons and human history that life is all about 'power, sex and money'—that dominant rank and social status, financial wealth and access to the female go together—is correct. Again, this is not unlike life in the lion's pride or that of other higher mammals and primates, where the dominant males and females control the access to resources and succession.

As a survival environment, society has a definite biological quality. Thus is the evolutionary reality that underlies our life and the organization of the world around us. This reality molds the basic features of human existence and, although sometimes obscured, stands behind everything of significance that happens in our world. The ethological reality of dominance and submission, property and boundary, sexuality and succession, aggression and competition, friend and foe overrides the sociological reality of society.

Human society is founded on biological principles. The organization of society is an extension of our biological behavior. The biological parameters of hierarchy, territory, sexuality, aggression and xenophobia shape our institutions, laws and practices, as well as, human conduct and transactions. In fact, like the functionally designed environment engineered by the intellect, the world of biological reality is also an extension of the human brain. It is an exact replica of the older midbrain—the seat of ethological behavior and evolutionary psyche. And like the left brain, the human midbrain is responsible for shaping important elements of our survival reality.

Evolution and biology are inerasable facts of human life. This makes the biological dimension of human society the dominant reality of individual survival, reducing the social, cultural dimension to a lesser, secondary reality. The ethological reality of human life supersedes cultural conditioning and intellectual design. The dominant reality of the human environment is the world established by the midbrain. It is this reality that determines individual survival and human destiny, and it is the foremost reality we must address. The sociological reality of society is reduced to an instrumentality for need gratification. It is not, however, the ultimate reality we have to reckon with. The world of cultural values and social norms turns out to be a surface reality, conducive to social adjustment, but in and of itself secondary to human survival.

Even though the sociological reality of life is not the dominant aspect of the modern survival environment, it is nevertheless the 'place' where we go to satisfy our needs, especially material, biological needs. These needs are related to issues and events like dating, courting, marriage and family, work and career, property and ownership that occur in the social arena. Since these needs are a vital aspect of our survival, these occasions are no longer social but survival events. The social situation provides the venue—often in disguised form, like in dating—for the ethological event. The sociological reality is instrumental for need gratification. Metaphorically speaking, the social world of institutions, work, recreation, entertainment, leisure, travel or pastime is the 'hunting ground' where the hunter goes to hunt for 'prey' and meet his needs. The biological reality is where he 'lives', the sociological reality is where he 'hunts'. Our needs will determine when a social occasion turns into a survival event. This is when we need evolutionary functioning. 'Showing up' at such an event with our socialized psychology alone will result in failure to meet our needs. Evolutionary functioning fortifies our survival: it provides the legs on which to stand.

Despite the fact that we find ourselves in the sociological aspect of society to meet our needs, the dominant reality of biology is ever present. It grits its teeth. Since survival is always about the competition for 'territory, resources and succession', issues and events such as dating, marrying, getting a job, making money, earning a living, and establishing a place gain ethological significance. Notably, mate selection, positioning and access to resources, territory and territorial defense are all determined and controlled by biological principle. Evolutionary conditions are the ultimate reality that determines and shapes the events of human life. Conversely, people tend to act and react in evolutionary ways when situations involve survival issues. Such situations relate to archetypal needs and conditions. Beneath the surface of human transactions lies the reality of evolutionary adaptation—the urge to survive.

When we look at the composition of the modern world, we find two competing realities intermingled—both extensions of the human brain. Each of these realities is involved in shaping the organization of the modern survival environment, each offering a different view of life. The cultural perspective advances rational knowledge and technological innovation. The evolutionary concept of life is bonded to the biology of our being and the archetypal intent of human life. Missing are the manifestations of the right human brain. Right-sidedness does not have a place of its own in the modern world. Lacking is a context for deepening the human experience. Western industrialized societies do not offer a concept of human life that rises much above the involvement in materialistic interests. The industrial life cycle turns life into a commodity, not acknowledging the personal, existential and metaphysical dimensions of human destiny. In this world of 'broken images', transformational and transcendental issues are left to the individual. Each person has to substantiate the meaning and purpose of life on his/her own. Modern society, neither as an institution nor collectively, has taken human evolution to the level of higher consciousness. This step has to be taken by the individual, posing significant survival issues.

Adaptation to life in today's society faces significant challenges. Rigorous strategy, however, can reduce the complexity of issues and keep confusion and frustration to a minimum. Most of all, it can prevent failure to adapt to modern life. Effective adaptation to the world of the modern survival environment involves several elements:

- Foremost in this process is an understanding of the world—sorting out relevant realities. Survivors know that biological principles determine the structure and functioning of the human environment. They understand that the biology of human behavior and human organization is the dominant reality individual survival has to address. It needs to be the focus of our involvement with the reality of the outside world. Survivors also understand that the world of society and culture is a world of our own making, an invented reality, forged by the intellect. Operating on the surface, it tends to screen out the more significant elements of human life and survival. Survivors understand the dissonance between surface reality and the survival reality underneath, between sociological pretense and biological fact.
- Second is a biological perception of life. Survivors have a biological orientation towards survival and society.

Survivors understand that survival is structured by biology. They also know that the world around them is structured according to biological principles. Survivors have learned to see the world in ethological terms. They have a biological perception of reality. In that, survivors perceive their world as a survival environment; they understand and approach social situations as survival events. The given historical context of society is taken into account: political, economic and social circumstances are factored as environmental conditions.

- Third is matching behavior to environment. Survivors know that society is the human version of the biological model found in nature and that its organization follows ethological parameters. Effective survival requires behaviors responsive to the environment. This brings up the relevance of evolutionary functioning. Survival in a world structured by biological parameters mandates a behavioral response pertinent to this type of environment. To match the biological, evolutionary qualities of society, survivors utilize evolutionary functioning. The survival advantage of evolutionary functioning, compared to cognitive functioning, is that it corresponds directly to the environmental realities that affect our survival: behavior matches environment and environment matches behavior. Both—behavior and environment—are biologically determined.

The differentiation between relevant realities in the survival environment also involves understanding our own psychologies. Our culturally conditioned psychology, socialized and learned, relates to the sociological reality of life in society—establishing social adjustment. Whereas, our evolutionary psychology, genetically preformed in the human psyche, relates to the biological dimension of human functioning and human organization—

enabling adaptation to life and environment. Understanding the environment and the adaptive responses it requires makes survival transparent and effective.

Survival Strategies

Every living organism must adapt to its environment. Evolution singled man out in a unique way. He "has a set of gifts"[1] which set him apart from the animal. While the world is full of those "exact and beautiful adaptations, by which an animal fits into its environment like one cog-wheel into another . . . evolution has not fitted man to any specific environment"[2]. Unlike other organisms, whose adaptation is controlled by the environment, man is equipped to adjust his adaptive responses to the environment, even alter the environment itself. Nature did not match or fix man to any specific environment nor did it specialize him in any particular way. On the contrary: all forms of human adaptation are aimed at versatility[3]. Man's unique mode of adaptation lies in being *non-specialized*. Generality of skills and a position of autonomy, in regard to the environment, are peculiar to the success of human adaptation. From this condition grew his tremendous adaptability.

Man's primary survival advantage is based on his ability to adapt to vastly different environments and to create the necessary 'artificial organs' of tools, weapons and clothing along with it[4]. Man's basic curiosity and exploratory behavior are intimately related to this mode of non-specific adaptation. It treats the environment and anything new in it as potentially relevant to survival—as enemy, prey or food[5]. We assess whatever we encounter as a possible threat or opportunity. This exploratory approach to the environment is coupled with "a biphasic mechanism for approach-withdrawal behavior"[6]. All survival depends on the ability to move towards what we need and away from what is harmful[7]. This biphasic adjustment mode of approach and avoidance operates across the whole spectrum of inanimate, biosocial and psychosocial survival conditions, encompassing the objects, events and people in our world[8].

Despite this remarkable adaptability, man is, at the same time, among the most fragile and vulnerable of creatures on earth. He has no scales, fur or hide for protection, nor does he have any claws or fangs for use as natural defense. Physically, man is not matched to the animal. Moreover, unlike the animal, he stands upright bringing "the most vulnerable side of the human body (the soft side) face-to-face with the world"[9]. Yet, his erect posture has increased his vision, perspective and mobility, giving him a particular survival advantage. Likewise, it has contributed to man's vulnerability by exposing his soft side to the world. The constitutional vulnerability of the human body offsets man's unique adaptability. This mixture of strength and weakness, ingenuity and vulnerability, makes up his basic survival constitution. It affects man's adaptation to the environment with unique implications for the development of his resources and personality.

Aside from these constitutional factors, there are numerous social and cultural issues that affect adaptation and survival conditions in today's world. These factors magnify man's inherent vulnerability and place a premium on adaptability by adding existential consequences. In the modern world, this vulnerability is no longer only physical.

- Originally invented as agriculture and intended to make life easier and survival more predictable, culture has since become an entity of its own. It has changed from being a means to being a condition of survival[10]. The industrial age has created a condition where man is dependent on a social system and its economy to provide for him. Characteristic of the modern world is the economic dependence of the individual on the environment, making individual survival subject to outside rule. The issues of modern survival are cultural and man-made. Modern society has imposed an *industrial life cycle* on human life that controls people's lives and defines their identities. Society is no longer an organic extension of individual and communal purposes and needs. On the contrary, society is an institution of political, economic and technological interests and innovations, which controls the modern survival environment.

Modern technology, keyed on progress and profit, is the pacesetter of innovation and change. The generations between new advancements and applications are becoming increasingly shorter. Meanwhile, the repercussions of these changes affect people's lives and livelihood. To keep up with the requirements of frequent change at work and at home, people are engaged in a constant process of learning and adjustment. Not only is our survival firmly controlled by outside factors and forces, but the environment itself is constantly changing, requiring human adaptation evermore to leapfrog behind those external conditions.

- Modern society functionalizes people into specific roles and performances. It requires specialization. The modern economy slots people into jobs and positions, and it eliminates them when they have lost their usefulness. The term 'obsolescence' is a most alarming addition to our vocabulary. It reveals, how priorities are set. Functional specialization begins early and lasts throughout life. It involves early Kindergarten training, instrumental school curricula, pre-programmed career paths and mobility levels, family size and consumption patterns, mortgage debts, fast foods, instant lifestyles, social status and the corresponding image. Individuals whose existence is clocked by the industrial life cycle are trapped in a network of cultural forces, controlling their destinies.

Awareness, often, takes on the form of regret after a person has suffered damage from job loss, bankruptcy, divorce or disease, or after most of life has gone—for "the environment exacts a price for the survival of the fittest; it captures them"[11]. The pressure towards specialization is pervasive. Specialization of skills and roles overturns fundamental requirements of individual survival—skill generality and field-independence—and causes massive survival disadvantage. Specialization creates vulnerability and increases dependence, subverting effective adaptation to the environment.

- Modern civilization has rearranged human survival. Guns and machines have cleared away the wilderness, eliminating the dramatics of survival in the natural environment. Survival has switched to the cultural environment of society. As a trade-off, civilization has enforced conformity to its values and way of life. Replacing the natural world, it has made people dependent on society and its system. The switch in survival environments has changed the demands survival exerts on the individual, making personality more important than the body. Civilization has taken charge of the entire process that through home, school and work forms our personality. Socialized in its values and norms, as well as, specialized in its roles and requirements, we have become a part of society and adopted its concepts of survival. The socialization and specialization, enforced by society, subject individual survival to external control. Moreover, the environment defines a person's values, norms and identity.

Part of the trade-off for life away from the wilderness, and subsequently from the farm, was the tacit consent to this form of economic and sociological dependence that comes with modern society. With dependence, however, comes heteronomy, the loss of autonomy. Dependence on the environment for livelihood, resources and supply subjects individual life and survival to external political and economic conditions. Environmental dependence compromises survival advantage. It undercuts field-independence and selective use of the environment. Moreover, society's tendency to involve the individual in various forms of psychological and institutional dependency is compounding the economic dependence on the marketplace and its impact on individual survival. Yet habitual or even prolonged dependency is debilitating and at the heart of survival problems in people as in societies. Dependency, encouraged by modern society, has significantly compromised individual survival capability. It jeopardizes effective adaptation by severely limiting the resilience, versatility and resourcefulness of the individual. Combined with cultural conditioning, dependency tends to suffocate the principal energy of the individual's life force handicapping his ability to cope with survival[12].

- Since its inception, Western civilization has favored the human intellect as its primary driving force. The preoccupation with scientific rationality and instrumental know-how set up a dominance of left-brain functioning[13]. Neurological inhibition and cultural repression joined in the attempt to eradicate human nature. The cognitive, cultural value system sidelined right-brain functioning as weak and 'tender-minded'[14] and condemned the instincts as brutal and primitive. Left-brain dominance has in effect undermined human survival capability, indispensable in today's world.

The instincts furnish evolutionary functioning, ethological behavior and the ability to maintain psychic balance. They are central to need gratification and psychological well-being under any conditions and in any environment. The right brain provides intuitive, perceptual and evaluative functions. But foremost, it is the strategic brain, invaluable to survival in the modern environment. It takes a holistic view of situations and envisions responsive action. It provides the ability to differentiate between relevant realities, to discern fact from fiction, appearance from meaning.

Modern society has blocked access to the resources of multiple brain functioning, trying to silence right brain and midbrain. The loss of survival capability is massive. The lack of right-brain functioning prevents a clear understanding of the modern survival environment. The suppression of midbrain functioning weakens our survival capacity and our chances for need gratification. Adaptation based on cognitive, left-brain functioning alone remains weak and ineffective. It typically involves stress and failure. Our socialized psychology is not equipped to handle adaptive functioning.

- The frontier of human survival has shifted. It had gone from the wilderness of bush and savannah to the agriculture of farm and field. From there it has moved to the offices and factories of urban existence and, lately, also to the involvement in a worldwide, global economy. The human ancestor faced the forces of nature in a constant struggle for survival as the hunter or the hunted. The discovery of grain and the domestication of animals aided in easing human survival—the harshness of life, however, remained. Survival in today's world is not much different. The conditions of survival, the circumstances that affect human life and the setting where it occurs, have changed. A new universe of factors and conditions affect human survival. More than ever, the world is complex and tenuous, life is uncertain and unpredictable, and people are dependent and vulnerable in the pursuit of their existence. Survival in today's world is as difficult as ever.

Culture has had a profound impact on the nature and essence of man. Generally, it has transformed and in significant ways weakened his ability to master his existence. Its influence has widely led to a sedation and atrophy of his survival skills. Yet, on the other hand, modern civilization has created survival conditions that are no less tenuous, uncertain, relentless and hard than those of the prehistoric past, when man had to face the threats and the hardships of the wilderness. Hardship and crisis have not disappeared in the modern world. The threats to survival have just taken on different forms. They include unemployment, work layoffs, economic recessions, obsolescence, inflation, deflation, corporate fraud, financial losses, bankruptcy, divorce, family dissolution, stress-related illness and disease, work-related stress, depression, despair, drug addiction, technological disasters, insecurity and anxiety during adolescence, illness and impoverishment in old age. Furthermore, the potential of nuclear destruction reflects on a global scale the profound crisis that has befallen human civilization in our time. The idea of survival has re-entered our language and our lives.

- The survival environment of the modern world is complex and constantly changing. Man's plan to simplify and stabilize human survival by inventing culture has failed. Survival today is most likely just as demanding, relentless and unpredictable as in prehistoric time, when the ancestor had to stake his life against the forces of nature and the cunning of the animal. Though in our day and age there is a difference. The world has become more complex and survival more complicated.

Man has created an environment of machines, materials, and money restructuring the playing field of survival in the modern world. The continuous expansion of this man-made environment has altered the make-up of our entire world. Individual self-sufficiency within a clearly defined local setting had to give way to a collective dependence on global political and economic conditions, affecting the need for a major adjustment of individual survival strategy. The relevance of external global conditions has backed the individual against the wall. Modern civilization has forced individual survival into a reactive position. Furthermore, modern technology tends to push the pace and scope of cultural evolution to a degree where the acquisition of new skills and the comprehension of new realities become on ongoing necessity.

Modern civilization has sharply divided rational and spiritual, as well as, cultural and biological values. Moreover, modern civilization has forced the individual to specialize his abilities, taking away the advantage of generalized skills. These cultural limitations on human life together with the pressure towards social conformity and urban existence severely cripple man's sense of self-reliance. More than ever, human adaptation has moved to a frontier where individual resourcefulness and resilience are at a premium. The modern world is unstable, often harsh, unforgiving and not particularly friendly to individual survival.

Modern society is a complex system of institutions, laws, relationships and activities on a grand scale and forever changing. Understanding the world around us has become a difficult, if not, insurmountable endeavor. The life of the individual is directly or indirectly interrelated with this world. The interdependence between the individual and the larger system puts personal survival on fragile ground. Any changes in the system will affect life and survival of the individual. Furthermore, since modern society itself is linked to a larger global context, individual life and survival are connected to worldwide conditions. If there is, for instance, a change in laws, production plans, export quotas, fashion or consumption patterns in one part of the world, this may affect the employment, livelihood and well-being of an individual in another part of the world. Everything in modern life reminds us of our basic vulnerability.

Each of these issues and conditions has implications for our survival in the modern world. Each issue needs to be considered when we fashion our approach to survival. Survival is the paramount task of the organism. The changes and conditions of modern life pose critical survival issues. The complexity of the modern survival environment necessitates strategic interventions to address the factors affecting human survival—the massive inherent vulnerability of the individual in the modern world, which is no less psychological, material, economic and political than it is physical. Effective adaptation in today's survival environment requires specific principles and strategies.

1. Survival is a deliberate strategic activity. The hunter knows what to hunt, where to hunt, and how to succeed. Strategic survival is preformed in the hunting way of life, the original 'master behavior pattern' of our species. Hunting involves a deliberately strategic approach to life and survival. Its key elements are a genetic program causing goal-directed behavior; a conscious behavioral strategy supported by generalized skills to facilitate goal achievement; a position of field-independence and selective use of the environment; social organization for communal activity, family life, shared responsibility, territorial defense; and a pragmatic view of the world focused on reality and results.

    Strategic adaptation leaves nothing to chance. It understands need gratification, the environment, and the relationship between them. Strategic survival produces the best and smartest way to live. Adaptation to the modern survival environment involves certain preliminary requirements. Just as the original hunter had to know about the wilderness and the prey he was after, we need to know the alphabet of the environment—the language, norms and technical skills to function in modern society. Moreover, we need to view society as a survival environment and assess it as a source of need gratification. Knowing the alphabet and understanding the composition of the survival environment provide the baseline for effective adaptation.

Adaptive strategy begins with a vision, evolves tactics, and eventually develops action steps. A survival strategy suited to modern existence needs to transcend the purely left-sided, materialistic definition of life goals set by the environment. It needs to reflect our basic need structure as physical and spiritual beings. Need gratification has to cover the entire archetypal spectrum of our nature and address our biological as well as our metaphysical needs. Survival efforts, that stop short at the transitory agenda imposed by society and do not include the permanent archetypal needs inherent in our make-up, are neither valid nor viable. The two cerebral hemispheres are the place "where the archetypal and the contemporary world meet"[15]. The strategy, therefore, needs to provide a formula for gratifying our material and our deeper psychological needs within the context of today's society. In that, the strategy includes a measure for assessing the survival value of the external environment. Need gratification must exceed the goals, and strategy needs to transcend the conditions set by the social environment.

A survival strategy that recognizes the reality of today's world and the reality of human nature provides a viable adaptation fitted to modern life. It places life on solid footing and furnishes complex understanding, able to relate reality to meaning, fact to symbol, event to purpose, biography to archetype. It sets up a dynamic interplay between the demands of human nature and the demands of society, between the temporary and the permanent, between practicality and spirituality. Strategic adaptation to modern life works with a design that incorporates all our basic biological and metaphysical needs and transcends the constraints and limitations of the social, cultural survival environment of modern society.

2. Survival must be on the terms of the survivor not on those of the environment. The hunter "is not at all like the

animals he is after . . . he is free, fluid, unpredictable"[16]. He is the initiator who asserts his purpose on the world. He seeks a stance and a positioning that make him the ultimate agent of his destiny. He does not allow himself to be cornered. Survivors approach survival with their own vision and plan. A position of autonomy and self-determination remains free from social influence and outer-directed conformity that limit perception and perspective. It rejects any form of specialization that eliminates options and destroys survival advantage. Autonomous positioning refuses the bondage of a singular, one-sided orientation and value system. It avoids conformity to the culture, as well as, continued conditioning of personality and psychology by the environment. It protects innate survival capabilities from neurological and cultural suppression.

The original hunter had to outwit the animal; the contemporary survivor needs to outmaneuver society. Self-reliant positioning determines its own values, sets its own goals, develops its own strategies, plans its own activities, and achieves its own results. The reference is to inherent values, visions and intentions. Self-referral fortifies individual survival. It sustains motivation, substantiates our reason for being, and shields us from distracting diversions from the outside. It helps us to differentiate between relevant realities and to prevent a condition where we succeed in terms of the world but fail our own history.

There is something rigorous, robust and direct about survival. It does not retreat from challenge or intimidation; it does not accept barrier or defeat; nor does it bow to rank or fate. Survival is about power and strategy. Survivors never underestimate the evolutionary reality of survival in the modern world. Successful survival requires an adaptive posture that transcends the dictates and confines of the environment—because the ultimate responsibility for success or failure goes to the individual.

3. Survival requires a strategic position, independent of its environment. The hunter "knows that the world is made to be used"[17], just as life belongs to those who take it. Central to the survival of the organism is need gratification through transaction with the environment. Strategy treats the environment as a source of gratification. The survivor views the environment as a resource for survival, not as a condition that controls his life. Modern society has become a condition rather than a means of survival, engendering economic dependence and social conformity. Survival strategy maintains alternatives and makes selective use of the environment, creating positioning for resources that reverses dependence on the system. It converts the function of the environment, turning society into a means instead of a condition of survival. Rather than being dependent on the environment, survivors use it to promote their survival. Effective adaptation establishes field-independence.

This reversal is at the core of survival issues in the modern world. It establishes the autonomy of the individual as the ultimate agent of his destiny. Without it, survival is in jeopardy. The modern world is profoundly unresponsive to the survival needs of the individual. Effective survival always depends on creating a viable adaptation that satisfies relevant needs within a given environment. In aligning the world to his purposes and needs, the survivor reverses a condition that works against him. Rather than adapt to the way of the world, he adapts the world to his own needs. He uses the world for his survival. Survivors do not conform and adapt to the world the way they find it. They create, instead, their own adaptation, fitting the environment to their survival needs.

4. Survival is based on understanding the world. Before he pursues his prey, the hunter scans his world. Survival depends on a reliable assessment of the environment. This

information provides the baseline for comparing the quality of the environment with the requirements of our survival. Understanding the survival environment of the modern world is difficult but essential. A one-sided vision based on intellect and left-brain functioning is not enough; it does not make it possible to perceive depth or perspective.

Effective adaptation in the modern world requires the integration of left-sided and right-sided functioning. The left brain hemisphere is the active mind, using its cognitive, analytical and abstract abilities to create the environment and get things done. It is "concerned with *doing*, with manipulating the environment"[18]. Its strength lies in its rational functions and the ability to make logical deductions. The right hemisphere is the receptive side, engaging its intuitive, holistic and synthetic qualities to perceive the 'whole picture', to transform experiences and thoughts into concepts and decisions, and to incorporate change[19]. It is "concerned with monitoring events as they happen, with perceiving the world as it is rather than subjecting it to some purpose or design"[20]. The main strength of the right brain lies in its superior perceptual and strategic capacity. Left-sidedness furnishes know-how and technical skill. Right-sidedness provides the know-why and a sense of the coherence of life.

The modern world is a world adverse to individual survival, where most feel overwhelmed, disoriented and helpless. Making use of both sides of the brain gives us a viable combination of cognitive and intuitive, analytical and synthetic, action-oriented and strategic abilities. Only the combined faculties of the brain let us see the world as it is. The unique structure of the human brain allows us to look at the world in various ways and to sort the reality we face. The collaboration between both sides of the brain makes it possible to distinguish between surface reality and those things that are important and meaningful to our lives. It provides the strong-line approach, the rigor and toughness, we need to meet the world of our survival.

5. Survival strategy needs to emphasize skill generality and minimize specialization. The hunter knows about the animal and its habits. He learned to use his weapons, set traps, skin game, prepare food, make clothing and build his shelter. Skill generality is at the core of human adaptability. It evolved as a distinct survival advantage peculiar to our species. The modern economy recruits workers just as the military inducts soldiers. It slots people into positions and roles, and it functionalizes them. The intent to functionalize translates into the pressure to specialize.

In contrast to other species, human adaptation to the environment formed on the principle of generality. Survivors protect this adaptive advantage. They pursue a strategy of skill diversity. The survivor functions as a generalist not as a specialist, a decathlon athlete rather than a sprinter. He lives life strategically, leaving nothing to chance. Adaptation aims to attain selective advantage in relation to the environment. Adaptive strategy pursues generality of skills and a position of autonomy in regard to the environment.

Skill and role specialization in modern society come with a price. It is the price of the overadjusted: they are the fittest, and yet the most vulnerable. Evolution exacts a price for excesses of adaptation and adjustment—the price is extinction. Specialization is fraught with problems and poses a danger to individual survival. Obsolescence and surprise changes in economic and technological conditions are only a few of the threats to consider. Survivors avoid any specialization that locks them into a segmental approach, takes away options, and eliminates survival advantage. They pursue a well-designed universality of skills to fortify their survival by creating both options and opportunities. They reject the narrow specialization of skills and abilities enforced by society. The survivor is the universal man who moves with precision. His every move is strong, crisp and exact, pivoted on a keen balance between power and discipline. He has learned "how to live to best advantage"[21].

Cultural conditions set the scenario of human survival. It is no longer possible to separate the life of the individual from global events. They have cascaded down to our lives and changed the world in which we live. Human existence is beleaguered by unique adaptive conditions endorsed and sustained by modern society. The frontier of modern survival has shifted to the offices and factories of urban existence and, in the recent past, also to the involvement in a now global economy.

Some people adapt to modern life on a day-to-day basis without strategy or design. They adjust, chiefly, by reacting to emergencies forced upon their survival, often after the fact and with limited skills. This ends up being an adaptation by trial and error, very costly at times. Other people adapt by conforming. They perceive advantage in adopting the material success values of society and in aligning their lives with the industrial life cycle of the marketplace. They face the future continually improving their ability to adjust to the socio-technical conditions and changes of modern life. This approach underscores dependence on the environment. It leads in the wrong direction each time the interests of the collective deviate from those of the individual—at this point, the last thing a person needs is to get there efficiently!

The survivor pursues survival in a different way. He recognizes the importance of material survival and success in the marketplace, but he reaches those goals without compromising the adaptive advantage of his position. Like the original hunter, he maintains a clear distinction, a demarcation line, between his life and the world outside—not because of bias or denial, but as a requirement of his survival. The environment remains a separate entity at his disposal, and adaptation becomes a strategic effort to make meaningful use of those external resources and opportunities.

The survivor's adaptive strategy retains an evolutionary posture in face of the modern world. His adaptation to contemporary life upholds the principles of skill generality and field-independence. The survivor protects his selective advantage, generic to human survival, against cultural pressures to the contrary. He avoids the limiting conditions of specialization, professional and otherwise. His adaptive strategy is designed to anticipate changes in the environment[22]. The generality and diversity of his skills can handle unstable economic and job-related conditions, as well as, changes in general life circumstances. The strategy prevents surprise from events beyond the survivor's control, such as forced retirement, loss of family or spouse, illness, or disability. It is designed to accommodate risk and eventuality.

Strategic adaptation further aims at maintaining a selective posture towards the external world. The relationship of the survivor to society is paradoxical—he uses it and he avoids it. He uses the environment—job market, economy, political institutions, etc.—as a means of survival without being colored or controlled by its values and practices. Adaptive efforts are directed at developing skills and at increasing strategic positioning and leverage.

The survivor moves between separate realities. His life involves a dual perspective on time. Just as modern civilization is the contemporary phase in the ongoing evolution of mankind, his life, too, has a current as well as an eternal aspect. Human life is situated in the historic context of the immediate world; yet, its meaning is determined by the permanent, non-historic dimension of evolutionary history. The events of the present relate to a permanent purpose; the experience of the moment is heightened by its eternal significance. Everything the survivor does checks against a larger background. The moment is translated into meaning. Nothing is wasted. Time and timelessness, action and purpose, blend into one. The merging of separate time dimensions gives his life a transcendent quality, a timeless intensity. The present opens into eternity, and eternity reflects on the present—like water that flows out to the sea and returns in the rain. This way, life loses nothing of its immediacy and gains everything in meaning. The life of the survivor is somewhat like a classical play—a contemporary plot projected on a timeless stage.

Rather than modeling his life after society's ideals and instructions, the survivor keeps nature as his guide. Although he appreciates the achievements of modern life, his personal story and his evolutionary heritage are the ultimate source of his power. The mythological and ethological dimensions supersede the cultural and social aspects of his life. The survivor's story, drawn from the eternal archetypes of human life, provides an ongoing sense of meaning and identity that he expresses in the daily circumstances of his world. His total involvement in life—at home, at work, or anywhere else—is illuminated by a transcendent consciousness. The personal myth is animated by an archetypal awareness. It understands the universal reality of mankind and species and the fundamental patterns of human needs and experiences inherent in the life cycle.

The individual's ethological nature is the biological underpinning of the mythological story. It enables him to scan, sense and understand the full environmental reality. It furnishes the potency and aggression to carry out his adaptation and survival. The fit between ethology and environment determines how well we adapt. Strategic adaptation treats the cultural and social aspects of our lives as mere options of conduct. In fact, the survivor frequently abandons these conditioned standards and techniques, because they are usually weak and ineffective choices compared to ethological measures. Through his resourcefulness, self-reliance, and resilience he has turned the world into a womb, where he moves with security confident that "he will lure game into his traps over and over again"[23]. It gives him a profound sense of confidence and power—a "total confidence without a reference point . . . like a tiger in the jungle"[24]. He has turned the world into his 'hunting ground'.

The individual's mythological self, the source of symbolic life, generates meaning from within. It furnishes a value system to screen the relevance of environmental events and demands. The ethological self, his fundamental biology, creates the life force from within. It offers a self-propelled energy independent of outside incentives. The mythological self provides the meaning behind the purpose. The ethological power supplies the energy behind the action. The symbolism and the biology of life—archetype and adaptation—are brought together and joined in harmony. This congruence of purpose and action, of energy and potency, accounts for the linearity and force in the life of the survivor. The ethological, archetypal dimension overrides the cultural and social aspects of any given situation; the environmental reality of survival is essentially determined by it. The survivor looks at life without bias or hesitation. The adaptive, evolutionary stance links survival in the modern world to the biological, archetypal imperatives of human life—which we neglect at our peril.

Man as the hunter is the archetypal survivor. And in modern life, he is the symbol of higher consciousness. This is now the point to where evolution has taken the frontier of human survival. In man, evolution has become conscious of itself, forcing him to create value and meaning in life[25]. Man as the hunter provides the "transcendent context for our brief existence here on earth"[26], both as an experience and as a metaphor. Hunting supplies the fundamental strategy for relating human needs to environmental resources, and it holds the essential mythology to guide our destiny.

Survival Skills

Survival strategies are one part of the adaptive know-how, survival skills are the other. Survival skills complement survival strategies. Survival skills provide the operational know-how. They support our survival strategies and determine how we approach our survival in any given environment. Strategic know-why and operational know-how inform and reinforce each other. Both work from the premise that man is "a generalized animal lacking the specializations that characterize other species"[1].

The relationship between skill and survival has taken on entirely new implications in contemporary society. The modern environment of highly developed occupations, massive bureaucracies, and urban settings has established survival conditions, which put a premium on skill development. In essence, we have created a scientifically designed life space. This techno-cultural survival environment demands a particular adaptation. We are expected to master specialized, adaptive skills that exceed the innate, biological survival equipment provided by human nature.

Furthermore, we have to turn away from the forms and methods of cultural adaptation that were still useful, not so long ago, in the time of our grandparents or even our parents. Modern technology and global political-economic conditions continuously alter the world in which we live. The survival parameters are constantly shifting. Human survival, today, confronts a techno-cultural environment, which forces specific and constant adaptation. It requires us not only to learn the rules of the game that is being played but, also, to learn the new rules as the game is being changed. In order to participate, compete and survive in this multi-faceted environment, the individual has to learn, execute and continuously update the intellectual, behavioral and professional skills society requires.

Society controls the survival conditions; the individual is forced to keep up with the adaptation. Moreover, society controls those conditions in such a way that it undermines the unique quality of human survival. Society's massive pressure toward specialization cuts into our adaptive strength, which depends upon being generalized and field-independent. And it does so at our expense. Being able to do only one thing involves a dangerous vulnerability in today's world. Though for various reasons, being employed as an accountant, a welder, or an engineer is just as precarious as solely being a housewife. Successful survival requires a fallback strategy, additional skills, to enable coping with different and changing conditions.

Survivors protect their survival advantage. They hold onto their positioning and ability to do and execute more than one job, trade, role, or position. Their skill development follows a conscious strategy. Survivors maintain the principle of non-specific, generalized adaptation by neutralizing the effects of specialization.

They stay ahead of environmental conditions by pursuing a counter-strategy: a universality of skills.

The basic skills of material survival today divide into two areas: the expressive skills, related to household and family, and the instrumental skills, related to work and achievement. The expressive skills center on the home: running the household, maintaining relationships between spouses, family or household members. The domestic skills involved in the management of the household create an indispensable repertoire of basic survival skills. These skills range anywhere from shopping, cooking, cleaning, washing and sewing, to financial planning, domestic budgeting and bookkeeping, preparing tax statements, communicating with agencies and authorities, and maintaining a car, house, garden or apartment.

The need for these survival skills may not always be present in our everyday lives. Division of labor within the household or other practices and circumstances, as the case may be, can create a situation where the individual remains uninvolved in these domestic activities and skills. Survivors, however, can perform them all. They are part of the survival equipment, which enables them to be self-sufficient. Being knowledgeable in these skills generates flexibility and adaptability.

Managing family relationships requires interpersonal competence and skills, such as the ability to communicate, listen, paraphrase, confront issues, solve problems, give support, express feelings, resolve conflict, including the skills involved in marriage, childcare and parenting. The intimacy of family and friends is vital to individual well-being and survival. The capacity to create intimacy and to maintain personal, marriage and family relationships over time depends directly upon the mastery of these skills. Survivors are keenly aware of this fact and their role in it. Solid competence of interpersonal, marital and familial skills is crucial for their survival and for the survival of their loved ones. Being able to maintain a relationship, a marriage, and a family is a critical part of survival. Survivors are consciously aware of these abilities and their importance as survival skills. They know that love is more than a feeling and success more than an accident.

The entire group of instrumental skills and methods of survival relates to a totally separate sphere of our lives, outside the boundary of the home. These modes of functioning refer to the public domain of work and institutions. Instrumental skills concentrate on instrumentality rather than intimacy, on achievement rather than support, on individuality rather than community, on objectivity rather than subjectivity, and on operational performance rather than intimate relationships.

Instrumental skills cannot be learned in the family because of its entirely different make-up. These skills are typically acquired through various types of formal schooling, such as elementary and high school, college, technical institutes and universities. The development of instrumental skills is a long, ongoing process. It begins with the instruction of writing, reading and arithmetic and other fields of complex and diverse skills. Instrumental skills include professional and work skills, as well as, skills of public conduct and operations. Professional and work skills involve technical or task-related skills, like fixing a car, operating a computer, designing a building, engineering a mineshaft or performing heart surgery. Instrumental skills also encompass managerial skills, like problem-solving, planning, decision-making, action-taking and people skills, such as supervision, communication and evaluation. Skills of public competence range anywhere from writing official letters, filling out forms, drafting formal applications, managing financial transactions, filing legal documents, to conducting meetings and public speaking. In a sense, all of these instrumental skills are adaptive skills, because they enable us to interface with the external environment: lack of the appropriate instrumental skills jeopardizes success and survival.

Survivors approach the external, cultural environment strategically and treat it as a means of survival. And although they do not succumb to its practices, values and belief systems, survivors are professionally and publicly skillful in dealing with the societal environment. Survivors can play on someone else's territory. They understand the instrumental environment of the public domain.

Modern society has shifted the major resources of material survival to the instrumental sphere of life. It is the place outside the home, where we work, earn money, buy food, goods and services, receive fuel and energy, obtain certificates and licenses, acquire permits and so forth.

At one time, the family, as a working unit, was the playing field of human survival. Successful adaptation in the contemporary world requires sufficient competence in the skills of the public domain: survivors do not underestimate this necessity. They acknowledge the need to interact with the instrumental environment and they have highly developed skills to do so. Their skill development is strategic and continuous. Like the original hunter, they confront the environment with versatility and anticipation. Their strategy aims to leverage their skills against the demands of a complex and changeable world. They have developed a set of professional skills, which allows them to alter their line of work, if they so choose, or when a change is forced upon them from outside.

Survivors have training or expertise in more than one type of work or profession, backed by the required certifications; and, they have positioned themselves for the eventuality of self-employment. Their strategy of skill diversity is designed to stay ahead of the unpredictability, which affects industry stability and employment conditions in today's society. They maintain their skills at a superior level to secure their material survival. Their repertoire of instrumental and expressive skills covers a wide frontier of potential survival conditions.

Material survival skills have traditionally been separated by the division of labor within the family, reflecting the biological differences between the genders. Both sexes "have evolved different anatomical, physiological and psychic features in order to perform their biologically appropriate functions"[2]. These biological differences have associated the expressive skills and activities with the woman and the instrumental and pragmatic functions with the man. Biologically, the female is responsible for bearing children and nurturing the young. Biologically, the male is responsible for providing food and shelter and for protecting the family against harm from outside threats and dangers. The predominant archetypal characteristics of the woman are "dominance, nurturance and the assumption of personal responsibility", indispensable "skills appropriate to motherhood"[3]. Her activities are centered around herself and the home. She is concerned with making clothing and utensils, preparing food, nurturing the children and managing family life. On the other hand, the primary archetypal features of the male are authority, leadership and territorialism directed at the external environment. Male activities focus on procuring food and protecting the family, on "the occupation of territory, establishment of the power structure, and the maintenance of the law"[4]. The man cooperates and competes with other men, using his superior strength and aggression, to explore and exploit the environment.

Human culture has traditionally supported distinctions between male and female roles, skills, and activities associated with their biological differences. The sexual role-differentiation reveals a fundamental aspect of the history of human evolution: the association of gender roles with nature and culture. Human evolution has made woman the custodian of nature, while man emerged as the creator of culture. "Woman creates and nurtures life; man can never parallel her triumphant achievement except in the use of ideas and technology."[5] Man has forever attempted to compensate for nature's gift to woman and "to emulate the great feminine mystery"[6]. And even though men are physically stronger, possess a greater capacity for abstract thought, and are "better equipped by nature to excel in a vast range of political, cultural and physical activities"[7]—the "central role will forever belong to women: they set the rhythm of things... women in all societies view male preoccupation with dominance and supra-familial pursuits in the same way as the wife in Western society views her husband's obsession with professional football—with a loving condescension and an understanding that men embrace the surrogate and forget the source. Nature has bestowed on women the biological abilities and psychophysiological propensities that enable the species to sustain itself. Men must forever stand at the periphery, questing after the surrogate powers, creativity and meaning, that nature has not seen fit to make innate functions in *their* physiology. Each man knows that he can never again be the most important person in another's life for long, and that he must reassert superiority in enough areas often enough to justify nature's allowing him to stay. There is no alternative; this is simply the way it is. At the bottom of it all, man's job is to protect woman, and woman's is to protect her infant; in nature all else is luxury"[8].

Cultural conditioning reflects masculine concerns. It has typically downplayed the role of the woman to upgrade man's importance in shaping the world. Young girls are brought up to focus on emotions, nurturance and intimate relationships, whereas boys are encouraged towards individuality, competition and achievement. Cultural conditioning has polarized the basic human survival skills, creating absolute distinction between female and male activities. Culture has associated expressiveness exclusively with the woman and instrumentality with the man, though differences in gender-related skills and behaviors are only relative.

This relativity has important implications for survival today. To survive in the modern environment, a person needs to bring expressive and instrumental skills together. During our evolutionary past, when man adapted to his ecological niche, nature brought order to his life. And later, when myth and religion set the guidelines for human conduct, community and culture provided the necessary continuity for human survival. In contrast, modern civilization has created a condition of discontinuity. It has overruled the natural order of things and replaced the traditional way of life with a secular and scientifically conceived world. In this world of enormous complexity and continuous change, without the ethical underpinnings to sustain a tangible continuity of human existence, the disruption of human life has become quasi-institutionalized. Nowadays, two or three career changes in a person's life are not unusual; and divorce is as normal as apple pie. Successful adaptation to this environment makes universal skill development a necessity.

The traditional role-differentiation between male and female skills and activities leaves many people helpless in light of the situation forced upon them. Men must do 'women's work' and women must do 'men's work'—and, often, they do so with little success. Divorce, in particular, highlights the discrepancy of contra-sexual skills and the inability to do what the other spouse had previously managed. Today, more often than not, women are faced with the necessity to earn money, obtain job training and locate work; conversely, men are confronted with child-rearing, housework and cooking. The conventional conditions of life have clearly changed: "In the evolutionary history of our species, man has depended for his security and sustenance on the environment; woman for hers on man"[9]. This is no longer an absolute condition of modern life. Biology and society are often at cross-purposes. The individual suffers from this lack of synchronization, which causes discontinuity of the human life cycle.

Survivors are aware of this change in the human condition and are prepared for it; they avoid being caught by surprise. Successful adaptation follows the principle of bipolarity. The survivor has developed bilateral skills, expressive as well as instrumental, to deal with the demands of modern life. Bilateral skills are not limited to gender; survival goes beyond sex roles. Today, the survivor, man and woman alike, needs to be able to function successfully both at home and in the outside world. The survivor does not seek out crisis or catastrophe, however, he or she is well equipped to deal with the changes forced upon his/her life in the event they occur. At times, survivors can 'be defeated, but never destroyed', because they have the skills and the spirit to cope with misfortune.

Our basic survival skills provide us with the material necessities to survive, such as food, shelter and community. There is more at stake, however. Human survival depends equally on spiritual strength and a sense of meaning. A life totally absorbed in material values and success soon turns into despair and disaster. The story of Dorian Gray, 'the man who gained the world but lost his soul', is no exaggeration. Examples of lives, that collapse because they lack psychic and spiritual fiber, are abundant. The rapid rush from riches to rags is common. To survivors, spiritual survival is just as important as material well-being; in fact, they view them as enhancing each other.

Modern culture does not promote spiritual survival. It does not offer any profound philosophical or spiritual values, nor does it encourage the quest for the inner meaning of life. Western civilization is built on technological progress, material production and ecological conquest. It concentrates on the historical present and strives for a scientifically designed world. It is preoccupied with the production of material things and defines human fulfillment as the pursuit of externalized values. Yet cars, microwaves, stereosets, fashionable clothing or other possessions do not, of themselves, bring about happiness. For it to reveal its full depth and significance, life must be seen in its eternal aspect[10].

Our culture does not relate to the fundamental and eternal meaning of life: "it despises the eternal and cares only for the here and now. Transhistoric and transcendental meaning are no longer considered. Inasmuch as we are interested in the past, it is a 'left-sided' interest, which seeks to pin man down to his place in that irreversible procession of events we call history: it goes no further than trying to explain how we came to be where we are. In this manner we have *provincialized* time and completely overlooked the wonderful circumstance that we also live in *non*-historical time—in the archetypal experiences of life, love and death, in our imagination, and, above all, in our dreams"[11]. Ever since the Fall, when "we sampled the forbidden fruit..., learned the secrets of agriculture and animal husbandry, relinquished our dependence on God, and started to bend nature to our will"[12], man has been plagued with the spiritual dilemma of the meaning of life. He lost the "primordial 'Paradise' in which our species lived out 99 per cent of its life"[13]. He lost the "state of balance with all other species of flora and fauna" through which he "was homeostatically adapted to his environment"[14]. He also lost the state of inner balance through which "the ego was homeostatically adapted to the Self"[15].

Ever since man began to inflict his will on the order of the universe, his mortal existence has been condemned to the ambivalence of salvation or despair. As his left-sided consciousness started to tamper with the mystery of life, he split mind from body, divorced emotion from intellect, and detached human life from its archetypal roots. Man has struggled with the push and pull between creation and chaos, meaning and futility ever since. Modern civilization is not designed for meaning; it does not help to turn to it for answers. This does not mean that modern culture is without spiritual reference or allusion. It becomes, however, a matter of finding the references to existential purpose and meaning it does have—a tantalizing task, somewhat like looking for a pearl in a mud puddle.

Spiritual survival is of quite a different nature than material survival. Spirituality and meaning are not commodities that can be acquired in the marketplace. There is no battery of skills to guarantee spiritual success. A precondition of the spiritual life, and somewhat a learnable skill, is the ability to postpone gratification. Sometimes, one has to wait and grow in order to find fulfillment. The 'here and now' is only a historic marker on the continuum of non-historic time, urging us to pursue our destiny and to not let it be wasted by tomorrow. Living in the present does not mean getting stuck in the 'provisional life', which stumbles over shortsighted gratifications, never obtaining a lasting and meaningful existence. Likewise, the 'here and now' does not refer to a reflex response to the lure of commercial pleasure and sexual adventure. True purpose and meaning involve timelessness. Shallow pleasures create shallow lives, just as 'violent delights have violent ends'. The ability and inclination to sacrifice short-term gain in order to protect the whole of one's life is a quality of the strategic side of the human brain[16].

The intuitive, creative and holistic faculties of the right brain enable us to postpone gratification. They also allow us to see the whole picture, the territory behind the map that stretches out in front of our lives. With this ability comes the capacity to discriminate between the important and the unimportant, the surrogate and the source, the transitory and the permanent. These judgments are steps and accomplishments on the road to spiritual well-being. There are, however, no hard and fast skills to achieve spirituality. Practices of Eastern yoga, meditation and prayer, or the exposure to mythic landscapes can only set the stage. They can teach the necessary discipline or open a door to spiritual and transcendental experiences. They are only, however, an introduction to the event. Spirituality is an inner capacity and an inner event. For that matter, it is not teachable and not accessible to the leverage of cognitive or instrumental skills—nor should it be.

Spirituality is an innate predisposition and gift available to anyone. It is somehow connected with the right brain and the older brain: it is joined with that somewhat forgotten language of the human soul. It is, therefore, not about learning but about accessing, about opening the door. Any spirituality begins, as T. S. Eliot writes: "At the still point of the turning world"[17]. We need to teach ourselves 'to sit still' and 'not-doing' in order to find meaning. Skills related to spiritual survival are really about 'stopping the world', 'turning off the noise', 'letting go' and 'dreaming'. It is then, when our left brain and all its pursuits have come to rest, that the gate to the world of our soul opens.

Meaning comes from the encounter with our archetypal nature. Meaning points to the inner self. To grasp it, we must take an Orphean journey into the depths of our own innermost mystery. Meaning is the source and purpose of spirituality. Meaning in human life comes from fulfilling one's destiny, from completing one's personal, yet archetypal history. We need meaning in life because we have been detached from our ancestral, archetypal roots. They were the bridge between inner and outer life. They offered a natural correspondence between life and environment, purpose and action, need and fulfillment. They provided an instinctive linearity, undisturbed by the keen imperialism of the left brain and safe from the abyss of spiritual despair. Meaning gives energy to life. It supports action, and it creates power and strength. It clicks with the purpose of life and creates the identity of a personal story. A life without meaning is like a frame without a picture, or a body without a soul. Spirituality is not about euphoria: rather it is about the contact with our inner self and about the inner purpose we assign to our life. It gives us, as T. S. Eliot says:

> "The inner freedom from the practical desire,
> The release from action and suffering, release from the inner
> And the outer compulsion, yet surrounded
> By a grace of sense, a white light still and moving."[18]

Spiritual survival is not a stand-alone, isolated endeavor. Material and spiritual survival are really the two sides of the same coin, mutually contributing to the value and wholeness of human life. Actually, they need to work hand in hand and support each other in establishing a congruence of outer and inner life. A good fit between material and spiritual survival stabilizes the alliance between purpose and action. It creates a linearity in life which stays on the main road towards lasting fulfillment—never sidetracked and entangled in the arterials of the 'provisional life'.

The fate of individual survival, however, is ultimately determined in the human brain. It is there, where our external and internal efforts must come together. Human survival depends upon our willingness to establish equality and interaction between the left and right sides of our brain. It rests on our effort to unite and align the conscious and unconscious of our personality. The two brain hemispheres, left and right, actually depend upon each other. They are "essentially *symbiotic*, each hemisphere performing functions that the other finds difficult"[19]. Yet, the left brain holds the key, the neurological inhibitor, to the functioning of the right brain. And furthermore: the left brain also controls access to midbrain activity[20]. And in that, it alone can unlock the gates to the unconscious mind, which is seated predominantly in the older sections of the human brain[21].

The integration of both cerebral hemispheres provides the groundwork, the neurological basis, for higher consciousness. The effort of breaking down the inequality between the two lateral hemispheres and of bringing them "into greater harmony"[22] is what Jung called the 'transcendent function'. The transcendent function creates the union of opposites. It unites the conscious and the unconscious, and reconciles their emotional and conceptual polarities through the use of symbols. "The unconscious can be reached and expressed only by symbols, which is the reason why the process of individuation can never be without the symbol. The symbol is the primitive expression of the unconscious, but at the same time it is also an idea corresponding to the highest intuition produced by consciousness."[23]

The transcendent function clears the path to the inner life of the soul. Jung recommended the use of spontaneous fantasies to activate the transcendent function: "You choose a *dream*, or some other *fantasy-image*, and *concentrate* on it by simply catching hold of it and looking at it. You can also use a *bad mood* as a starting point, and then try to find out what sort of fantasy-image it will produce, or what image expresses this mood. You then fix this image in the mind by *concentrating your attention*. Usually it will alter, as the mere fact of contemplating it animates it. The alterations must be carefully *noted down* all the time, for they reflect the psychic processes in the unconscious background, which appear in the form of *images* consisting of conscious memory material. In this way conscious and unconscious are united"[24]. This type of process, faithfully practiced, encourages the integrating of the human mind: "dreams, phantasy-images, bad moods, are all right hemispheric functions; concentrating, attending, contemplating and writing down are all left hemispheric functions. 'In this way conscious and unconscious are united'. So are the left and right hemispheres"[25].

At one time, man's survival was directed by his archetypal nature. With the development of rational consciousness, man's link to his natural self weakened. Man lost the instinctive linearity given to him by his own nature—the innocence he once had in the Garden of Eden. Human survival, today, depends upon the attainment of higher consciousness. It is the closest we can come to the instinctive certainty human nature provides. It alone can reconcile the split between culture and nature. It alone can sustain our daily life with meaning and vitality; and, it alone can unify our material and spiritual efforts to survive.

The survivor is the universal human being. Survivors have sought out numerous experiences and developed a fund of adaptive skills. They have consciously exposed themselves to the world to acquire and to test their skills on the front line. Their skill development is positioned to enable self-sufficiency and to cover all aspects of their survival. They have developed universality in their mental and physical skills. The strategy is to cover the whole spectrum of modern survival conditions with a solid equipment of adaptive skills and, yet, still retain a reserve.

Survivors confront life with versatility and resourcefulness. They have a keen sense of reality and know how to apply their skills to selective advantage. They anticipate change and the future, and they do not believe or accept that being 'naïve' is an excuse. Their skills span all areas—professional, public, domestic, scholastic, interpersonal, psychic, aesthetic, athletic, technical, mechanical, etc. They are experts in some and above average in all. The survivor is like the Olympic decathlon athlete, the Odyssean hero of the Games, who can compete in all disciplines and beat the specialists in some.

The enormity of these adaptive skills is designed to ready and fortify the survivor for as many aspects of the human endeavor as possible and to experience the fullness of life along with it. All experiences are aligned with a master plan—converging in the thrust of the personal story. Similarly, all skills support the existential purpose and the ongoing survival. The universality of mental, behavioral and physical skills establishes a survival position of remarkable flexibility and adaptiveness. It allows the survivor to protect his survival advantage—of being 'generalized' and 'field-independent'—in a world, which presses for specialization and conformity.

Survival Scenarios

Survival scenarios are mental concepts and part of survival consciousness. They are the ways we envision the world and how it works. We use them to gauge our survival chances and to determine how to fulfill our needs. A survival scenario is a set of concepts, theories and assumptions about the environment and how it relates to our survival. It reflects our understanding of the dynamics of the world as a 'marketplace' and the environment where we transact our survival activity. Survival scenarios contain information and personal opinions about most areas of life, the way things work, and what might affect our chances to succeed. They reflect our insights and convictions about economics, politics, world affairs, work and social life. Most importantly, they aid us in our assessment of survival in the outside world—in such matters as making a living, getting a job, receiving a promotion, finding a spouse. Survival scenarios are our explanations of the world and how it functions with respect to our lives and well-being.

Survival scenarios are adaptive concepts. They commonly refer to assumptions and expectations regarding need gratification and the possibility or impossibility to fulfill these needs. A major portion of their content is dedicated to issues of the supply and availability of the things we need. These considerations frequently include an assessment of opportunities and notions on how to prevent failure. Some survival scenarios make reference to the source of supply and opportunity. This may be hard work, favorable economic conditions, a friendly universe or a benevolent God. We use survival scenarios to assist us in our adaptation to society. They provide the map for need gratification in our transactions with the environment. They tell us if things are real, doable, and worth it or not. They are the mental concepts we refer to and consult when we interact with the world while pursuing our needs. Survival scenarios tend to influence our approach to need gratification and to affect our relationship with the outside world: frequently, they are the determinants of our survival efforts and outcomes.

Survival scenarios form as a result of general information, personal experience, observation and numerous other sources. They have a qualitative, contextual quality, usually in the form of a narrative rather than an exact mathematical, economic or sociological model. Survival scenarios have a certain philosophical quality and emotional tone: they are usually either optimistic or pessimistic. Aside from the information they contain about the outside world, survival scenarios have a psychological component. They reflect our feelings and attitudes. Often these scenarios are projections of our confidence or anxieties concerning our success in getting what we need. Survival scenarios also reflect perceptions about our own capabilities. They gauge how successful a 'hunter' we are and how competent we feel to fulfill our needs and find satisfaction in life. Furthermore, some survival scenarios also make reference to the degree of ease or difficulty entailed in the undertakings we pursue or envision.

Typically, survival scenarios vary in nature and content from person to person. The quality of survival scenarios tends to correspond to personality factors—such as the level of psychological development, personal interest and initiative, experience and knowledge, and so forth. It is important that we pay attention to our beliefs about survival: the way we approach "making a living, maintaining a reputation, achieving goals, and getting things done"[1]. Dysfunctional concepts may obstruct successful adaptation: "only the fittest attitudes survive"[2].

Survivors operate with a constructive, optimistic survival scenario, ensuring that they achieve selective advantage and gratification of their needs. They view the world without limitations as an abundant supermarket of commodities, people, events, experiences, chances and opportunities, with more than enough for everyone[3]. The survivor knows that everything he/she needs is available to him/her, and he/she makes sure that he/she gets it. He has confidence in his ability and in the abundance of the world, knowing that he will always have what he needs: "A hunter knows he will lure game into his traps over and over again, so he doesn't worry"[4]. His thinking and his attitudes are not constricted by fear or anxiety. Without fear, the idea of scarcity disappears. The survivor knows that security comes from the "ability to deal with the world, not from a guarantee by someone else"[5]. He does not cling to people, the past or possessions. The survivor relies on his innate capacity to survive, which nature, that is biological evolution, fitted "to meet all the exigent demands of life"[6]. He draws on the evolutionary intelligence inherent in human nature to advance his adaptation to the modern world. The purpose of adaptation is always the survival of the organism, "the real content of evolution (biological as well as cultural) is the elaboration of new behaviour"[7].

Modern society suggests a survival scenario where security is dependent upon status enhancement and struggle against a hostile world, evoking fantasies of scarcity and failure[8]. It has created a world where material success is featured as the ultimate trophy and reason for being, and where human survival takes on the form of a chase after the Golden Fleece. Life itself is about "clawing upward toward status and survival"[9]. The implications of this scenario are many and far-reaching. When getting and accumulating material possessions are the primary objective, and everyone competes for the same, a notion of scarcity develops. With the notion of scarcity comes a fear of failure and non-being. Moreover, from this fear ensues a sense of deprivation and helplessness. The entrapment is first of all mental. This is a mental set desperate to find security in the attempt to control everything—events and emotions. It sees "survival as the result of a successful struggle against a hostile environment—the real world"[10]. In this notion of life, "we find ourselves killing germs, conquering nature, and struggling for survival. Existence becomes a commodity that is in short supply"[11]. In the end, it all turns into a vicious cycle of fear, stress and suffering with a paradoxical twist: "He or she develops a heart attack and dies, forfeiting the very survival which was the purpose of the fearful struggle"[12].

The Western notion of causality has not only led man to dominate and control the material world, it has also instigated a survival concept geared toward control and attachment. This concept creates the notion that security results from trying to fix and control the flow of events and from forming attachments to people and things. Fears of letting go of control and possessions, that is, resistance to change and essentially to the flow of life, cause 'diseases of adaptation' like rheumatism, arthritis, ulcers, coronary heart disease, cancer, and so forth[13]. 'Left-sidedness' generates a concept of human survival with serious implications for individual health and well-being.

Adaptation needs to be understood in relationship to health and well-being. Health, like survival capability, is a measure of our adaptation to life. Research on adaptation and stress suggests that illness originates from within the person rather than from outside. It also states that physical and mental states are closely related, suggesting a psychosomatic model of life in which the close alignment between body and mind, individual and world, becomes a determining factor of human health. Health rests on successful adaptation to life.

Adaptation creates stress as a normal condition of exerting effort and energy. Distress, as a subjective experience of stress, relates to the values and beliefs a person brings to his/her life, especially his/her attitudes towards survival. Health is ultimately anchored in the organic processes of the body and in the adaptation of the individual to life. It is, thus, directly related to harmony with the flow of life and the realization of its archetypal intent. Any attempt to resist or override human nature threatens our health. If our experience remains disconnected from the "common needs, instincts and potentials" universal to human nature and "departs from the norms of the species"[14], we initiate pathological imbalance. Connection with the organic and spiritual essence of life releases the powers inherent in the biology and psyche of our nature: this determines the "duration of the life-span, the measure of vital energy at one's disposal"[15] and, ultimately, the condition of our health and the fabric of our destiny.

Conventional medicine insists that all illness is caused by an outside agent or stressor—a germ, virus, your mother-in-law, or your boss—and that it "must be treated by finding a specific cause and applying the specific cure"[16]. Psychosomatic medicine maintains the existence of a mental component in the causation of physical disease. It contends "that *disease and distress can flow from our psychological attitudes toward environmental events*"[17]. Distress, like all other stress-related forms of human suffering, comes from our beliefs about survival.

The human mind plays a crucial role in the development of illness and disease: the "problem is rooted in attitudes, not organs"[18]. The left brain, logical, sequential and verbal, "has to do with our socialization, language and movement in our world"[19]. It is commonly "the weaver and keeper of our beliefs, opinions, and shoulds"[20]. The right brain, intuitive, timeless and visual, "has to do with our ties to our limbic system and emotions"[21]. It "is responsible for the body" and ultimately our health[22]. The material, scientific culture of Western society, concerned with causality and space-time matters, favors left-brain dominance. The left hemisphere, the 'male side', "deals with space-time concerns like making a living, maintaining a reputation, achieving goals, and getting things done"[23]. Giving little credence to the right hemisphere, the 'feminine side', and its functioning, our rational-technological culture implicitly relegates the human body to a position inferior to the intellect. The cultural suppression of right-brain qualities and the subsequent inhibition of our innate homeostatic and archetypal systems obviously have significant consequences for our health and our adaptation to the environment.

Adaptation needs to be seen in light of the psychosomatic model of life. Illness comes with a frame of mind. "The most compelling factors of the environment, the most commonly involved in the causation of disease, are the goals that the individual sets for himself, often without regard to biological necessity."[24] Our modern lifestyle is a child of the left-hemispheric brain—rational, action-prone, segmental, with most of its functioning consisting of activity that originates on the outside. The individual who is swept into this whirlwind of modern existence is "engaged in a continuous here and now struggle against time, other people, or both, always accompanied by an emotional overlay of frustration, hostility, or both"[25]. The classical distinction between body and mind treats physical illness without reference to the emotional, mental or spiritual aspects of a person's life. A disease model that denies psychosomatic involvement and a survival scenario that is driven by insecurity, a need for control and attachment, and feelings or fantasies of scarcity, hostility and non-being form a fateful combination. These, however, are the prevalent notions about survival in modern society and, likewise, a major source of illness and disease.

The psychosomatic model of health recognizes the role of the patient in the healing process. Each person carries his/her own doctor inside, the immune system—the inborn ability of the human body to heal itself. The human immune system is an adaptive mechanism with close anatomical and biochemical ties to the human brain. Immunity, the body's resistance to illness and disease, is responsive to our feelings, attitudes, thoughts and beliefs. The "human factor—the psyche—controls the off-on switch that activates the body's natural immune system"[26]. Generally, disease reflects problems of adaptation. The body informs the mind through its afflictions.

"All disease is metaphor"[27] and it contains a message coded in symbolic, somatic language. Ulcers, hypertension, and heart disease, for instance, are maladaptive responses that reflect impatience, hostility and competitiveness[28]. The affected organ carries the symbolism: the colon that had to swallow all the anger and anxiety, the heart that collapsed after being abused like a machine. Diseases, like allergies, arthritis or cancer, are related to passivity and feelings of defeat and inadequacy[29]. They symbolize a sense of depression and helplessness in life, an inability to cope with survival and a feeling of being overwhelmed by its demands. Understanding the physical symbolism, the body presents, requires an integrated, unified view of human life and functioning. Health and disease are the body's response to the process of adaptation and a consequence of the human psyche, which governs this process. Healing is something between the person and the illness, rather than something between a patient and a doctor—"all medicine is too late. It is used when we are ill"[30]. Disease reflects problems of adaptation. Healing is largely self-healing.

Survival scenarios are a part of mental adaptation. In order to improve the adaptation to the environment and to maximize need gratification, it is useful to take the following steps:

(1) Review the content and emotional tone of the current survival scenario with respect to the beliefs and assumptions about the outside world, the underlying emotions and attitudes, dominant themes and the general outlook.
(2) Construct a viable survival scenario as a strategic action plan and as a forecasting tool for longer time horizons. Include in this scenario: an environmental assessment, a competence review, psychological factors; involve empirical evidence, and control for negativity.

Survival Frontiers

The survival environment is an external condition and refers to the make-up of the outside world. Survival frontiers originate on the inside and relate to our inherent make-up as both physical and mental beings. In contrast to the animal, human survival is not merely a biological process: our mental abilities, the facts that we are conscious of our existence and aware of our experiences, add another dimension to our survival.

Survival frontiers are associated with the two sides of our being, specifically, with the particular needs affiliated with each aspect of our nature. The biological, material needs correlate with the physical side of our being and involve everything related to livelihood and physical well-being, family, space, security, community, economics and defense, mating and procreation, and religion and ritual. The emotional, cognitive and spiritual needs, associated with the mental side of our being, involve existential and metaphysical matters, which result from the experience of life and from the innate predisposition to seek a relationship with the supernatural and a higher order of being.

In order to satisfy these needs, we turn to the outside world. The frontiers of this pursuit are either biological or metaphysical reflective of our fundamental needs. There is a symmetry and correspondence between inner and outer realities, between internal needs and external adaptation. Survival frontiers are not physical or geographical locations nor are they identical with the survival environment, but they direct how we interact with it. Survival frontiers are the focal points of our involvement with the world and for our adaptation to life. They are, like all frontiers, both a physical condition and a state of mind. Survival frontiers are the relevant realities that provide the resources we require to satisfy our needs.

The 'worlds' designated for survival involve primarily the realms of instinct and spirit. In the former, we are faced with the biological necessity of need gratification and the fact that survival is essentially a matter of biology. Adaptation related to this domain puts a premium on ethological behavior. In the latter, we are confronted with the ramifications of metaphysical adaptation and the necessity to generate mental equivalents for life experiences that engender psychic balance in the face of uncontrollable and unpredictable human events. Here, adaptation requires the resources of human consciousness.

Survival is a goal-directed activity. It is launched by an internal organic intent that seeks realization on the outside. We must select the external context and the means to facilitate need gratification. Survival has an outward thrust, driven by the biology of the instincts, which underlies all of our needs. We must direct this instinctual thrust towards the frontiers of our survival to satisfy those needs.

It is up to us to make these choices. Modern society typically offers ample opportunity and supply to satisfy our biological, material needs. The problem with it is that all this material abundance comes with an externalized, materialistic value system which makes it hard to stop and know when enough is enough.

On the other hand, modern society offers very little to satisfy our spiritual needs. It lacks the existential, moral and metaphysical context to deepen the human experience. In sum, modern society offers too much of one and too little of the other. What we need, both physically and mentally, is, of course, out there and available. We need to find it. The survival frontiers provide the focal points for this pursuit. They supply the map to find what we are looking for; they furnish the orientation to focus the organic thrust of our survival efforts.

Nature has designed, in us, a being that is both physical and mental, with needs that are both material and spiritual, and it has given us the tools, both ethological and psychic, to fulfill those needs. Our basic organic constitution, our basic needs and our basic tools all correspond to the biological-metaphysical polarity. Survival frontiers are extensions of our nature and our needs. Survival frontiers, too, are aligned with this polarity, which is the archetypal polarity between instinct and spirit at the core of human life—making biology and metaphysics the ultimate frontiers of human survival. Survival frontiers frame the process of effective adaptation and need gratification and help forge a viable alignment with the archetypal intent of human life.

Chapter Eight

> I found that the more I looked into my own spirit and the spirit of my patients, I saw stretched out before me an infinite objective mystery within as great and wonderful as a sky full of stars spread out above us on a clear and moonless winter's night.
>
> Carl G. Jung
> Personal Correspondence

Recovering Human Nature

Evolutionary intelligence, our natural psychology, addresses the survival demands of life and it gives us the ability to cope with them. Our adaptive requirements are measured by the life we live. Ultimately, our physical, material and mental well-being depends on our ability and resiliency to adapt to life. Strength and viability of this adaptation stand on how successful we are in fulfilling our needs, in functioning within our world, and in establishing a sense of coherence to account for the experiences in our lives. Seen in the evolutionary context, life is a conditioning force that commands continuous adaptation to changing circumstances, needs and demands. There is an unyielding inevitability to this process, pressing for maturation and success. Here nature is relentless. Failure to adapt to the demands of life ends in distress, disease and death. Central to life is the challenge of learning how to live.

The Survival Value of Human Nature

Survival is the primary function of the organism. Survival involves a bio-program of innate capabilities that support life and well-being. This adaptive bio-program enables evolutionary functioning—the capacity for behavioral and mental adaptation. It sets up a dual mode of human functioning, joining the biological and metaphysical dimensions of human existence. Successful survival addresses the physical as well as the spiritual dimensions of all aspects of life including health, relationships, family, community, work and money. The innate bio-program also facilitates fundamental adaptive processes. Effective adaptation focuses on need gratification, strategic positioning and psychic balance.

This adaptive bio-program is seated in the human midbrain—in the primary or evolutionary psyche, as Jung called it. The human psyche functions as the primary adaptive agent in our lives. Its adaptive capacity is available to us. Evolutionary intelligence taps into the human psyche to recover our inborn survival abilities that are there to be called upon when we need them. Utilizing these innate biological resources enables us to adapt effectively to the demands and experiences of life.

Effective adaptation favors the biological response. It resorts to human nature and its powers, present in the evolutionary psyche and the genetically consolidated survival capability it contains. Effective survival emulates the adaptive principles found in nature, setting forth a strategic mode of problem solving that puts us in charge of our lives. The biological response to life circumstances is always superior to the conditioned response of social learning and acquired behavior, because it relies on our natural life force and its innate resources.

Our capacity for adaptation has biological origins. The essential capabilities to live and survive are innate. Like any other form of life, we are equipped with an inherent survival capacity. There is a certain comfort in knowing that we do not have to go outside ourselves to obtain this capacity—we only need to develop and use what is already there.

The psyche provides the tools for human survival. We are equipped with instinct and intuition. They come with the archetypes, which form the genetic basis of human survival psychology. We come into the world with the ability to survive.

The archetypes have distinct survival value. They are part of human nature. Recovering evolutionary intelligence resurrects the natural self and its capabilities.

Aside from the major and more obvious functions of mediating our relationship to the environment and of maintaining psychic balance and existential coherence, instinct and intuition assist us in understanding and addressing human situations. They let us sense what happens, what we're up against, what works, and how to react in a given situation. They tell us how to handle problems, how to move in relationships, how to solve conflicts. They also inform us how to deal with difficult or dangerous people, how to succeed in particular situations, how to make friends, how to win a prospective mate. They let us know what's being said, what's not being said, what's between the lines, what makes a person tick, what to watch for, what a person really wants, what goes on around us, how to avoid trouble, whom to trust, when to say what needs to be said, when to take a stand, where to go from here. They prompt us when to hold on or to let go, when situations are adverse or toxic, when there is danger, when we are with the wrong people. And they trigger us to protect ourselves, to respond to harm and abuse, to stand up for ourselves, to stop exhausting ourselves, and so forth. Instinct and intuition reflect the evolutionary reality of human life, while bonding us to the biological and psychic energies of the body—our life force. It is essential to honor them and to enlist them in our survival. Recovering human nature fortifies our adaptation to life.

But there is a dilemma. Most of the time, we are not aware of the functioning of the brain and what it does for us at any given moment. This is especially true for the older parts of the brain. Most of these functions are automatic, such as our vital functions, metabolism, and similar processes. The older and more remote the brain, the less we are aware of its operations. This, too, applies to the midbrain and its functions. The midbrain, the seat of the evolutionary psyche, controls, among other things, responses to the environment. It determines instinctual behavior and adaptive functioning. Most of it is dormant and unconscious.

Human survival functioning is part of the older brain. Our innate survival psychology is largely unconscious. This is why most of us don't know about it. There is another reason, too. Western culture has never looked favorably on human nature. It either ignored or wrongly rejected our instinctual biology as something negative. A social persona was put in front of the natural self. As a result, we lack knowledge and awareness of our own biological intelligence. Recovering the evolutionary intelligence of human nature, our innate survival capacity, therefore, involves several aspects. Given the split from our evolutionary self, it becomes a process of reinventing ourselves in a new way.

- The recovery of our innate adaptive psychology begins with the awareness of our natural survival capabilities. Evolution has put a set of behavioral, attitudinal and mental capabilities in the service of human self-preservation, invaluable to life and survival. Bringing these innate survival capabilities into conscious awareness turns them into a powerful dependable resource. The process of making the unconscious conscious is like claiming land from the sea. It retrieves that part of our nature, which has been sealed off by socialization and cognitive process.

  For most of us, this means cutting through the cognitive and conditioning processes we have become accustomed to and reconfirming the validity and integrity of our inborn capacity for self-preservation. This involves a significant reorientation process and an examination of our relationship with ourselves, with people, and with the world around us. Recovering the innate capacity for self-preservation and survival restores an important sense of confidence and security to human psychology. Awareness of our own capabilities changes our way of functioning and the way we look at the world.

- Youngsters in early hunting societies go through a process of ethological rehearsal[1]. All children the world over, including those in the animal kingdom, play at being grownups. Ethological rehearsal is a specific kind of play or training. Its objective is to activate innate survival behavior. Ethology signifies behavioral adaptation and specifically refers to a set of biological survival behaviors, which evolved to secure need gratification and effective adaptation to the environment. Ethology relates to behavioral survival. Ethological rehearsal involves our natural instincts and survival behaviors. It puts us in touch with the territorial, hierarchical, aggressive, sexual and xenophobic aspects of our nature.

  Ethological behavior forms the instinctive pole of the archetypal psyche. The expression of these adaptive behavioral features is usually involuntary and stimulated by the outside. They are activated by significant stimuli that prescribe survival behavior. These innate abilities present a natural adaptive response to survival conditions, unless, they are overruled by social training and conditioned behavior. Survival is essentially an instinctual response.

  Ethological rehearsal reinforces that human survival rests on a powerful natural foundation. Ultimately, it intends to restore the behavioral confidence and the instinctive trust in our ability to fulfill our needs. Education and training in ethological knowledge are indispensable for survival. While the human instincts are innate, specific instinctual behaviors are not. Since instinctive behavior itself "is not inherited", only "the potential to develop . . . behavioural systems"[2], ethological training is instrumental in activating innate survival behaviors. Rehearsing the use of our instincts reinforces the presence of a powerful dependable resource.

- Nature matches attitudes to behavior. Once we become aware of our innate ability to survive and once we start acting as survivors, our attitudes have to follow suit. Survival behavior needs to be reinforced by survival attitudes. Biological behavior corresponds to the natural order and quite explicitly to the demands nature puts on adaptation and maturity. Nature's primary command is that the organism is responsible for its survival. Nature drives for self-reliance and self-sufficiency of the organism. For it to be effective, survival needs to be field-independent. Nature insists on individuality and self-reliance. It demands responsibility for the life it gives. Alongside the biology of behaviors aimed at need gratification, nature has placed a set of attitudes to reinforce viable adaptation.

  These attitudes are evolutionary traits of human nature. They stress individuality, initiative and responsibility to achieve self-reliance and self-sufficiency. These attitudes form the motivational core of evolutionary functioning. Attitudinal adaptation is the bridge between the behavioral and mental aspects of human survival. *Total confidence* and *total abandon*, the highest levels of behavioral and mental adaptation, come down to maturity and personal responsibility.

- A large portion of human survival is mental. The innate capacity to maintain psychic balance enables mental adaptation. It is the ability to adapt to circumstances of great impact beyond our control, to cope with situations that are emotionally stressful and potentially damaging, to come to terms with the hardness of life, and in the end to make sense of it all.

  Neurologically, mental adaptation involves two levels of brain functioning. The adaptive capacity itself originates in the midbrain—involving instinctive, archetypal functions. The content, the interpretation we put on our experiences, is furnished by the left and the right brain hemispheres—engaging our ability to reason, sift, sort, evaluate, attach value and meaning. Survival consciousness involves genetic and acquired elements. The instinctual function is nature's gift; the content is our contribution.

Coming to terms with difficult or changing conditions involves an adaptive process of several stages: Impact, reaction, reversal (genetic component), recovery, resolution (content component). The quality of mental adaptation is directly related to our psychological, mental and spiritual development. Increased maturity means increased mental and spiritual adaptation.

- The final step: the integration of new adaptive functioning into the structure of our personality. Having been brought up by social training, it will take some time for most of us to recover the behaviors, attitudes, and the consciousness that compose our evolutionary intelligence. After recognizing these adaptive features, we need to practice and reinforce them.

The process of restoring our inherent survival abilities moves from awareness to conscious utilization. Practice and repetition establish intentional usage and eventually make these adaptive features a part of our personality and of our way of functioning. We need to use these features consciously and eventually turn them into ongoing habitual patterns. Where survival has mostly been a spontaneous reaction to unforeseen events and conditions, conscious use of our innate adaptive resources facilitates proaction. This turns survival from reflex into strategy.

Integration of these adaptive qualities restores the functional integrity of the natural self. This restoration establishes an innate system of adaptive functioning in the psychology of the individual—replacing socialization and conditioned psychology as the primary reference and mode of operating in life. Conscious practice and repetition aim to recover the natural self as the agent of our survival and to establish a true sense of functional autonomy. The purpose of this practice is to realign our life with the evolutionary impulse and the adaptive potential of our species—bringing to bear all the strengths and achievements of a two million year-old history.

Human nature has inherent survival value. Its adaptive capability was honed by evolutionary process. It contains the entire survival experience of our species.

Ten Steps to Recover Human Nature

Although mostly unconscious, our natural powers of survival are comparable to those of the animal. To connect with our innate survival psychology and to put it to use in our lives, we need to do several things:

1. The first step is to create awareness and remove the mystery. We need to understand that we have an inherent survival capacity like all living organisms. We also need to appreciate the value and importance of our innate psychology despite the cultural rejection it has received. In it, we possess a real and reliable source of personal self-reliance.
2. The second step is to pay attention to our adaptive abilities and to bring them to the surface. The job is to make the unconscious conscious. Once we know we possess inherent behaviors and mental abilities that respond to survival issues, we can observe how they operate in us and others.
3. The third step is to rehearse and activate survival behavior. Remember playing grownups or watching lion cubs practice for the hunt, all in preparation for adulthood? Rehearsing survival behavior puts us in touch with our

hierarchical, territorial, sexual, xenophobic and aggressive instincts. It reinforces what is already there. It also releases the energy that powers our vitality.
4. The fourth step is to add attitude to ability. Nature insists on self-reliance and self-sufficiency. It demands initiative and responsibility for the life it gives. Survival behavior needs to be reinforced by survival attitudes. They form the bridge to mental survival.
5. The fifth step is to engage with the innate ability to maintain psychic balance. It emerges in situations of distress effecting recovery after the initial shock. It is there when we need it. Trusting its lead provides security and confidence. Adding personal growth amplifies the genetic abilities for mental adaptation. Increased maturity and wisdom enhance our ability to cope with the events and eventualities of life.
6. The sixth step is to switch from intellect to innate intelligence. The intellect inhibits the adaptive capacity of the older brain. As long as the intellect dominates our approach to life, evolutionary functioning remains dormant and unavailable. Using instinct versus intellect is not an either/or matter. It is an issue of the right approach in the right circumstance. Survival issues fall to the instinct.
7. The seventh step is to practice what we have. Practice and repetition reinforce our innate abilities and make them part of our normal behavior. Eventually, continued use transforms the instinctual response to survival into conscious action and deliberate strategy.
8. The eighth step is to align our life with our innate psychology. Human life is ultimately structured by biology. The issues of hierarchy, territory, sexuality, xenophobia and aggression form not only our core behavior but also the way we organize our society and our affairs. Once we realize that our innate psychology is also manifest in our environment, this alignment falls into place. Our

survival behavior matches the survival conditions of our world. The long-term issues of our life and destiny require a similar alignment. The stages and events of the natural life cycle resonate with our innate psychology and its spiritual demands. Bringing our life in line with our inherent survival psychology, both behavior and consciousness, makes it strong and effective.

9. The ninth step is to regain trust in our nature. Western civilization developed at the expense of nature. It has also undermined the trust in our own nature. Fear and doubt result in limitation and failure. Nature forever puts a premium on reality, and adaptation is its ultimate test. What passes that inspection is fit to live and survive in the real world. We are no exception; moreover, we passed the test. Human nature has significant survival value. Trusting the adaptive capacity of our evolutionary intelligence makes it a reliable resource.

10. The tenth step is to live life from within. Instinct and intuition are the cornerstones of human nature. They form the baseline of human life. Instinct and intuition are the ultimate resource and reality reference of human survival. They sustain us from within and they relate us to the larger realities of nature and cosmos. The intellect is a valuable ally in negotiating the man-made world of modern life. Effective survival is based on instinct and intuition with the intellect on standby.

Our innate psychology contains the powers of nature. It provides behaviors to compete for resources, to defend our interests and property, to sustain sexual potency and partnership, and to protect our security. It also provides the spirituality to sustain confidence and inner peace. It gives us the ability to stake our claim and to hold our own.

Even though cultural suppression and conditioning may have concealed this innate psychology, its instinctive potency, however, remains resistant to extinction. Though dormant and concealed, nobody ever completely loses this original, evolutionary capacity. Therefore, it can be resurrected and become available again. Instinct and intuition are inerasable features of human nature.

Adaptation is the everpresent frontier of life. It is there where our fate and fortune are decided. Restoring the instinctive trust in our ability to fulfill our needs has to be at the top of the list. At the very bottom, survival is an instinctual response. It has to come from there to be successful.

Chapter Nine

'This is your world', he said, pointing to the busy street outside the window. 'You are a man of that world. And out there, in that world, is your hunting ground. There is no way to escape the *doing* of our world, so what a warrior does is to turn his world into his hunting ground. As a hunter, a warrior knows that the world is made to be used. So he uses every bit of it. A warrior is like a pirate that has no qualms in taking and using anything he wants, except that the warrior doesn't mind or he doesn't feel insulted when he is used and taken himself'.

Carlos Castaneda
Lessons

The Way Of The Hunter

The hunter is a principal figure of mythology. He symbolizes the struggle for survival and the path to success. The hunter is the primordial survivor. He represents the evolutionary history of our species. The struggle of human survival has found expression in mythology because it is a universal struggle. The mythic figure of the hunter is immortalized in ancient mythology, even in the heavenly constellation of the stars.

The appearance of the hunter in mythology reflects man's interest in this figure, who is so much like us—embroiled in the ongoing effort to survive. It also reflects the solution to human survival, presented by the figure of the hunter. Hunting is man's superior survival behavior. Evolution has established hunting as the 'master behavior pattern' of the species. It is a pattern geared for survival. The hunter is a generalist, not a specialist. Despite the universality, there is balance. It was for this reason that Odysseus, the classical man of action and proponent of survival in ancient mythology, was to become the carrier of the Greek allegory: "Why Odysseus, seeing that he was by no means the greatest of the heroes who fought on the great plains of Troy? He is instinctively chosen, perhaps, because he represented the hero in his legitimate, individual and most diversified proportions more accurately than any other. Others had more courage and strength; were more compulsive and dedicated warriors, or wiser and more experienced as was Old Nestor. But Odysseus had all of these qualities and none in excess. All aspects were subject to his awareness of reality, and an intelligence acute enough for him to be referred to as the fox. His advice was constantly sought, and it was he who ultimately thought up the fatal Wooden Horse, and he is obviously chosen for being so many-sided an individual without hubris"[1].

The adaptation of the hunting way of life to the modern world pivots on the transformation of the original hunter into an inner hunter. The hunter within is the man of higher consciousness who has realigned himself with the evolutionary impulse of his species. "At one time everybody knew that a hunter was the best of men."[2] The ancient hunter has never left. He has been subdued, but still lives on in the deep recesses of the human psyche.

Becoming a Hunter: The Journey into Life

The process of hunting in early societies involved programming of children, scanning, stalking, immobilization (killing, capture) and retrieval. The system was designed to secure the survival of both the hunter and the group. The "instant one begins to live like a hunter, one is no longer ordinary"[1].

About Seeing and Scanning

Before he pursues his prey, the hunter scans his world. He then knows what to hunt and where to hunt. He becomes familiar with the habits and movements of the animal, and he learns about the features and conditions of the territory. Scanning is an essential part of hunting and requires keen ability of observation, inspection and judgment. It helps him collect, sort and evaluate information about the environment and get the facts to guarantee the success of the hunt. By knowing the reality of the world he lives in, the hunter secures his survival.

Hunting is a strategic activity. The hunter "lives his life strategically"[2]. He depends on his ability to know and understand his world. For that, he trusts his knowledge and his intuition. He also has a plan to satisfy his needs and a strategy on how to succeed. Survival aims for a specific outcome and does not allow for error or illusion. The hunter "is not at all like the animal he is after"—he "has no routines"[3]. Survival requires a strategic position, independent of the world. The hunter takes a stance that makes him the ultimate agent of his destiny. He does not allow himself to be cornered. He rejects anything that takes his options away or destroys his survival advantage. He sees for himself and retains his own judgment. He makes sure that survival is on his terms, not on those of the environment. The original hunter had to be smarter than the animal; the modern hunter needs to be smarter than society. The hunter relies on human nature. He uses all his innate abilities to survive, unobstructed by cultural influence and training. He knows that the only security we have is our "ability to deal with the world"[4]. The "hunter knows he will lure game into his traps over and over again, so he doesn't worry"[5].

About Meaning and History

The hunter is not a solitary figure who roams the plains and hills on his own. The hunt is a communal event. But he is man with a story. The story is his most precious possession. It is the source of his power. The story tells him who he is and where he is going. That way, he has a history as his tribe has a history. Like the animal and his weapons, the story is part of the hunt.

The hunter has a story and that story changes his world. As his personal myth unfolds, it takes on shape in the outer world.

The story finds expression in the activities, things and events of his life. The story is a map and it gives him a sense of ongoing identity over time. The hunter keeps a larger view of himself than society would want him to have. The hunter is the universal man. He rejects a narrow functional self-concept that would stamp, shrink and measure his being. He avoids the collapse of identity through catastrophe, crisis or old age. The hunter moves far from the crowd. His values and identity derive from his own nature and abilities. His story gives him a power that propels his life. The biography becomes the expression of the story. The hunter relates to the world on his terms, measuring his participation in its affairs. He remains involved and detached at the same time—he treats the world compassionately and sparingly. "Therein lies the secret of great hunters. To be available and unavailable at the precise turn of the road."[6]

The hunter knows that the story spans his entire lifetime. The story is his own evolution. It reflects the universal life of the species, giving him a profound sense of history. He regards his story with affection. It is the primordial guide that leads him on his path of destiny. It links him to a higher order. The story is really an inner story and the hunter is ultimately an inner hunter.

About Versatility and Competence

The hunter knows a lot depends on him, if not everything. He has prepared himself well for the hunt. His spirit and his body are as precise as the arrow and as flexible as his bow. Every nerve, sense and sinew has been trained to meet the jungle and his prey. "He is not at all like the animals he is after, fixed by heavy routines and predictable quirks; he is free, fluid, unpredictable."[7] A hunter leaves nothing to chance. He knows it is his hunt. He is ready and he knows how to survive.

The hunter avoids conformity to culture. He resists being molded by the environment. He stays clear of the limitations society puts on personality and behavior. Hunters "transcend the environment rather than just coping with it"[8]. The hunter uses all his abilities and brings them in line with the requirements of his survival. The universality of his personality and skills allows him to handle situations well. His mental, emotional and behavioral versatility makes the hunter seem fluid and unpredictable. He reads the situation carefully and does whatever he must to deal with it successfully. His personal story enables him to "function without a stable external frame of reference"[9] and to steer a clear course while others might flounder when the external world begins to shift.

The hunter moves with precision. He is competent in many areas, in many ways. His involvement with the world is precise, crisp, decisive and purposeful. He has "no doubts about his mastery"[10]. This competence gives him a profound sense of confidence: "Just fully being skillful involves total lack of inhibition"[11]. He is not afraid to be, he is not afraid to live. He "dares to *be*, like a tiger in the jungle"[12]. The hunter comes from the evolutionary wisdom of his nature. He has learned what no one can teach him[13]. There comes a point in life, when the student needs to leave the master. He knows that survival remains his own doing and that ultimately only he can provide the answers. Human nature is his mentor. The hunter relies on his inner resources to give him strength and guidance. He has compassion for people and identifies with mankind. He avoids strong attachments to objects, procedures and beliefs. He resists conformity but obeys the law. He views the world without judgment. He knows the odds and he makes himself accountable for his results. He can see 'below the horizon of time and round the corners of life'. He has no heroes[14].

The hunter is a generalist, not a specialist. Despite the complexity, there is balance. Like Odysseus, the proponent of survival in ancient mythology, he is the 'many-sided individual without hubris'. For a person "to be a hunter means that one knows a great deal"[15]. His versatility and competence give him the power to withstand the rigors of life. He has left the perimeters of dependency and lives on a separate frontier.

About Skills and Methods

Hunting takes great skill. From early on, the hunter learned about his way of life, first from play, then in the wilderness. He got to know about the animal, its habits, how to stalk it and how to kill. He learned to use his weapons, set traps, skin game, prepare food, make clothing and build his shelter. Play and exercise helped him to condition his body for hunt and combat. Since childhood he had learned about his tribe, its life, its rituals and its customs. Nothing was unimportant. With time, he also learned to know about the land, the rivers, the sky, the stars, the weather and the wind. And soon he began to understand that his success as a hunter would depend not only on his spirit and the strength and speed of his body, but equally on his skill.

The hunter protects his survival advantage. He holds on to his independent position and the ability to do more than one thing—more than one job or trade, more than one role or position. He develops his skills strategically. He adapts to the world by pursuing many skills rather than specialized competency. The hunter approaches the environment strategically. He treats it as a means for his survival. Like the original hunter, he confronts the environment with versatility and anticipation. His strategy aims to leverage his skills against the demands of a complex and changeable world.

The hunter views his skills as essential tools in his effort to survive. He improves them to secure his material survival. The hunter is aware of changes in the human condition and he is prepared for them, never to be caught by surprise. He does not seek out crisis or catastrophe, but he is well equipped to deal with changes forced upon his life. He has the skills and the spirit to cope with misfortune. He meets life with resourcefulness and versatility. He has a keen sense of reality and knows how to apply his skills to selective advantage. The generality of his skills gives him flexibility and a superior position to adapt to the world.

About People and Predators

The hunter encounters the world with all his senses. He sees it, hears it, feels it, touches it, smells it, and dreams it. Early in life, he learned what he had to watch for. He learned about the animals, their ways, how to read them and what it took to live amongst them. He got to know about the difference between predators and game. He learned the stories and legends of his tribe, and he was taught how to observe the world around him. In time, he learned about the things that work in the real world. He learned about other people, the good ones and the bad ones. He learned about hunting and being hunted. And he got to understand about the use and meaning of power. All these things were important in becoming a hunter.

We are born with the tools to face the world and to adapt to it. We come into the world armed with the biology and psychology of our instincts. Instinctive behavior helps us to adapt to external conditions. Our instincts can adjust to the survival conditions of modern life. The hunter respects his instincts and enlists them in his survival. They bond him with the biological and psychic energy of his life force. Instincts reflect the evolutionary reality of life—they let him understand what happens and what he must do.

The instincts supply an invaluable and inexhaustible fund of wisdom and vitality. They have an uncanny power about them—a vigor and crispness, coupled with certitude in action. The hunter embraces his instinctive nature. He sees it as a source of his power and resourcefulness. He underlines its strength by accepting that he is by nature hierarchical, territorial, aggressive, xenophobic and sexual. And he expects others and life to be the same. But there is a twist—the hunter is aggressive about life, not toward people or environment. His aggression is directed at survival. Higher consciousness curbs the raw biology of the instincts, as nature did before modern man began to override its norms and inhibitions. Aggression plays a role in all aspects of instinctive behavior. Like his skills, his instinctive potency is another resource for his survival. He can be aggressive in competition and defense, if he has to, or he can be territorial to protect what is his.

The instincts exist to preserve life. The hunter knows that every survival situation involves the evolutionary dimension of human life. He does not change personality in social situations or when he moves in his world. He holds his power. He looks at the world in evolutionary terms. Everything is about survival. The hunter does not leave anything to chance. Survival happens everywhere and at all times. Geared for survival, the hunter is always in touch with his power and his skills. He never abandons his nature. He understands the evolutionary facts behind human events. The hunter expects hierarchical, territorial, aggressive, xenophobic or sexual behavior in others. He is aware of the way of the world. And he knows, too, that "there's no plan when it comes to hunting power": the hunter "must always be in a state of readiness"[16].

He is also ready to protect himself against danger and harm coming from other people. Nature has equipped us with the ability to perceive danger[17]. The most common of these inherited warning systems among many animal species is the predator archetype. We have a similar inborn warning system. Human predators are as dangerous as their animal counterparts. They misuse their innate biological behavior to attack and prey on other people. In situations like these, the hunter needs to rely on his innate fight-flight response, knowing that "his fear would immediately turn him into a prey"[18].

About Environment and Universe

The hunter assumes total responsibility for his existence. His life is pitted against the wilderness, his place of survival. The hunter lives life strategically, leaving nothing to chance. He calculates everything, and then he acts. The hunter knows the wilderness. He knows he needs a plan to give him advantage and control for his life in the wilderness. He knows he cannot be without a plan if he is to survive successfully. A hunter "is tuned to survive, and he survives in the best of all possible fashions"[19].

The hunter recognizes the importance of material survival and success in the marketplace. He achieves those goals without compromising the adaptive advantage of his position. Like the original hunter, he maintains a clear distinction between his life and the outside world. The environment remains a separate entity at his disposal. Adaptation becomes a strategic effort to make meaningful use of those external resources and opportunities. The hunter protects his selective advantage, generic to human survival, against cultural pressures to the contrary. His adaptation to contemporary life is *generalized* and *field-independent*. His relationship to society is paradoxical: he uses it and avoids it at the same time[20]. The hunter moves between separate realities—his world and the world outside. Rather than modeling his life after society's ideals and instructions, he keeps nature as his guide.

The hunter treats both the environment and the universe as outside realities. He does not conduct his relationship to the universe as a matter of principle or personal conviction. He stays impartial to many of the theories that attempt to explain the effect of the universe on human life. He treats them as relative theories. His ultimate frame of reference is the principle of human survival. Adaptation is concerned with what works in the real world. It selects the best possible answer for any given situation—like the river that finds its way to the sea. When nothing is for sure, the hunter remains alert. A hunter "does not catch game because he sets his traps, or because he knows the routines of his prey, but because he himself has no routines"[21]. Refusing to reject or adopt any theory, that sensibly explains how things happen in life, leaves him with a set of theories that he can rotate depending on the conditions he faces—a "good hunter changes his ways as often as he needs"[22]. The hunter uses all of them, because "one explanation of anything is inadequate"[23]. Adaptation is not concerned with judgment, only with survival.

About Health and Healing

The hunter is deeply involved in his life. He keeps his mind clear, his body strong and life simple. He has adapted himself well to the way of the wilderness. His body and soul are one. He lives the earth, the water, the animals and the skies. He cares for his world and the people around him. His life touches on nature and eternity. Hunting is his life and destiny. "It is difficult for him to miss his aim, because his two feet are held firmly planted on the ground by the weight of his whole body."[24]

To the hunter, health is part of his power. Health is not a singular, isolated aspect of a person's life, nor is it merely the absence of illness and disease—it is a way of life. "Health is not something you do, it is how you are."[25] The hunter is not part of the imaginary race, the hectic pace, that keeps people on the run. He does not understand his life in terms of material success, nor does he look for security in the attachment to status or things, nor does he see the world as either hostile or friendly. To him the world is a place to transact business. He views the world as a place of abundance and he has abundant means to get what he needs. There is always a market for what a person can do and what people need[26]. The hunter views material survival as one aspect of a larger effort, not as an end in itself. His security comes from trust in his own resourcefulness and his "ability to deal with the world"[27].

The hunter shields his life from the influence of society. He keeps it away from external demands, appeals, distractions and seductions. His life is well-rounded and reaches into many aspects. His lifestyle is balanced between 'left-sided' and 'right-sided', practical and spiritual involvements. There is a strong kinship with people, traditions and particularly with nature. His lifestyle resonates with his being and philosophy of life. Health is an important part of it. On balance, his life is more strongly rooted in the physical than in the mental. He went to Zorba's school[28]. The hunter understands health as a way of being in the world. It is a vital source of his power.

Being a Hunter: Mastery of Two Worlds

The hunter has a profound biological orientation towards life. In the end, life is an organic matter subject to biological intent. We live not only our own lives but also the life of our species. Whenever we satisfy the archetypal intent of life, we gain a sense of complete satisfaction. We know then that it is the 'real thing' rather than the substitute. The hunter is in harmony with his nature, accepting "the nature of the animal we are"[1].

The hunter understands nature as the authority to set the pace and purpose of his life. His life is grounded in biology. He seeks compliance with nature rather than conformity to society. He treats human nature as the baseline of his life and remains indifferent to cultural influence. But he knows how to move in the world. He has the skills to function and succeed in society. He responds to environmental conditions with strategy and skill. His approach to secure material survival is on his own terms. He remains in charge of his survival throughout life. Continuous involvement in his survival, for which he assumes final responsibility at all times, makes everything he does meaningful. "A hunter must not only know about the habits of his prey, he also must know that there are powers on this earth that guide men and animals and everything that is living."[2]

About Survival and Being

The hunter sets up his own world. He collapses the world as it is and puts a different one in its place. To him, survival remains the ultimate and eternal reality. The environment around him is the setting and the scene where it takes place. The environment is the world of the day—the values an era attaches to things and events, the practices of how things are organized, treated and done. To the hunter, none of that is a given. That is to say, he does not conform and adjust to the world the way he finds it. Instead, he creates his own adaptation, fitting the environment to the needs of his survival.

The hunter has trust in himself and faith in the natural order of things. His early efforts were directed at building his attitudes and skills, at resolving internal liabilities and conflicts, and at matching needs with responsibility. It was a process of developing and fine-tuning his personality and methods. He has reached an eminent state of precision in his way of being in and with the world. Unresolved people are messy. They leave a trail of destruction behind. The hunter moves with precision: he "uses his world sparingly and with tenderness, regardless of whether the world might be things, or plants, or animals, or people, or power"[3]. Survival is about the business of living, both material and mental. Yet, the hunter is neither a materialist nor a mystic. He has overcome the ambivalence of life and turned his world into a womb. The hunter moves between inner and outer events. He is both practical and spiritual, his life is both personal and universal, his world both transitory and eternal. Combining these polarities, he has achieved a mastery of two worlds. He has turned the world into his hunting ground.

The Hunter Within: The Essence of Power

The hunter is the archetypal survivor. Like his ancestor of the past who stalked the animal and set the traps, he is the initiator who asserts his purpose on the world. As the original hunter, he views the environment as a source of survival, not as a condition that controls his life. Taking complete charge of his existence, he does not entrust his fate to the hands of outside powers or conditions nor does he leave anything to chance. He faces the world equipped with strategy and skill, relying on his own resources to fulfill his needs and achieve his aims. "A man is only the sum of his personal power, and that sum determines how he lives and how he dies."[1]

The hunter's approach to life is deliberate, simple and direct. The story and strategy, that guide him, uphold the coherence of his world opposite conditions he cannot control. He respects the natural order of things and the laws of life. The hunter is a man of high integrity, which he stakes against the world. The hunter traces his lineage to his ancestral past. He sees himself as part of a larger process and cosmos of events. He has a sense of belonging to a timeless and transpersonal universe. He relates to a larger heritage and history. He knows that in his own story and in the story of his time he is about to repeat 'the eternal life of the species'. His strength derives from the biological, instinctive and psychic resources of his own nature and from his relationship to a higher order of being.

About Power and Energy

Hunting is about power. It is a way of life geared for survival. The hunter is familiar with the secrets of power and the mysteries of the world. He knows it is ultimately his personal power that will make him succeed in the world. Whatever the conditions, circumstances or choices, he needs to match them with a power of his own. He knows he cannot depend on props or chance when it comes to his own survival. For him, power originates from his own organic and psychic nature, and from his trust in the universe.

The hunter knows about nature as a source of power and strength. It contains the energy and the meaning of life; in it we find "that age-old animal power which drives the migrating bird across the sea"[2]. If tapped, our nature provides an enormous resource for survival. The hunter has an unadulterated relationship with nature, with his own body and biology, and with the earth and all of life. He is part of nature and nature is part of him.

In his life, the hunter reconciles nature and culture—not by denying his evolutionary origins but by relying on the ethics of biology inherent in his nature, which engender social order in the service of survival. Culture to the hunter is a matter of higher consciousness, not an antithesis to nature. The hunter perceives nature as orderly and harmonious. He deeply appreciates nature and life and his own natural self. He knows that man is, first of all, an animal, a descendant of Mother Nature, like any other creature on earth. As an animal, man is biologically equipped to master the organic task of survival. And survival is what the hunter is all about.

The original hunter is still alive in him in many ways. There is something of the raw, untamed wilderness in him—the roar of the lion and the fury of the sea. And there is in him, too, the gentleness of the flower and of the wind. Trust in nature is rewarded with reliability. As part of nature, as an animal, possibly a very special one, the human being possesses the same kind of biological energy and life force bestowed on any living organism. This energy is the very essence of life itself. It is the fuel in the engine, the power that drives the organism and generates vitality. It is the life instinct converted into energy, the force installed in the organism to sustain its survival.

The hunter treats nature's investment wisely. His natural energies are not obstructed by outside conditioning. The purpose of the instincts is to preserve life. They are the core behavior in man. The instincts have definite survival value in daily life. The hunter is never far from his instincts. They assure him that he is matched to handle any situation that comes his way.

The hunter has a strong sense for the physical and practical side of things. He sees the world not only as a mental event of ideas, schedules and objectives, but no less as a physical reality of objects, activities and experiences. As a survivor, the hunter stays close to the ground, finding reality in simplicity. The body is the primary contact with reality. The hunter is a physical person—practical, earthy and robust. The body lives and remembers, yet unless it moves and acts and feels it remains a dormant asset. A world of urban lifestyles and synthetic environments, where things are highly artificial, automated and amputated, deprives people of real experiences. It makes them lose touch with their natural selves. The hunter avoids the mental bias of the modern world. He knows bodily experiences reinforce the energy and certainty of life and, on an even deeper level, the biological reality of survival.

The hunter is a man close to the earth, drawing on the powers of nature, ever respectful of its mysteries and laws. He is part of the seasons, the soil, the sky and the sea, and they are part of him. His love of animals, flowers and trees, his fascination with sunshine and rain, winter, spring, summer and fall, his rapture from the force of ocean and storm, from the grandeur of mythic landscapes—all are part of his power, essence and magic. In nature the opposites of life merge, polarities harmonize and energy flows. The humanity of the hunter does not depend on the rejection of his nature nor on a sterile intellectualism under the skull. He relies on a workable balance between the powers of body and mind. Just as much as mind and soul are a source of power and strength, so is the human body with all its natural forces—for there is a Zorba in all of us.

About Power and Meaning

Man is not only an animal confined to a biological destiny. He belongs to a larger history, which distinguishes him as a human being.

Both body and psyche are the product of evolution—the nature within. The hunter's life follows the innate patterns of his nature. He lives an archetypal life, reflective of the universal themes and events of the eternal life of the species. The collective psyche is a force field in the life of man ever since his time began. The "psychic depths are nature, and nature is creative life."[3] *The hunter sees his life as part of the natural process of all life.*

The hunter understands the meaning of life in relation to the biological intent of nature. The power he draws from nature is enhanced by his story. This inner story creates a path and a journey. Being on the path that is your path brings special powers other people do not have[4]. For the story and the journey to occur there must be a bond between personal life and the fabric of events. The story links the hero to the meaning and energy of life. Having a story makes dealing with the hardships and difficulties of survival somewhat easier and less awesome. But it does not make things any less demanding. The spirituality of the hunter is, thus, grounded in biology and in the actual experiences of life. He understands the survival value of having a story. It combines the necessities with the essence of life and provides a stable source of psychic energy.

Evolution has impressed on the human psyche a clear distinction of what is useful, effective, desirable, moral, and what is not. It has established what works and what doesn't. This is why we can trust nature. The hunter knows that the psyche has the answers he needs. It has been there before him. Doing right by nature and right by the heart is the meaning that inspires his life. Capable not only of intellectual understanding and rational effectiveness but also of compassion and 'understanding through life', the hunter has created in himself an unfailing well of energy and creativity. He is strong on the outside because he is strong on the inside—knowing full well that survival forever originates from within.

Expanded consciousness allows him to see and know more than one reality and to move with ease in the world. He creates and attracts conditions that promote his survival. He remains, however, removed from the noise, hustle and trivia of modern life, nor does he assume its externalized values and beliefs. They get in the way of where he seeks to take his story and his life. His commitment is to humanity and its evolution. It is part of his story to give to mankind and support the same world that sustains him.

About Power and Faith

A shadow on the floor, a two-dimensional reality of length and width, represents a reflection of a three-dimensional object like a chair or a vase. Likewise, our world of three dimensions is a reflection of a four- or more-dimensional universe. And just as the shadow does not 'know' how it got here nor anything about the world it is a reflection of, we do not understand about the higher order reality that affects our existence[5]. Our intelligence fails to comprehend whatever lies beyond the boundary of our three-dimensional world. Yet, the things that really affect us come from there. We need to have faith in the existence of a higher order and intelligence that impacts us from beyond our world. This means there is a player on the other side whom we do not know and cannot control. This, too, means that we "do not have to concern ourselves with the cosmic world, the world of gods, psychic powers, angels and devils. To do so may be to lose track of the physical world in which we live, and this results in madness"[6].

And this from the hunter: "The other side of faith is trusting oneself. It is the belief that we deserve good things to happen to us in life. Fate is not an external force; it springs up from inside. When things go wrong, it is not a bad fate at work. There is something inside that is doing it.

Emotional injuries of childhood or later life are wounds of the spirit. They affect a person's trust in the world and outlook on life. Often they leave a sense of bitterness, cynicism or disillusionment behind, which, untreated, is perpetuated into adult life. The wounds of the past cut deeply into the human soul with feelings of being unworthy, unloveable, impotent, unwanted or doomed and with a view of the world as unrelenting, ungiving and hostile. Early injuries create a set of attitudes that largely determine the conduct and course of a person's life—a hopeless sense of desperation and defeat that 'no matter what I do, things won't work out anyway'. Treating the emotional injuries of childhood, the parental wound, is a matter of healing attitudes. It is in the person's attitudes where the pain, damage and distortion, caused by the original injuries, remain alive.

In order to heal yourself, you need to reach out to the wound inside of you. You need to make a relationship with the unconscious—your soul. Healing the wound means going inside to the soul. It is there where the wound occurred and where your fate was affected. It all happened on a level inaccessible to the conscious mind. So if you work with your fantasies and dreams, you see fate in formation. And if you relate to them and try to understand them, you can make a dialog with them and articulate the wound in images and emotions. And you can see that the shape of fate does change. The outcome changes because of the different relationship with the things inside which have been creating it. To put it another way: healing yourself is 'mothering' yourself. You are giving time and attention to your feelings in the way a mother should have done and didn't. It is giving yourself a 'feeding', holding the wound.

Without this inner work, the wound buried in the soul of your unconscious simply creates a product. Then it hits you in outer life, and it feels like fate. If you keep staring at the outer things, nothing is going to shift. It first comes from inside: the practical things in life fall into place when you get the inner things sorted out. Healing the wound changes your attitudes about yourself, about life and your place in the world—and good things will happen to you. As you believe that you deserve it and that you have something to offer, of course, it will come. Maybe, not this week but sometime soon.

Healing the cynicism and bitterness, which afflict your attitudes, rectifies the wound and recaptures a sense of inner wholeness. This rewards you with a belief and a trust in yourself. Moreover, it engenders the religious attitude, a regained faith in the natural order of the universe and in the meaningfulness of life. It is an inner faith born from the soul, not a clever rationality. It is the kind of faith that inspires your hopes and your dreams and that is with you in times of hardship and sorrow. It is a faith that you can actually bring down into life. So that when things are difficult and painful, you somehow know it will be alright in the end. It is the kind of faith that decides your fate"[7].

The survival value of faith is such that it can make a difference between life and death. The hunter knows about the power of faith in good times and in bad times—"there is no time for timidity"[8]. Faith is the spring of life, the inside peace that knows things will work out. It is a shield against hardship and doubt. And it is "the faith that looks through death"[9] which helps us to come to terms with the side of life that is unredeemable—with the sadness over the problems between people that remain unresolved, over the pain that continues and festers unhealed, over the times that will never return, over the losses we can never retrieve.

Real faith is a spiritual attitude with an instinctual base. The reverse side of faith is the moral attitude. The hunter has a keen moral sense. It directs his conduct of life and his relationship to the world. The earth and all of life are sacred to him and evidence of a larger design. Faith bridges the gap of doubt and despair and mediates the relationship between man and universe.

Faith together with the moral attitude—the principles of belief and responsibility—are the basis of love. The ability to give and receive love is inborn in all of us. Love is the generating force that connects us with the reality and mystery of life. The love of life is the principal prerequisite of human survival. It alone enables the conscious mind to accept the hardness of life and the inevitability of death. Love is an innate capacity of the human psyche. It is the connecting principle that joins us with the world, that transforms the polarities of life—that forgives, redeems, heals and makes whole. Love is the principle of the eternally feminine within, which offers us support and understanding and, thus, enables us to cope with the masculine endeavor of facing the world of survival.

About Power and Survival

Nature is relentless with her creatures. After only a short period of nurturing, she confronts the upcoming offspring with the unforgiving ultimatum: 'fly' or 'die', forcing the youngster to take the jump into reality and self-sufficiency. Those, who fail, fall easy prey to other animals or to the traps and weapons of man.

The human survival instinct took shape in the hunting way of life. Evolution made hunting into the 'master behavior pattern' of the species. Acquired by evolution, hunting behavior reflects the decrees of nature, mandating survival as the ultimate reality of life. The hunter looks at life from the standpoint of survival. There is nothing more real and final than nature itself. It gives life, it determines life, and it ends life. The hunter anchors his life in the biology of his being. He runs his life as a business knowing that survival is his business. The real influence in his life is life itself. He is at one with his destiny and so without worry or fear. Both his practicality and spirituality are deliberate, precise and effective. They interact in partnership as the masculine and feminine principles of life.

The hunter does not fit his survival into the world, instead, he fits the world into his survival. His approach to survival is that of the original hunter. It spans "the entire biobehavioral continuum"[10] and emphasizes the importance of comprehensive survival capabilities. The hunter is conscious of the complexity of modern life and the demands it puts on his resources. He knows that the modern world requires a high degree of competence and effectiveness in all areas of life. The hunter has prepared himself well. "A hunter hunts whatever presents itself to him. Thus he must always be in a state of readiness."[11] The hunter knows something about most things. He can do more things than most people, and he is able to function effectively in all aspects of life.

The hunting way of life is a strategic approach to survival. The hunter applies strategy not only to those things in life that are controllable, but also to those that are not. Some things in life need to be accepted the way they are. Sometimes, these are major things. This does not mean being passive or relying on luck or chance. It is a form of active waiting. It means being expectant, receptive and ready for the opportunity when it occurs. A hunter "when he stalks in the wilderness would never walk into any place without figuring out his points of protection"[12]. Alternative and fallback strategies are always necessary in life and they are part of his overall approach. Yet they never stray too far from the main direction of his life. Generally, he trusts his instincts more than his intellect and depends on innate more than on learned abilities. Both instinct and intuition are important resources of human life. Both are innate. Both are readily available.

The hunter treats spirituality as a resource not as a pastime—soft, convenient and expendable. His psyche, the combination of instinct and spirit, relates him to the archetypal reality of life. Instinct and spirit are the two basic poles of his life with the conscious mind as a powerful ally. The life of the hunter is not immune to difficulty or hardship, yet this does not bewilder him. He accepts the paradoxical nature of life. He knows that survival is an instinctual response, and, as such, it can rely on the biological potency of nature. Nature is the final judge of survival. Forever putting a premium on reality, it rewards our successes with happiness and well-being, and it punishes our failures with illness and despair. And it is ultimately in our own nature where we have to look for strength and find the answers.

About Transformation and Transcendence

> *Survival is the governing principle of all of life and the ultimate task each living organism is contracted to achieve. The environment sets the conditions of where and how it takes place. Human life in the modern world happens on two frontiers split into separate realities with individual and global survival directly in the middle. On the biological frontier, we are faced with the principles of nature and subject to the paradox of life and death, growth and decay, permanence and change. On the cultural frontier, we are confronted with the evolution of human consciousness and forced to contend with the dilemma between creation*

and chaos, meaning and futility, salvation and despair. We hold life for only a short while and we try our best to cherish it and make it worthwhile before it all disappears. The capriciousness of nature makes life somehow seem like a cosmic tease, while the creations of culture turn it into a somewhat dubious experiment. Yet the wonders of nature endow life with a sense of magic and mystery, and the achievements of culture give it a quality of freedom and autonomy.

Everything in life reminds us of our basic vulnerability and everything points to the immense adaptability modern survival requires. Man as the hunter is the archetypal survivor. In modern life he is the symbol of higher consciousness—because that is where evolution has taken the frontier of human survival. In man, evolution has become conscious of itself, forcing him to create value and meaning in life[13]. Both as an experience and as a metaphor, man as the hunter provides the "transcendent context for our brief existence here on earth"[14]. This behavior pattern is still as valid today as it was in man's distant past, because evolution has not ended and the need to survive has not disappeared.

Hunting remains the fundamental strategy for relating human needs to environmental resources. In the hunter, evolution has created the ultimate format of human survival. The pattern enshrines man's unique capacity to penetrate the environment with strategy and to mold its conditions to his purposes. It enlists man's fundamental survival instinct and marshals all his resources to ensure success. It enables him to make his world coherent amid and against adversity and change. And it holds the essential ethics to preserve and protect the world in which he lives. Paramount to the hunting way of life is its goal-directed quality. Hunting is purposeful and integrates all available capabilities to fortify man's survival effort aimed at the environment in front of it and over time.

Advanced consciousness is the evolutionary frontier of the modern hunter. Higher consciousness transcends the ambivalence of modern life. It aligns our world making it whole and manageable, and it gives us a feeling of competence, well-being and peace. Expansion of consciousness requires expansion of personality. Achieving the transformation of consciousness shifts life to a higher plain where we are at one with the universe, and where life is a meaningful destiny and death no longer a threat. Wholeness is both the end of a journey and the threshold to a new life. It is where the personal ends and the universal begins. The transition is preexistent in the human psyche. The psyche contains "the collective history of the species"[15] which, in essence, is the experience of man as the hunter. The human psyche is both personal and universal. The feeling of belonging to life and time and nature is inherent in us.

Modern man is no longer at one with nature, the flowers and the seasons. Gone, too, is man the hunter, the eternal survivor who led the way for mankind along the frontiers of time and evolution—vanished in the man-made world of a technological age. Only in the depths of man's natural self there still resides the original power and wisdom of that now silent and forgotten figure high up on a distant hill at the horizon of history.

EPILOG

For even though we are the first animals to begin to understand the physical processes underlying our experience of life, and though we are developing the psychological and biotechnological capacities for self-transformation, the genome still has us in its grip. We are still the animals that we were. Our ability to influence the course of history and avert the disasters just ahead is far more circumscribed than most of us care to admit. But the creation of a better, safer world will not come through political rhetoric or inhabiting a Rousseauesque cloud-cuckoo land. It can only come, if come it can, through a deep understanding of the nature of the animal we are.

Anthony Stevens

In the long history of our species we have come to a turning point. The bases have shifted. Ever since the inception of culture, we have staged our own evolution determined to improve on nature. Now, evolution has put us on notice. We have changed the world so completely that in a sense 'we meet only ourselves'. Whatever we do, wherever we turn, we encounter man-made creations. We no longer confront nature and adapt to its laws. We now live in a world of our own making—a world within a world, disconnected from the universe of natural and cosmic realities. Only if we 'come to terms with this new situation in every sphere of life' will we recover that 'certainty in the strivings of the soul' of which the Chinese sage has spoken. These observations, stated by W. Heisenberg[1] over seven decades ago, are as true today as they were then.

What occurred on the grand scale of the outside world also happened to the human being on the inside. The fate of the natural world and the fate of the natural self are closely interwoven. Man's willfully imposed domination over nature left unmistakable markings on environment and personality. The cultural rejection of our evolutionary nature has inflicted permanent wounds on the human psyche. The injury affects both instinct and spirit. The infraction is fundamental. It disables our grounding in the biological process of life; and it dislodges our standing with the world of the supernatural. Ever since civilized man began to impose his will on the designs of nature, the species has lived with a wounded psyche.

Healing the wounds of instinct and spirit is at the core of human survival in our time.

If there was ever a time to revisit human nature and to review the results of human civilization, that moment is now. The evolution of our species has reached a critical point where the fate of the human race and the future of our habitat on this planet are in question.

> Just as the purpose of a plant is to grow, so it is that the main purpose of every human being is to survive and grow until death.
>
> Dalai Lama
> Public Interview

Issues And Conclusions

Human survival has reached a turning point. The survival of the individual is pitted against the enormity of a complex, constantly changing world that far exceeds his comprehension and control—and frequently his adaptive capability. The survival of the species hinges on the willingness and ability of modern man to reshape his destiny and avoid the abyss of self-destruction and extinction by his own hands. The issues in both individual and collective survival are much the same—so is the required remedy: the advancement of human evolution.

The following gives a summary statement of the main ideas of the book, an assessment of human survival in the modern age, and an outlook on what must be done.

Evolutionary Intelligence

Survival has always been real to me. For most of my life I have lived on the boundary between countries, cultures and languages. The frontier was never very far away. There were impasses, setbacks paired with achievements. My work as a psychotherapist helped me to understand human behavior as well as my own. This knowledge made it easier to live and win the battles of life. But it was my work with suicidal patients that more than anything clarified my understanding of human functioning. People who approach suicide are cut off from their natural life force and the innate intelligence of their biological being. It was through the negation of life these people faced, that I began to see the value of human nature and understand the importance of evolutionary intelligence.

Life comes without instruction, leverage or guarantee. To be healthy is to learn and know how to live. All of us struggle with the enigma of our existence and how to best make it to the end. Society is a great source of information and influence. Some of what we learn is useful but enduring recipes for life are hard to come by. My own inquiry has taught me that going beyond the cultural models for living back to the evolutionary experience of our species produces the most productive answers. In fact, my work in psychotherapy made it clear that, in the final analysis, most problems of living are due to a lack of evolutionary functioning. When evolutionary functioning is intact, people tend to live strong and effective lives.

The Essence of Human Nature

Human nature is a biological entity made for survival. Over two million years or 99% of human history went into its formation. It contains the survival experience of our species. Our history goes back to the time when our ancestors survived as hunters and gatherers. They confronted the forces of nature in search of shelter and food, and survival was the order of the day. It was then that our basic anatomy, behavior and psychology were formed. These features and abilities entered our genetic make-up and have stayed with us ever since. Like that of all other living organisms, our nature was formed by the adaptive forces of evolution. For that, we possess the same natural powers to adapt and survive that we admire in animals. Formed by evolutionary process, our nature holds the biological intelligence of life. Evolution shapes the organism for survival. It makes sure that the organism is matched to its environment and its needs are met. And it checks this adaptation for maximum fit. This makes evolution the most rigorous test of reality. What passes that inspection is fit to live in the real world.

Evolution secured our survival and we made out rather well.

Nature gave us a unique brain. Other species are bigger, stronger or faster. We, on the other hand, are smarter. Rather than developing the physical advantages of size, strength or speed, we started out with a larger, more capable brain. This added other advantages. All other forms of life are fixed to a particular environment or specific routine—we are not. In fact, the enlarged brain makes it possible to manipulate and change the environment. The evolution of other species concentrated primarily on the formation of body and anatomy. The demands on our survival were different. Relative size and lack of relevant physical features required additional capabilities. This made our evolution different from that of other species. Human survival depended foremost on the evolution of the brain rather than that of the body. Our specific survival advantage as a species lies, therefore, in our behavior and psychology—the human psyche.

The Evolution of Our Survival Capacity

The evolution of the human psyche makes for an impressive story. It established us as a viable species with the biological capacity to survive, giving us the same natural powers of adaptation and survival as animals. It also constituted the duality of human nature between biology and consciousness, separating us from the animal by a different destiny. In the process we went from a nomadic past to the urban existence of today. It all began during the hunting period of our species. Our distant ancestors forged the brain we have today. The exposure to a harsh, unforgiving world in an unrelenting struggle for survival set the stage for the unique evolution our species would undertake.

The competition for "territory, resources and succession"[1] required effective responses to the environment. This is how we acquired our instincts—behaviors based on biology. They developed to secure protection and the gratification of basic needs. The instincts are survival behaviors and respond to specific survival situations. Each instinctual behavior satisfies particular survival needs:

- *Hierarchical* behavior, which involves issues of dominance and submission, establishes position and access to resources;
- *territorial* behavior, which relates to issues of space and boundaries, claims property and defends it against outsiders;
- *sexual* behavior, which relates to family and child-rearing, secures attachment, community and succession;
- *xenophobic* behavior, which responds to safety needs, protects against danger from people and environment;
- **aggressive** behavior, which responds to threat, injury and deprivation, prompts self-protection, recovery and need fulfillment.

The instincts are survival responses of the evolutionary psyche. Alongside, the primary psyche developed the ability for mental adaptation. This, too, involved an instinctual response to outside conditions. Catastrophic experiences encountered by early humans, such as disaster, death and disease, were overwhelming and annihilating at first. The exposure to the unpredictable and uncontrollable events of life required the ability to cope with the mental and spiritual repercussions of their existence. Here, too, evolution matched abilities to the demands of event and environment. This was quite an accomplishment. And again, it was the instinct that produced the survival response. The instinct instigates the recovery from setback and loss and subsequently involves other parts of the brain to come to terms with the experience. The adaptation to difficult and changing conditions sets off a sequence of several steps:

- First, the *impact* of the external event,
- followed by the internal *reaction* to the event;
- once the experience has bottomed out, the instinct activates the genetic ability to maintain psychic balance, thus, initiating a *reversal* in the response;

- the reversal leads to *recovery* from the initial impact of the event, and finally,
- to a coming to terms with the given situation and achieving *resolution* through problem solving, decision making and cognitive expansion.

We know that ancient peoples worshipped sun and moon and animated the forces of nature to appease them. This tells us about their hardships and fears as well as their attempts to mediate the effects of powers and circumstances they could not control. Over time, the human psyche furnished the ability to adapt not only behaviorally but also mentally to the conditions of the environment. This innate capacity to maintain psychic balance in the face of unforeseeable, catastrophic events makes it possible for us to function within the context of a larger macrocosm beyond our control.

The Biology of Human Society

Now, about our world. Although favoring us with a unique brain, nature did not let us lose our spots. Neither a special brain nor civilization with its efforts to erase human nature have altered the fact that biology remains the ultimate reality of our life. Like other living organisms, we tend to live in hierarchically organized groups and communities, establish families to secure succession, protect territory and resources with rules and boundaries, and defend our security and property against outsiders. The evolutionary qualities of human behavior are reflected in the organization of our public institutions, the structure of political, bureaucratic systems, in the functioning of business life, the stratification of status, power and wealth, the fabric of urban existence, and even in the affairs of daily life. The biological reality of dominance and submission, property and boundary, sexuality and succession, aggression and competition, friend and foe supersedes all cultural conditioning and sociological reality.

We live in an invented world. We may think that culture, society, and intellect have fashioned a world beyond nature and biology only subject to our will and creation. But this is not so. It is true that we have created a world of our own making—a functional, rationally designed environment based on science and invention. But this has never changed the facts of our biology. The world may have shifted from savannah to skyscraper, human society, however, remains forever based on the biological model found in nature. We mark rank with symbols of power and status; we regulate access to resources through position and influence; we protect territory and property with fences and laws; we establish family for child-rearing and ties of belonging—not unlike other species. As a survival environment, society has a definite biological quality. In other words, we are facing a reality different from the one we think we are.

The Ethics of Biology

Human nature has had a rough going throughout the history of civilization. Political and religious interests, especially, found the human instincts objectionable. Evolutionary functioning stresses self-reliance and independence, making a person autonomous and less controllable. References to the evil and bestiality of human nature abound. Human aggression and sexuality were usually singled out as the most deviant aspects of our instinctual nature. This demonization of human nature was put out to repress our natural self. For the most part, this campaign was successful, convincing us that we needed civilization to protect us from ourselves. This notion is self-serving, but most of all, it is wrong.

There is an ethic in biology; it safeguards community, territory and property and, foremost, it protects life and the continuation of the species. Because the instincts have evolved to support the life of the individual and that of the group, they are vested with rules and inhibitions[2]. Most prominent is the inhibition against killing, which curtails human aggression with definite limits and boundaries. The biological inhibitions of the instincts have been overruled by civilization. This interference with the biological design set up the infamous pairing between the intellect and human aggression. Ever since, man has used his innate aggression as a destructive force.

As a species we have spent more ingenuity on designing methods of torture and destruction than on those of love and compassion. In fact, most of civilized history is a seamless succession of wars, torture, devastation, cruelties and destruction instigated by the intellect. All this is the work of the left brain, exploiting the instinct. It has nothing to do with the natural aggression of the instinct needed to survive. Cruelty and violence come from the mind, not the instincts. The inadequate coordination between intellect and instinct has been called the fateful invention of our species[3]. As a result we acquired a 'unique, murderous, delusional streak'. Culture has corrupted the human instincts, overturned their normative foundations, and joined them with the intellect. In essence, civilization has brutalized human nature. In short, there is nothing inherently base or barbarous about human nature. The violence we see today is not biological in origin; it is acquired and learned. While the combination of the instincts with the left brain, the intellect, tends to lead to destruction, the combination of instincts and right brain leads to higher consciousness and morality.

The Archetypes: Our Innate Bio-Program

The brain maintains a record of our species. Different parts of our brain are linked to different stages of evolution. Arranged in sequence, they are the reptilian, the mammalian and, as the last addition, a uniquely human brain. Each part serves special functions; all work together to sustain body and mind. The make-up of our brain lets us know that we share the evolution of life on this planet, showing us what we have in common with other species and what sets us apart. But it does not stop there. The evolution turned from the organic matter to the human psyche. The collective survival experience of our species over two million years put the psyche through its own evolution. Endless repetition has engraved these experiences into our psychic constitution, so Jung.

The evolutionary psyche is thus a collective psyche common to all of us. It is the common ground of human experience. We all inherit the same psyche. It is in this sense that, according to Jung, "every individual life is at the same time the eternal life of the species"[4]. As the seed contains the natural configuration of the whole, there is something in us to which the unfolding of our life conforms. Jung called these inherent patterns of life the archetypes of the human psyche. The archetypes are the 'living stuff' in us that initiates and controls the typical behaviors and experiences of our species, even though we are largely unaware of them and what they do.

The archetypes evolved in adaptation to outer reality and are inherited modes of functioning much like "the inborn way in which the chick emerges from the egg"[5]. They determine the fabric of our existence, prompting the significant events and experiences in a person's life along the human life cycle. Being parented, forming attachments, exploring the environment, adolescent rebellion, courting and erotic behavior, marrying, child-rearing, establishing a place in the social hierarchy, territorial defense, assuming the responsibilities of adulthood, participating in religious rituals, maturity and old age, preparation for death—are all subject to control by the human psyche[6]. The archetypes are universal elements of the evolutionary psyche shared by all humanity as part of a common biological and psychological history. They are genetically established and make up the innate bio-program contained in the psyche, fashioning our adaptation to life.

Ours is an evolution from biology to consciousness. From its biological beginnings, the human psyche extended to the realm of rational thought and spiritual awareness, expanding from the old brain to the new. The evolution is reflected in the polarity of the archetypes. They reach from the behavior of the instincts to the symbolic expressions of human consciousness. The instincts evolved to address the biology of life—everything related to livelihood and physical well-being, family, space, security, community, economics and defense, mating and procreation, religion and ritual. Consciousness advanced to allay the metaphysics of life—the emotional, mental and spiritual repercussions of human existence.

The archetypes manifest in biological behavior but also in the universal myths and symbols of the human experience. They not only give us the wherewithal for self-subsistence, they also furnish the code for the layout of our lives. We meet the symbolic expressions of the archetypes in our fantasies and dreams; and we find their symbolic representations in the universal themes of folklore, literature and art. They reflect the inner, unconscious drama of the human psyche. The archetypal life cycle contains the complete scenario of human life. Myths represent this journey of the human psyche and symbolically tell the common story of all of us.

Personal Mythology

The evolution of our species is the journey from instinct to spirit, from biology to metaphysics—the two frontiers of human survival. The process is replicated in our own life. The genetic bioprogram of the archetypes sets the course. It begins with the biology of childhood. Directed by the archetypes, we follow the evolutionary path. The path takes us through the biologically and psychologically relevant experiences of life.

Our individual process plays off the universal blueprint of human evolution. Alongside the evolutionary master plan of our species, we need to create our own story and fulfill our own destiny. We are called upon to repeat the evolutionary journey in our own lives.

Mythology depicts the process as the hero's journey of 'departure', 'initiation' and 'return'[7]. The cultural myth represents in symbolic form the steps of human development toward wholeness: Separation from parents and home, initiation into adulthood, courtship, marriage, and the assumption of the responsibilities for family, work, home and community. On the psychological level, this corresponds to the resolution of dependency, the acceptance of autonomy and adult responsibility, the successful transition into the public sphere of achievement and social commitment, and the final breaking of the psychic bond with the parents to allow individual investment in a marriage and family of our own. This concludes the first half of life; the second half, "when no longer life but death is the challenge"[8], involves engagement in the social responsibilities of advanced maturity, preparation for death and dying.

Even though the archetypal bio-program is innate, we need to activate it. We activate it by engaging in the events and experiences prescribed and prompted by the archetypes. The hero's journey is the evolutionary journey. There are many ways to do this: the hero has 'a thousand faces'. Evolution is always biologically driven. Its purpose is invariably the adaptation and survival of the organism.

Personalizing the evolutionary process strengthens and elevates our adaptation to life. Central to this undertaking is a sense of destiny based on an enduring commitment to personal survival and growth, turning evolution into a personal story. Having a story makes a difference. A personal story creates a sense of involvement, coherence and enduring identity. It ends up being the salient guide to lead the person on the path of destiny, providing a unique continuum through mortal existence. As a story of human development and survival, it is an inner story that manifests on the outside. It seeks expression and reveals itself in the activities, actions and events of the outer life.

The story is directed from within, as if by an inner director-producer, who, given the outline, is charged with giving it reality and form, with shaping a life story that projects into an uncharted future. A story of personal evolution takes its cues from transpersonal principles and parameters, combining them with the personal needs and aspirations of the individual. Drafted as an archetypal vision of life, a personal story incorporates the universal themes of the human experience. It views human life in relation to the higher order of nature and cosmos and enshrines a person's ultimate reason for being. Likewise, it proceeds from an understanding of oneself, people, events and experiences set against the larger background of life's purpose and meaning. There is an awareness that one's life needs to concur with the relevant events and stages inherent in the archetypal blueprint of human existence. And there is a sense that life resonates with a symbolic process of recurrent images, metaphors and themes—that the very personal is truly universal.

Inner and outer events combine in a resilient action-philosophy, relating experience to meaning and continuously creating the generative force to extend the story. As a dynamic master plan, the personal story contains intent and strategy and a concept of the expression it seeks in actions, relationships and commitments. Such a story is not a specific, rationally derived life plan in pursuit of definite goals and objectives. Though only an outline not specific in detail, a personal story gives a clear sense of direction and a framework for decisions. Ultimately, it instills a linearity of purpose and action.

As an account of human evolution and development, the story reflects the universal life of the species depicted in mythology and represented in the figure and journey of the hero. The ultimate purpose of the story is the quest for wholeness, becoming what one is destined to become from the beginning[9]. It is a process of illumination and transfiguration—the hero has to come back with wisdom. As the story progresses, and one's own development and survival move toward a realization of the universal human story, it becomes a mythology of its own: a personal mythology.

Higher Consciousness and Morality

Left and right brains, both parts of the new brain, have assumed different functions. The left brain is primarily cognitive, analytic and operates on the principle of cause and effect, establishing a world of intellectual distinctions and relationships. The right brain with its intuitive, holistic, synthetic qualities lets us see the whole picture and transforms experiences and thoughts into concepts and decisions[10]. Words are the language of the left brain, pictures that of the right brain. One is the center of speech, the other the hub of our visions and dreams. The left brain enables rational thought; the right brain creates symbolic expression. We need both parts of the new brain to operate effectively in the world: the right brain is strategic, the left brain action-oriented. Both evolved from the older midbrain, the seat of the evolutionary psyche.

Because of related qualities, evolutionary psyche and right brain make a natural match. There is no relationship between left brain and midbrain; the intellect inhibits evolutionary functioning[11]. The left brain set up our cultural evolution, separate from our biological past. The evolution of the human psyche extended to the right brain. Natural adaptation followed the biological line. The archetypes carried this evolution, expanding from instinct to spirit. Survival was to include biology and metaphysics, behavior and mind. Normal consciousness goes back to the organic ability of the brain stem to keep us alert and animated; higher consciousness results from the expansion of the evolutionary psyche to the new brain. Higher consciousness involves the awareness of our being and existence.

Mental adaptation reaches its highest level in advanced consciousness and spirituality. Higher consciousness resonates with the myths and symbols reflecting the universal life of the species. It also connects us to the larger realities of the cosmic universe. As we know from modern physics and metaphysics, psyche and cosmos obey the same laws and are not separated "by any fixed barriers"[12]. Higher consciousness enables us to maintain psychic balance and to function within the larger context of a macrocosm beyond our control. Spanning from instinct to spirit, the evolutionary psyche relates us both to the biology of life and nature and to the metaphysics of the cosmic order that surrounds us. It integrates worlds.

Included in the expansion of biology to higher consciousness is the moral issue. The ethics of biology are based on the preservation of the species. The instincts are life-enforcing and designed to promote the existence of the individual and that of the group, calibrated to mediate between individual and collective interests. Because the instincts are meant to support the life of individual and community they are vested with rules and inhibitions. The ethics of biology center primarily on the protection of life, property and community. Basic norms of biological behavior—regulating (a) the inhibition to kill, (b) the possession of property, and (c) the possession of the partner—imply that by nature we seek peace and respect property, honesty, loyalty and obedience[13]. The human intellect broke with the laws of nature. It has subverted the biological inhibition against killing, and it has employed our innate aggression for destructive designs. While the pairing of left brain and instincts suggests destructive consequences, the combination of midbrain and right brain furthers the moral evolution of human conduct.

Higher consciousness engenders a spiritual ethic, which puts human life in the context of the natural and cosmic order. Its hallmark is a moral sense to protect and not to harm, which not only extends to our fellowman but to all living things that share our world. Moral evolution expands the ethics of biology. Not only are we charged with the responsibility for our own survival, we are also given the responsibility for the impact of our lives and our actions on the world. Moral integrity is the sign of advanced personal evolution and maturity. It combines compassion with respect and reaffirms our common bond with all other forms of life on the planet. Spiritual ethics are based on a sense of personal responsibility and integrity, and they start at home.

Survivor Personality

Compared to the time when our adaptive capabilities evolved, human survival has not become that much easier. In fact, it may be just as uncertain, relentless and hard as it was then. Our prehistoric ancestors faced the threat of the animal and the vicissitudes of nature. Threats to survival have since taken on different forms—layoffs, job loss, bankruptcy, divorce, family dissolution, stress-related disease, drugs, prolonged illness, poverty in old age, to mention just a few. Seen in the evolutionary context, life is a conditioning force that continuously demands the ability to adapt to changing circumstances and requirements. We are all genetically programmed to survive, however, we also need to do our part. Nature insists on self-reliance and self-sufficiency. It demands initiative and responsibility for the life it gives. Survival, at its hardest, is a reaction to crisis and disaster. At its highest, it is the best and smartest way to live.

People who survive successfully do several things well. They take a deliberate approach to survival. Survivors succeed because:

- they take full advantage of their innate survival psychology;
- they understand the world they live in;
- they treat survival as a strategic undertaking;
- they see their life as part of a larger process;
- they turn survival into a personal evolution.

All this, together with the notion that everyone is responsible for his/her own survival and that 'nobody can do it for you'.

Following these adaptive principles shapes the survival activity and creates distinct survival advantage:

- Most people rely on their intellect to get them through life. They depend on it for everything they do, think and feel. Survivors live life differently. They understand that nature has given us what we need to survive. Survivors rely foremost on the biological intelligence inherent in human nature. Our innate survival psychology comes from the evolutionary intelligence of our instincts and intuition.

  The instincts furnish the behavior to respond to the environment and fulfill our needs. Intuition, the mental and spiritual function of the human psyche, enables us to face difficulty and overcome hardship. Survivors limit the intellect to a specific role in their approach to survival. It adds instrumental intelligence to negotiate the interface with modern life.
- Survivors perceive their world as a survival environment. They know that the world around them is structured

according to biological principles. Society is the human version of the biological model found in nature. For the most part we have ignored this biological fact and we have created a separate reality of social norms, values and lifestyles. The world of society and culture is a world of our own making, forged by the intellect. It is an invented reality. The environment we create is only a surface layer.

The biological reality remains the dominant structure in our life, requiring evolutionary functioning to satisfy our needs. Survivors have learned to see the world in biological terms, understanding social situations as survival events. The historical context of society is taken into account: political, economic and social circumstances are factored as environmental conditions.

- When it comes to survival, survivors don't leave anything to chance. Their approach to survival is strategic and deliberate. As a strategic activity, effective survival takes its lead from the hunting way of life—"the master behavior pattern of the human species"[14]. As such, survival is a goal-oriented behavior, governed by a genetic program to sustain the life and welfare of the hunter; it is based on a conscious behavioral strategy, supported by generalized skills to facilitate the achievement of goals; it makes selective use of the environment, retaining control of opposite external conditions; and it incorporates a practical view of things, with a keen eye for reality and results.

Strategic survival views the environment as a source of gratification. This stance creates a platform for positioning which reverses dependence on outside conditions. It treats the environment as a means rather than a condition of survival. Rather than being dependent on the environment for survival, the environment is used to promote survival. This reversal in positioning is at the core of the survival issue in the modern world. It establishes the autonomy of the individual as the ultimate agent of his destiny. Without it, survival is subject to economic dependence and in serious jeopardy.

- Survivors understand that survival comes from within and is based on instinct, intuition and intellect. Each faculty relates us to a separate reality, a different world. Each world puts different demands on our survival; each faculty serves our survival in a different way. The instincts connect us with nature and biology, intuition relates us to the realm of spirit and cosmos, and finally, the intellect takes us into the man-made world of society and culture.

  We need the instincts to pursue our practical needs within a given environment; we need our intuition to address the spiritual issues of life and to maintain inner balance in difficult situations; and we need the intellect to function in the social and occupational aspects of our lives. We can access each of these faculties, enter each of these worlds, at will, as we would shift gears in a car with 'three on the floor'. Survivors live life primarily from their instincts and intuition, with the intellect on standby. The intellect does not have the unique backing of biological evolution that fortifies instinct and intuition. It is not embedded in the archetypal process of life.

  In the larger scheme of things, survivors live in a world of different dimensions. They place their life in the larger context of natural and cosmic realities. Their perspective on things keeps them close to biology and metaphysics—the ultimate frontiers of human survival. Survivors bring their life in line with the timeless, universal issues of the human experience. There is the realization that human destiny needs to transcend the transitory appeal of society and culture.

- Survivors are people on the frontier. They see their life

as an opportunity to learn and to grow. Survivors combine the biological imperative to survive with the spiritual quest to fulfill one's individual destiny. They turn survival into a personal evolution. As such, the frontier is both a physical condition and a state of mind. The efforts to survive and the opportunities to learn reinforce each other. Survival becomes as much a challenge for growth as personal development becomes a measure for effective adaptation. Joining the efforts to survive and to grow in a conscious endeavor turns survival into a proactive, strategic activity. Rather than being a reaction to deprivation and necessity, survival becomes an undertaking with a vision and a plan.

Somehow, we all determine the size of our life—its reach and its depth. Survivors tend to seek a large life, a scenario that expands the field for evolution and survival. There is a sense of adventure that somehow recalls the hero's journey. The survivor dares to be "like a tiger in the jungle"[15]. There is also a feeling of certitude about living, born from maturity and mastery. Pairing evolution and survival engenders an intimate involvement with life and a deep appreciation of the human experience against the backdrop of mortal existence. It provides, as Jung suggested, the opportunity to 'understand through life' rather than through the intellect and to know that which is unteachable.

The reward for successful survival is a strong, effective life and a profound confidence that carries over to whatever we do.

A Call for Evolutionary Functioning

Why do we need all this? There are two compelling reasons for the use of evolutionary functioning:

- Instinct and intuition are innate survival faculties and, thus, inherently stronger and more effective than any

acquired, socialized psychology when it comes to survival.
- The human environment is biologically determined and underlies the world of culture and society we have created.

At one time or another, we all have been told to trust our instincts[16]. The advice is to handle a particular situation by relying on a faculty that is reliable and innate to human nature. Somehow, we acknowledge the fact that our instincts provide certain powers and advantages when it counts. The notion also suggests that our instincts are superior to learning and intellectual functioning when faced with a critical situation. The instincts, however, are much more than the occasional backup to keep us out of trouble. Our instincts are a life-supporting system of behaviors and abilities inherent in the evolutionary psyche. They are the result of the survival experience of our species, which is firmly engraved in our psyche. Evolutionary adaptation has furnished the human psyche with the biological intelligence of life.

Although we know of the inherent wisdom of our nature, few of us take the step to embrace our instincts as a guiding action system and to make full use of their benefits in our lives. Endorsing our instinctual nature bestows on us the evolutionary intelligence it contains. Our evolutionary behavior and psychology constitute the survival advantage of our species in the pursuit of the practical and spiritual needs of life. This was true for our ancestors, and it is still true today. Evolutionary functioning puts us in the position to secure our material and mental survival. Human nature contains "the collective wisdom of our species", the basic bio-program "enabling us to meet all the exigent demands of life"[17].

We also need to realize that the organization of society is an extension of our biological behavior. The survival advantage of evolutionary functioning becomes even more apparent, once we realize that society is built on biological principles. That is, behavior matches the environment and environment matches the behavior. Both are biologically determined. The biological parameters of hierarchy, territory, sexuality, aggression and xenophobia are issues in both. The match-up of behavior and environment magnifies the survival advantage of evolutionary functioning. Understanding its dynamics makes survival transparent and effective.

We live in a world that reflects our basic human nature. This should be of benefit to us; it was after all biology that engineered our survival in the first place. We normally don't look at our world that way. To take advantage of our innate survival capacity, we need to see the environment in biological terms. Social events and issues—such as dating, courting, marriage and family life, work and career, property and ownership—provide the venue for the gratification of our primary needs. All these seemingly social occasions are, of course, matters of biology. Social and cultural events are based on biology and as such are staged to ensure that these essential needs are met—staged by the biology of the archetypal psyche.

As the world gets more and more complex, survival becomes increasingly complicated. For 99% of our history as a species we survived on the strength and wisdom of our nature. Understanding the basics of human survival is a necessity for successful living.

Survival in The Modern World

The human condition in the modern world is under siege by complex factors and forces, which extend far beyond the comprehension and control of the individual. We live in a world of global political and economic conditions, dominated by a progressive technology and international markets, and, of late, by renewed military involvements and threats to our personal security. This world determines our livelihood and the welfare of mankind. The constellation of today's world is global. The environment, which determines our survival, has become increasingly remote and elusive. There is a gap between the individual and 'the world'. The world, relevant to individual survival, has expanded, putting distance between cause and effect. The individual finds himself subjected to a condition where outside factors control his existence.

The widening gap between private and public spheres is paralleled by an increasing interdependence between them. The human condition in modern society pivots on a precarious ambivalence of conflict and control. More than ever before, the world is complex and tenuous, life is uncertain and unpredictable, and people are dependent and vulnerable in the pursuit of their existence. The emotional tone has also changed. Insecurity and anxiety are the mood of the age.

The increase in distance and dependence between individual life and global events has created a new universe of factors and conditions with profound implications for individual survival and the future of mankind as a whole. The changes in the make-up of our world have established a condition of *heteronomy*—a condition wherein outside factors and influences suspend the autonomy of the individual.

Heteronomy, the opposite of autonomy, causes loss of control in those areas of life that are central to our survival and destiny. The single most critical aspect of heteronomy in modern society is the economic dependence of the individual on the environment. Wage and salary systems tie the individual household into the larger scale of national and international economies and determine its survival in the short- and long-term. Financial and economic viability are at the core of material survival in today's world. The dependence of the individual on global economic conditions puts survival in definite jeopardy. Most people define survival in terms of job security and overall economic stability. Neither can be affected by the individual. Decisions and events outside our sphere of influence control our lives. Today, many people feel helpless in deciding their direction in life, because we have lost control over vital aspects in our lives that determine our security and survival. Individual security and welfare are tied to global events; the control over fate and survival has changed hands. In addition, the state of these global affairs has increasingly become more volatile and unpredictable, exposing the livelihood and material security of the individual more and more to the turbulence of environmental conditions.

Throughout this process, the matrix of human life has shifted. The focus of action has moved to the global context, away from the hands-on reality of self-subsistence and self-determination within the bounds of a defined place that had formed the basis of human survival throughout history. The familiar world of individual control and autonomy has given way to a fragmentation of our existence into anonymous dependencies of a political, economic and social nature. As the sphere of personal influence disintegrates, the sense of isolation and helplessness intensifies. The shift of focus and activity away from individual control and commitment has led to an amputation of life, eliminating many aspects vital to our survival.

Meanwhile, we are being sidetracked by the attempt of the modern mass media to compensate for the loss of rootedness and vitality in our lives. They let us partake in the pageant of global affairs. The media provide the vehicle for this kind of vicarious living, superimposing the makeshift of an illusory world on the fragile framework of modern life. By creating a whole cosmogony of irrelevant detail and lesser fears, they provide the fateful distraction of a substitute reality. It masks the powerlessness and it numbs the fear and despair that scar the human condition in modern time.

The current condition started with the Industrial Revolution, an event that changed the world. Early on, capitalism had formed a close alliance with technology, stimulating the growth of democracy, the mass production of goods, and mass communication via newspapers, radio, and eventually television. By then, modern civilization was well on its way to becoming a global community. Geography and marketplace opened up, spawning migration and mobility as new forms of adaptation. The alliance between technological potential and profit motive has since taken a firm grip of our culture. Its values of material and social success have become the dominant belief system and expression of life in the industrialized world.

The make-up of the modern world is not oriented towards the individual. The focus is on global dimensions. The world modern man has created is no longer organically grown and an extension of human nature and needs. In fact, it is a world unfriendly to human survival. The human condition, the way people live and survive, has become a distant adjunct to modern civilization. It usually gets left behind. Progress and change tend to proceed at their own accord, leaving the consequences like orphans to fend for themselves. We live in a complex, constantly changing world. Technology is the driving force, which transports our civilization into the future, rapidly and relentlessly, seemingly without concern for ethics, ecology, or mankind itself.

Technology has emerged as the prime pacesetter of the human evolution in modern time. Technological innovations and applications continuously change the parameters of our world and of our survival, demanding constant adaptation to new realities and requirements. The impact of technology on our lives is exacerbated by a now super-regional, global economy. Together they constellate a human environment and survival conditions beyond our choice and control. The exposure to rapid technological change and the dependence on global economic conditions account for the basic vulnerability of the individual in today's world.

The enormous complexity of the modern world makes understanding very difficult. The multitude of structures, issues, demands, choices and changes confronting the individual creates a surplus reality, making comprehension and orientation almost unmanageable. Understanding is complicated by the fact that society, the survival environment, is constantly changing. This creates a relativity that makes strategy development and the ability to plan, target, and maneuver extremely difficult.

Not only is our survival firmly controlled by outside factors and forces, but this environment is itself constantly changing, requiring human adaptation forever to leapfrog behind. While the world around us is changing, the circumstances and conditions of human survival are changing along with it. Heteronomy implies that the life and the survival of the individual are subject to outside rule. Our life and welfare are tied to global events. Even though we enjoy a reasonable measure of political stability, security of any kind—job, career, financial, marital, etc.—is more elusive than ever. The intricate dependence on global complexities outside his sphere of control exposes the survival of the individual to a heteronomous condition unique in human history. The relevance of external, global conditions has backed the individual against the wall. Modern society has forced individual survival into a reactive position.

The effects of heteronomy, the absence of autonomy and control in our lives, are magnified by the tendency of modern society to entrap the individual in a state of dependency, socially and psychologically. A world, which is "materially preoccupied, spiritually impoverished and technologically possessed"[1], fosters developmental dependency and immaturity in the individual. It stands in contrast to the premise of personal responsibility and self-reliance essential to individual survival. Heteronomy and dependency together constitute a fateful combination, jeopardizing successful adaptation. It puts the individual at definite risk.

The issues of modern survival are man-made. We have, to a large extent, created a world heavy on technology and trivia, where materialism replaces meaning and morality, and where the preoccupation with power, profit and possessions drives progress and change. But most of all, modern man has created a world unfriendly to human survival. Individual life has become an appendix to a complex world of political, industrial and economic conditions subject to external control.

Modern civilization has changed the make-up of the world. For "the first time in the course of history modern man on this earth now confronts himself alone... In previous times man felt that he confronted nature alone. Nature populated by creatures of all kinds was a domain existing according to its own laws, to which he had somehow to adapt himself. In our age, however, we live in a world which man has changed so completely that in every sphere... we are always meeting man-made creations, so that in a sense we meet only ourselves"[2]. Human life and human nature are no longer in harmony—nor are man and his world.

Modern man has imposed his own design on the world and on the human condition. Since the onset of the scientific, industrial revolution we have come "to view nature as something to be 'mastered', social institutions as things to be 'engineered' and traditional values as constraints to be overthrown"[3]. Particularly Western culture developed at the expense of nature—nature as an environment and in all its manifestations in human life. Culture set out to reorganize human life by inventing a world of its own. Modern civilization ushered in a new reality. It has created a rational, instrumental world founded on the laws of causality and time. It has defined human life in functional, industrial terms reflective of economic, technological conditions. It has reshaped the human environment, and it has rewritten the human biography.

The effects on the human condition, however, have long been coming. From early beginnings in agriculture, the rural society converted into the industrial society, and now we live in a global world with all its promises and problems. Modern civilization has created survival conditions that are no less tenuous, uncertain, unyielding and hard than those of the prehistoric past. Individual survival is just as unpredictable, fierce and relentless now as it was then. Human civilization has failed to deliver on its promise[4]. Hardship and crisis have not disappeared in the modern world. The threats to survival are different now, but there are many, and they are everywhere. Prehistoric survival *was* hard; modern survival *is* hard.

The cultural and societal orientation of the modern world has come to overshadow the biological reality of life and to distract from its relevance. But there is a catch. It is culture that has a big hold on modern man, but it is nature that we have to reckon with in the end—nature as archetypal intent and ethological reality. What are the values we pursue, and how well do we adapt to life and environment? Having choices is about paying the price. The vulnerability of the individual in the modern world is exacerbated by the ethological reality of life. The human environment is biologically determined and underlies the world of society and culture we have created. The sociological reality of life is only a quasi-reality superimposed on the biological reality of life. Social organization is an extension of biological behavior. Fact is, we live in a world that reflects our basic human nature. Irrespective of the historical make-up of human society at any given time, the ultimate reality of human life and survival is always structured by biology. Nature, not society or culture, is the final determinant of human existence.

Even though modern civilization attempted to restructure the human survival reality and to erase the immanence of biology in human functioning, the relevance of human ethology has not disappeared. It remains the preeminent principle of existential adaptation in the modern world. The survival reality of human life, like that of animal life, is essentially determined by the ethological parameters of territory, hierarchy, aggression, sexuality and xenophobia. Beneath the surface of human transactions lies the reality of evolutionary adaptation, the need to survive. The biological reality of life is just as dominant as it ever was, and biological behavior is just as relevant as before. Despite its overlay of cultural values and socialized behavior, the modern survival environment is determined by human biology—but we do not have the tools to deal with it. They lie buried and dormant in the human psyche. Trying to fulfill our needs and trying to cope with a complex, constantly changing world are polarities of increasingly unmanageable proportions.

Cultural evolution was designed to improve on nature. From its inception, modern civilization rejected man's evolutionary nature just as it sought to control and dominate nature on the outside. Culture tamed and domesticated man like the animal before him, determined to eliminate his instinctive, ethological side and any traces of his animal ancestry. It vigorously pursued to replace man's natural self with a social persona, intended to reflect distance from his biological evolution and a presumed superiority of cultural, rational functioning. And by doing so, it simultaneously suppressed his innate adaptive capability, while the ethological reality of human survival remained as it always was, leaving him defenseless against conditions that overreach his abilities to cope. The biological reality of life sets up ethological parameters and adaptive conditions, which require distinct survival capabilities to match them. This is the very reason nature has equipped us to be territorial, hierarchical, aggressive, sexual and xenophobic. Biological survival behavior ensures that we survive and get what we need.

Both societal and ethological issues compound the challenge to individual survival in the modern world. Then, there is life itself. Human life is an event that comes without instruction, leverage or guarantee. Effectively, we control very little in life. Our reality is the reflection of a higher order reality, just as a shadow is a two-dimensional representation of a three-dimensional object. We inhabit a three-dimensional world, controlled by a higher-dimensional order and universe. The forces of natural and cosmic law determine most of what happens to us. Beyond the biology of ethological survival stand the metaphysics of human consciousness—the effort to cope with the immensity of life.

Survival is the paramount task of the organism. Every age needs to review the changes and conditions of life and reaffirm the coherence of its world[5]. Today's survival reality compounds several adaptive dimensions: the modern global society, pushing us into an experimental world of ever-increasing complexity and unpredictability; the ever-present biology of survival which ultimately structures the ethological parameters of human organization and behavioral adaptation; and, finally, the metaphysical ramifications of life as a consequence of human consciousness.

In each domain, the individual is part of a larger context, and the key events of human existence are predominantly subject to outside rule[6]. In each domain, we work from a position of heteronomy with little or no control over the things that happen to us or in our lives. Controlled either by the laws of biology, the principles of metaphysics and cosmic law, or by the conditions of society, the individual finds himself in a situation where external facts and forces set the terms of his existence—generally a condition of long odds. The magnitude of these issues and their implications for the human condition are enormous. With minimal or no control over existential conditions, life itself becomes a matter of survival.

The adaptive challenges and demands in the modern world are massive. The survival conditions are societal, ethological and existential. Socialization and cultural conditioning do not even begin to prepare the individual for the survival reality of modern life. A life without reference to nature and biology lacks grounding in the reality of survival.

Evolutionary adaptation has furnished the human psyche with the biological intelligence of life. The complexity of human survival in the modern world requires the evolutionary survival capability of the human psyche. Effective adaptation in the modern survival environment depends on our innate evolutionary intelligence. Once we realize that society is built on biological principles, that survival is determined by ethological parameters, and that the larger mythological and metaphysical issues of life are preformed in the human psyche, then the relevance and survival value of evolutionary functioning become even more apparent. Nature has prepared us to deal with all the important demands of life.

Discussion

We are now in the fishbowl of evolution as have been other generations and civilizations before us. Man has strayed from the evolution of nature to design one of his own. Along with it, he has created his own values and destiny. And this is what it is: a world of technological progress, material appearances and global complexities, suffering from spiritual impoverishment, existential despair and a sense of fundamental rootlessness. It is a world adverse to survival, where the individual feels overwhelmed, disoriented and helpless. We live in an age largely characterized by noise, movement and knowledge but not by action, harmony and wisdom. The problem of this world is, as an old movie says, that 'there are too many people in a hurry to get there but they don't know where they are going'.

The problem of modern man is that he has lost the connection with his natural history. Culture has cut him off from his evolutionary past, pretending that it never existed. Severed from his roots, he is like a tree about to fall. He lacks nourishment, strength and support. Not grounded in his evolutionary heritage, he has become feeble and clay-footed. He is a tamed and domesticated animal, handicapped in his ability to survive. It is only when man renews the link with his basic nature, and when he learns to balance its positive and negative sides, that he will come to terms with the issues of his own survival and regain a sense of relevance and proportion. Without this, he is left with his own destructive tendencies, constantly at war with others and forever at odds with himself and the universe.

Modern man is at a turning point where the human condition jeopardizes his own survival, individually and collectively. Evolution has put us on the spot[1]. The challenge is unprecedented: modern man is forced to transcend the very conditions he himself has created. Cultural evolution has pushed man to the very limits of his own evolution as a living organism. The survival of the species again depends on the evolution of the human brain—this time, on the evolution of higher consciousness. The cure of modern man rests on his willingness and ability to reconnect with the biological foundations of his life.

The direction human evolution must take is rather self-evident. We need to come to terms with the natural evolution of our species; we need to enhance the cultural evolution, which modern man began but has not finished; and we need to combine the two. The formula is simple: (1) Accept evolution number one, (2) advance evolution number two, and (3) assimilate both. The process follows the principal paradigm of human evolution from instinct to spirit and their integration towards wholeness.

Step one is to acknowledge our biological history and its results. Natural evolution spans the longest period in the history of our species. More than 99% of human history is prehistoric. The most essential features of our being are prehistoric, recorded in the DNA of our species. Homo sapiens, dated 35,000 years ago, is our closest ancestor; human culture itself began only ten to twelve thousand years ago with the introduction of agriculture. Before that came more than two million years of natural history when the human race evolved as a distinct, viable species. This evolutionary history is part of our genetic make-up, anatomically, physiologically and psychologically.

From a historical perspective, it seems that accepting our biological evolution and its results would be accepting the obvious. We should not be surprised that "every human action goes back in some part to our animal origins"[2]. After all, the transition from life in the trees to life on the plains was not clean or abrupt, and there were parts of evolutionary history that man shared with the animal. Unfortunately, for many "the animal has always symbolized the psychic sphere in man which lies hidden in the darkness of the body's instinctual life"[3], and as such has no place in their lives. They have, instead, declared social and cultural values as the final goal of human striving and fulfillment, which, of course, they can never be.

The solution to the endless debate, whether we are the product of evolution or environment, rests on a clear acceptance and "a deep understanding of the nature of the animal we are" and of the archetypal principles "governing the organic and psychic processes of life"[4]. All this would be of little importance, except that any default against nature will eventually come back to haunt us. It is, however, not the issue what we *are*, but what we *do*: "What matters, after all, is not that we *are* aggressive, xenophobic, sexual, hierarchical and territorial but what *attitude* we adopt to these fundamental *a priori* aspects of our nature—how we live them, and how we mediate them to the group. It is the ethical orientation that counts."[5] The issue is, how we relate to our evolutionary nature and how we make use of it.

Human nature is a fact of biology. Our instinctual nature has genetic roots and is inerasable. Human aggression, for instance, like sexuality, is "an ineradicable feature of human nature" and "an unavoidable fact of human life"[6]. It is, "therefore, as Freud says, an 'educational sin' if one does not prepare a person for the aggression with which he will sooner or later have to come to grips. All attempts to underrate aggression by referring to the alleged fact that it is learned—in the face of the available evidence to the contrary—are in the highest degree irresponsible"[7]. The instincts are an undeniable fact of human nature.

We need to acknowledge "the nature of the animal we are"[8], but we also need to realize and acknowledge what culture has done to the animal side of our being. Modern civilization has taken the human instincts, robbed them of their biological norms and inhibitions[9], and joined them with the human intellect. Without the innate constraints to balance their enormous potency, the instincts have been put to unintended, destructive use. In effect, modern civilization has brutalized human nature by removing its ethical foundations. Recorded human history—essentially an uninterrupted succession of wars and devastations—provides the evidence that neither culture, nor the intellect, nor a socialized morality can control or repress the human instincts. The instincts are an 'ineradicable feature of human nature'. It stands, therefore, to reason that it is more constructive to accept our instinctual nature than to deny it.

Denial of our instincts does not eliminate them. Yet, having stripped the instincts of their natural constraints, they can only run rampant—unless we accept them and give them a new context to function in. For that, we need to acknowledge that we have tampered with the instincts in the past and that we have the ability to make them potentially destructive and dangerous in the future. Only if we admit to the evidence that we tend to abuse instincts and obviate their biological intent, can we appreciate their life-preserving, adaptive purpose, which is neither good nor bad. As long as we deny our instincts and our part in perverting their intended use, they will manifest in corrupt, destructive ways.

Human nature has survival value. Used properly, the human instincts are of obvious survival quality. They enable us to adapt to external conditions. The instincts in animals and in humans are biological behaviors related to the life and survival of the organism. The major instincts cover significant behavioral aspects of our relationship to the environment. The instincts have enormous power and force. They are part of our life force. That is why we want to use them in our survival. But we also need to take responsibility to use them in their intended way and not to abuse them.

Step two is to advance human consciousness. The evolution of higher consciousness completes the formation of the human being. It realizes the archetypal paradigm of human evolution, advancing from instinct to spirit, from biology to metaphysics. Biological evolution produced our innate capability to survive. Cultural evolution has produced the scientific, technological and social achievements we have today. The evolution of higher consciousness is meant to advance and enhance the cultural evolution beyond the material level. The specific issues of spiritual evolution are: existentially, to deepen the human experience; metaphysically, to enable a connection with the supernatural; morally, to counterbalance destructive tendencies of human behavior.

In revising nature, culture has created its own way of life and existential landscape, clearly underselling the capability and nobility of our species—the blind materialism of ever-increasing status, power and possessions that knows the price of everything and the value of nothing; the fixation on vicarious living which takes its inspiration from the illusory world of the mass media and ends up in the tedium of making and spending money to break the paralysis of boredom; the mysticism of a profuse spirituality which abhors the reality demands of mundane life and is forever on the lookout for new answers and gurus; and the withdrawal into alcohol and drugs that avoids the reality of life and survival by disappearance into oblivion.

But the challenge of survival is by no means over, and the principles of evolution are just as tough and awesome as ever. The rivalry for power and position, the lust for wealth and material possessions, have much of the rawness of the wilderness—with one exception. Modern man lost the sense of balance and proportion that comes from nature. The cultural repression of man's basic nature has served few and hurt many. On balance it seems, modern civilization has not led man to the moral and spiritual refinement of higher consciousness as it purported to do when it rejected man's evolutionary past. Instead, it has enforced a primitivism of purpose and practice in human and political conduct, reminiscent of the cave man. Instead of creating a world where the value of meaning and considerations of love and compassion prevail, modern civilization has unleashed a jungle mentality that engenders greed, disharmony and fear. But there was nothing wrong before when man lived in harmony with nature; in fact, "the only thing that is wrong with the world is man"[10]. In a world where things are the important things, the loss of meaning endangers survival. The ingenuity of modern man is technical, not spiritual. In short, we have created a world, which is "materially preoccupied, spiritually impoverished and technologically possessed"[11].

The efforts to resolve the cultural denial of human nature must be paired with the endeavor to transcend the confining grip of a predominantly materialistic culture. To facilitate evolution towards higher consciousness, individually and collectively, modern civilization needs to provide the existential, metaphysical and moral context for deepening the human experience. Society continuously engineers its own culture and way of life. The establishment and transmission of values are critical. The choices are constantly being made. The accentuation of increased understanding, compassion and cooperation as the goals for individual and collective evolution furthers the attainment of a spiritual perspective and attitude. The emphasis on humanistic, aesthetic, philosophical values provides the existential context to enhance individual awareness and conduct in the service of survival and well-being. Yet—the public display and merchandizing of human corruption, violence, horror, terror and destruction through mass media and popular art, on the other hand, do not contribute to the evolution of higher consciousness. They lessen and lower the human experience and reinforce materialistic aspirations and destructive tendencies.

The scientific, industrial revolution has destroyed the traditional way of life and changed the fabric of human existence. T. S. Eliot speaks of 'a heap of broken images' and his *The Waste Land* is the obituary on the myths, rituals and values, which had once served as a guide and anchor for a way of life. But nothing substantial has taken its place. Modern civilization got stuck on the physical level of reality, not advancing the human condition much beyond the pursuit of material values. It brought on "a sociological stagnation of inauthentic lives and living that has settled upon us, and that evokes nothing of our spiritual life, our potentialities, or even our physical courage—until, of course, it gets us into one of its inhuman wars"[12].

Modern man has lost his spiritual, metaphysical bearings. He no longer has the rituals of the ancient peoples to fend off the fear, chaos, and terror that come with life. All the advancements of the modern age did not dispel the existential and metaphysical vulnerability of the human condition. The ability to deal with the paradoxical reality of human existence, and not be paralyzed by the fear of death or the fear of life, is at the core of survival in the modern world. In its efforts to render man's evolutionary heritage extinct and irrelevant, human civilization has suppressed the adaptive capacity of the human psyche to come to terms with these metaphysical issues—the supernatural facts and forces beyond human comprehension and control, which impact our life and shape our destiny. The evolution of higher consciousness enables us to reconnect with a larger, cosmic order and to bring a sense of certainty to our survival.

Modern man has disavowed his natural history, deeming it unacceptable. The denial of man's instinctual nature did not erase its existence, but led to the perversion of its use. Modern civilization has subverted the natural, biological, life-preserving intent of the human instincts. Especially, the removal of the natural inhibitions of human aggression through the intellect has furthered destructive tendencies in our species. Since the biological ethics of human nature have been corrupted, we need to have a new normative base to regulate instinctual behavior. Only the advanced morality of higher consciousness can provide these ethical foundations. Only evolution to a higher context can take the sting out of the destructive aggression set off by man. The evolution to attain a higher moral sense needs to be executed individually and collectively. Even if collective evolution does not happen, we still must achieve it individually.

The evolution of higher consciousness provides the moral equivalent to the normative foundations of human nature, originally provided by the biology of the instincts. It compensates for the loss of biological ethics, caused by the intervention of modern man. Advanced consciousness establishes a moral sense, based on personal responsibility. It provides the morality to protect and not to harm. On the transpersonal level, advanced consciousness holds the essential ethics to preserve and protect the world in which we live. The natural world shares a fate similar to that of the natural self in the modern age: sometimes we treat our world as if we had a spare one in the basement[13]. Higher consciousness rehabilitates human nature, the basis of evolutionary functioning, and restores it to the biological purpose it was meant to have—the survival of the individual and that of the group. The human instinct, especially aggression, is meant as a life-enhancing driving force not as a destructive force to harm others. The biological intent of the instincts is life-enforcing and life-preserving. That is where they need to be brought back to. Higher consciousness enables us to preserve the integrity of the human instinct and to retain the survival value of evolutionary functioning in the life of the individual.

It is upon modern society to take its share of responsibility. Society cannot continue to blame human nature as cruel, brutal and destructive, while modeling and advertising violence and destructiveness at the same time. It is the very same violence that we create on one side and that we condemn on the other. Modern civilization needs to take responsibility for removing the biological inhibitions of the instincts, especially in regard to violence and killing. It also needs to assume responsibility for the inherent arrogance of wanting to upstage nature and improve on its designs. Modern culture obstructs our alignment with nature and the biological foundations of life. If we want a more peaceful, cooperative world, culture needs to induce the existential, moral and metaphysical context for the evolution of advanced consciousness, individually and collectively. Modern society needs to lead the way towards higher consciousness, not toward more materialism, violence and destructiveness as it does now.

Step three is to merge the natural and cultural evolutions of our species. The fusion of both evolutions at the level of higher consciousness completes the archetypal integration. The assimilation of our evolutionary history and its biological results restores the validity of human nature and credits it with survival value.

The acceptance of human nature is the starting point for advanced evolution. It is from this level where the journey to higher consciousness and mature morality begins. The integration of the evolutionary psyche with the spirituality of advanced consciousness completes the natural progression of the human archetype from instinct to spirit. The assimilation of both evolutions forges the neurological connection between old brain and new brain, nature and culture, biological endowment and human achievement. It recognizes the essence of our being, our species, in its duality as a biological animal and a creature of higher consciousness.

The redemption of the animal in us is the story of Chiron, the centaur—half man and half horse. Chiron stood out amongst the centaurs, known for their savageness and violence. He was the wise man of Greek mythology and famed teacher of Greek heroes. The myth is about probing our animal nature and combining it with the spirit. It is the clearest example of the archetypal paradigm, the hero's journey form instinct to spirit. The intent of the journey is to engender harmony between man and animal and to demonstrate the potency that comes from combining both. The story foreshadows the realignment of civilized man with his biological history. The significance of accepting our evolutionary nature, the natural self, and combining it with our cultural self is to complete the human evolution and to establish a sense of wholeness.

We who have the good fortune to live in the modern era are obliged to appreciate the ancestor who came before us to pioneer the human experience, and we are well advised to honor what he left behind for us to use. Moreover, we need to do our part and complete our own evolution—in tribute to the nobility of a creature that managed to survive the rigors of life in full awareness of its beauty, its hardness, and its terror.

J. Campbell reminds us, that "it's a very grim thing to be a modern human being"[14]. The ambivalence of life and the pressure of survival weigh on the individual: "The world into which we are born is brutal and cruel, and at the same time of divine beauty"[15]. But despite the cruelty and terror, there is sanity in nature. Despite the changes in human life and history, there is a "sense of something that lives and endures underneath the eternal flux"[16]. And in spite of "the impression of absolute nullity"[17], there is a sense of meaningfulness in all that happens.

Modern man has lost the untamed power of his primal nature that would protect him in the world and the symbolic life "that would inform him of a deeper self"[18] and guide his destiny. Yet, given his innate resources and capabilities, he is still as strong and indestructible as the original hunter before him, and his life as potentially vital and purposeful as he wants it to be. In order to survive successfully and live sanely, modern man needs to recover the soundness and simplicity of nature and to resurrect what lies dormant in his being—for "'at bottom' the psyche is simply 'world'"[19]. He needs to rediscover the age-old power, wisdom and meaning contained in his original self which is both the endowment and the mandate of nature to man. He needs "to replace the detached, materialistic world view imposed by modern science with a *Weltanschauung* capable of revitalizing the near-moribund notions of life's meaning and purpose, and of providing an ethical standpoint from which to face the mortal problems which confront us"[20].

Somehow, there needs to be a snap inside that throws the internal switch, a reversal of figure and ground between appearance and meaning, ideology and reality, old and new ways—a 'journey to Damascus' for modern man to realize the call of the hour. For in life as in mythology, it is man's blindness and ignorance of his self and his story that the gods punish with disaster as his hubris. Life is a story that begins and ends somewhere, and however fragile it may be, we are called upon to fill it with our own destiny—because the worst thing that could happen to you, to me, to any of us is that "we had the experience but missed the meaning"[21].

APPENDIX

The new humanity will be universal and it will have the artist's attitude: that is, it will recognize that the immense value and beauty of the human being lie precisely in that he belongs to the two kingdoms, nature and spirit.

Thomas Mann

NOTATIONS FOR THE PROFESSIONAL

This section brings together information of particular interest to the professional and the reader, who looks for additional background to what has been presented in this book.

Scientific Epistemology

The book presents a metapsychology based on phylogenetic principles. Specifically, it depicts an innate adaptive psychology referring to universal, genetic features in the psychological constitution of the human being. The focus is on generic survival capabilities inherent in human nature. This psychology is different and separate from the socialized psychology of cultural conditioning, and as a metapsychology supersedes it.

Scientifically, this book is based on evolutionary epistemology stressing the influence of biology on human behavior and psychology, and emphasizing the concepts of phylogeny and adaptation as underlying human development and survival. The book combines the fields of ethology, sociobiology, C. G. Jung's analytical psychology and J. Campbell's work on comparative religion and mythology coalescing their various contributions to an understanding and appreciation of human behavior and human consciousness. All these various disciplines are essentially evolutionarily oriented placing the psychological model into the realms of biology and philosophy rather than in the fields of physics and laboratory experimentation[1] as behavioristic psychology has done in the past.

It further utilizes a psychosomatic model proposing a phylogenetic structure that is replicated in the course of ontogenetic development[2]. The phylogenetic structure, inherent in the human psyche, consists of archetypes[3]—innate bio-programs and releasing mechanisms—which control the events of the human life cycle and manifest in adaptive behavior in response to environmental circumstances. Individual life is an expression of the biological pattern of the species. Jung equated this *a priori structure* underlying all ontogenetic development to the archetypal determinants of the evolutionary or phylogenetic psyche[4].

Human Psychology and Brain Functioning

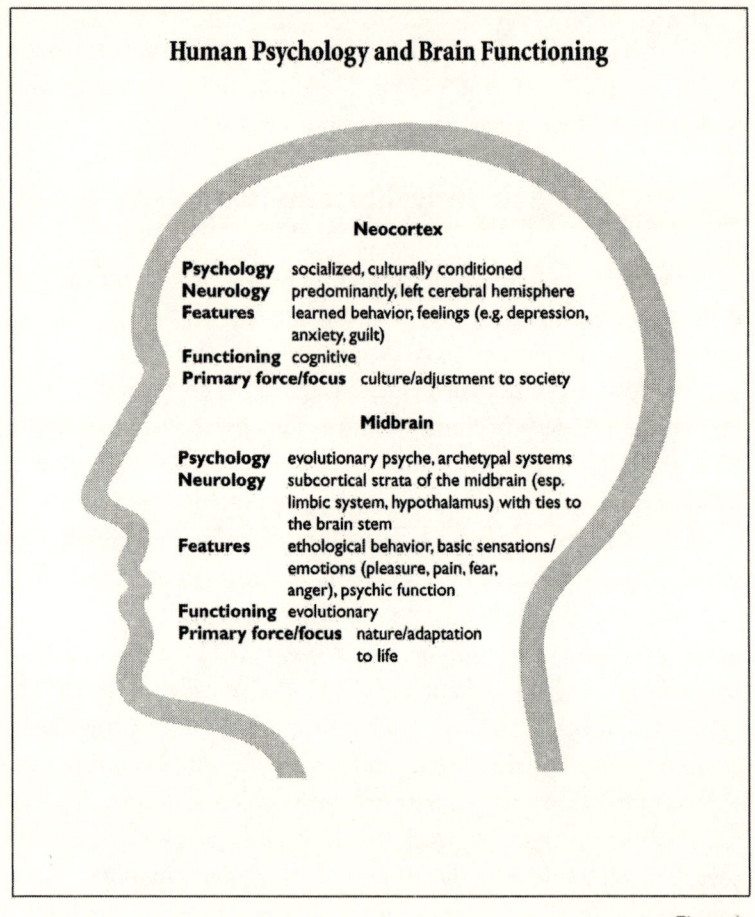

Neocortex

Psychology	socialized, culturally conditioned
Neurology	predominantly, left cerebral hemisphere
Features	learned behavior, feelings (e.g. depression, anxiety, guilt)
Functioning	cognitive
Primary force/focus	culture/adjustment to society

Midbrain

Psychology	evolutionary psyche, archetypal systems
Neurology	subcortical strata of the midbrain (esp. limbic system, hypothalamus) with ties to the brain stem
Features	ethological behavior, basic sensations/emotions (pleasure, pain, fear, anger), psychic function
Functioning	evolutionary
Primary force/focus	nature/adaptation to life

Figure 1

The book takes psychology to a new frontier—the boundary where biology and metabiology, instinct and spirit, body and mind, behavior and consciousness, individual and species are joined. Psychotherapy is perceived as a process of advancing the adaptive capability of the individual by activating the innate biological, psychic structures developed by evolutionary process. In the evolutionary psyche, Jung believed, resided "the collective wisdom of our species, the basic programme enabling us to meet all the exigent demands of life"[5]. The objective of psychotherapy is seen as advancing human evolution both on an individual and a collective level.

Genetic endowment and biological epistemology acknowledge the evolutionary aspect of human nature and the homologues of features and characteristics with other species. Analytical psychology, ethology, and mythology make it possible to appreciate the complexity and the unity of life and enable us to reestablish the connection with ourselves, nature and the cosmos, thus, healing the rift which has opened up since the beginning of the modern age.

The Neurology of Human Survival

Human nature is a product of evolution. The basic nature of our species developed during that period of our history when the primordial ancestor survived as a hunter and gatherer. It is a nature geared for survival. Body and mind were shaped by evolution. This basic biology of anatomy, behavior, and psyche differentiates us from other species and gives us our distinct survival advantage. Evolution did not fit humans to any particular environment or specific routine like all other forms of life[1]. And rather than providing us with particular physical features like strength, size or speed as the animal, nature gave us the advantage of a unique brain. Human survival depended on the evolution of the brain rather than that of the body. Our selective survival advantage, therefore, lies in our behavior and psychology.

Neurological research[2] during the last few decades has significantly contributed to our understanding of brain functioning and human behavior. Elaborate research has revealed the intricate anatomy of the old and new, the right and left parts of the brain, and the delicate interaction of their neurophysiology. It has also established the structure and functioning of the human brain as a manifestation of the evolutionary history of our species.

Basically, the human brain consists of several parts; all are linked to different stages of evolutionary development. The reptilian brain, which we share with all vertebrates, belongs to the oldest section of the human brain. Located in the brain stem, it regulates the basic vital functions of the body. It controls the cardiovascular and respiratory systems, and it maintains consciousness. The operations of this part of the brain are largely automatic and deeply anchored in the organic processes of life.

The mammalian brain, which makes up the midsection of the human brain, represents a further evolutionary stage. This part of the brain provides balancing mechanisms and as such regulates hormone levels, the sensations of hunger and thirst, sexual drive, and sleep. In addition, it controls the emotions of anger and fear along with the related behaviors of fight and flight. The midbrain is also the province of instinctive and affective behavior. In that, it controls in all mammals as well as in humans important responses to the environment. It is responsible for such inborn and biologically relevant behaviors as "maternal attachment, courting and erotic behavior, dominance and submission, and territorial defence"[3]. These are genetically inherited behavior patterns and species-specific. The midbrain is the center of ethological behavior and the neurological foundation of man's archetypal nature.

The neocortex, which constitutes the outer layer of the human brain, is the most recent formation in the development of the brain. This new portion of the brain is common to all higher mammals, including humans, and responsible for cognition and perception on a more sophisticated level. Unique to humans and to the evolution of the human brain, finally, is the division of the neocortex into the left and right brain hemispheres. This lateralization of the neocortical structures of the brain is the result of man's particular adaptation to the environment, which differentiates him from the animal.

The development of weapons, tools, social organization, language, and speech led to a specialization of the left brain hemisphere in humans, setting the two halves of the neocortex apart. Right-hemispheric specialization, on the other hand, is based on the development of perceptual, sensory, intuitive, and synthetic abilities as well as the formation of higher consciousness. The left cerebral hemisphere is closely associated with the cultural evolution of our species, which it initiated. Its key abilities are language, cognition, and memory. The right brain carried on the natural evolution of our species. It took on sophisticated adaptations refining our abilities to relate to the environment. The right hemisphere is the center of intuition, sensation, and perception.

Each part of the brain carries out essential survival functions. The older sections of the brain, brain stem and midbrain, are responsible for biological survival related to organic maintenance and environmental adaptation, essentially controlling physiology, consciousness, and behavior. These subcortical strata involve the organic and archetypal structures basic to the process of life. The midbrain in conjunction with the neocortex is responsible for mental survival, sustaining psychic equilibrium by fashioning cognitive-affective coherence in response to human events and experiences. The more recent parts of the brain, the right and left cerebral cortex, facilitate instrumental survival by providing such advanced functions as perception, orientation, language, and by controlling essential processes like learning, movement, and memory. The neocortex, especially the left brain, confers the competence to interface and interact with the survival environment of the modern world which is its own creation[4].

The neurological substrate of the archetypal system, referred to by Jung, has been identified with the phylogenetically older parts of the brain[5]. It is located primarily in the limbic system and the brain stem[6]. Survival behavior and phylogenetically determined behavior patterns, "such as maternal attachment, courting and sexual behaviour, dominance and submission, and territorial defence, together with the emotions which accompany them"[7], originate from the "neuronal systems in the midbrain (especially the limbic system and the striatal complex)"[8]. Survival consciousness involves subcortical and neocortical strata[9]. The instinctive pole of the archetypes is

Survival Functions of the Human Brain

Table 2

	Subcortical Brain		Neocortical Brain	
Neurological Complex	brain stem reticular activating system *lower brain*	midbrain limbic system hypothalamus pituitary gland *inner brain*	left cerebral hemisphere Broca/Wernicke areas *outer brain*	right cerebral hemisphere frontal/parietal lobes *outer brain*
Evolutionary Stage	reptilian brain	paleomammalian brain	neomammalian brain/human brain	neomammalian brain/human brain
Survival Category	organic biological	behavioral affective environmental	cognitive instrumental verbal/social	mental spiritual metaphysical
Adaptive Function	consciousness organic processes vital functions	ethological behavior primary emotions and sensations psychic function	action-oriented technical analytical rational thought	strategic intuitive synthetic higher consciousness

Brain Region

associated with the limbic system and the brain stem; while the spiritual pole involves both cerebral hemispheres[10], especially the right. The archetypal structures of brain stem and midbrain combine with the intuitive, synthetic, strategic activities of the right hemisphere and the abstract, analytical, verbal activities of the left brain[11], assimilating archetypal preformation and neocortical specialization in the perception and interpretation of the survival reality. Higher consciousness involves the complex neurology[12] of fully integrated functioning between all parts of the human brain.

The survival value of the neocortical brain results from its lateral specialization. Hemispheric functioning provides adaptive compatibility of almost symbiotic proportions[13] with each part of the cortex providing significant contributions to the survival of the individual[14]. The right brain has intuitive, creative, and visual-spatial properties; because of its visionary, holistic, and synthetic qualities, it is the strategic brain. The left brain is the "locus of the manipulatory, linguistic and logical skills necessary for survival"[15]; given its empirical, analytical and rational abilities it is action-oriented. The survival contributions of both cortical hemispheres are important for effective adaptation. Since the scientific and industrial revolutions, cultural conditioning, in the West, has favored the development and utilization of the left brain at the expense of right-hemispheric functioning[16]. This left-sided dominance, however, goes beyond cultural influence. Neurological inhibition across the corpus callosum, executed by the left brain, can intercept and shut out hemispheric interaction and input from the right brain. Additional inhibition of neurological pathways can affect transmission of adaptive processes between cortex and the older brain—limbic system and brain stem[17].

Dominance of the left brain hemisphere, even though culturally favored and promoted, produces a significant survival disadvantage by suppressing vital adaptive (instinctual, archetypal, affective, and creative) processes. It emphasizes and isolates left-hemispheric functioning at the expense of the other parts of the brain essential to human survival[18]. In effect, it reduces survival capability and undermines effective adaptation. That is, it weakens the neurophysiological foundations of human survival and our stance in the world. Cultural reinforcement and neurological inhibition set up an exclusivity of the left brain with significant consequences. Left-sided dominance severs us from our evolutionary past and from the powers of our inborn nature. It also implies that left-hemispheric functioning is the only capability of the human brain and that our 'left-sided' world[19] is the only reality there is. Left-hemispheric dominance has profound evolutionary significance. It has not only affected the neurological balance of brain functioning, but also has created a cultural bias[20] with critical repercussions for the individual and society.

The anatomical complexity of the human brain shows the imprint of evolutionary adaptation. Developmentally and functionally, modern neurology speaks of three[21], even four[22], brains in one—"each with a different phylogenetic history, each differing in kind from the other despite the myriad interconnections linking them together"[23], each with "its own special intelligence, its own special memory, its own sense of time and space, and its own motor functions"[24]. The survival value of the neocortex exists in conjunction with the subcortical systems of the phylogenetically older brain. Optimization of survival advantage and survival ability depends on psychic homeostasis and the functioning of the brain as a total entity. Full utilization of the human brain is less a matter of using the millions and millions of brain cells as of employing the various parts of the brain[25].

Effective survival and adaptation—material, environmental, and spiritual—"are dependent upon the psyche functioning as a balanced totality"[26]. The neurophysiology of human survival rests indispensably on the "horizontal integration between left and right hemispheres and (the) vertical integration between the phylogenetically old and recent brains"[27]. Inasmuch as the corpus callosum contributes to lateral hemispheric integration, providing us with the necessary awareness and instrumentality to function in the world, likewise, the neurological linkup between brain stem, midbrain, and neocortex establishes the fundamental hierarchical integration. Vertical integration of the human brain provides the biological and metabiological resources of the psyche, as well as, the connection between life and nature, instinct and spirit, psyche and cosmos, biology and survival[28]. The greatest survival value and adaptive capability of the human brain exist when all its parts function as a whole.

Adaptive Therapy

The following discussion of therapy-related issues is based on the concepts and content presented in this book. Of particular relevance are the sections on adaptive functioning and the role of the human psyche in the survival process.

Reason for Therapy

Adaptive therapy presents a biological, ethologically oriented model of psychiatry. It is designed to enable effective adaptation. The focus of adaptive therapy is the recovery and rehabilitation of our innate adaptive capabilities, bringing to bear what biology has developed in the human psyche and the survival capabilities embedded in it. Adaptive therapy puts psychotherapy back in line with the reality of human life and survival. It takes psychology to a new frontier—the boundary where biology and metabiology, instinct and spirit, body and mind, behavior and consciousness, individual and species are joined. Psychotherapy is perceived as a process of advancing the adaptive capability of the individual by activating the innate biological, psychic structures developed by evolutionary process. In the evolutionary psyche, Jung believed, "resided the collective wisdom of our species, the basic programme enabling us to meet all the exigent demands of life"[1]. The objective of psychotherapy is seen as advancing human evolution, both on an individual and a collective level.

General Purpose

Traditionally, psychotherapy has focused on the individual's history, personality and functioning with the objective of modifying dysfunctional behavior, restructuring erroneous thinking, reversing mood disorder and the general purview of removing concomitant symptomatology. Webster's Dictionary gives a definition of psychotherapy as "the treatment of psychological disorders or maladjustments"[2]. The emphasis is on developmental and cognitive processes, essentially left-hemispheric features and functioning of the cerebral cortex[3].

In contrast to traditional psychology, adaptive therapy places primary emphasis on the inherent processes and capabilities of the subcortical brain and its relevance to human adaptive functioning. Adaptive therapy redefines the role of therapy. It is less interested in personal ontogenetic development, as it is in the role of the phylogenetic psyche in human life and ultimately in individual survival. Rather than focusing on learned behavior and modes of functioning, adaptive therapy concentrates on innate, biologically relevant patterns of behavior and awareness[4]. The focus of therapeutic intervention and methodology is on biologically inherent rather than on culturally acquired features of the individual. Adaptive therapy emphasizes the notion that human life, like that of other living organisms, is ultimately determined by its biology and that human biology spells out the parameters not only of physical but also psychic adaptation. Given these principles, therapy is designed to provide a set of functions, which differ quite distinctly from those of traditional psychotherapy.

1. The paramount objective of adaptive therapy is to strengthen the person's adaptation to life. Therapy facilitates this process in several different ways. Foremost is the effort to increase the individual's survival capability through the utilization of adaptive features inherent in the genetic psyche. These features are preexistent in the older, subcortical parts of the human brain. Human survival, much like that of all other forms of life, can rely on evolutionary resources. The patterns of behavior and consciousness necessary to adapt to the environment and 'to meet the exigent demands of life' are preformed in the archetypal structures of the human psyche[5]. The biological

and metabiological dimensions of human life are not only replicated but also resourced in the genetic make-up of our being.

The utilization of these innate resources and forging the archetypal integration of instinct and spirit, behavior and consciousness, increase human survival capability and adaptation to life. The genetically inherent configurations of development and wholeness, present in the biology of the organism, promote the survival of both individual and species within its given environment. That is, the primary function of adaptive therapy is to relate psychotherapy to adaptation and survival.

2. A second function of adaptive therapy is to relate survival to health. Health, like survival capability, is a measure of our adaptation to life. H. Seyle's work on adaptation and stress has provided the evidence that health, both physical and mental, is inextricably associated with wholeness and harmony. He made it clear that illness originates from within the person rather than from outside[6], postulating a psychosomatic model of human life. Health results from complete alignment with the vital and instinctual processes of human nature and from a full realization of our mental and psychic processes as sentient, conscious beings.

The wholeness, which underlies health, comes from the biological and metabiological connection with the outer realities of nature and cosmos. Human nature and human life are both a replication as well as a component of the larger context of nature and universe in which we participate as physical and mental beings. Jung maintained "that nature is not only outside but inside; that the phylogenetic human psyche is a portion of nature itself; and that, consequently, there exists, in a very profound sense, a hidden connection between human nature and the nature of the cosmos"[7].

Health rests on successful adaptation to life. At the core of health and survival stands the relationship of the organism to life itself—the congruence of individual life with the natural life cycle of the species, which is preformed in the archetypes of the evolutionary psyche[8]. Health is ultimately anchored in the organic processes of the human body and in the adaptation of the individual to life. It is, thus, directly related to a harmony with the flow of life and the realization of life's archetypal intent[9].

If individual experience remains disconnected from the "common needs, instincts and potentials", universal to human nature, and "departs from the norms of the species" a "pathological state of imbalance ensues"[10]. Connection with the organic and spiritual essence of life releases the powers inherent in the biology and psychology of human nature, which determine "the duration of the life-span, the measure of vital energy at one's disposal"[11] and, ultimately, the condition of our health. Health comes from harmony between body and mind, and from successful adaptation to the world around us[12].

3. A third function of adaptive therapy is to relate survival to reality. The human survival reality is structured by biological and metabiological dimensions[13]. The baseline of human survival is determined by the nature of our constitution and needs. Need gratification correlates with environmental adaptation, specifically, adaptation to relevant realities. The duality of our constitution as physical and mental beings relates us to specific realities. The gratification of material, biological needs refers us to the biological reality of life[14], fulfillment of our mental and spiritual needs to the metabiological reality of human existence. One is structured by evolutionary conditions, whereas, the other by metaphysical principles and cosmic laws.

Both realities stand in contrast to the man-made reality of the socio-cultural environment, which is essentially structured by rational, scientific values. The socio-cultural system of society is an instrumentality for the gratification of our biological and spiritual needs, and, as such, has the quality of an intermediary or secondary reality. Alongside the sociological reality exists the archetypal world of nature and cosmos in which we partake through our biology and spirituality, specifically, through the subcortical and right-hemispheric functioning of the human brain.

Therapy needs to address the reality issue in order to enable effective adaptation. The individual needs to understand that social reality and survival reality are not identical, and that human instincts and intuition, not the intellect, are the main agents of successful adaptation. The individual must also know that the ethological reality always supersedes the sociological reality of the environment. Adaptive therapy emphasizes reality differentiation and facilitates a perceptual figure-ground switch to direct a person's attention to the relevant realities and determining factors of human survival.

Adaptive therapy relates individual survival to the key determinants of adaptive functioning: the adaptive capability of the individual, health as the baseline of adaptation and therapy, and the perception of relevant realities that affect human life.

Theoretical Foundations

The main focus of psychotherapy is the adaptive capacity inherent in the phylogenetic psyche. The Jungian concept of the archetypes[15] is central to the theoretical framework of adaptive therapy. Archetypes constitute the essential elements of the phylogenetic psyche fashioned by the biological processes of evolution. Their purpose is to furnish the behavioral and mental capabilities for successful adaptation to the environment. The human psyche contains the relevant bio-program to ensure our survival: archetypes are "the neuropsychic centers responsible for co-ordinating the behavioural and psychic repertoires of our species in response to whatever environmental circumstances we may encounter"[16]. The duality of the archetypal structure, consisting of a behavioral, instinctive, unconscious and a mental, spiritual, conscious pole, determines the therapeutic paradigm. The paradigm addresses the behavioral and mental adaptation of the individual. The instinctive aspect of the archetypes manifests in behavior; the spiritual aspect fashions symbolic expression. The archetypes are biological entities, formed by evolutionary process in response to environmental conditions. The archetypal system of the human psyche is, thus, directly relevant to human survival.

Adaptive therapy differs from traditional psychotherapy by focusing on innate rather than learned psychological processes. It addresses evolutionary functioning[17], which constitutes the primary neurology of human survival. Evolutionary functioning is an innate adaptive psychology contained in the primary psyche. Its psychological features are genetic, universal, impersonal, and stable[18]. It consists of innate behaviors, sensations, emotions, attitudes, and psychic functions. Evolutionary functioning originates in the midbrain—the seat of the archetypal psyche. Evolutionary functioning comprises the functional aspect of the archetypes.

Evolutionary functioning is the primary reference system of adaptive therapy. Eventually, all behavioral and emotional reality has to be understood at the biological level in order to reveal its teleological significance. The five types of ethological behaviors together with the four categories of biological sensations and emotions constitute the neurobehavioral substratum of our natural life force. Complemented by biological values and imperatives, and expanded by related psychic functions, this biobehavioral system, seated in the midsection of the human brain, comprises the essential human survival psychology. Evolutionary functioning represents the relevant reality of the organism. It also establishes the reality parameters and the clinical focus of psychiatric intervention and psychotherapy. It is on that level of neurological functioning where body and mind are connected, where the organism connects with the world and with the metaphysical

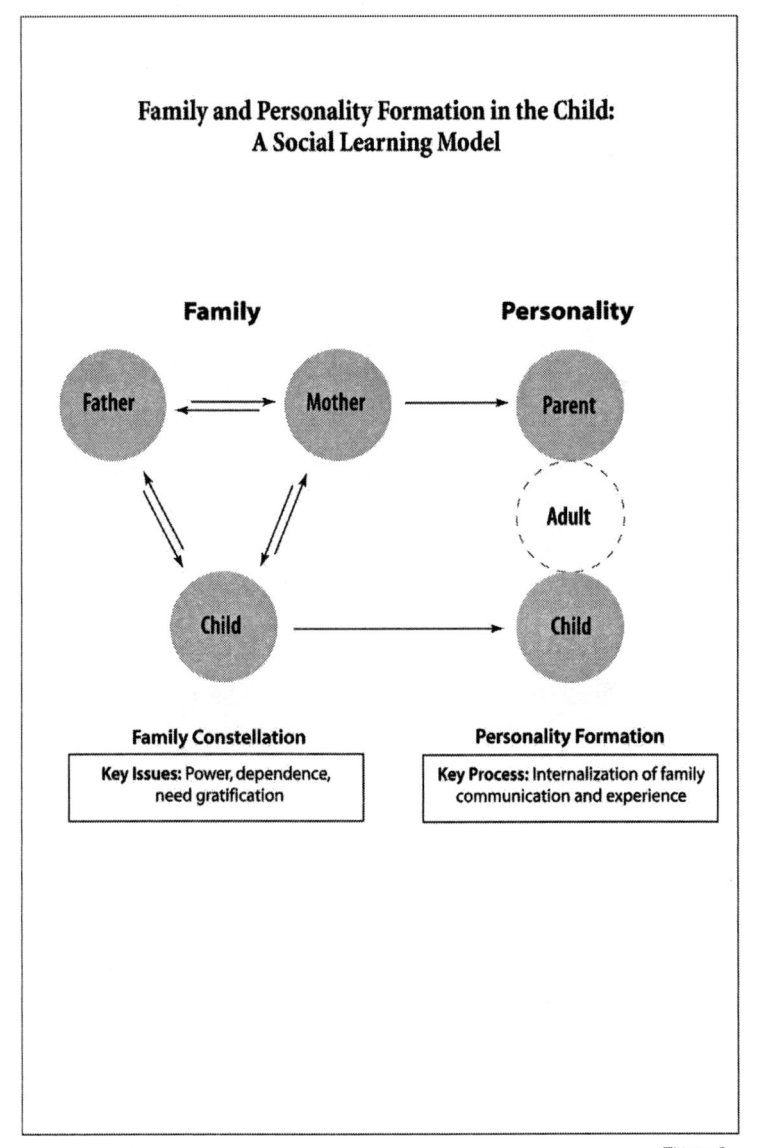

Family and Personality Formation in the Child: A Social Learning Model

Family — Father ⇌ Mother, both ⇌ Child

Personality — Mother → Parent; (Adult, dashed); Child → Child

Family Constellation
Key Issues: Power, dependence, need gratification

Personality Formation
Key Process: Internalization of family communication and experience

Figure 2

dimension of human existence. It is on that level where health, human survival, and well-being originate. The organic relevance of these innate mechanisms is to advance adaptive capability and human survival. This biological reference is indispensable in psychotherapy.

Evolutionary functioning stands in contrast to cognitive, culturally conditioned psychology, which is the product of socialization. Figure (2) illustrates the social learning process in the development of an individual's conditioned psychology, primarily based on family experience and other environmental influences[19]. Adaptive therapy uses the socialized psychology of the individual as a source of personal and medical history, and, at times, as an entry-point to treatment.

Goals of Therapy

The goal of adaptive therapy is to optimize the individual's adaptation to life. This involves strengthening survival capability and increasing survival advantage, essentially, issues of ability and strategy.

- The initial step of psychotherapy consists of creating an awareness of the innate adaptive capabilities of the individual. This involves confirming their existence as genetic, permanent attributes of human survival[20]. The role of therapy is aimed at focusing human behavior and consciousness on innate genetic processes.
- The human survival capability exists preformed in the archetypal structures of the phylogenetic, evolutionary psyche. The archetypes contain a genetic survival program. As biological entities, the archetypes are not under the control of reason or will. The human archetypes are comparable to 'innate releasing mechanisms'[21] and are activated by significant stimuli that prescribe survival behavior[22]. The organic relevance of these inborn mechanisms is to promote life and survival. The role of therapy is to protect the functional

integrity of these innate adaptive processes and to render them accessible to the individual[23].

- Furthermore, therapy must take an active role in rehabilitating the older subcortical parts of the human brain and in providing permission to utilize them. In other words, therapy must be instrumental in reversing a cultural bias and taboo, which has suppressed and restricted the instinctual and spiritual aspects of human nature and, consequently, the adaptive capability of the individual[24].

- Adaptive therapy creates access to the archetypal world of instinct and higher consciousness, the principal resources of human survival. It facilitates a process by which the individual is able to reconnect with the biological foundations of his life. Jung viewed the task of the psychotherapist "as achieving a reconciliation between the patient and the '2 million year-old man that is in all of us'"[25]. "Our difficulties, he argued, 'come from losing contact with our instincts, with the age-old unforgotten wisdom stored up in us'."[26] As a cure for our collective ills, Jung recommended that people be enabled to establish contact with the resources inherent in human nature.

- Additionally, therapy needs to help forge within the individual personality the archetypal connection between instinct and spirit, behavior and consciousness. This internal process is designed to unify nature and culture, as well as, individual and world as the basis for the effective adaptation to life. Adaptive therapy aims to achieve archetypal integration by simultaneously encouraging instinctual life and biological behavior and by helping to evolve a person's spirituality and higher consciousness.

- Finally, therapy supports adaptive efforts of increasing survival advantage. Most transactions with the environment are concerned with need gratification. The achievement of survival advantage depends upon a biologically determined relationship to the environment. Selective advantage is established, for instance, through strategic positioning, skill generality, and enhancing access to resources. Adaptive therapy elaborates on the variances between the industrial and natural life cycles; it outlines the value implications and the existential repercussions that are involved. Adaptive therapy advocates the adaptive advantage of non-specificity in an individual's life. It favors a form of adaptation, which accommodates the skill demands of modern life and the ability to transition between separate realities without jeopardizing the selective advantage of generality.

In general, adaptive therapy aims to optimize the fit between ethology and environment. It reinforces the evolutionary principles of human survival, and it promotes the notion of the archetypal survivor who is adept in all areas of life.

Role of Therapy

Adaptive therapy is concerned with the existential adaptation of the individual, as well as, the corresponding innate capabilities and processes of the human psyche[27]. As part of the older brain, these adaptive features have retained their "full functional integrity"[28] throughout evolution, while other cerebral functions were added. The therapeutic task is to activate what is already there and to actualize the archetypal potential preexistent in the psychophysiological organism[29].

The objective, therefore, is to facilitate the ontogenetic development of phylogenetic features in the psychic constitution and, consequently and most importantly, to surface the full innate adaptive capability already available in the human psyche. This alters the role of psychotherapy, which is thus not engaged in changing acquired dysfunctional behavior and personality features, rather its function is to attend to organic and psychic processes that are an innate part of human nature.

Biological psychology involves an informational, facilitative role of therapy and clinical intervention[30]. The therapeutic role is to educate the individual to the existing adaptive capacity and to encourage and maximize its utilization. Conceptually, it operates from the long-term perspective of evolutionary principles, viewing human life as unfolding according to a species-specific pattern within the context of a given environment. The archetypal life exists inside and outside of personality and society as a genetic time capsule driven by the teleology of survival. Personal experience and history give it complexion and flesh out the details[31].

The archetypal life provides grounding in the timeless dimensions of biology and metabiology. It allows the individual to fasten life to lasting parameters and to gain a sense of mastery in daily and lifelong affairs. The archetypal life comes with the instruction to heed its biological, evolutionary intent in order to achieve viable adaptation and self-completion. It also includes the moral imperative to preserve the continuation of the species and to not cause harm to others in the course of personal pursuits and individual survival. The archetypal life exists in accord with nature and cosmos. It bestows a sense of sovereignty, serenity and ease when facing existential conditions and the adaptive task of fulfilling our needs. One of the primary objectives of adaptive therapy is to help the individual reach a level where he/she can connect with his/her natural self and relate to the evolutionary, archetypal principles of life as part of the same process.

Neurological Model

The neurological model underlying adaptive therapy is based on a dual integration of cerebral structures and functions: the vertical integration of the older and newer parts of the human brain, as well as, the horizontal integration of left and right cerebral hemispheres via the corpus callosum. The model incorporates the entire evolutionary history of our species with its various stages of adaptation and development as manifest in the various sections of the brain[32]. The integration of the major parts of the human brain brings the total available adaptive capacity into play. Effective integration looks for the proper balance and deployment of the various adaptive cerebral functions[33].

The older subcortical section of the human brain, which is given much prominence in this model of psychotherapy, provides the fundamental framework of human life. It contains the entire collective survival experience of our species; it establishes the essential parameters of human adaptation; and it furnishes the necessary capabilities to execute the adaptation. The older brain provides the behavioral repertoire, the existential values, the mental predisposition, even the configuration of the entire life cycle, necessary 'to meet all of the exigent demands of life'.

Central to the reclamation and rehabilitation of the older regions of the human brain, and in protecting their 'full functional integrity', is the dissolution of left-hemispheric dominance. The left brain not only gives prominence to 'left-sided' reality[34], but it also can inhibit subcortical interaction[35] with other parts of the brain. The neurological inhibition of cerebral functioning, exerted by the left hemisphere, similarly may affect the right brain. Overextension of left-hemispheric functioning is counterproductive. It controls the reality, open to perception, and the cerebral functions, available to the adaptive process.

Horizontal integration of both cerebral hemispheres increases adaptive functioning, bringing the unique survival value[36] of each side of the brain into play. Part of the rehabilitation of the right brain is in the acknowledgment that its survival value has largely gone unrecognized. The right brain offers an understanding of the world, which the left brain completely fails to perceive. Survival in modern society requires integration of left-sided and right-sided functioning of the brain. The left brain is capable of technical ability and know-how; its empirical principle of cause and effect spawns action and motivates growth. The right brain, conversely, provides a notion of the coherence of life, a deeper sense of purpose and meaning, and a vision and strategy for human existence.

Finally, vertical integration of the old and new brains completes the adaptive composition, resonating with the larger transpersonal context of human life and the particular local and historical circumstances of its manifestation. The older brain provides the innate genetic survival capacity, validated by evolution and experience. The new brain contributes the learned survival capabilities, acquired from, and tailored to, the specific environment of modern society. The full horizontal and vertical integration of the human brain establishes the place "where the archetypal world and the contemporary world meet"[37]. The alignment and balance between all parts of the brain present an organic view of life and environment. Integration accommodates the dynamic interplay between the demands of human nature and the demands of the world.

The particular composition and functioning of the brain have allowed the human being to prevail over his environment. Adaptive therapy promotes the successful survival and adaptation of the individual. Foremost are the rediscovery, reclamation and rehabilitation of our evolutionary adaptive capabilities, which have been sidelined by modern civilization. The innate biological and metabiological survival capabilities are indispensable for the effective adaptation to life, where our social and scientific abilities are insufficient to the task.

Adaptive therapy facilitates cerebral integration of the various regions of the human brain to function as a unified entity. It supports the survival of the individual by expediting the utilization of the full adaptive capacity of the brain and by bringing to bear the specific capabilities of each of its parts. Adaptive therapy also, somehow, functions as a gatekeeper of cerebral functioning and as a guard against its cultural stereotyping. On one hand, it oversees left-brain functioning, monitoring for its tendency to dominate brain performance. On the other hand, it pursues actualization of the old brain. Finally, adaptive therapy encourages right-brain functioning. This form of therapy protects the individual from the blindness of a purely left-sided perception and, instead, promotes an "understanding through life"[38] rather than through the intellect.

Treatment Objectives

The role of therapy in behavioral and mental adaptation consists of diverse functions. Survival behavior does not have to be learned or acquired. It is essentially biological behavior and operates from the level of our instincts. Survival consciousness, on the other hand, requires personal growth. It is a function of genetic endowment and psychological development, inasmuch as it involves subcortical and neocortical functioning.

Ethological behavior evolves in order to adapt the organism to its environment. We are no exception. Humans are, by nature, territorial, hierarchical, aggressive, sexual and xenophobic. Behavioral adaptation is central to the gratification of our material needs. Ethological behavior represents the instinctive pole of the archetypes of the evolutionary psyche. It developed in response to environmental conditions. It corresponds to the ethological reality of the survival environment. The biology of human behavior largely determines the sociological reality of society.

- Adaptive therapy promotes awareness of human ethology and the behavioral survival capability inherent in the human psyche. Furthermore, it facilitates the activation of biological behavior through the process of ethological rehearsal, designed to recapture and mobilize innate adaptive behaviors. Adaptive therapy is also instrumental in emotional management, assisting the individual to differentiate between basic feelings and pseudo-emotions, organic sensations versus socially acquired, cognitively induced emotions such as anxiety, depression, sadness or guilt.

Most psychotherapies never enter the field of human consciousness[39], as their main focus is on psychopathology rather than adaptation, leaving this arena to the religious and spiritual professions. A person's higher consciousness and spirituality are an essential part of the adaptive process of coping with the events and experiences of his/her life. The religious archetype[40] is the genetic, biological foundation of human survival consciousness; the individual's particular adaptive concept is the mental, metabiological formulation of his/her survival consciousness.

The role of psychotherapy, related to a person's survival consciousness, assumes developmental, informational, facilitative and supportive functions. This involves several issues:

- Therapy must entail the overall maturation process of the individual, because the survival concept is determined by the level of psychological development. Dependent psychology, for instance, produces maladaptive conceptual systems. It understands the world in symbiotic, familial terms, espousing dysfunctional responses of anxiety, insecurity and conformity.
- A more immediate role of psychotherapy in facilitating the functioning of an individual's survival consciousness involves creating an awareness of the innate survival capability inherent in the human psyche. Survival is an instinctual response and, as such, it can rely on the biological potency of nature. By facilitating awareness of this innate capability, psychotherapy promotes a reorientation and shift in the person's adaptive functioning.
- A related function of psychotherapy is to stimulate and activate the archetype, in this case, the religious archetype[41]. Most genetic capabilities and characteristics of our biological nature are a potentiality: called upon

in time of need. The functional structures of the archetypal psyche, both behavioral and mental, operate much like 'innate releasing mechanisms'[42], instantly activated when environmental circumstances necessitate a response.

- Moreover, therapy needs to concern itself with the content aspects of the survival consciousness. The conceptual content of survival consciousness is a derivative of the person's psychology and developmental maturation. Psychotherapy needs to facilitate articulation and awareness of the survival concept the person is using to operate and function in his/her world. A review of the attitudes and beliefs an individual holds about life—events, people, and self—reveals the adaptive viability of the conceptual system.

- An important role of therapy consists in facilitating the reconstruction of the survival concept both during and after an individual experiences crisis or upheaval. Crisis, per definition, constitutes the breakdown of the existing conceptual system. At times, a person is confronted with situations that go beyond his/her comprehension and coping abilities. These are junctures in the individual's life experience and personal development, which surface the limits of the current survival concept. A breakdown of the adaptive concept forces replacement and the necessity to either revise the existing or to construct a new conceptual system. This process benefits greatly from facilitation and intervention of psychotherapy.

The role of psychotherapy in mental adaptation needs to address both the genetic and the developmental aspects of survival consciousness. Therapy takes on either a facilitative or a supportive function to promote the survival ability of the individual. Like survival behavior, survival consciousness is essentially about need gratification. The integration of survival behavior and survival consciousness generates the behavioral and mental abilities along with the interpersonal and ethical parameters essential to human survival[43]. It establishes the foundation for an action-philosophy of adaptive capability and resilience and for a moral code that is informed both by the ethics of biology and the moral sense of higher consciousness[44].

Treatment Issues

The greatest psychological obstacle to individual survival is dependency. It weakens initiative and independent action and misleads with an illusory view of life, where others come to the rescue and provide care and support. Dependency reinforces a sense of helplessness and passivity that subverts resilience and survival activity[45]. Prolonged dependency is debilitating. Psychiatrically speaking, dependency is the root cause of mental illness[46].

Freud maintained that mental illness was a defense against anxiety, which resulted from threatened or failed transaction with the external world for the purpose of need gratification[47]. Intrigued by his discovery, Freud elaborated on his theory of defense mechanisms[48]. However, rather than strengthening the individual's adaptive capabilities to reduce and eliminate the anxiety, he focused on the dysfunctionality and its pathological consequences, inadvertently setting the course for modern psychiatry. Freud's list of psychological defenses was eventually extended and converted into a system of psychiatric diagnoses, establishing a preoccupation with pathology.

Adaptive therapy turns toward the opposite direction. What people needed then and need now, is to have more adaptive capability in order to be less afraid of living and to be more effective in satisfying their needs. It is like learning how to ski—teaching people techniques reduces their fear of the mountain. The same is true of living—enhancing an individual's survival abilities minimizes his/her anxieties, basically his/her fear of life. Or, as a patient stated in therapy: "The way to get healthy is to learn how to live." Adaptive therapy helps people overcome by anxiety to overcome anxiety.

Freud's point that psychological pathology and mental illness essentially result from a dysfunctional reaction or resistance to life[49] is well taken. Contrasting adaptive therapy and conventional psychotherapy highlights the difference in approach to the clinical situation. Conceptually, there is the emphasis on the adaptation to life versus a focus on the defense against life. While traditional psychiatry concentrates on the pathological reaction and its potential causes and consequences, adaptive therapy pursues evolutionary adaptation and successful gratification of the individual's needs. Compared to the complexity of clinical diagnoses, the diagnostic system of adaptive therapy is quite simple and stated as: in the present condition capable or incapable of conducting a functional life and of achieving need gratification. A deficitary diagnosis is followed up with a treatment plan on how to increase the patient's adaptive capability.

A person's defenses against life, no matter what diagnostic classifications are used to describe them, indicate foremost the individual's inability to live a functional life. Adaptive therapy focuses clinical intervention on the diminished survival ability and its activation. The goal of successful therapy is to make the person fit to live. Adaptive therapy defines cure as achieving the ability to live and survive effectively. Effective living means getting needs met. The primary objective of therapy is to develop adaptive competence and, like the decathlon athlete, to reach adaptive effectiveness in all areas of life, such as relationships, finances, skills, career and work.

A further difference between adaptive and traditional psychotherapy exists in regard to the type of psychology that is being addressed. Conventional therapy is exclusively engaged with the person's culturally conditioned psychology. This psychology is seated in the neocortex and consists of learned behaviors and socialized ways of thinking and feeling. Adaptive validity and viability of this type of psychology are minimal. The individual's socialized psychology is only an adjunct to his/her life rather than its main driving force. As a psychological system, it is reflective of cultural convention, which is designed to achieve efficient adjustment to society. Culturally conditioned psychology is, however, not related to the biological and existential reality of adaptation and survival—a function, which is carried out by the evolutionary psyche, located in the midsection of the human brain. The human psyche is the workshop of life; its adaptive biology corresponds to the dynamics and demands of human existence. Adaptive therapy is involved with the person's evolutionary functioning, the innate survival psychology of the human psyche.

The clinical objectives of adaptive therapy are directed at two specific issues: Elimination of dysfunctional adaptation and the establishment of effective adaptation with respect to individual functioning. Traditional psychotherapy targets the existing symptomatology, presented by the patient, and defines it as the relevant psychopathology[50]. The pathology, however, actually lies in the individual's dysfunctional adaptation to life[51]. That is to say, the pathology is on the adaptive, rather than on the physiological, emotional or psychosocial level.

Whatever is specified as pathology determines the process and outcome of treatment. The treatment focus of conventional psychotherapy practice is to target the symptomatology of the alleged disorder with the intent to remove the existing pathology and to reestablish the baseline of the premorbid condition. This approach does not capture or question the rudimentary etiology of the presenting mental illness. By not addressing the real issues in the person's life, there is the danger of returning the patient to the *status quo ante*, rendering him/her just as helpless and bewildered as before. The treatment paradigm of traditional psychotherapy fails to ameliorate the underlying condition and incapacitation, which is affecting the patient, and to impact any real, durable changes in the individual's life and functioning. The shortfall of traditional therapy is evident in the misdiagnosis of the presenting pathology and in the misplacement of treatment interventions: The *condition* causes the *disorder*; the *treatment* treats the *disorder*; the *condition* remains untreated.

When a person is suffering from anxiety and depression, because he/she feels lonely and poor, then improvement or removal of symptoms and a change in affect represent insufficient clinical objectives to address the existential and experiential issues at hand. The depression or anxiety may be a reaction to a difficult, stressful or unfortunate situation such as divorce, separation, the death or loss of a loved one, career, financial or medical problems. The treatment solution, however, must not consist of focusing on the reaction to existential events or changes in condition, i.e. symptoms, but in enhancing the individual's approach and adaptation to life. The therapeutic issues involved in most treatment scenarios and clinical conditions require a response on a strategy rather than on a symptom level.

Adaptive therapy addresses the distressed existential condition, as well as, the adaptive incapacitation of the patient as the two critical points of clinical intervention. It shifts the rationale and focus of treatment to strategic issues of adaptive repositioning, need gratification and the general survival requirements of the individual. The emphasis is on the rectification of life circumstances and the rehabilitation of adaptive capability rather than on symptom removal or mood reversal. The deficit of adaptive functioning in the patient's life is the foremost target of therapeutic intervention.

Adaptation and survival are primary functions of the organism. They involve an innate bio-program of biological capabilities and processes. This bio-program, which supersedes social learning and cultural conditioning, facilitates fundamental adaptive processes such as strategic positioning, ethological functioning and maintaining psychic balance for the purposes of need gratification and personal well-being. It furnishes the natural biological and metabiological resources essential to sustain life and survival. The seat of this adaptive bio-program is the human midbrain[52] or, what Jung referred to as, the primary or evolutionary psyche. The evolutionary psyche not only contains the collective survival experience of our species, it also functions as the primary adaptive agent in our lives.

Adaptive therapy focuses foremost on the evolutionary psyche of the individual. It is designed to activate the full adaptive capacity of the human brain and to make it available in the person's life. Adaptive therapy facilitates the use of these innate adaptive resources. It aids the individual to adapt effectively to the demands and experiences of his/her life. Bringing the existential experience of the individual in line with the natural adaptive processes of the brain transforms the individual's response to the circumstances and events in his/her life.

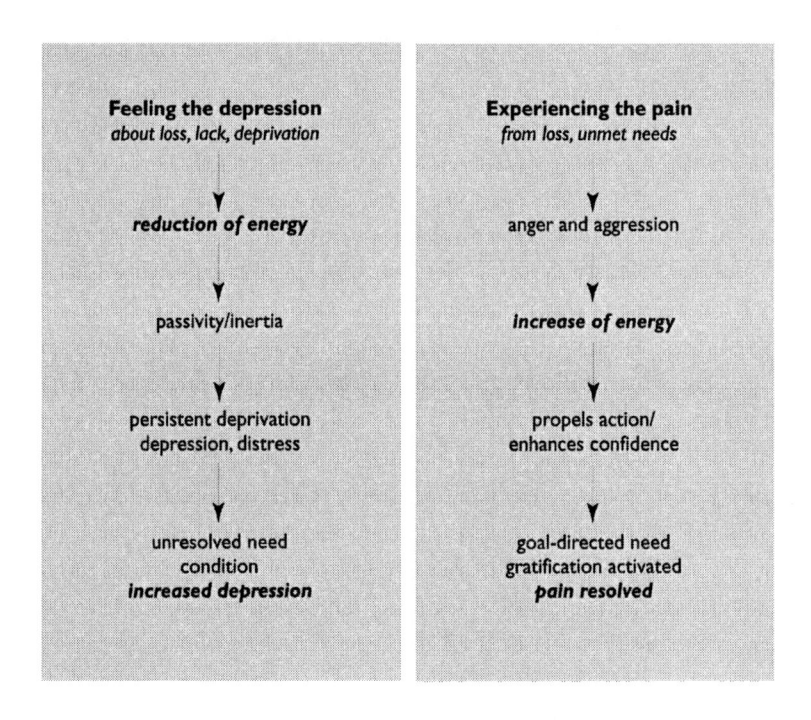

Feeling the depression *about loss, lack, deprivation*	**Experiencing the pain** *from loss, unmet needs*
▼	▼
reduction of energy	anger and aggression
▼	▼
passivity/inertia	**increase of energy**
▼	▼
persistent deprivation depression, distress	propels action/ enhances confidence
▼	▼
unresolved need condition **increased depression**	goal-directed need gratification activated **pain resolved**

The accompanying flow chart demonstrates two distinct ways in which experiences and events can be processed and responded to, depending on what functional parts of the brain are being engaged. A situation of loss, lack, deprivation, change of status or condition may result in two entirely opposite responses to the same event.

Subjective responses to existential circumstances are either conditioned and acquired or evolutionary and biological. Conditioned responses involve neocortical functioning and initiate cognitive processing of events and experiences. By contrast, evolutionary responses to external events are tied into the organic processes of the subcortical brain and activate adaptive functioning[53]. Thus a person may either feel depression or experience pain as the result of loss, lack or deprivation depending on how he/she chooses to respond[54].

Depression is a mental event and involves thought process; pain, on the other hand, is an organic experience that engenders biological and/or metabiological adaptation. The subsequent process in each case is markedly different. Depression, in the end, leads to more depression; pain, on the other hand, converts into action. The conditioned response leads to dysfunctional stagnation; the evolutionary or organic response generates effective adaptation[55].

The therapeutic principles underlying adaptive therapy emulate the adaptive principles found in nature: (a) setting forth a problem-solving mode designed to maximize the selective survival advantage of the individual and (b) establishing an overall treatment process, which follows and models the adaptive processes of the organism. From the individual's viewpoint, the therapy experience also takes on a different quality. At its best, therapy not only copies life, it also enables relevant learning transfer to the particular life situation of the individual. In that sense, adaptive therapy provides a form and a forum of learning about life, which is essential to the adaptive functioning of the individual inasmuch as modeling—showing the way—is in itself an important function of therapy.

Clinical Methodology and Treatment Interventions

Adaptive therapy represents a radical departure from traditional psychotherapy. It takes recourse to innate adaptive capabilities aimed at facilitating personal maturity and mastery of the human experience. Adaptive therapy addresses the adaptive requirements of the individual. A person's physical, material and mental well-being is ultimately contingent on the strength and viability of her adaptation to life. Well-being depends upon how successful the person is in achieving need gratification, in her ability to function within a given environment, and in establishing a sense of coherence to account for the experiences in her life. Seen in an evolutionary context, life functions as a conditioning force that requires continuous adaptation to changing circumstances, needs and demands.

Like disease, mental illness reflects dysfunctional adaptation to life[56]. Failure to respond to and adapt to the circumstances of life causes mental distress and disorder. Problems of living and their emotional, psychosocial fallout result from dysfunctional adaptation. An essential function of therapy, therefore, is to teach people how to live.

The therapeutic methodology of adaptive therapy is predicated by the fact that the capacity for adaptation has biological origins and is innate. Given the condition of innate genetic structures, there is no need to modify existing features or functions[57]. Adaptive therapy is designed to increase survival capability, promote survival advantage, and strengthen effective adaptation using the inherent adaptive capabilities of the individual. To a large extent, psychotherapy is directed towards the reactivation of this adaptive potential and its confirmation as part of the human psychological make-up. Its main function is to activate what is already there.

The treatment process involves several elements. At the core of therapeutic interventions are behavioral, attitudinal, mental and spiritual issues. A significant function of adaptive therapy is to reinforce and enhance survival behavior, survival attitude, and survival consciousness. Creating awareness and the subsequent practice of innate adaptive abilities are collateral interventions. The central aspect of the therapeutic process reflects the archetypal structure of the evolutionary paradigm.

The clinical interventions of adaptive therapy involve: (a) educational reorientation, (b) ethological rehearsal, (c) attitudinal reinforcement, (d) mental and spiritual amplification, and (e) practice.

(a) Educational Reorientation

Objective: the purpose of educational reorientation is to increase awareness of natural, innate survival capabilities—behavioral, attitudinal, mental and spiritual. Human survival functioning is an inherent capacity of the older brain. Subcortical functioning, as it involves brain stem and regions of the midbrain, is essentially involuntary and automatic. Vital functions, metabolic processes, instinctive behavior and adaptive functioning, to name just a few, proceed outside conscious awareness and control. The adaptive capability of the human brain, therefore, remains generally unknown and unrecognized.

Bringing the innate survival capabilities into conscious awareness turns these features into a powerful dependable resource in response to existential conditions, which require adaptive functioning. Instinctive knowledge becomes conscious knowledge; the automatic, involuntary reaction turns into conscious process and deliberate action. Making the unconscious conscious is somewhat like claiming land from the sea. In making the unconscious conscious, we make contact with the archetypes in us and retrieve that part of our nature, which has been sealed off by socialization and cognitive process.

Therapy must facilitate awareness of the individual's inherent capacity for adaptation. It has to educate people about the adaptive features and abilities of the human brain and to explain how people can utilize them in conducting their daily affairs. Additionally, therapy needs to inform people about the intrinsic survival value of these adaptive features compared to any learned and acquired psychological competencies. This information also needs to include the notion that we possess—whatever we require to live and survive—inside our own nature.

Adaptive therapy returns something to the individual that the culture at large, historically, has denied him/her—awareness and acceptance of his/her innate survival capacity. It acknowledges the fact that the distinct survival advantage of humans, as a species and as an individual, lies in our inherent behavior and psychology. Most importantly, it confirms the validity and integrity of our inborn capacity for self-preservation and survival. In that, adaptive therapy restores an important sense of confidence and security to human psychology, providing a real and reliable foundation for personal self-reliance. It strengthens the overall survival ability of the individual, advancing competency for successful adaptation and maturation[58]. Essentially, adaptive therapy reorients the person to a different dimension of functioning, reconfiguring the individual's relationships to self, environment and universe. Accessing the innate survival capability of the individual through education and reorientation sets the stage for effective adaptation and living.

(b) Ethological Rehearsal

Objective: the goal of ethological rehearsal is to access and activate innate survival behavior. Adaptive therapy seeks to increase the adaptive capability of the individual by resorting to his/her innate capacity for adaptation and self-preservation. The human ethology is a significant part of the adaptive repertoire provided by the brain. Ethology signifies behavioral adaptation and specifically refers to a set of biological survival behaviors—territorial, hierarchical, aggressive, sexual and xenophobic—that evolved to secure need gratification and effective adaptation to environmental conditions[59].

Ethological behavior forms the instinctive pole of the archetypal structure contained in the evolutionary psyche. The organic relevance of this biobehavioral system is to promote life and survival. The expression of these adaptive behavioral features is usually involuntary and stimulated by the outside. They are activated by significant stimuli that prescribe survival behavior. The biobehavioral survival features of the human brain, which help to regulate our relationship to the environment, present a natural adaptive response to survival conditions unless they are overruled by social training and cultural conditioning[60].

Ethological behavior equates to instinctive behavior. With regard to the structure and functioning of the human instincts, it is important to note two relevant issues:

- Instinctive behavior and attitude originate in the regions of the brain stem and the midbrain. As part of the archetypal structure, the instinctive system is an element of the collective, unconscious psyche. In essence, instincts are part of the human unconscious.
- The instincts are a component of the genetic constitution of the human psyche. The human instincts are innate, yet particular instinctive behavior patterns are not inherited. According to J. Bowlby, "what is inherited is the potential to develop . . . behavioural systems, both the nature and form of which differ in some measure according to the particular environment in which development takes place"[61]. Instinctual behavior needs to be activated and developed.

In conjunction with the behavioral elements of environmental adaptation, therapy needs to raise the awareness that the reality of human life is ultimately structured by ethological not sociological premises and parameters[62]. It also must point out that it is exactly those survival conditions in the environment that the individual has been equipped and prepared for by evolutionary process. Much of human life and behavior clearly indicates that evolutionary conditions are the ultimate reality that determines and shapes the events of human existence. Given the quality of the human survival reality[63], therapy needs to alert the individual to these adaptive conditions and make the natural adaptive capabilities of the individual readily available for conscious action.

Ethological rehearsal is used to reinforce innate survival behavior[64] and to substantiate the effective adaptation of the individual. Therapy activates and amplifies what is already there. Ethology involves behavior and environment; it refers to the adaptive response capability of the organism to external conditions. In humans, ethological behavior is regulated by the midbrain. As a therapeutic methodology, ethological rehearsal involves both behavioral and observational training. Specifically, ethological rehearsal is used: (1) to sensitize the person to the existence and functioning of innate adaptive behavior; (2) to practice effective and appropriate utilization of adaptive behavior[65]; and (3) to enhance ethological scanning, i.e. observation and awareness of environmental conditions. Ethological training aims to strengthen the overall survival behavior of the individual and his/her successful adaptation to life[66].

Human ethology also involves an archetypal bio-program[67] of biological values, which coordinates a lifelong sequence of ethological events. Archetypes regulate the human life cycle and constitute the essential matrix of human experience[68]. Human biology defines the primary needs, values and occurrences[69] essential to the human existence. These biological patterns of human life have distinct survival value.

Contemporary society is no longer organized on natural principles[70], rather, modern life is considerably out of sync with human nature[71]. Discrepancy exists between social and natural ideals both on the level of values and life cycle. In its effort to promote health and healing, therapy needs to reinforce values. Adaptive therapy reinforces the archetypal intent of human life to ensure effective adaptation. It helps the individual to accept the notion that the biology of his/her being is the primary reality of his/her life. Adaptive therapy incorporates the biological imperatives of life into the therapeutic process both as a baseline and as an objective. Human health and fulfillment, ultimately, refer to a life that achieves its natural archetypal intent.

Ethological training reinforces a biological orientation towards life, perceiving it as an organic matter subject to biological intent. It recognizes the evolutionary reality of human events—the eternal principles of life. Ethological rehearsal assists the individual to reconnect with the biological foundations of his life and to realign himself with the evolutionary impulse of the species. It reinforces our biological capacity to survive.

Given the cultural bias against the instinctual, archetypal side of our psychological constitution and given the societal pressure to act against the biological intent of our own nature, therapy must advance the acceptance of these adaptive capabilities in the individual, despite the convention of social conditioning which tries to hide and discredit them. Furthermore, it needs to rehabilitate human instinctive behavior as a vital part of human psychology and human functioning because of its intrinsic survival value. This adaptive biology not only determines the state of our health, it essentially impacts all aspects of our lives and how we function in the world and conduct our affairs, such as family, marriage, child-rearing, relationships, work and finances.

Ethological rehearsal is aided by activating sensory experiences. Sensation, the bodily experience of reality, facilitates access to biology and the instinctive level of ethological behavior. The mere physicality of it also reinforces the biological orientation towards life and environment[72].

(c) Attitudinal Reinforcement

Objective: the purpose of attitudinal reinforcement is to match survival attitudes to survival behavior. Biological behavior corresponds to the order found in nature and quite explicitly to the demands nature places on adaptation and maturity. The significance of ethological behavior is underscored by a set of evolutionary principles, which emphasize self-reliance and self-sufficiency of the organism. In nature, the organism is responsible for its own survival.

After a brief period of attachment and protected growth, survival becomes the task of the organism itself. This is true for all living organisms and humans are no exception.

Modern society has established an intricate system of dependency[73], which makes it increasingly difficult for the individual to take hold of his/her life[74] and to relate to the world[75]. While nature models self-reliance, society fosters dependency. This marks a significant departure from the natural foundations of life. We have replaced the biological imperative for self-reliance with various forms of institutionalized dependency, contrary to the designs and demands of nature.

Both health and well-being are contingent upon effective adaptation to the circumstances and exigencies of life. Survival places a premium on self-reliance. Biological behavior is reinforced by a set of attitudes that match the demands of existential adaptation. These attitudes stress individuality, initiative and responsibility in order to achieve self-reliance and self-sufficiency. They are evolutionary traits of human nature that are supportive of successful adaptation. These attitudes form the motivational core structure of adaptive functioning, driving both need gratification and effective adaptation. This internal structure provides motivation and direction. It also generates the necessary field-independence of action and goal-achievement to effectively position individual survival relative to environmental changes and conditions. The function of attitudinal adaptation is, thus, threefold: (1) to motivate need fulfillment, (2) to reinforce ethological behavior, and (3) to facilitate field-independence.

Attitudinal adaptation is the bridge between the behavioral and mental aspects of human survival. Attitude stands between instinct and spirit, joining both dimensions of adaptive functioning. The pairing of survival behavior and survival attitude fortifies confidence in our ability to fulfill our needs. The combination of survival consciousness and survival attitude consolidates our resolve to negotiate life in the larger context of experiences and events. The notions of *total confidence* and *total abandon*, as the highest manifestations of behavioral and mental adaptation, are founded on the concept of personal responsibility. *Total confidence* and *total abandon*, essentially, embody the idea and the ability of approaching life without fear[76]. They result from healing the *instinctual* and the *spiritual wounds* in our psychological make-up, from overcoming the culturally induced impairment of our constitutional survival capability. In the final analysis, both come down to the attitudinal prerequisites of maturity, personal responsibility and the willingness of the individual to do whatever it takes to achieve effective adaptation to life.

It is the role of therapy to elucidate and reiterate these attitudinal predispositions of human survival. In a society that does not consistently propagate the notion of self-reliance and personal responsibility, these evolutionary features do not appear to be self-evident. Effective adaptation and successful survival, however, cannot be achieved without them. Adaptive therapy moves in tandem with nature. It reinforces the evolutionary survival attitudes to underscore the survival capability of the individual. Given the modern trend towards dependency, attitudinal reinforcement constitutes a significant psychological intervention[77].

Attitudinal reinforcement is a crucial part of the therapeutic process. It is used to draw attention to the reciprocity between individual survival and personal responsibility and to establish the relationship between awareness, attitude and adaptation. Attitudinal reinforcement is to be positioned in such a way that it (a) supports motivation and the individual's active role in his/her survival efforts, and that it (b) indicates the pivotal function of attitudes in the interaction of behavior and consciousness.

(d) Mental and Spiritual Amplification

Objective: the function of mental and spiritual amplification is to increase, expand and fortify survival consciousness. A large portion of human survival is mental. Survival consciousness stems from an innate genetic capacity to maintain psychic balance[78]. It enables us to cope with life circumstances, which are emotionally stressful and potentially damaging. This capacity puts us in the position to adapt to existential situations and conditions of great impact often beyond our control. The capability for mental adaptation is based on biological predispositions of the human psyche. The actual content of survival consciousness, however, varies and depends upon the individual's life experience, existential philosophy and religious belief system.

Survival behavior involves the behavioral adaptation to the survival conditions of the environment. The utility of survival consciousness lies in the mental adaptation to the events and experiences of life. Neurologically, survival consciousness involves two levels of brain functioning in the maintenance of psychic balance. The adaptive capacity itself originates in the midbrain, the seat of the evolutionary psyche and of the archetypal structure it contains. The content of survival consciousness is supplied by both cerebral hemispheres.

The role of therapy is, thus, twofold. Chiefly, therapy must enable awareness of the innate capacity for mental adaptation and the nature of its functioning. This usually takes on the form of illustration and self-experiment[79]. Therapy must underscore the primary genetic properties of this adaptive capability. It needs to confirm that all the essential features of human survival—behavioral and mental—are instinctive and inborn. The notion of the genetic origin of this adaptive capacity contains the reassurance that we have what we need to survive.

Furthermore, therapy can be instrumental in increasing a person's adaptive capability to cope with difficult, unpredictable and uncontrollable life circumstances. The expansion of the capacity for mental adaptation goes to the content component of survival consciousness. The content of survival consciousness generally corresponds to the level of the individual's psychological development[80]. The role of therapy in this context is more indirect and long-term. It is aimed at the expansion of survival consciousness by aiding the psychological development of the individual—a process from dependency to maturity that manifests in a person's relationship to life and symbolically expresses in his/her conceptual understanding of the world. Increased psychological maturity leads to expanded conceptual content, and, in turn, a stronger survival concept results in improved mental adaptation. Mental and spiritual amplification enhances the adaptive capability to deal with the events and eventualities of life.

(e) Practice

Objective: the purpose of practice is to improve and integrate new adaptive functioning. Adaptive therapy seeks to recover our innate ability to survive. Educational reorientation creates awareness of this inherent capacity for survival, which encompasses the whole spectrum of human functioning including behavior, attitudes and higher consciousness. A final step of therapy consists of extending awareness into conscious utilization. Practice and repetition are used to establish intentional usage and eventual habitualization of these adaptive features[81]. Practice-feedback loops assist in the integration of these adaptive qualities into the personality structure and functional repertoire of the individual.

Adaptive therapy is designed to realign the individual's life with the evolutionary impulse and adaptive potential of the species and to bring to bear all the strengths and achievements of a two million year-old history[82]. It is aimed at restoring the functional integrity of the natural self as the agent of survival and at establishing a true sense of functional autonomy in the individual. Therapy enables the individual to constitute an internal structure of adaptive functioning and to replace socialization and conditioned psychology as the primary frame of reference and mode of operation in his/her life.

Central to both the methodology and the overall concept of adaptive therapy is the notion of the archetype[83]. The archetypes of the evolutionary psyche represent the different dimensions of life in which the human being participates. The structure of the archetype is dualistic and combines the realms of instinct and spirit, and, in that, it determines our connection to both worlds. The archetypal structure refers to our biological and metabiological constitution as both physical and mental beings. The archetypes of the human psyche capture the wholeness of life and, as such, create the foundations of our health and well-being. Reintegration of the natural self into the psychology and life of the individual provides the basis for wholeness and health. Nature founded these adaptive qualities and capabilities for us. It awaits our recognition to use them. Adaptive therapy facilitates the integrative process of bringing these inherent behavioral, attitudinal, mental and spiritual features together and to make them available for individual survival.

Rationale for Adaptive Therapy

The notion of adaptive therapy suggests the need for healing the human psyche in a fundamental way. As a species, we are faced with the evolutionary paradox of having to rediscover and relearn what should be normal, common day practice. A variety of factors make this evolutionary requirement a necessity rather than an option.

The human condition is overshadowed by multiple predicaments: (1) the organic paradox of life and death, (2) the existential ambivalence of meaning or futility, and (3) a pervasive condition of heteronomy in most aspects of life. The psychological enormity of the human experience predicates the survival of the individual. The complexity of the human condition is paired with yet another paradox: the mismatch between the massive survival demands of modern life and the diminished survival capability of the individual due to cultural repression[84]. The *instinctual* and *spiritual wounds* of the human psyche are the combined damage to our survival capability. As a result of the cultural and neurological inhibition of human nature, we are instinctually 'amputated', as well as, spiritually dissociated from the very sources that engender and support life. Evolution is urging us to fulfill the Darwinian inspiration from the Jungian perspective of becoming, "spiritually no less than physically, . . . the culmination of the great, lumbering, evolutionary pageant"[85] by joining and integrating our animal origins with the heights of human consciousness in full awareness that the human spirit evolved from a biological base[86].

Adaptive therapy operates against the background of this cultural and historical context. The human condition in modern society not only spells out the survival requirements, which face each one of us, it also points out the inherent cultural issues that either promote or impede human survival. The archetypal paradigm of instinct and spirit, underlying adaptive therapy, not only reflects the history of human evolution from our animal origins to higher consciousness, it also provides the template for a healthy life and for successful adaptation as it relates the human existence to the larger context of nature and universe. Adaptive therapy aims to heal the rift within the psyche of the individual—a rift, which has disconnected the human being from the source of his own life, as well as, from the ground of his being.

Adaptive therapy is forging the biological and metabiological connection, which is present in all aspects of human functioning despite longstanding cultural claims to the opposite[87]. The connection exists on the instinctual level and on the spiritual level[88]. Recovering the relationship with our own nature by recognizing and accepting "the nature of the animal we are"[89] restores the integrity of the evolutionary psyche and our alignment with life. Healing the *instinctual wound* brings back the primordial trust of the creature and the behavioral confidence in our ability to survive and fulfill our needs. Making "the mythological connection"[90] with the ground of our being in nature and cosmos reaffirms the coherence of our world and our relationship with a larger process in which we exist and participate. Healing of the *spiritual wound* restores the unity with all things and our trust in the process of life to provide for our needs.

Adaptive therapy aims at eliminating the deficit and the damage which modern civilization has inflicted on the human psyche. The integration of instinct and spirit pursues a specific therapeutic objective: healing is aimed at reversing the domestication of the natural self and the ensuing loss of survival capacity. Healing is further directed at dissolving the division, created by human culture, that separates us from life, nature and universe. This makes therapy a corrective agent of the cultural process in the service of individual survival. Cerebral integration thus becomes a neurological metaphor with larger relevance: the healing of human nature in the therapy office is symbolic of the healing that needs to take place in the culture at large.

Depression As a Case in Point

Understanding mental illness is essential to its treatment. A comparison of animal and human behavior elucidates the issues and causes of depression, anxiety, and other emotions or psychosocial conditions. Observing the feeding situation of infant animals gives us an instructive picture of their survival behavior and quite often their further fate in life. Watching, for instance, wolf cubs fending for food at their mother's breast, we notice that most of the cubs make it to the nipple while few move to the side and go without. The young animals reaching the mother's nipple use their natural aggression to get what they need.

The animal that does not get to the food source does not apply its inborn survival behavior and goes hungry. Stepping aside, the infant animal surrenders its place in the supply of food. The withdrawal is signaled by deferential gesture. Nodding, crouching its body into a cowering position, the retreating animal exhibits a display of defeat. Relinquishing its claim for need gratification, demonstrating submission, and moving away from the center of action to the periphery of the feeding situation typify its survival position. The fact that its needs remain unfulfilled is manifest in its depressed physical posture and weakened response to the feeding event. The animal that fails in the competition for food, shelter, and mate demonstrates defeat by showing signs of deference and submission. It withdraws from the group to the periphery of life. This is the basis for depression.

Survival behavior and depression in humans resemble the animal analogy. Depression, the existential opposite of aggression, is intimately related to the individual's need structure. Any imbalance in the fulfillment of a person's needs through lack, loss or deprivation is likely to cause depression. The depression is first perceived, cognitively, as an absence of desired objects or a desired state of being; subsequently it is registered, neurologically, as a retardation or acceleration of metabolic, motor and mental processes; and, finally, it is experienced, emotionally, as a state of dejection and despondency. The emotional and behavioral features of depression are very similar to the physical and gestural characteristics of the retreating animal, relinquishing its territory and claim on resources while displaying defeat.

People with depression present a withdrawal from life and from the survival activity of getting their needs met, and commonly settle at the psychosocial periphery of the world they live in. They act much like the animal that does not apply its natural survival behavior to fend for itself. Depression in a person indicates poor or impaired survival ability. It signifies that the individual's inherent survival behavior has been either blunted or stunted most commonly by excessive cultural conditioning[1]. Reversal of depression, therefore, is accomplished by reestablishing balance within the person's need structure. Treatment of depression, thus, needs to focus on increasing the individual's ability to fulfill his needs, generally, on strengthening his survival behavior.

Clinical work with suicidal patients, people whose involvement with life and its adaptive imperative has become so weak and tenuous as to be severed, clearly shows the existence of inherent adaptive structures—biological behaviors designed for self-preservation and survival. Konrad Lorenz referred to these biobehavioral strata as ethological behavior. Clinical experience verifies that people whose survival responses are muted or weak are more prone to depression than persons whose adaptive behavior is intact. Clinical work also shows that socialization and cultural conditioning tend to submerge and suppress these biological adaptive capabilities with layers of learned, socially acquired forms of behavior. Careful, successive removal of these formations of culturally conditioned thinking, feeling and behavior eventually reveals a core of adaptive, biological behavior of unmistakable vitality and power. Successful psychotherapy of people with suicidal intent reconnects the individual with his life force. It reactivates his biological survival behavior and reestablishes his ability to fulfill his needs.

Adaptive and traditional therapy view depression quite differently. Both forms of psychotherapy start out from different premises and end up with different objectives and outcomes. Conventional psychotherapy deals with the person's conditioned psychology of learned and socially acquired ways of functioning, which is generally controlled by the neocortex, mainly the left cerebral hemisphere. Traditional therapy understands depression as an intra-psychic process, defining it as a mood disorder with concomitant cognitive, emotional, behavioral, and physiological symptoms that range anywhere from diminished pleasure, lethargy, psychomotor retardation to listlessness and insomnia[2]. Depression is seen as a reaction to personal tragedy or unfavorable events and conditions, affecting reduced psychosocial functioning and emotional imbalance. There is also consensus about the debilitating nature of depression, which potentially may affect familial, social, and occupational functioning. Disability and distress may last from a few days up to several months or years.

The treatment goals, as defined by traditional psychotherapy, call for symptom removal and mood reversal. The clinical focus is on mood changes, concomitant symptomatology, and on various treatment modalities. Issues regarding the etiology or epidemiology of depression, however, receive little attention. This includes questions such as why some people tend to be affected by depression while others are not, why some individuals react to life status changes like death, divorce, financial loss, mobility, etc. with depression rather than with grief or bereavement.

Adaptive therapy, on the other hand, involves the evolutionary psyche, the neurological center of ethological behavior and archetypal functioning, controlled by the subcortical structures of the midbrain. Ethological behavior equates to survival behavior, a biologically inherent adaptive capability. Adaptive therapy perceives depression as an ethological event involving the renunciation of resources and territory, a display of defeat, and subsequent withdrawal from the survival activity or event. An ethological or survival event is defined as a situation or condition where adaptive issues of a person's life are at stake. Depression is seen as a result of ineffective survival behavior and unresolved need issues. Treatment objectives aim at increasing adaptive capability, strengthening strategic positioning and survival activity, and rectifying imbalance of the individual's need structure. Adaptive therapy differs significantly from the conventional treatment of depression: depression as emotional experience (mood disorder) is a secondary issue; depression as deprivation (due to lack or loss) and imbalance in need gratification is the primary issue.

The treatment focus of adaptive therapy is the person's evolutionary psyche and the respective biological survival behavior. The objective of psychotherapy is to strengthen the individual's adaptive capability and to undo any conditioned behavior responses that may inhibit its full expression and functioning. In the case of depression, it may mean mobilization of the person's natural adaptive aggression to affect repositioning with regard to events, conditions, objectives and to facilitate the fulfillment of needs and goals. In cases, where culturally conditioned responses are resistant, certain forms of therapeutic interventions and methodologies, like ethological rehearsal, are required to activate the instinctive behavioral response.

When a person is suffering from depression as a result of divorce or separation, the death of a loved one, work or financial problems, a medical condition, i.e. actual existential events and changes of condition, then symptom removal and mood reversal do not suffice as an adequate form and outcome of treatment. The existing condition needs to be addressed on a strategic level in order to set adaptive responses in motion. Effective therapeutic intervention needs to enable the person to address the loss situation, to rectify distressed circumstances, and, if at all possible, to restore the former quality of life. Depression requires an adaptive response. Depression needs to be addressed in terms of need gratification and strategic repositioning rather than through mood alteration and symptom removal.

The adaptive and psychosocial benefits of conventional treatment usually tend to be short-lived, unless therapy establishes the notion of personal responsibility and adaptive functioning. The benefits involve a temporary relief and at the same time a false sense of hope because the underlying cause of the depression, which is the deficit of adaptive capability, remains unaddressed. This is evidenced by the fact that people experience frequent relapses even after extensive medical and psychological intervention. Conventional treatment of depression tends to return the person to the *status quo ante*, the condition that caused the depression in the first place. Effective treatment must go beyond the reactive symptomatology: it needs to address the incapacitation, the adaptive deficit, of the person, her inability to live and survive as both the cause and consequence of the affliction.

Most types of conventional psychotherapy deal with the culturally conditioned psychology of the individual, involving socialized forms of behavior, thinking and feeling. The objective of treatment is to change the impact of certain behavioral, cognitive and emotional processes on the mental status and psychosocial condition of the individual. Psychotherapy, often complemented by antidepressant medication, proceeds by modifying behavior, restructuring thought content, and verbalizing emotions. Treatment success consists of achieving the baseline of the premorbid condition by removing existing symptoms and reversing the mood alteration.

Addressing the culturally conditioned psychology of the individual is not enough. Psychotherapy needs to reach the material and symbolic levels of the evolutionary psyche. It contains the human survival capabilities as part of the individual's genetic make-up. The emphasis needs to be on adaptive rehabilitation, on a strategic rather than a symptomatic approach. Therapy must: (1) advance the individual's ability to fulfill his needs by accessing his innate adaptive psychology, (2) strengthen his positioning and

Comparative Treatment Models of Depression

	Adaptive Therapy	Traditional Psychotherapy
Focus of Psychotherapy	evolutionary psyche; evolutionary functioning	culturally conditioned psychology; cognitive functioning
Origin of Psychological System	nature/evolution	culture/socialization
Neurological/ Behavioral Stratum	midbrain, brain stem innate, biological behavior	neocortex/left brain learned, socially acquired behavior
Concept of Depression	ethological event: renunciation of resources/territory; demonstration of submission; display of defeat	intra-psychic process: mood disorder; concomitant cognitive, emotional, behavioral, physiological symptomatology
Content and Symbolism of the Illness	retreat to periphery of life; ineffective survival behavior; unresolved need issues	reaction to personal tragedy or unfavorable event/condition; reduced psycho-social functioning; emotional imbalance
Therapeutic Objectives	increase adaptive capability; strengthen survival behavior; mobilization of life force	symptom removal; mood reversal; adjustment to society
Psychological Treatment Interventions and Methodologies	ethological rehearsal; others	cognitive restructuring; others, often in combination with antidepressant medication

Table 3

functioning with regard to the environment, and (3) provide the reference for putting himself in the context of a coherent archetypal life plan. Ideally, psychotherapy fosters the individual's confidence in his/her survival capability and engenders reliance on and resolve in its use.

What has been said about depression similarly applies to anxiety. Like depression, anxiety is a culturally conditioned response. Anxiety is a learned, socially acquired feeling. Its origin is cognitive; in essence, it is a way of thinking. Fear is the primary emotion. Fear is controlled by the midbrain, the province of the evolutionary psyche. Anxiety, according to Freud, is the anticipation of frustrated or failed need gratification because of inadequate transaction with the environment[3]. Anxiety results from a lack of confidence in adaptive capability[4]. Essentially, depression stems from the experience that we don't have what we need and anxiety from the expectation that we won't have what we need. Orientation to time, present or future, is not within the realm of the evolutionary psyche, neither are depression and anxiety. The sole purpose of the genetic psyche is set on adaptation and survival. Effective elimination of anxiety or depression depends on activating the person's inherent survival ability and on restoring confidence in its effectiveness and reliability.

The Normative Foundations of Biological Behavior

Human instinct and human intuition, the most significant psychological manifestations of nature in us, have incurred a reluctant, unfavorable, at times, even hostile acknowledgment in Western culture. Most of us do not really understand what instinct and intuition are and how they work. A complex history of political suppression, religious condemnation, and scientific denial has as much as driven them into intellectual obscurity.

Instincts have genetic roots and are an undeniable fact of human nature. The instincts in animals and humans are biological behaviors related to the life and survival of the organism. Instinctual behavior originates in the subcortical structures of the human midbrain, the seat of the evolutionary psyche. The instincts constitute behavioral adaptations developed in response to environmental conditions. They are behaviors based on biology. The major instincts cover significant behavioral aspects of our relationship to the environment. The territorial instinct is aimed at the protection of property and boundary; the hierarchical instinct establishes access to resources, cast in terms of dominance and submission; the aggressive instinct fuels the impetus towards need gratification and provides the necessary energy and forcefulness to assure success; the sexual instinct pursues partnering, succession and community bonding; the xenophobic instinct, finally, addresses safety issues in our relationship to the world around us. The instincts are neither good nor bad. They are an evolutionary reality of the human psyche and the result of our collective survival experience as a species over a period of more than two million years.

Because of their enormous potency, biological evolution has fitted the instincts with certain constraints, balancing the requirements of individual survival with the demands of the group. The biology of behavior is regulated. In order to control the vital force of the instincts, biological behavior comes with ethical standards and natural inhibitions[1]. They serve to curb and curtail non-adaptive deviations of instinctual behavior. Biological behavior is normative. The teleology of biological norms lies in the preservation of the species.

Biological norms relate to specific aspects of existence and prescribe conduct. The ethics of biology center primarily on the protection of life, property and community. Foremost are (1) the norm, instituting the inhibition to kill, (2) the norm, sanctioning the possession of objects, and (3) the norm, establishing possession of the partner[2]. These inhibitions "are still present"; they "are given to us as phylogenetic adaptations"[3]. These biological norms imply a desire for peace, respect for the property of others, and regard for honesty, loyalty and obedience. These human behaviors and attitudes have biological foundations[4]. Other "basic ethical attitudes" that "are determined by phylogenetic adaptation"[5] include an innate sense of pity, a natural antidote to aggression and killing. Animals, especially higher primates, "can be both sociable and aggressive"[6]. This is true for humans: "As a social being with aggressive tendencies man, too, has to cope with the problem of controlling aggression"[7]. Like in animals, there are in man certain genetically established rites and attitudes such as greeting and bonding behaviors to maintain inter-specific harmony and cooperation[8].

Nature contains definite inhibitions against killing, stealing, and other excesses of instinctual behavior that could jeopardize the survival of the species. The instincts are life-advancing and life-preserving. Aggression, or any other instinct, is not designed to be destructive. The instincts are meant to serve the survival of the organism. The fact, that the functioning of the instincts is biologically controlled, coordinates the survival of individual and group and secures the preservation of the species. Biological ethics anticipate, of course, many of our own legal practices. In fact, most cultural norms have natural antecedents and go back to biological norms. A return to the instincts, therefore, does not imply a license for anarchy. It rather means reestablishing the normative foundations of biology and observing the inhibitions nature has installed to secure the preservation of the species through adaptive calibration of individual and collective interests.

Modern civilization has downgraded the standing of nature in man's life. Western culture, especially, has not produced the appropriate reverence to appreciate what it finds in nature. At best, Western civilization has had an ambivalent relationship to nature. Generally, it developed at the expense of nature, both as an environment and as an aspect of personality. Culture in the West, more than anything, was founded on the attempt to improve on nature. Western civilization set out to shape the human being as a purely cultural creation devoid of behavioral biology and the animal ancestry of the species. Moreover, as reflected in our language, it has consistently demonized human nature as brute, base, and bad.

In fact, we reserve terms like 'bestial' or 'animalistic' to denote our deepest contempt for the worst forms of deviant behavior.

Stigmatizing them as aberrant and destructive, Western civilization did not take well to the human instincts. Ever since the inception of human culture, people have been instructed to distance themselves from the natural history of the species and from their evolutionary heritage. Politically, the human instincts have always been an irritant to any form of social organization that intends to establish obedience and to control human behavior. The instincts endow the human being with powers that enable self-reliance and autonomy. The repression of the human instincts despite their importance for the survival and self-preservation of individual and species has stamped enduring repercussions on the human condition.

Western civilization has established its own reality and initiated its own history. The gap between culture and nature is enormous and the rejection of biological evolution is complete. Cultural norms have replaced biological norms. A socialized morality has taken the place of the inherent ethics of human nature. The normative bases have shifted. Yet, the evidence does not show that cultural morality or a socialized conscience can contain human aggression any more successfully than the natural inhibitions and norms of the instincts. Moreover, moral development in the modern age has sidestepped significant biological imperatives and engaged in a fateful tour de force. The human intellect has penetrated the province of the instincts. Exploiting the unfettered force of instinctual aggression, the intellect has invented and executed more cruelty and brutality than natural aggression is ever capable of. In fact, civilized human history is predominantly a history of wars, devastations, tortures and cruelties instigated by the human intellect—not by human nature. This brings up the poignant question whether 'primitive man' really ever was as violent and cruel as civilization would have us believe—or has 'civilized man' himself assumed this dubious distinction?

Cultural man has subverted the human instincts, interfering with their biological norms and inhibitions, by joining them with the human intellect. This fateful combination of intellect and instinct has shaped modern human history. It unleashed an enormous natural force without the proper constraints. The intellect was used (1) to overturn the natural killing inhibition through indoctrination to bestialize the enemy, turning him into an object that deserves to be killed, (2) to design ever more sophisticated forms of killing, torture and cruelty, as in the schematism of the Inquisition or the designs of modern warfare, and (3) to create distance weapons, whose use ejects the biological inhibitions and turns killing into an anonymous act[9]. In effect, cultural man has brutalized human nature. As "a result of an inadequate co-ordination between two areas of the brain—the 'rational' neocortex and the 'instinctual' hypothalamus—Man had somehow acquired the 'unique, murderous, delusional streak' that propelled him, inevitably, to murder, to torture and to war"[10].

Culture has removed all remnants of human nature from its rationale, replacing nature's ethics and influence on man. Thus, instead of natural norms and inhibitions, we are left with a socialized morality that constantly requires either priest or police. But "we are equipped with aggression-inhibitions, even vis-à-vis strangers, provided we do not erect barriers which prevent contact and do not employ weapons that so distance us from the enemy that we cannot take account of his human reactions"[11]. Biological ethics are reliable, and they function and endure unless we interfere with them: "Of the factors mentioned that enable man to overcome his innate inhibitions, I consider his capacity for mentally dehumanizing his fellow-men to be the most dangerous. In the last analysis it is this capacity to switch off pity that makes him into a cold-blooded murderer. It is with this in mind that Lorenz, too, has pointed out that the purely reasonable man of the future, predicted in the rationalists' utopias, who pays no attention to his inner voices, would certainly be no angel but much more likely the opposite"[12].

The rehabilitation of the instincts as an integral part of the human psychology is of fundamental importance to human survival. This includes respecting the natural inhibitions of instinctual behavior and the biological norms that reinforce them. Underlying is a full appreciation of the nature of our being as a biological animal and as a creature of higher consciousness and advanced morality—linking natural and cultural evolutions as the unique achievement of our species.

Glossary Of Terms

Adaptation: the process allowing organisms to become better suited for survival and reproduction in their given environment. Adaptation involves the formation or alteration of features and abilities in response to environmental conditions to optimize survival. Generally, adaptation is a biological process of maximizing the fit between the organism and its environment. Effective adaptation equates to increased survival prospects for the organism.

Adaptive: conducive to survival.

Archetypes: adaptive components of the human psyche. The archetypes are universal genetic structures comparable to the genetic code in the seed of a plant. They control significant behavioral expressions and experiences of life characteristic of the species, including the sequence and occurrences of the human life cycle.

Ethology: the study of animal behavior in the natural environment from the evolutionary perspective. Within the last few decades, ethology has been extended to look at biological behaviors in humans.

Ethological behavior: biological survival behavior in response to environmental conditions.

Ethological event: survival situation related to need gratification. Frequently, social situations function as ethological events.

Evolutionary functioning: innate survival psychology originating in the human psyche. It involves inherent behavioral, attitudinal, affective and psychic capabilities of human functioning.

Human nature: the evolutionary intelligence inherent in humans as the result of the collective survival experience of the species. Human nature evolved through evolutionary adaptation. It contains the biological intelligence of life.

Ontogeny: individual development and adaptation following the pattern of the species (phylogeny).

Phylogeny: evolutionary development of species-specific patterns. Jung introduced the concept of phylogeny (phylogenesis) into psychology to suggest that evolutionary development and biological inheritance do not only apply to physical, anatomical features but equally to psyche and archetypes.

Survival: the biological imperative to sustain the life and well-being of the organism. Survival is the governing principle that determines the structure and functioning of all forms of life.

Notebook
Of Evolutionary Functioning

Evolutionary intelligence is the stronger of the two psychologies we have. When evolutionary functioning is intact, people tend to live strong, healthy lives.

Like all living organisms and forms of life, we possess an innate survival capacity. The human psyche contains the collective wisdom of our species, the basic bio-program enabling us to meet the essential demands of life. C. G. Jung

Both our body and our psyche are a product of evolution. The psyche was molded and shaped much the same way as were our physical features. As it turns out, the human psyche is the sum total of our collective survival experience as a species.

Our distant ancestors forged the brain we have today. Over two million years or 99% of human history went into its formation. It was then when our survival experience was founded and our basic anatomy, behavior and psychology were formed. The exposure to a harsh, unforgiving world in an unrelenting struggle for survival required effective responses to the environment. This is how we acquired our instincts—behaviors based on biology. They developed to secure protection and the gratification of basic needs.

Evolutionary adaptation has furnished the human psyche with the biological intelligence of life. Although mostly unconscious, our natural powers of survival are comparable to those of the animal. Evolution is the most rigorous test of reality. What passes that inspection can survive in the real world.

Nature has given us its own psychology. Seat of this psychology is the evolutionary psyche. This innate psychology provides two things: one, the survival behavior to satisfy our basic needs and, two, the mental *ability to cope with the difficulties and tragedies of life. Jung called these bipolar structures of behavioral and mental adaptation the archetypes of the human psyche.*

Survival is the ultimate mandate of the organism. At the very bottom, survival is an instinctual response. Whenever our life and survival are at stake, this ancient psychology goes to work. The evolution of the human psyche produced a psychology that enables self-reliance and self-sufficiency.

Ours is an evolution from biology to consciousness. Our innate survival psychology comes from the evolutionary intelligence of instinct and spirit—the two aspects of the archetypes.

Most people rely on their intellect to get them through life and depend on it for everything they do, think and feel. Survivors live life differently. Survivors rely foremost on the biological intelligence inherent in human nature. They keep the intellect on standby, limiting it to the interface with modern life. In the larger scheme of things, survivors live in a world of different dimensions. They place their life in the larger context of natural and cosmic realities. Their perspective on things keeps them close to biology and metaphysics—the ultimate frontiers of human survival.

Much of human life and behavior makes it clear "that we are innately territorial, inclined to mate for life, potentially co-operative with allies and hostile to foes, prone to congregate in hierarchically organized communities, and so on, much in the same way as many other mammalian and primate species". A. Stevens

Society is the human version of the biological model found in nature. The organization of society is an extension of our biological behavior. Evolutionary conditions are the ultimate reality that determines and shapes the events of human life. As a survival environment, society has a definite biological quality, requiring evolutionary functioning to satisfy our needs. The world of society and culture is a world of our own making—forged by the intellect. It is an invented reality.

The frontier of survival has shifted from the wilderness of bush and savannah to the offices and factories of urban existence. The original hunter had to be smarter than the animal; the modern survivor needs to be smarter than society.

The animal that fails in the competition for food, shelter and mate demonstrates defeat by showing signs of deference and submission. It withdraws from the group to the periphery of life. This is the basis for depression.

People who survive successfully do several things well. Survivors succeed because they take full advantage of their innate survival psychology, understand the world they live in, treat survival as a strategic undertaking, see their life as part of a larger process, and turn survival into a personal evolution.

The hero's journey is the evolutionary journey. There are many ways to do this—the hero has 'a thousand faces'.

For it to reveal its full depth, significance and beauty, life must be seen in its eternal aspect. L. Wittgenstein

* * *

NOTES

Note: Books that appear in the Selected Bibliography are quoted without the usual reference data once they have been cited.

PART I

(1) C. G. Jung, *Psychological Reflections*, J. Jacobi, ed., Routledge & Kegan Paul, London, 1971, p. 76.
(2) See Chief Seattle's letter to the President of the United States in about1852 in response to the inquiry of the United States Government about buying tribal lands from the Indians. Chief Seattle "was one of the last spokesmen of the Paleolithic moral order". From: J. Campbell with B. Moyers, *The Power of Myth*, Doubleday, New York, 1988, pp. 32, 34.
(3) Organic food now needs USFDA approval.

DISCOVERING HUMAN NATURE

(1) The term 'survival' is used throughout this book in its biological sense as the adaptation of the organism to the environment. 'Survival' is defined as effective adaptation to life.
(2) See Hans Seyle's research on health, stress and adaptation. Seyle views life and survival as the continuous adaptation to the changing conditions of the environment. H. Seyle, *The Stress of Life*, McGraw Hill, New York, 1955; H. Seyle, *Stress Without Distress*, Lippincott, New York, 1974; H. Seyle, *The Physiology and Pathology of Exposure to Stress*, Acta, Montreal, 1950.

The Essence of Human Nature

(1) See: A. Stevens, *Archetype: A Natural History of the Self*, Routledge & Kegan Paul, London and Henley, 1982, p. 34; for a more detailed discussion of C. G. Jung's view on human nature and the evolution of the human psyche, see: A. Stevens, *Archetype*, pp. 29-61.

Our Natural Psychology

(1) A. Stevens, *Archetype*, p. 231.

The Natural History of Our Species

(1) See: A. Stevens, *Archetype*, p. 23. Stevens refers to Charles Darwin's fundamental conclusion "that the guiding principle governing the structure and function of all living organisms is, quite simply, the survival of the species".

(2) W. S. Laughlin, Hunting: *An Integrating Biobehavior System and Its Evolutionary Importance*, in: R. B. Lee and I. DeVore, eds., *Man the Hunter*, Aldine Publishing Company, New York, 1982, p. 304. "Man evolved as a hunter; he spent over 99 per cent of his species' history as a hunter; and he spread over the entire habitable area of the world as a hunter." (From a statement attributed to W. S. Laughlin, from: L. Binford, I. DeVore, et al., *Primate Behavior and the Evolution of Aggression*, in: R. B. Lee and I. DeVore, eds., *Man the Hunter*, p. 341.) Hunting as a form of behavior has never left man, not even in modern civilization. But it no longer serves survival. Instead, hunting tends to show up in a variety of unrelated circumstances. Whenever instinctive behavior is not aimed at its organic intent, it tends to release itself into substitute activities (K. Lorenz, *Das Wirkungsgefuege der Natur und das Schicksal des Menschen*, Piper Verlag, Munich/Zurich, 1983, p. 193). So, a dog, prevented from hunting, will satisfy his prey-seeking behavior by chasing his master's slipper. Likewise, men chase after a ball in a sport stadium or engage in similar activities. On the somber side, man's hunting heritage comes through as a penchant for killing in the form of sport, crime and war. See:

S. L. Washburn and C. S. Lancaster, *The Evolution of Hunting*, in: R. B. Lee and I. DeVore, eds., *Man the Hunter*, Aldine Publishing Company, New York, 1982, p. 299.

(3) W. S. Laughlin, *An Integrating Biobehavior System and Its Evolutionary Importance*, in: R. B. Lee and I. DeVore, eds., *Man the Hunter*, p. 304.

(4) S. L. Washburn and C. S. Lancaster, *The Evolution of Hunting*, in: R. B. Lee and I. DeVore, eds., *Man the Hunter*, p. 299.

(5) A. Stevens, *Archetype*, p. 231.

(6) A. Stevens, *Archetype*, p. 7.

(7) A. Stevens, *Archetype*, p. 52.

The Natural Foundations of Human Life

(1) C. G. Jung, *The Collected Works 9, Part I*, Routledge & Kegan Paul, London, 1968, para. 99.

(2) Different regions of the human brain correspond to various stages of evolutionary development, suggesting a connection with other forms of life on this planet. The brain stem, the oldest formation of the human brain, equates to the reptilian brain; we share it with all vertebrates. The mammalian brain makes up the midsection of the human brain; we share it with all other mammals. Finally, we share the most recent evolutionary formation of the human brain, the neomammalian part, with higher mammals and primates.

(3) The unalterable structure of the human psyche owes its "existence exclusively to heredity". From: C. G. Jung, *Collected Works 9, Part I*, para. 88.

(4) C. G. Jung, *The Collected Works 11*, Routledge & Kegan Paul, London, 1968, para. 146.

(5) Archetypes are the essential matrix of human experience and basic to all the "typical situations in life". See: C. G. Jung, *Collected Works 9, Part I*, para. 99. Archetypes are, so Jung, 'active living dispositions' with "the capacity to initiate, control and mediate the common behavioural characteristics and typical experiences of our kind, even though we are, for the most part, unaware of them. As the basis of all the usual phenomena of life, the archetypes transcend culture, race and time". From: A. Stevens, *Archetype*, p. 39.

(6) C. G. Jung, *The Collected Work 18*, Routledge & Kegan Paul, London, 1953-78, para. 1228.
(7) E. W. Sinnott, *Biology of the Spirit*, Viking Press, New York, 1955, p. 26; quoted in: A. Stevens, *Archetype*, p. 53.
(8) See: A. Stevens, *Jung*, Oxford University Press, Oxford and New York, 1996, p. 44.
(9) A. Stevens, *Archetype*, p. 60. Jung suggested that the archetypes are "the neuropsychic centers responsible for co-ordinating the behavioural and psychic repertoires of our species in response to whatever environmental circumstances we may encounter". From: A. Stevens, *Archetype*, p. 17.
(10) A. Stevens, *Archetype*, p. 34.
(11) A. Stevens, *Archetype*, p. 62.
(12) See: A. Stevens, *Archetype*, p. 62.
(13) See: A. Stevens, *Archetype*, p. 62.
(14) A. Stevens, *Archetype*, p. 61.
(15) The collective unconscious of our species contains archaic and primordial contents, eternal or "universal images that have existed since the remotest time" (C. G. Jung, *Collected Works 9, Part I*, para. 5). The collective representations of these themes and images are the universal myths of mankind. The source of mythic form is the human psyche. Myths, fairytales, and fables concretize the archetypes. They hold the collective wisdom of the community and culture.
(16) C. G. Jung, *Collected Works 9, Part I*, para. 7.
(17) A. Stevens, *Archetype*, p. 62. That is to say, "viewed from the strictly biological standpoint, the archetype is an ancient, genetically determined releaser or inhibiter. From the purely psychological point of view it is, of course, a good deal more than that, since the survival of the species, and the life of each member of the species, depends upon our capacity to 'know' situations, to recognize the essence of what we may find ourselves up against, and our ability to select from a vast repertoire of possible responses the behaviour and strategy most suited to the problem in hand". From: A. Stevens, *Archetype*, p. 54.
(18) Survival scenarios are subjective interpretations of the environment and how it relates to our survival. Also, see Chapter 7, Survival Scenarios, pp. 211-17.

(19) As so ably demonstrated in the works of C. G. Jung, Joseph Campbell and others. See, for instance: C. G. Jung, *Man and His Symbols*, Doubleday & Company, Garden City, New York, 1979; J. Campbell, *The Hero With a Thousand Faces*, Princeton University Press, Princeton, New Jersey, 1973; J. Campbell, *Myths to Live By*, Bantam Books, New York, 1980; J. Campbell with B. Moyers, *The Power of Myth*, Doubleday, New York, 1988.

(20) A. Stevens, *Jung*, Oxford University Press, Oxford/New York, 1996, p. 44.

(21) A. Stevens, *Jung*, p. 47.

The Effects of Human Civilization

(1) A. Stevens, *Archetype*, p. 278.

The Ethics of Biology

(1) See: I. Eibl-Eibesfeldt, *Die Biologie des menschlichen Verhaltens: Grundriss der Humanethologie*, Piper Verlag, Munich, 1986, pp. 863-83; I. Eibl-Eibesfeldt, *Love and Hate: The Natural History of Behavior Patterns*, Aldine de Gruyter, New York, 1996, pp. 90-105; also see pp. 107-28 and pp. 129-69 for a detailed discussion of natural inhibitions.

(2) I. Eibl-Eibesfeldt, *Love and Hate*, pp. 102-5.

(3) Quoted in: B. Chatwin, *The Songlines*, Elisabeth Sifton Books, Viking Penguin Inc., New York, 1987, p. 211.

(4) The adaptive function of the instincts is remarkably resistant to modification. It takes extraordinary measures to corrupt the instinct and to convert its adaptive qualities into destructive deviance. But it can be done: "Among the military fraternities of Ancient Germany a young man, as part of his training to stifle inhibitions against killing, was required to strip naked; to dress himself in the hot, freshly flayed skin of a bear; to work himself into a 'bestial' rage: in other words, to go, quite literally, berserk. 'Bearskin' and 'berserk' are the same word. The helmets of the Royal Guards, on duty outside Buckingham Palace, are the descendants of this primitive battle costume." From: B. Chatwin, *Songlines*, p. 217.

The Biological Reality of Life

(1) A. Stevens, *Archetype*, p. 40.
(2) See: K. Lorenz, *Beitraege zur Ethologie sozialer Corviden*, Jahrbuch der Ornithologie, Vol. 79, 1931, pp. 67-127; K. Lorenz, *Er redete mit dem Vieh, den Voegeln und den Fischen*, Borotha-Schoeler, Wien, 1949; K. Lorenz, *Man Meets Dog*, New York and London, 1954.
(3) See: I. Eibl-Eibesfeldt, *Grundriss der vergleichenden Verhaltensforschung: Ethologie*, Piper Verlag, Munich/Zurich, 1987; I. Eibl-Eibesfeldt, *Der vorprogrammierte Mensch: Das Ererbte als bestimmender Faktor im menschlichen Verhalten*, Deutscher Taschenbuch Verlag, Munich, 1976.

EVOLUTIONARY FUNCTIONING

(1) D. Attenborough, *Life on Earth: A Natural History*, Little, Brown and Company, Boston, Toronto, 1980, p. 294.
(2) D. Attenborough, *Life on Earth*, p. 294.
(3) D. Attenborough, *Life on Earth*, p. 295.
(4) D. Attenborough, *Life on Earth*, p. 294.
(5) D. Attenborough, *Life on Earth*, p. 295.
(6) D. Attenborough, *Life on Earth*, p. 300.
(7) D. Attenborough, *Life on Earth*, p. 299.
(8) D. Attenborough, *Life on Earth*, p. 305.
(9) D. Attenborough, *Life on Earth*, p. 304-5.
(10) D. Attenborough, *Life on Earth*, p. 302.
(11) D. Attenborough, *Life on Earth*, p. 307.
(12) D. Attenborough, *Life on Earth*, p. 293.
(13) D. Attenborough, *Life on Earth*, p. 307.
(14) A. Stevens, Archetype, p. 265.

Ethological Behavior

(1) A. Stevens, *Archetype*, p. 17, referring to K. Lorenz's concept.
(2) See: A. Stevens, *Archetype*, p. 17.
(3) A. Stevens, *Archetype*, p. 231.
(4) I. Eibl-Eibesfeldt, *Die Biologie des menschlichen Verhaltens*, pp. 212-536;

I. Eibl-Eibesfeldt, *Grundriss der vergleichenden Verhaltensforschung*, pp. 449-621; A. Stevens, *Archetype*, pp. 224-33. Despite the scientific evidence to the contrary, popular opinion has traditionally argued against the existence of human instincts. However, this has never been the real issue. It does not matter what we *are* but what we *do*. "What matters, after all, is not that we are aggressive, xenophobic, sexual, hierarchical and territorial but what *attitude* we adopt to these fundamental *a priori* aspects of our nature—how we live them, and how we mediate them to the group. It is the ethical orientation that counts." From: A. Stevens, *Archetype*, p. 240.

(5) W. S. Laughlin, *Hunting: An Integrating Biobehavior System and Its Evolutionary Importance*, in: R. B. Lee and I. DeVore, eds., *Man the Hunter*, Aldine Publishing Company, New York, 1982, p. 304.

(6) A. Stevens, *Archetype*, p. 132.

(7) A. Stevens, *Archetype*, p. 154.

(8) A. Stevens, *Archetype*, p. 229.

(9) See: A. Stevens, *Archetype*, p. 185.

(10) See: A. Stevens, *Archetype*, p. 231.

(11) See: I. Eibl-Eibesfeldt, *Love and Hate*, pp. 72-89.

(12) See: D. M. Buss, *The Evolution of Desire: Strategies of Human Mating*, Basic Books, A Subsidiary of Perseus Books, L.L.C., New York, 1994; J. Clark, *What the Hell Do Women Really Want*, Island Flower Books, San Francisco, 1997.

(13) Also see: D. M. Buss, *The Evolution of Desire*. Failure to understand the ethological significance of human sexuality frequently results in dysfunctional approaches to sexuality, including the repression of sexuality. Judging from the widespread sale of drugs to address the condition, erectile dysfunction has seemingly reached alarming proportions in Western societies. Modern potency medications are a sad commentary on modern civilization and what we have done to the human body and the nature of our instincts. We have now come to a place, for whatever reasons, where we have to support and prop up the strongest drive nature has given us.

(14) See: K. Lorenz, *Das Wirkungsgefuege*, p. 304.

(15) I. Eibl-Eibesfeldt, *Love and Hate*, pp. 106-167.

(16) I. Eibl-Eibesfeldt, *Love and Hate*, pp. 90-105.

(17) A. Stevens, *Archetype*, p. 227.

(18) A. Stevens, *Archetype*, p. 226.
(19) R. Ardrey, *The Social Contract: A Personal Inquiry into the Evolutionary Sources of Order and Disorder*, Collins, London, 1970, p. 259. Quoted in: A. Stevens, *Archetype*, p. 227.
(20) R. Ardrey, *Social Contract*, p. 259.
(21) A. Stevens, *Archetype*, p. 227.
(22) A. Stevens, *Archetype*, p. 226.
(23) A. Stevens, *Archetype*, p. 234. For a more detailed discussion on human aggression, see: I. Eibl-Eibesfeldt, *Love and Hate*, pp. 63-89.
(24) A. Stevens, *Archetype*, p. 240.
(25) I. Eibl-Eibesfeldt, *Love and Hate*, pp. 98-102; also see: A. Plack, *Die Gesellschaft und das Boese*, Paul List Verlag, Munich, 1968. "The problem of man is not that we are aggressive but that we break the rules", from: R. Ardrey, *Social Contract*, p. 259, quoted in: A. Stevens, *Archetype*, p. 227.
(26) A. Stevens, *Archetype*, p. 240. Most people had experiences when they trusted and found themselves betrayed; given a lot and had it blown in their face; paid too high a price and came out with nothing; loved too much and saw it all destroyed. Many had experiences of being intimidated, insulted or attacked; mislead, deceived and taken advantage of; abused or violated. All these are lessons in reality, often expensive and very costly in many respects. The lesson that needs to be understood and relearned is twofold. The first part rests on the acknowledgement that life is ultimately about survival. Human transactions are primarily directed at gaining selective advantage. The evolutionary intent preempts cultural training and individual psychology. Secondly, the issue, therefore, is not to mistrust people but to appreciate human nature. "All of us behave like the prey we are after. That, of course, also makes us prey for something or someone else. Now, the concern of a hunter, who knows all this, is to stop being a prey himself." (C. Castaneda, *Journey to Ixtlan*, A Touchstone Book, Simon and Schuster, New York, 1972, p. 101.) Ceasing to be a victim begins with an acceptance of human nature. This means we accept that we are fundamentally "aggressive, xenophobic, sexual, hierarchical and territorial" (A. Stevens, *Archetype*, p. 240), and we abandon the illusion that expects anything else. (Only the evolution of higher consciousness can transform the quality of human interaction, not cultural conditioning or a socialized morality.)

(27) See: A. Stevens, *Archetype*, p. 102.
(28) The patterns of human perception "like many of our patterns of behaviour have been programmed by evolutionary pressures" (A. Stevens, *Archetype*, p. 55). In other words, "we, like all other animals, perceive only what we have been equipped to perceive". From: A. Stevens, *Archetype*, p. 54.
(29) K. Lorenz, *Behind the Mirror: A Search for the Natural History of Human Knowledge*, Methuen, London, 1977, p. 28.
(30) See: N. Tinbergen, *The Study of Instinct*, Oxford University Press, London, 1951.
(31) A. Stevens, *Archetype*, p. 101.
(32) A. Stevens, *Archetype*, p. 102.
(33) A. Stevens, *Archetype*, p. 102.
(34) J. Bowlby, *Attachment and Loss, Volume I: Attachment*, Hogarth Press and the Institute of Psycho-Analysis, London, 1969; quoted in: A. Stevens, *Archetype*, p. 49.
(35) J. Bowlby, *Attachment and Loss, Volume I: Attachment*, p. 45; quoted in: A. Stevens, *Archetype*, p. 50.
(36) See: E. Mayr in: A. Stevens, *Archetype*, p. 51.
(37) See: A. Stevens, *Archetype*, p. 51.
(38) This refers to the issue that both evolutionary and right-hemispheric functioning are subject to "the surveillance and control of the *left* frontal cortex". From: A. Stevens, *Archetype*, p. 265.

Biological Imperatives and Attitudes

(1) This instruction is unmistakable. It is reinforced by the evidence of distress, disease, even death. Nature is actually quite relentless with its creatures. After only a short period of nurturing, it confronts the upcoming offspring with the unforgiving ultimatum to either 'fly' or 'die', forcing the young animal to take the jump into reality and self-sufficiency. Those, who fail, fall prey to other animals or to the traps and weapons of man. Although faced with the same basic reality, we have never come clear with these issues, which so definitely affect the life and welfare of the individual.
(2) Nature does not support what is not fit to survive. It weeds out weakness to secure the health and viability of the species. Nature, which is always more in line with life than culture, terminates all prospects of continued

dependency beyond the point of biological necessity. Nature exhibits a definite relentlessness about its premises for life and survival, which our species often fails to perceive. It teaches us to take our cues from the reality of life as biology presents it to us. In that world adaptation and survival dictate the parameters of life. Nature prescribes self-sufficiency; it does not tolerate 'bandaged eagles'. Modern society, on the other hand, has for all practical purposes quasi-institutionalized dependency through its institutions and way of life. We have not replicated the evolutionary principles of life in the social fabric of our values and norms. Modern society has set up an intricate system of dependence and dependency, which makes it increasingly difficult to attain self-reliance and autonomy. (Examples include: the transition from domestic self-sufficiency to industrial employment, adolescence as an institutionalized form of delayed maturity, a generalized condition of heteronomy.) This marks a significant departure from the natural foundations of life. While nature emphasizes adaptive capability and skills, culture promotes dependency under the guise of development. We have replaced the biological imperative of self-reliance with various forms of institutionalized dependency quite contrary to the designs and demands of nature. In fact, as a society, we have never come clear with the issue of dependency and for that matter have fudged the quality and significance of human survival often to the detriment of the individual.

Biological Values

(1) A. Stevens, *Jung*, Oxford University Press, New York/Oxford, 1996, p. 44.
(2) C. G. Jung, *The Collected Works 11*, Routledge & Kegan Paul, London, 1968, para. 146.
(3) This means "to actualize the archetypal potential already present in the psycho-physical organism . . . in a manner similar to that by which a photographer, through the addition of chemicals and the use of skill, brings out the image impregnated in a photographic plate". From: A. Stevens, *Archetype*, p. 16.
(4) E. W. Sinnott, *Biology of the Spirit*, Viking Press, New York, 1955, p. 26; quoted in: A. Stevens, *Archetype*, p. 53.
(5) See: J. Campbell, *Way of The Animal Powers, Part 1 of 2, Mythologies of the Great Hunt (Historical Atlas of World Mythology)*, HarperCollins, New

York, 1988, P. XII.
(6) C. G. Jung, *Collected Works 9, Part I*, para. 88.
(7) See: A. Stevens, *Archetype*, p. 17.

Primary Sensations and Emotions

(1) See: A. Siebert, *The Survivor Personality*, Northwest Magazine, 1/1980.

Psychic Function

(1) The fact that key human events are subject to outside rule defines the context of human life. It turns the world into a chessboard: "the pieces are the phenomena of the universe; the rules of the game are what we call the laws of Nature. The player on the other side is hidden from us. We know that his play is always fair, just and patient. But also we know, to our cost, that he never overlooks a mistake, or makes the slightest allowance for ignorance" (see: T. H. Huxley, *Lay Sermons, Addresses, and Reviews*, Appleton & Company, New York, 1895). Modern physics perceives the cosmos "as one inseparable reality—for ever in motion, alive, organic; spiritual and material at the same time". All the things we can see or touch "are but different aspects or manifestations of the same ultimate reality". From: F. Capra, *The Tao of Physics*, Fontana Paperbacks, London/Oxford, 1984, p.29.

(2) Poets and mental patients provide an instructive account of human life in the absence of such an adaptive mental system: without a functional survival concept, life seems more stark, the ambivalences and horrors of life more visible. There is diminished motivation to accomplish the biological tasks of life; existence runs on minimum energy. There is a sense of indifference, an almost surrealistic perception of life outside the frame; there is the sense that eventually everyone walks into the ocean alone and disappears into oblivion; there is little consolation to be found in anything. Everything seems unreal, a cruel fraud, a scene of horror in nature and among people, with God nowhere in sight.

(3) C. G. Jung, *The Undiscovered Self*, Routledge & Kegan Paul, London, 1982, p. 28.

(4) C. G. Jung, *The Undiscovered Self*, p. 26.

ADVANCED ADAPTIVE FUNCTIONING

(1) Also see Chapter 2, pp. 56-57, for a description of brain functioning.

The Evolution of Higher Consciousness

(1) B. B. Tregoe and J. W. Zimmerman, *Top Management Strategy: What It Is and How to Make It Work*, Simon and Schuster, New York, 1980, pp. 103-5.
(2) See: A. Stevens, *Archetype*, pp. 251, 255-6.
(3) See: A. Stevens, *Archetype*, p. 265.
(4) See research by P. MacLean and J. P. Henry, discussed in: A. Stevens, *Archetype*, p. 264.
(5) See: A. Stevens, *Archetype*, p. 254. For a more detailed discussion of these issues, see Appendix/The Neurology of Human Survival, pp. 301-07.
(6) See: B. B. Tregoe and J. W. Zimmerman, *Top Management Strategy*, pp. 103-5.
(7) See: A. Stevens, *Archetype*, p. 265.
(8) R. Wilhelm (trans.) and C. G. Jung, *The Secret of the Golden Flower: A Chinese Book of Life*, Harcourt Brace Jovanovich Publishers, New York, 1962, p. 11.

The Evolution of Advanced Morality

(1) See Chapter 1, The Ethics of Biology, pp. 46-47.
(2) See: I. Eibl-Eibesfeldt, *Die Biologie des Menschlichen Verhaltens*, pp. 863-83; I. Eibl-Eibesfeldt, *Love and Hate*, pp. 90-105.
(3) See: A. Stevens, *Archetype*, p. 256.
(4) See: C. G. Jung, *Man and his Symbols*, Doubleday & Company, Garden City, New Jersey, 1979; J. Campbell, *Myths to Live By*, Bantam Books, New York, 1980; J. Campbell, *The Hero With a Thousand Faces*, Princeton University Press, Princeton, New Jersey, 1973; J. Campbell with B. Moyers, *The Power of Myth*, Doubleday, New York, 1988.
(5) See: C. G. Jung, *Collected Works 11*, para. 146.

PART II

(1) C. G. Jung, *Collected Works 13*, para. 2.
(2) A. Stevens, *Archetype*, p. 38.

BEHAVIORAL ADAPTATION

Operating Life As a Business

(1) Once we engage and identify with the scenario of the industrial life cycle, several things happen. First and foremost, we hand over the control of our survival to the goodwill and judgment of others. At the same time, we become vulnerable to the vagaries of firings, obsolescence, or industrial layoffs. Wanting to succeed in this system, the individual feels compelled to adopt the achievement expectations of the industrial world. He, thereby, takes on a *functional identity*, a one-sided self-image, based on productivity, efficiency and usefulness. The individual begins to perceive and understand himself in terms of society. This assumed identity streamlines the self-definition of the individual. It shapes the individual's values, aspirations, lifestyle, interests and sense of self-worth. A functional identity involves a diminution of personal identity and autonomy. It is a one-dimensional self-concept stipulated by the outside world, consistently attuned to the expectations of the environment. Taking on a functional identity has profound and lasting effects. It creates a lifelong preoccupation with external requirements, demands and prescriptions. A functional identity already affects the young person as he prepares for adult life through schooling, goal-setting, and career planning. Adulthood, the main productive and commercial period in a person's life, is more or less summarily defined by it. The effects of a functional self-definition, however, even tarnish the later years. This kind of identity rears its head upon retirement, when suddenly, after being dismissed from active work life and no longer commercially useful, the person feels unproductive and disposable. It is extremely difficult to restore a sense of solid and stable identity after it has been broken or frozen in stagnation. Hobbies and travel rarely can fend off the depression, which is likely to set in after retirement. The industrial life cycle reflects society's view of life. It favors

adulthood, the productive years, and discredits old age, turning its generation into a marginal group on the outskirts of life. Lacking social respect and integration into the mainstream, aging becomes a difficult period of life. The industrial life cycle arbitrarily shortens the active and productive life span of the individual, setting up retirement as an endpoint where everything stops. And frequently it does. The notion of retirement as a final destination with nowhere else to go or as a threshold into a lonely, forgotten existence has deep psychological effects. Along with the actual wear and tear of industrial life and employment, it often lowers a person's life expectancy. Apprehension about retirement and fearing dismissal, in turn, frequently cause a backup condition as early as midlife— the panic of 'running out of time', followed by a romantic return to youthful endeavors. In effect, the industrial-economic cycle of production and consumption, which tends to absorb our lives, has totally altered the human condition. It has changed the nature of human survival and altogether life itself. It has thrown off the natural life cycle, the linear progression of developmental stages from childhood to old age. See also Chapter 7, pp. 170-74.

(2) See also: H. Browne, *How I Found Freedom in an Unfree World*, Macmillan Publishing Company, New York, 1973, pp. 236-46.

(3) Mainly doubt and anxiety, which commonly present as negative self-talk ("Can I do it?", "Am I good enough?") and/or social phobia. Also see Chapter 2, Primary Sensations and Emotions, pp. 76-78.

(4) Cultural conditioning is designed to repress ethological processes and to replace instinctive behavior with cognitive functioning. The adaptive objective is to reverse the process, to activate evolutionary functioning, and to overturn our socialized psychology for survival to be successful. Adaptive, transactional aggression is essential to successful survival. It counteracts anxiety and promotes self-preservation. Generally, material survival and effective economic adaptation highlight the pivotal adaptive dichotomy between the active pursuit of need gratification and its renunciation through withdrawal, between aggression and depression. The aggression is about life and is directed at adaptation and survival, not toward people or environment. It is adaptive aggression in the truest sense in that it promotes the survival of the individual and, at the same time,

follows the biological norms that inhibit excessive or destructive deviation of the instinct. Also see Chapter 1, The Biological Reality of Life, pp. 48-53.
(5) I. Eibl-Eibesfeldt, *Welt am Sonntag*, July 13, 1980, p. 25.
(6) B. B. Tregoe and J. W. Zimmerman, *Top Management Strategy: What It Is and How to Make It Work*, Simon and Schuster, New York, 1980, p. 39.
(7) Statement attributed to Peter Drucker, professor of management sciences.

Family and Child-Rearing

(1) A. Stevens, *Archetype*, p. 154.
(2) C. G. Jung, quoted in: A. Stevens, *Archetype*, p. 62.
(3) C. G. Jung, *Modern Man in Search of A Soul*, Ark Paperbacks, Routledge & Kegan Paul, London and Melbourne, 1984, pp. 109-131.
(4) C. G. Jung, *Modern Man*, p. 119.
(5) A. Stevens, *Archetype*, p. 122.

MENTAL ADAPTATION

(1) C. G. Jung, *Modern Man*, p. 109.
(2) C. G. Jung, *Modern Man*, p. 109.
(3) C. G. Jung, *Modern Man*, p. 110.
(4) C. G. Jung, *Modern Man*, p. 110.
(5) C. G. Jung, *Modern Man*, p. 110.
(6) C. G. Jung, *Modern Man*, p. 110.
(7) C. G. Jung, *Modern Man*, p. 111.
(8) C. G. Jung, *Psychological Reflections*, by J. Jacobi, ed., Routledge & Kegan Paul, London, 1971, p. 76.
(9) W. S. Washburn and C. S. Lancaster, *The Evolution of Hunting*, in: R. B. Lee and I. DeVore, *Man the Hunter*, Aldine Publishing Company, New York, 1982, p. 303.
(10) See: J. Campbell, *The Hero With a Thousand Faces*, p. 18, footnote; J. Campbell with B. Moyers, *The Power of Myth*.
(11) A. Stevens, *Archetype*, p. 239.
(12) C. G. Jung, *Modern Man*, p. 243. Our basic psychology is biological. It consists of a genetic program that controls the biologically relevant

occurrences of life. Events and experiences, such as marriage, family and religion, are preprogrammed in the collective human psyche, which exists in all of us. What we do with these genetic predispositions, and how far we can take them, is an issue of our own personal development and spirituality.

(13) C. G. Jung, *Modern Man*, p. 126.

Marriage As a Biological and Spiritual Union

(1) B. Bettelheim during a Seattle lecture on modern marriage and family, 1975.
(2) J. Campbell, ed., *The Portable Jung*, Penguin Books, Harmondsworth and New York, 1986, p. 173.
(3) See for an additional discussion of these issues: D. M. Buss, *The Evolution of Desire: Strategies of Human Mating*, Basic Books, 1994.
(4) You do that by finding out what unconscious fantasies and feelings you have about the opposite sex. This way you know what you really, that is unconsciously, bring to the relationship or marriage. Making these psychic contents conscious and working them through enables us to withdraw our own psychological projections from the relationship, which we tend to put on the partner in terms of expectations, emotions and behavior. As long as these feelings, fantasies and images remain unrecognized and unresolved, they tend to get in the way of the relationship.

Religious Attitude and Survival

(1) S. Stevens, *Archetype*, p. 284.
(2) C. G. Jung, *The Undiscovered Self*, Routledge & Kegan Paul, London, 1982, p.29.
(3) C. G. Jung, *The Undiscovered Self*, p. 19.
(4) C. G. Jung, *Modern Man*, p. 151.
(5) C. G. Jung, *Modern Man*, p. 145.
(6) C. G. Jung, *Modern Man*, p. 146.
(7) C. G. Jung, *Modern Man*, p. 154.
(8) C. G. Jung, *Modern Man*, p. 160.
(9) C. G. Jung, *The Undiscovered Self*, p. 20.

(10) C. G. Jung, *The Undiscovered Self*, p. 26.
(11) The religious experience is one way in which we adapt to our world. It takes over where our ability to determine our lives leaves off. The creation of myths and symbols is the psychic adaptation, which makes the encounter with the unknown, the leap of faith, possible. The religious attitude exists genetically preformed and preprogrammed in human nature. Ultimately, it is the power of his own psyche that gives man the ability to believe and relinquish the need for control. It allows him to come to terms with the "dependence on and submission to the irrational facts of experience". From: C. G. Jung, *The Undiscovered Self*, p. 19.
(12) K. Armstrong, *A History of God*, Alfred A. Knopf, New York, 1993, pp. XVII-XXIII.
(13) C. G. Jung, *The Undiscovered Self*, p. 26.
(14) For the importance of "man's myth-making capacities", see: A. Stevens, *Archetype*, pp. 35-37.
(15) F. Capra, *The Tao of Physics*, Fontana Paperbacks, London/Oxford, 1984, p.65.
(16) F. Capra, *The Tao of Physics*, p. 65.
(17) C. G. Jung, *Modern Man*, p. 149.
(18) C. G. Jung, *Modern Man*, p. 151.
(19) C. G. Jung, *Modern Man*, p. 145.
(20) C. G. Jung, *Modern Man*, p. 149.
(21) A. Stevens, *Archetype*, p. 284.
(22) From a letter by C. G. Jung to Laurens Van der Post, in: L. Van der Post, *Jung And The Story of Our Time*, Penguin Books, Harmondsworth/New York, 1985, p. 216.
(23) A. Stevens, *Archetype*, p. 284.
(24) From the *Eschatological Laundry List*, quoted in: S. B. Kopp, *If You Meet the Buddha on the Road, Kill Him*, Bantam Books, Toronto/New York, 1985, p. 223.
(25) J. Campbell, ed., *The Portable Jung*, pp. 505-18.
(26) See: W. Pauli, *The Interpretation of Nature and Psyche*, London and New York, 1955, p. 152.
(27) A. Storr, *The Essential Jung*, Princeton University Press, Princeton, 1983, p. 331.
(28) See: C. G. Jung, *Collected Works 14*, pars. 767-80.

(29) See: C. G. Jung, *Collected Works 14*, pars. 767-80.
(30) R. Wilhelm and C. G. Jung, *The Secret of the Golden Flower: A Chinese Book of Life*, Harcourt Brace Jovanovich, Publishers, San Diego/New York/London, 1962, p. 11.
(31) F. Capra, *The Tao of Physics*, p. 29.
(32) A. Storr, *The Essential Jung*, p. 335.
(33) F. Capra, *The Tao of Physics*, p. 93.
(34) See: C. G. Jung, *Collected Works 8*.
(35) L. Greene, *The Astrology of Fate*, Mandala Books, Unwin Paperbacks, London/Boston/Sydney, 1985, p. 271.
(36) L. Greene, *The Astrology of Fate*, p. 278.
(37) See: L. Greene, *The Astrology of Fate*, p. 278.

PERSONAL ADAPTATION

(1) See Chapter 7, pp. 171-72.
(2) A. Stevens, *Archetype*, p. 255.

Survivor Personality

(1) See: A. Stevens, *Archetype*, p. 23.
(2) W. S. Laughlin, *Hunting: An Integrating Biobehavior System and Its Evolutionary Importance*, in: R. B. Lee and I. DeVore, *Man the Hunter*, Aldine Publishing Company, New York, 1982, p. 304.
(3) J. Bronowski, *The Ascent of Man*, British Broadcasting Corporation, London, 1980, p. 20.
(4) See: A. Stevens, *Archetype*, p. 281.
(5) A. Stevens, *Archetype*, p. 37.
(6) R. Wilhelm and C. G. Jung, *The Secret of the Golden Flower: A Chinese Book of Life*, Harcourt Brace Jovanovich, New York, 1962, p. 11.
(7) A. Stevens, *Archetype*, p. 111; also see pp. 140-173. Archetypal intent is "concerned with the formation of attachment bonds, the establishment of basic trust, and the development of a secure ego conceiving itself as being both acceptable to others and capable of coping with the eventualities of life". From: A. Stevens, *Archetype*, p. 111.
(8) C. Castaneda, *Journey to Ixtlan: The Lessons of Don Juan*, A Touchstone

(9) From: S. Maugham, *The Razor's Edge*.
(10) C. Castaneda, *Journey to Ixtlan*, p. 254.
(11) C. Trungpa, *The Myth of Freedom and the Way of Meditation*, Shambhala Publications, Boulder & London, 1976, p. 121.
(12) W. Wordsworth, *Ode on Intimations of Immortality from Recollections of Early Childhood*.

Personal Evolution and Mythology

(1) C. G. Jung, *Collected Works 11*, para. 146.
(2) See: A. Stevens, *Archetype*, pp. 40, 52.
(3) J. Campbell with B. Moyers, *The Power of Myth*, p. 37. J. Campbell has elaborated on this process in his famous book, *The Hero With a Thousand Faces*, which depicts the psychological development of the individual as the hero's journey of 'departure', 'initiation' and 'return'.
(4) J. Campbell with B. Moyers, *The Power of Myth*, p. 59.
(5) J. Campbell with B. Moyers, *The Power of Myth*, p. 126.
(6) J. Campbell with B. Moyers, *The Power of Myth*, p. 139.
(7) A. Stevens, *Archetype*, p. 140.
(8) J. Campbell with B. Moyers, *The Power of Myth*, p.142. "The infant knows what to do when a nipple is in its mouth. There is a whole system of built-in action which, when we see it in animals, we call instinct. That is the biological ground. But then certain things can happen that make it repulsive or difficult or frightening or sinful to do some of the things one is impelled to do and that is when we begin to have our most troublesome psychological problems. Myths primarily are for fundamental instructions in these matters. Our society today is not giving us adequate mythic instruction of this kind." From: J. Campbell with B. Moyers, *The Power of Myth*, 142.
(9) See: J. Campbell with B. Moyers, *The Power of Myth*, 148.
(10) A. Stevens, *Archetype*, p. 36.
(11) A. Stevens, *Archetype*, p. 34.
(12) J. Campbell, *The Hero With a Thousand Faces*, p. 3.
(13) L. Van der Post, *Jung and The Story of Our Time*, pp. 150, 151.
(14) See: C. G. Jung, *Collected Works 11*, para. 144.

(15) A. Stevens, *Archetype*, p. 129.
(16) J. Campbell, *The Hero With a Thousand Faces*, p. 12.
(17) A. Stevens, *Archetype*, p. 124.
(18) See: J. Campbell, *The Hero With a Thousand Faces*, p. 193.
(19) L. Van der Post, *Jung and The Story of Our Time*, p. 145.
(20) C. G. Jung, *Collected Works 9, Part I*, para. 56.
(21) L. Van der Post, *Jung and The Story of Our Time*, p. 121.
(22) L. Van der Post, *Jung and The Story of Our Time*, p. 73.
(23) L. Van der Post, *Jung and The Story of Our Time*, p. 166.
(24) J. Campbell, *The Hero With a Thousand Faces*, p. 207.
(25) J. Campbell, *The Hero With a Thousand Faces*, p. 228.

PART III

(1) Jung believed that the human psyche contained "the collective wisdom of our species, the basic bioprogramme" for human survival. From: A. Stevens, *Archetype*, p. 34.
(2) W. S. Laughlin, *Hunting: An Integrating Biobehavior System and Its Evolutionary Importance*, in: R. B. Lee and I. DeVore, *Man the Hunter*, Aldine Publishing Company, New York, 1982, p. 304.

THE PARAMETERS OF HUMAN SURVIVAL

Survival Environment

(1) See: A. Stevens, *Archetype*, pp. 255-9.
(2) D. Attenborough, *Life on Earth*, p. 305.
(3) The right brain offers an understanding of the world, which the left brain totally fails to perceive. Rarely does the intellect comprehend the full meaning of a given situation, nor does it ever see the grand scheme of things. The left-brain dominance, encouraged by modern society, has created a cultural prejudice against right-sided traits. The left brain favors extroversion and action over insight and contemplation. The intuitive, creative and symbolic qualities of the right brain have, in the main, been seen as effeminate and weak; its holistic, synthetic and strategic capacities have remained unappreciated. In all, the survival value of the right brain

has largely gone unrecognized. Moreover, the reluctance to include right-brain aspects into our lives has reinforced the prevailing left-sided view of the world. Overall, left-sidedness has become identified with being 'tough-minded' and right-sidedness with being 'tender-minded'. Also see: J. Campbell, *The Flight of the Gander*, Regnery Gateway, Chicago, 1960, p. 62.

(4) See also: F. Capra, *The Tao of Physics*, Flamingo published by Fontana Paperbacks, London, 1984, pp. 33-52.
(5) C. G. Jung, *Collected Works 13*, para. 2.
(6) J. Bronowski, *The Ascent of Man*, p. 31.
(7) A. Stevens, *Archetype*, p. 7.
(8) A. Stevens, *Archetype*, p. 231.

Survival Strategies

(1) J. Bronowski, *The Ascent of Man*, p. 19.
(2) J. Bronowski, *The Ascent of Man*, p. 19.
(3) See: K. Lorenz, *Das Wirkungsgefuege*, p. 238.
(4) See: K. Lorenz, *Das Wirkungsgefuege*, p. 237.
(5) See: K. Lorenz, *Das Wirkungsgefuege*, p. 239.
(6) L. R. Aronson, E. Tobach et al., eds., *Development and Evolution of Behavior: Essays in Memory of T. C. Schneirla*, Freeman & Company, San Francisco, 1970, p. 163.
(7) See: A. Siebert, *The Survivor Personality*, Northwest Magazine, 1/1980.
(8) See: L. R. Aronson, E. Tobach et al., eds., *Development and Evolution of Behavior*, p. 250.
(9) A. Lowen, *Depression and the Body*, Penguin Books, New York, 1980, p. 301.
(10) Originally intended to make life easier and survival more predictable, culture has more and more become an entity of its own. Culture has changed from being a means to being a condition of survival.
(11) J. Bronowski, *The Ascent of Man*, p. 26.
(12) Adolescence, as the transitional phase between childhood and adulthood, is a creation of modern society and probably the most obvious example of quasi-institutionalized dependency. It is designed as a preparation phase to ready the young person through myriad forms of schooling and training

for the professional, financial, social and intellectual demands of the adult world. Adolescence does not exist in tribal societies. To them, youth is only a chronological matter. Marked by initiation rites, the transition from childhood to adult status is instant. One day the young boys and girls are still children, the next day they are grownups assuming adult responsibilities. The duration of adolescence in modern industrialized societies has grown proportionately to the preparatory requirements society demands. As modern society becomes more and more complex, those requirements have grown steadily over the years—and along with them the length of adolescence and the time young people remain away from adulthood. The longer the period of adolescence, the harder it becomes to grow up. Modern society delays psychosocial maturity of the young and contributes to immaturity and dependency in adult life. Coupled with cultural conditioning, psychological and institutional dependency poses a significant detriment to individual survival in modern life. Cultural conditioning tames the natural potency in us, diminishing our ability to address survival. Layers upon layers of cultural conditioning—the 'shoulds', 'have to's' and 'ought to's' of civilized life—have stifled and weakened man's natural constitution and vitality. Judging from its psychosocial results, incessant socialization is not unlike the process of domestication that tames the animal. Work with suicidal patients invariably shows that as soon as the layers of environmental conditioning, which are affecting their depression and despair, are stripped away, the natural fiber returns. Invariably, people bounce back with vigor and vitality. This is to say, once "the external props collapse, (people) fall back on life itself". From: T. Des Pres, in: A. Siebert, *Newsletter*, Association for Humanistic Psychology, San Francisco, 8/1983, p. 22.

(13) See: A. Stevens, *Archetype*, pp. 251, 255, 274-5.
(14) See: J. Campbell, *The Flight of the Gander*, Regnery Gateway, Chicago, 1960, p. 62.
(15) A. Stevens, *Archetype*, p. 274.
(16) C. Castaneda, *Journey to Ixtlan: The Lessons of Don Juan*, A Touchstone Book, Simon and Schuster, New York, 1972, p. 100.
(17) C. Castaneda, *Journey to Ixtlan*, p. 254.
(18) A. Stevens, *Archetype*, p. 253.
(19) See: B. B. Tregoe and J. W. Zimmerman, *Top Management Strategy: What*

It Is and How to Make It Work, Simon and Schuster, New York, 1980, pp. 102-5.
(20) A. Stevens, *Archetype*, p. 253.
(21) From: S. Maugham, *The Razor's Edge*.
(22) Bronowski views anticipation as a prime promoter of human adaptation and survival. See: J Bronowski, *The Ascent of Man*, p. 54.
(23) C. Castaneda, *Journey to Ixtlan*, p. 95.
(24) C. Trungpa, *The Myth of Freedom and the Way of Meditation*, Shambhala Publications, Boulder & London, 1976, p. 121.
(25) Lorenz refers to H. Tuppy, in: K. Lorenz, *Das Wirkungsgefuege*, p. 35.
(26) A. Stevens, *Archetype*, p. 37.

Survival Skills

(1) W. S. Laughlin, *Hunting: An Integrating Biobehavior System and Its Evolutionary Importance*, in: R. B. Lee and I. DeVore, *Man the Hunter*, Aldine Publishing Company, New York, 1982, p. 312.
(2) A. Stevens, *Archetype*, p. 184.
(3) A. Stevens, *Archetype*, p. 191.
(4) A. Stevens, *Archetype*, p. 187.
(5) A. Stevens, *Archetype*, p. 190.
(6) A. Stevens, *Archetype*, p. 190.
(7) A. Stevens, *Archetype*, p. 189.
(8) S. Goldberg, *The Inevitability of Patriarchy*, Maurice Temple Smith, London, 1973, p. 218. Quoted in: A. Stevens, *Archetype*, p. 190.
(9) A. Stevens, *Archetype*, p. 192.
(10) "'The work of art', wrote Ludwig Wittgenstein, the eminent Cambridge philosopher, 'is the object seen *sub specie aeternitatis* (in its eternal aspect); and the good life is the world seen *sub specie aeternitatis* (in its eternal aspect).'" See Ludwig Wittgenstein, philosopher, quoted in: A. Stevens, *Archetype*, p. 283.
(11) A. Stevens, *Archetype*, p. 283.
(12) A. Stevens, *Archetype*, p. 280.
(13) A. Stevens, *Archetype*, p. 280.
(14) A. Stevens, *Archetype*, p. 280.
(15) A. Stevens, *Archetype*, p. 280.

(16) See: B. B. Tregoe and J. W. Zimmerman, *Top Management Strategy: What Is It And How to Make It Work*, Simon and Schuster, New York, 1983, p. 104.
(17) T. S. Eliot, *Four Quartets*.
(18) T. S. Eliot, *Four Quartets*.
(19) A. Stevens, *Archetype*, p. 255. Jung further suggested that both cerebral hemispheres "supplement each other to form the transcendent function" (C. G. Jung, *Collected Works 8*, from a reference by E. Rossi, quoted in: A. Stevens, *Archetype*, p. 272). The complementary relationship between both hemispheres stands in contrast to their disproportional functioning enforced by modern society.
(20) See: A. Stevens, *Archetype*, p. 265.
(21) See: A. Stevens, *Archetype*, p. 274.
(22) See: A. Stevens, *Archetype*, p. 272.
(23) C. G. Jung, *Commentary on The Secret of the Golden Flower*, (trans.) C. F. Barnes, Collins and Routledge & Kegan Paul, London, 1962, p. 107.
(24) C. G. Jung, *Collected Works 14*, para. 706; quoted in: A. Stevens, *Archetype*, p. 273.
(25) A. Stevens, *Archetype*, p. 273.

Survival Scenarios

(1) I. Oyle, *The New American Medicine Show*, University Press, Santa Cruz, 1979, p. 96.
(2) I. Oyle, *Medicine Show*, p. 118.
(3) "If you realize that there will always be people willing to pay to have things done, and if you're willing to find out what they're willing to pay for, you have nothing to be afraid of." From: H. Browne, *How I Found Freedom in an Unfree World*, Macmillan Publishing Company, New York, 1973, p. 241.
(4) C. Castaneda, *Journey to Ixtlan: The Lessons of Don Juan*, A Touchstone Book, Simon and Schuster, New York, 1972, p. 95.
(5) H. Browne, *How I Found Freedom*, p. 237.
(6) As Jung postulated, see: A. Stevens, *Archetype*, p. 34.
(7) J. Bronowski, *The Ascent of Man*, p. 41.
(8) See: I. Oyle, *Medicine Show*, pp. 110-133.
(9) I. Oyle, *Medicine Show*, p. 111.

(10) I. Oyle, *Medicine Show*, p. 111.
(11) I. Oyle, *Medicine Show*, p. 131.
(12) I. Oyle, *Medicine Show*, p. 115.
(13) See: H. Seyle, *The Physiology and Pathology of Exposure to Stress*, Acta, Montreal, 1950.
(14) J. Campbell, ed., *The Portable Jung*, Penguin Books, New York, 1986, p. XXII.
(15) R. Wilhelm and C. G. Jung, *The Secret of the Golden Flower: A Chinese Book of Life*, Harcourt Brace Jovanovich, Publishers, San Diego/New York/London, 1962, p. 13.
(16) I. Oyle, *Medicine Show*, p. 102.
(17) I. Oyle, *Medicine Show*, p. 101.
(18) I. Oyle, *Medicine Show*, p. 110.
(19) P. Pearsall, *Superimmunity: Master Your Emotions & Improve Your Health*, McGraw-Hill Book Company, 1987, p. 31.
(20) I. Oyle, *Medicine Show*, p. 96.
(21) P. Pearsall, *Superimmunity*, p. 31.
(22) I. Oyle, *Medicine Show*, p. 96.
(23) I. Oyle, *Medicine Show*, p. 96.
(24) Attributed to Rene Dubos, quoted in P. Pearsall, *Superimmunity*, p. 43.
(25) M. Friedman and R. H. Rosenman, *Type A Behavior and Your Heart*, Alfred Knopf, New York, 1974, quoted in: I. Oyle, *Medicine Show*, p. 111.
(26) I. Oyle, *Medicine Show*, p. 48.
(27) P. Pearsall, *Superimmunity*, p. 20.
(28) See: P. Pearsall, *Superimmunity*, pp. 126 and 181.
(29) See: P. Pearsall, *Superimmunity*, pp. 126 and 181.
(30) P. Pearsall, *Superimmunity*, p. 336.

RECOVERING HUMAN NATURE

The Survival Value of Human Nature

(1) W. S. Laughlin, *Hunting: An Integrating Biobehavior System and Its Evolutionary Importance*, in: R. B. Lee and I. DeVore, *Man the Hunter*, Aldine Publishing Company, New York, 1982, pp. 305-7.
(2) J. Bowlby, *Attachment and Loss, Volume 1: Attachment*, Hogarth Press and

the Institute of Psycho-Analysis, London, 1969, p. 45, quoted in: A. Stevens, *Archetype*, p. 50.

THE WAY OF THE HUNTER

(1) L. van der Post, *Jung and The Story of Our Time*, p. 162.
(2) C. Castaneda, *Journey to Ixtlan: The Lessons of Don Juan*, A Touchstone Book, Simon and Schuster, New York, 1972, p. 79.

Becoming a Hunter: The Journey into Life

(1) C. Castaneda, *Journey to Ixtlan*, p. 267.
(2) C. Castaneda, *Journey to Ixtlan*, p. 269.
(3) C. Castaneda, *Journey to Ixtlan*, p. 100.
(4) H. Browne, *How I Found Freedom in an Unfree World*, Macmillan Publishing Inc., New York, 1973, p. 237.
(5) C. Castaneda, *Journey to Ixtlan*, p. 95.
(6) C. Castaneda, *Journey to Ixtlan*, p. 90.
(7) C. Castaneda, *Journey to Ixtlan*, p. 100.
(8) C. S. Hall and G. Lindzey, *Theories of Personality*, John Wiley & Sons, Inc., New York, 1970, p. 328.
(9) A. Siebert, *The Survivor Personality*, Northwest Magazine, 1/1980.
(10) C. Castaneda, *Journey to Ixtlan*, p. 105.
(11) C. Trungpa, *The Myth of Freedom and The Way of Meditation*, Shambhala Publications, Inc., Boulder & London, 1976, p. 121.
(12) C. Trungpa, *The Myth of Freedom*, p. 121.
(13) See: A. Siebert, *Newsletter*, Association for Humanistic Psychology, San Francisco, 8/1983, p. 21.
(14) See: A. Siebert, *Newsletter*; A. Siebert, *The Survivor Personality*; C. S. Hall and G. Lindzey, *Theories of Personality*, p. 328; B. Siegel, *Love, Medicine and Miracles*, Harper & Row, New York, 1986, pp. 162-4; L. van der Post, *Jung and The Story of Our Time*, p. 243; L. D. Olsen, *Outdoor Survival Skills*, Brigham Young University Press, Provo, 1973, pp. 1-5.
(15) C. Castaneda, *Journey to Ixtlan*, p. 76.
(16) C. Castaneda, *Journey to Ixtlan*, p. 152.
(17) See: A. Stevens, *Archetype*, pp. 101-3.

(18) C. Castaneda, *Journey to Ixtlan*, p. 102.
(19) C. Castaneda, *Journey to Ixtlan*, p. 150.
(20) Survivors use their environment—job market, economy, political institutions, etc.—as a means of survival without being colored or controlled by its values and practices.
(21) C. Castaneda, *Journey to Ixtlan*, p. 100.
(22) C. Castaneda, *Journey to Ixtlan*, p. 106.
(23) See: P. Pearsall, *Superimmunity: Master Your Emotions & Improve Your Health*, McGraw Hill, New York, 1987, p. 252. The theory of complementarity (Neils Bohr) suggests that our understanding of the world needs to include polarity and complementarity to comprehend the paradoxical nature of reality. Every theoretical explanation represents a different account of reality and tends to exclude everything else that remains outside its scope. So, any given set of facts can be interpreted by any number of theories. The various efforts to understand man's relationship to the universe account for the events in human life as a result of either magic, individual effort, chance or fate, luck or circumstance, cause and effect, meaningful coincidences, preordained destiny, Divine Providence, etc. None of these explanations is fully substantiated or able to validate everything that happens in a person's life. The seam is missing that shows the connection between life and the universe. The workings of the world stay concealed in the mystery of life. With each explanation, the universe changes. Human life, too, takes on a different quality. See also Chapter 5, Religious Attitude and Survival, pp. 133-41.
(24) N. Kazantzakis, *Zorba the Greek*, Faber and Faber, London, 1995, p. 65.
(25) P. Pearsall, *Superimmunity*, p. XIV.
(26) "If you realize that there will always be people willing to pay to have things done, and if you are willing to find out what they're willing to pay for, you have nothing to be afraid of. You'll know that you can always strike a bargain with someone to do something—even if you're flat on your back." From: H. Browne, *How I Found Freedom in an Unfree World*, Macmillan Publishing, Inc., New York, 1973, p. 241.
(27) H. Browne, *How I Found Freedom*, p. 237.
(28) "My life is wasted, I thought. If only I could take a cloth and wipe out all I have learnt, all I have seen and heard, and go to Zorba's school and start the great, the real alphabet! What a different road I would choose. I

would keep my five senses perfectly trained, and my whole body, too, so that it would *enjoy and understand*. I should learn to run, to wrestle, to swim, to ride horses, to row, to drive a car, to fire a rifle. I should fill my soul with flesh. I should fill my flesh with soul. In fact, I should reconcile at last within me the two eternal antagonists." From: N. Kazantzakis, *Zorba the Greek*, p. 77.

Being a Hunter: Mastery of Two Worlds

(1) A. Stevens, *Archetype*, p. 38.
(2) C. Castaneda, *Journey to Ixtlan*, p. 106.
(3) C. Castaneda, *Journey to Ixtlan*, p. 95.

The Hunter Within: The Essence of Power

(1) C. Castaneda, Journey to Ixtlan, p. 192.
(2) L. van der Post, *Jung and The Story of Our Time*, p. 141.
(3) C. G. Jung, *Modern Man*, p. 248.
(4) J. Campbell with B. Moyer, *The Power of Myth*, pp. 91-121.
(5) This illustration of the metaphysical realities, which impinge on the human existence, was given to the author by Charles Shields, a wise man and friend.
(6) C. Trungpa, *The Myth of Freedom*, p. 113.
(7) This is not an actual quote. The content is related to a conversation with Liz Greene, Jungian scholar and author.
(8) C. Castaneda, *Journey to Ixtlan*, p. 112.
(9) W. Wordsworth, *Ode on Intimations of Immortality from Recollections of Early Childhood*.
(10) W. S. Laughlin, *Hunting: An Integrating Biobehavior System and Its Evolutionary Importance*, in: R. B. Lee and I. DeVore, eds., *Man the Hunter*, Aldine Publishing Company, New York, 1982, p. 304.
(11) C. Castaneda, *Journey to Ixtlan*, p. 152.
(12) C. Castaneda, *Journey to Ixtlan*, p. 102.
(13) See: H. Tuppy, in: K. Lorenz, *Das Wirkungsgefuege*, p. 35.
(14) A. Stevens, *Archetype*, p. 37.
(15) Reflecting "Jung's view (as opposed to Plato's) that the mental events

experienced by every individual are determined not merely by his personal history, but by the collective history of the species as a whole (biologically encoded in the collective unconscious), reaching back into the primordial mists of evolutionary time". From: A. Stevens, *Archetype*, p. 39.

EPILOG

(1) German physicist, 1901-76, Nobel Prize laureate.

Evolutionary Intelligence

(1) A. Stevens, *Archetype*, p. 231.
(2) See on the biological basis of ethical norms: I. Eibl-Eibesfeldt, *Love and Hate*, pp. 90-105. The adaptive function of the instincts is remarkably resistant to modification. It takes extraordinary measures to corrupt the instinct and to convert its adaptive qualities into destructive deviance. But it can be done: "Among the military fraternities of Ancient Germany a young man, as part of his training to stifle inhibitions against killing, was required to strip naked; to dress himself in the hot, freshly flayed skin of a bear; to work himself into a 'bestial' rage: in other words, to go, quite literally, berserk. 'Bearskin' and 'berserk' are the same word. The helmets of the Royal Guards, on duty outside Buckingham Palace, are the descendants of this primitive battle costume." From: B. Chatwin, *The Songlines*, Elisabeth Sifton Books, Viking Penguin Inc., New York, 1987, p. 217.
(3) Statement by Arthur Koestler during a public lecture, quoted in: B. Chatwin, *The Songlines*, p. 211.
(4) C. G. Jung, *Collected Works 11*, para. 146.
(5) C. G. Jung, *Collected Works 18*, para. 1228.
(6) See: A. Stevens, *Archetype*, pp. 40, 52.
(7) See: J. Campbell, *The Hero With a Thousand Faces*, pp. 47-243.
(8) J. Campbell, *The Hero With a Thousand Faces*, p. 12.
(9) See: C. G. Jung, *Collected Works 11*, para. 144. Also see Chapter 6, p. 160.
(10) See: B. B. Tregoe and J. W. Zimmerman, *Top Management Strategy: What*

It Is And How To Make It Work, Simon and Schuster, New York, 1980, pp. 103-5.

(11) See: P. Flor-Henry, *Lateralized Temporal-Limbic Dysfunction and Psychopathology*, in: *Annals of the New York Academy of Sciences, Vol. 380*, pp. 777-97. Quoted in: A. Stevens, *Archetype*, p. 265.

(12) R. Wilhelm and C. G. Jung, *The Secret of the Golden Flower: A Chinese Book of Life*, Harcourt Brace Jovanovich, New York, 1962, p. 11.

(13) See: I. Eibl-Eibesfeldt, *Die Biologie des menschlichen Verhaltens*, pp. 863-85; I. Eibl-Eibesfeldt, *Love and Hate*, pp. 106-69.

(14) W. S. Laughlin, *Hunting: An Integrating Biobehavior System and Its Evolutionary Importance*, in: R. B. Lee and I. DeVore, eds., *Man the Hunter*, Aldine Publishing Company, New York, 1982, p. 304.

(15) C. Trungpa, *The Myth of Freedom and the Way of Meditation*, Shambhala Publications Inc., Boulder & London, 1976, p. 121.

(16) The uncanny wisdom of instinct and intuition is part of human tradition and folklore: "Heroes in moments of crisis are said to hear 'angel voices' telling them what to do next. The whole of the Odyssey is a marvellous tug of war between Athene whispering in Odysseus's ear, 'Yes, you'll make it', and Poseidon roaring, 'No, you won't!' And if you swap the word 'instinct' for 'angel voice', you come close to the more psychologically-minded mythographers: that myths are fragments of the soul-life of Early Man". From: B. Chatwin, *The Songlines*, Elisabeth Sifton Books, Viking Penguin Inc., New York, 1987, p. 216.

(17) See reference to C. G. Jung in: A. Stevens, *Archetype*, p. 34.

Survival in The Modern World

(1) A. Stevens, *Archetype*, p. 279.

(2) Statement made by W. Heisenberg, 1901-76, German physicist, Nobel Prize winner.

(3) A. Stevens, *Archetype*, p. 278.

(4) Human civilization is founded on the development of agriculture—the attempt to make human survival more *predictable* and *reliable* through settling, growing crops and domesticating animals.

(5) See: J. Bronowski, *The Ascent of Man*, p. 20.
(6) Particularly at the macro-level, making personal value/goal structure transitory and short-term. Example of heteronomy at the macro-level: no/minimal control over resources.

Discussion

(1) See: A. Stevens, *Archetype*, p. 281.
(2) J. Bronowski, *The Ascent of Man*, p. 31.
(3) C. G. Jung, *Collected Works 9, Part I*, para. 444.
(4) A. Stevens, *Archetype*, p. 38.
(5) A. Stevens, *Archetype*, p. 240.
(6) A. Stevens, *Archetype*, p. 234.
(7) I. Eibl-Eibesfeldt, *Love and Hate*, pp. 63-89; quoted in: A. Stevens, *Archetype*, p. 234.
(8) A. Stevens, *Archetype*, p. 38.
(9) See on ethical foundations in biology: I. Eibl-Eibesfeldt, *Love and Hate*, pp. 90-105.
(10) C. G. Jung, *Collected Works 10*, para. 441.
(11) A. Stevens, *Archetype*, p. 279.
(12) J. Campbell with B. Moyers, *The Power of Myth*, p. 131.
(13) There exists in Western civilization a certain cultural arrogance, frequently pointed out by Richard Leakey, that assumes a natural superiority of the human species and a right to manhandle the planet. This arrogance is reflected in the notion of having to improve on nature and in man's relationship to other species. Native peoples used rituals to atone for the killing of an animal. Taking the life of animals was restricted to self-preservation and survival. Killing was related to need, not greed as in Western societies where animals are killed for profit or sport.
(14) J. Campbell with B. Moyers, *The Power of Myth*, p. 131.
(15) C. G. Jung, *Memories, Dreams, Reflections*, A. Jaffe, ed., Vintage Books, New York, 1965, p. 4.
(16) C. G. Jung, *Memories, Dreams, Reflections*, p. 4.
(17) C. G. Jung, *Memories, Dreams, Reflections*, p. 4.

(18) L. van der Post, *Jung and The Story of Our Time*, p. 246.
(19) C. G. Jung, *Collected Works 9, Part I*, para. 291.
(20) A. Stevens, *Archetype*, p. 31.
(21) T. S. Eliot, *Four Quartets*.

APPENDIX

NOTATIONS FOR THE PROFESSIONAL

Scientific Epistemology

(1) As an illustration, the well-established approach of the cognitive-behavioral treatment model: "Cognitive-behavioral therapy merges two theories. Cognitive theory supposes that behavior is secondary to a person's thoughts while behavioral theory infers that behavior is not a result of how we think, but is contingent upon rewards and punishment." From: C. Gore-Felton, *Acute Stress Reactions Among Victims of Violence: Assessment and Treatment*, in: *Directions in Clinical and Counseling Psychology*, The Hatherleigh Company, Long Island City, 2000, Vol. 10, p. 6.
(2) See: A. Stevens, *Archetype*, p. 64.
(3) C. G. Jung, *Collected Works 9, Part I*, para. 1-110.
(4) C. G. Jung, *Collected Works 7*, para. 300, quoted in: A. Stevens, *Archetype*, pp. 44-5.
(5) Stevens referring to Jung, in: A. Stevens, *Archetype*, p. 34.

The Neurology of Human Survival

(1) Nature—"that is, biological evolution—has not fitted man to any specific environment" nor has it specialized him in any particular way (J. Bronowski, *The Ascent of Man*, p. 19). Instead, man has evolved with the advantage of being a 'specialist in universality', a specialist in not being specialized, equipped with the capacity to create, manipulate and change the environment according to his own terms. From this grew his tremendous adaptability (see: K. Lorenz, *Das Wirkungsgefuege*, pp. 237-245). This is our selective advantage as a species. While other animal species developed with specific anatomical features such as size, strength

or speed to gain the necessary advantage to survive, man's survival depended mainly on the capacity and evolution of his brain. The particular make-up and functioning of the human brain has allowed man to prevail over his environment.

(2) See: R. W. Sperry, *Hemisphere Disconnection and Unity in Conscious Awareness*, in: *American Psychologist*, 23, 1968, pp. 723-33; P. D. McLean, *Brain Mechanisms of Primal Sexual Functions and Related Behavior*, in: M. Sandler and G. L. Gessa, eds., *Sexual Behavior, Pharmacology and Biochemistry*, Raven, New York, pp. 1-11; R. E. Ornstein, *The Psychology of Consciousness*, Freeman, San Francisco, 1972.

(3) A. Stevens, *Archetype*, p. 265.

(4) The development of science and technology has had a profound impact on the development of Western civilization. The cultural emphasis on rational thought and scientific knowledge has established a dominance of the left cerebral hemisphere. The preoccupation with left-hemispheric functioning has contributed to the creation of a 'left-sided', man-made world, which is, in essence, an extension of the human intellect with all its characteristic traits. Moreover, the preponderance of rational, scientific elements of modern culture has established the primacy of cognitive functioning as the predominant mode of psychological functioning.

(5) Confirmation of Jung's biological approach to human psychology is increasingly forthcoming and has consistently been substantiated by recent neurological research. Reviewing his research into the neurophysiology of brain functioning, Henry concludes that "the metapsychological foundations built by Carl Jung are proving to be soundly conceived. There is a rapidly growing body of evidence linking our mammalian inheritance of basic brainstem functions with man's unique religious, social and cultural achievements. Society has scarcely begun to consider the implications of these discoveries". (From: J. P. Henry and P. M. Stephens, *Stress, Health and the Social Environment: A Sociobiological Approach to Medicine*, Springer Verlag, New York, 1977, p. 111. Quoted in: A. Stevens, *Archetype*, p. 267.) Neurological evidence further confirms the existence of phylogenetic structures determining human ethology. See I. Eibl-Eibesfeldt, *Die Biologie des menschlichen Verhaltens*, pp. 115-120.

(6) See: J. P. Henry's research, quoted in A. Stevens, *Archetype*, pp. 262-3.

Archetypal structures "have their neuronal substrate located primarily in the phylogenetically much older parts of the brain. It is not, of course, possible to designate any precise neurological location for any of the archetypes. Inasmuch as one archetypal system can be differentiated from another, each must have an extremely complex and widely ramifying neurological substrate involving millions of neurons in the brain stem and limbic system (the instinctive or biological pole) and both cerebral hemispheres (the psychic or spiritual pole)". Quoted from: A. Stevens, *Archetype*, pp. 265-6.

(7) A. Stevens, *Archetype*, p. 265.

(8) See: P. D. MacLean's research, quoted in: A. Stevens, *Archetype*, p. 265.

(9) "Consciousness is not a simple, unitary phenomenon which can be assumed to possess a discrete cerebral location, but a richly complex process dependent upon a vast network of neuronal structures which are probably hierarchically arranged." From: A. Stevens, *Archetype*, p. 261.

(10) A. Stevens, *Archetype*, p. 266.

(11) A. Stevens, *Archetype*, pp. 274-5.

(12) "These cerebral processes, functioning as an enormously complex and integrated totality, are evidently the very stuff of consciousness, and are the consequence of brain functioning as a whole rather than of processes occurring in any specific group of neurons (apart from those of the reticular activating system of the brain stem, which seems to be the powerhouse driving the whole complex of systems subserving consciousness) . . . consciousness (*according to R. Sperry*) is a property of brain circuitry and brain chemistry working as a whole." It is, as Jung stated, "dependent upon the psyche functioning as a balanced totality". Both quotes from: A. Stevens, *Archetype*, p 262.

(13) A. Stevens, *Archetype*, p. 255.

(14) Each hemisphere contributes important functions to the survival of the human being. The left brain hemisphere is responsible for rational and empirical thinking. The intellect, "whose function it is to discriminate, divide, compare, measure and categorize", provides the basis for rational knowledge. It makes logical and abstract thought possible. The left brain is primarily analytic. It operates on the principle of cause and effect and in that creates a world "of intellectual distinctions", of objects and events "which can only exist in relation to each other". (For above see: F. Capra,

The Tao of Physics, Fontana Paperbacks, London, 1984, p. 34). The right brain hemisphere is the center of intuition, sensation and perception. With "its intuitive, creative and holistic qualities", it is basically "the strategic side of the brain". It enables us to perceive things and people as they are. It lets us see the whole picture, unconstrained by details. The right brain makes it possible to transform experiences and thoughts into concepts and decisions. It works effectively without complete information, and it enables us to incorporate change. The right brain is predominantly synthetic. It takes a holistic view of situations and attends to the future. (For above see: B. B Tregoe & J. W. Zimmerman, *Top Management Strategy: What It Is and How to Make It Work*, Simon and Schuster, New York, 1980, pp. 103-4.) Together, the joint faculties of the left and right brain support survival in supreme fashion. Making use of both sides of the brain gives us the ability to be cognitive and intuitive, analytical and holistic, action-oriented and strategic. The unique structure of the human brain allows us to look at the world in two different ways and to screen the reality in front of us, relative to our needs and survival.

(15) A. Stevens, *Archetype*, p. 255.

(16) "Cerebral dominance, like all biologically determined human characteristics, is susceptible to environmental influences. . . . Our own culture is a case in point: ever since the Renaissance, stress has increasingly been laid on the need to develop left hemispheric functions at the expense of the right. Encouragement of the left hemisphere begins early in life with the emphasis placed in all Western primary schools on the need for proficiency in the three Rs (writing, reading and arithmetic). Although right hemispheric activities such as art, drama, dancing and music are given a place in the curriculum, fewer resources and fewer hours are allocated to them than to left-sided disciplines such as mathematics, languages, physics and chemistry; . . . Education reflects the ruling obsessions of society; and a culture such as ours which stresses the importance of rational, analytic processes rather than aesthetic, synthetic ones, and which places a higher value on material achievement than on symbolic expression, inevitably promotes a form of left hemispheric 'imperialism'." (From: A. Stevens, *Archetype*, pp. 255-6.) Some people live exclusively in this left-sided reality of our man-made world, unaware

of the additional realities, which impinge on human existence and their neurological receptors in the human brain.

(17) See P. Flor-Henry's research, quoted in: A. Stevens, *Archetype*, p. 265. Modern brain research has "demonstrated that human emotional responses are dependent on neuronal pathways linking the limbic system of the midbrain with parietal and frontal areas of the right cerebral hemisphere. Moreover, Flor-Henry has made the truly fascinating discovery that this whole complicated right hemispheric/limbic affectional system is under the surveillance and control of the *left* frontal cortex—thus lending further weight to the conclusion that the left hemisphere can, via the corpus callosum, 'repress' or inhibit the activities, and especially the *emotionally toned* activities (which are the vital concern of psychiatrists), of the right".

(18) Early childhood training (socialization and school) establishes left-hemispheric functioning at the expense of total brain functioning, suppressing the instinctual, archetypal brain and discrediting the right. It is very much a process of colonization so characteristic of Western culture—a process of invasion aimed at subjecting existing, so called, 'primitive' elements to outside rule. This is more than an analogy inasmuch as the human brain and what happens there is, of course, the template for the actions and endeavors on the outside, creating the external manifestation of the neurological process. Colonization as a concept and as a reality first started in the human brain. The colonization of many parts of the world by imperialistic powers with subsequent imposition of their culture is a result of the neurological colonization of the human brain, which preceded it.

(19) The man-made world is an extension of the left human brain, virtually designed by its concepts and abilities.

(20) The effects of left-hemispheric dominance and its cultural bias on science, politics, on our economic and social affairs are unmistakable and pervasive. These effects are evident in the left-sided value system of competition, goal-setting, and the achievement principle characteristic of the protestant ethic and the rise of industrialized economies (Max Weber). They are also evident in medicine and issues of psychosomatic illness, in the way we understand reality, our body, our being, and our health.

(21) See P. D. MacLean's research, quoted in: A. Stevens, *Archetype*, p. 264.

(22) See J. P. Henry's and P. M. Stephens' research, quoted in: A. Stevens, *Archetype*, p. 264.

(23) A. Stevens, *Archetype*, p. 264.
(24) P. D. MacLean, *Sensory and Perceptive Factors in Emotional Functions of the Triune Brain*, in: R. G. Grenell and S. Gabay, eds., *Biological Foundations of Psychiatry*, Raven, New York, vol. 1, pp. 177-98. Quoted in: A. Stevens, *Archetype*, p. 264.
(25) The adaptive functions provided by the human brain involve foremost the neuronal centers of the midbrain (especially limbic system and hypothalamus) and of the brain stem (especially the reticular activating system) responsible for ethological behavior, primary emotions and sensations, psychic equilibrium and metabiological consciousness. They include, further, the strategic, intuitive and spiritual qualities of the right brain; and last, but not least, the instrumental and action-oriented capabilities of the left hemisphere.
(26) Reflecting Jung's view of personal development and higher consciousness, in: A. Stevens, *Archetype*, p. 262.
(27) A. Stevens, *Archetype*, p. 254. Organically, this means the "establishment of integrated neurological connections between the various brain centers and neurological systems". From: A. Siebert, *Newsletter*, Association for Humanistic Psychology, San Francisco, 8/1983, p. 21.
(28) The biological approach to dreams and dreaming, stated by Jung, exemplifies the importance of the neurological connection between old and recent regions of the brain. Dreams, he believed, "are the means by which the psyche maintains its equilibrium . . . Night after night dreams put us in touch with our phylogenetic past, with the 'unitary soul of humanity', and it is in this extraordinary achievement that their therapeutic importance lies". (See: A. Stevens, *Archetype*, p. 270). Dreams, according to Jung, possess the crucial function "of linking the inherent biogrammar of the species with the conscious awareness of the individual". From: A. Stevens, *Archetype*, p. 274.

Adaptive Therapy

(1) See: A. Stevens, *Archetype*, p. 34.
(2) *Webster's Encyclopedic Unabridged Dictionary of the English Language*, Gramercy Books, New York, 1996, p. 1561.
(3) "While the cerebral cortex is undoubtedly of the greatest significance for

human psychology and neuro-physiology, containing as it does not less than 75 per cent of all the 10 or 12 thousand million neurones in the brain, it must not be forgotten that in all primates the phylogenetically much older parts of the brain still exist and still possess their full functional integrity. Yet for the greater part of this century psychologists have done their best to overlook this fact, devoting themselves tirelessly to the study of cognitive and perceptual processes while leaving emotion and instinct to the biologists." From: A. Stevens, *Archetype*, p, 263.

(4) The archetypes of the phylogenetic psyche refer to universal elements of human life, common to all people, everywhere at all times. Human life and growth then become a matter of developing what is already there. Each person does that differently. Thus, in one sense we are all the same, in another, we are all different. Each "individual life is at the same time the eternal life of the species" (C. G. Jung, *Collected Works 11*, para. 146) and, simultaneously, a unique reenactment of the same story.

(5) All adaptive processes, whether physiological, behavioral or mental, involve the evolutionary principles of self-preservation and self-completion universally present throughout nature—the organic "system incorporates genetic instructions for all the programmes it is potentially capable of executing: the exigencies of life are already 'planned for', the apparent goal being the (survival and the) *wholeness of the individual organism*". From: A. Stevens, *Archetype*, p. 73.

(6) Distress, like all other stress-related forms of human suffering, comes from our beliefs about survival. The psychosomatic model maintains the existence of a mental component in the causation of physical illness and disease. It contends "*that disease and distress can flow from our psychological attitudes towards environmental events*" (I. Oyle, *The New American Medicine Show*, University Press, Santa Cruz, California, 1979, p. 101). The human mind plays a crucial role in the development of illness and disease: the "problem is rooted in attitudes, not organs" (I. Oyle, *Medicine Show*, p. 110). The left brain, logical, sequential and verbal, "has to do with our socialization, language and movement" in the world (P. Pearsall, *Superimmunity: Master Your Emotions & Improve Your Health*, McGraw-Hill Book Company, 1987, p. 31). It is commonly "the weaver and keeper of our beliefs, opinions and shoulds" (I. Oyle, *Medicine Show*, p. 96). The right brain, intuitive, timeless and visual, "has to do with our

ties to our limbic system and emotions" (P. Pearsall, *Superimmunity*, p. 31). It "is responsible for the body" and ultimately our health (I. Oyle, *Medicine Show*, p. 96). Adaptation needs to be seen in light of the psychosomatic model of life. Illness comes with a frame of mind. "The most compelling factors of the environment, the most commonly involved in the causation of disease, are the goals that the individual sets for himself, often without regard for biological necessity" (R. Dubos quoted in P. Pearsall, *Superimmunity*, p. 43). Generally, disease reflects problems of adaptation. The body informs the mind through its afflictions. "All disease is metaphor" (P. Pearsall, *Superimmunity*, p. 20) and it contains a message coded in symbolic, somatic language. Ulcers, spastic colon, irritable bowel syndrome, hypertension, and heart disease, for instance, are maladaptive responses that reflect impatience, hostility and competitiveness (P. Pearsall, *Superimmunity*, pp. 126, 181). The affected organ carries the symbolism: the colon that had to swallow all the anger and anxiety, or the heart that collapsed after being abused like a machine. Diseases, such as allergies, arthritis, infections, diabetes, multiple sclerosis, lupus, or cancer, tend to relate to passivity and feelings of defeat and inadequacy (P. Pearsall, *Superimmunity*, pp. 126, 181). They symbolize a sense of depression and helplessness in life, an inability to cope with survival and a feeling of being overwhelmed by its demands. Understanding the physical symbolism, the body presents, requires an integrated, unified view of human life and functioning. Health and disease are the body's response to the process of adaptation and a consequence of the human mind that governs this process.

(7) Stevens' summary of Jung's view of the relationship between the human being, nature and life. (From: A. Stevens, *Archetype*, p. 35.) The human psyche, like the human body, has a definable structure "which shares a phylogenetic continuity with the rest of the animal kingdom" (A. Stevens, *Archetype*, p. 22), that is, with the rest of creation. Furthermore, modern physics, esp. quantum physics, wave and particle theory, confirms Jung's notion of the essential commonality between psyche and universe: we are made of the same stuff as the universe. See: D. Chopra, *Magical Mind, Magical Body: Mastering the Mind/Body Connection for Perfect Health and Total Well-Being*, tape series, produced by Nightingale Conant Corporation, Niles, Illinois, 1990.

(8) The archetypes of the phylogenetic psyche determine the basic patterns of human life. The archetypes are our tie to biology, nature and life. Jung referred to the archetypes as 'primordial images' inscribed in the brain, later developed by experience (see: A. Stevens, *Archetype*, p. 16). That is to say, the universality of the species represented in the phylogeny of the human psyche becomes individualized in the ontogeny of personal life and development. The evolutionary psyche "contains the whole spiritual heritage of mankind's evolution, born anew in the brain structure of every individual". From: C. G. Jung, *Collected Works 8*, para. 342, quoted in: A. Stevens, *Archetype*, p. 47.

(9) 'Archetypal intent' involves "those archetypal imperatives, inherent within the biogrammar of the maturing Self, which are concerned with the formation of attachment bonds, the establishment of basic trust, and the development of a secure ego conceiving of itself as being both acceptable to others and capable of coping with the eventualities of life". From: A. Stevens, *Archetype*, p. 111.

(10) J. Campbell, ed., *The Portable Jung*, p. XXII.

(11) R. Wilhelm and C. G. Jung, *The Secret of the Golden Flower: A Chinese Book of Life*, Harcourt Brace Jovanovich, Publishers, New York, 1962, p. 13.

(12) Modern society has restructured the conditions and redefined the objectives of human survival by imposing the scientific and economic demands of the industrial life cycle on the life and survival of the individual. See Chapter 7, pp. 170-74.

(13) Human survival rests on the successful effort of the individual to establish a lifelong continuity of integrating the biological and spiritual aspects of life with the cultural reality of society.

(14) The evolutionary qualities of human behavior are reflected in the structure and functioning of society. The rational, scientific design of the modern world has not erased the principles and effects of evolution in human life. Biology, that is biological evolution, has given us territorial, hierarchical, xenophobic, aggressive and sexual propensities we cannot escape. These ethological features are only partially hidden behind the rational facade of the institutions and interactions that form the world modern civilization has created to replace human nature. The evolutionary reality of man's basic ethological nature stands permanently behind the curtain of human life, constituting a deeper and profound dimension of human conduct.

Beneath the surface of human transactions lies the reality of evolutionary adaptation, the urge to survive. People tend to act and react in evolutionary ways when situations involve survival issues. Such situations relate to archetypal needs, values and conditions. The protection of family and property, the performance of work roles, and relationships in courtship, marriage and child-rearing call up evolutionary responses.

(15) For a discussion of archetypes, see Chapter 1, The Natural Foundations of Human Life, pp. 39-43. Both Jung and Freud shared the notion of the unconscious, but differed in its conceptual understanding: "The difference between the Jungian archetypes of the unconscious and Freud's complexes is that the archetypes of the unconscious are manifestations of the organs of the body and their powers. Archetypes are biologically grounded, whereas the Freudian unconscious is a collection of repressed traumatic experiences from the individual's lifetime. The Freudian unconscious is a personal unconscious, it is biographical. The Jungian archetypes of the unconscious are biological. The biographical is secondary to that." From: J. Campbell with B. Moyers, *The Power of Myth*, p. 51.

(16) A. Stevens, *Archetype*, p. 17.

(17) See Chapter 2, pp. 58-87.

(18) Suicide is the human antithesis of survival. Work with suicidal patients is very informative about the validity of psychological systems. Suicide manifests the breakdown of socialized psychology. At a time when a person is questioning all her psychological constructs, she discovers that all learned behaviors, attitudes and values fail her in this moment of crisis. It is only when the effects of cultural conditioning are removed and undone, that the person can reconnect with the powers of her innate psyche and find the strength to move through crisis and to go on living. Suicidal behavior is out of touch with the biological ground of life, divorced from the inherent life force and the law of nature, because of the cultural and neurological suppression of the natural self. The clinical picture of dementia also confirms the stability of these innate psychic structures. Despite hemispheric damage, evolutionary functioning remains intact. The midbrain regulates relationships with the environment. Demented persons continue to respond to contact, support, trust and affection unaffected by the disease even though they may be confused, incoherent and disoriented.

(19) Evolutionary functioning is an innate adaptive capacity of the human psyche. By contrast, culturally conditioned psychology results from social acquisition. Social learning theories, like Transactional Analysis, describe the acquisition process in detail. The conditioned psychology of the individual comes within the domain of the cerebral cortex. Its content is mostly cognitive and partly experiential.

(20) See Chapter 2, pp. 58-60, 74-75, 81-83.

(21) N. Tinbergen, *The Study of Instinct*, Oxford University Press, London, 1951. "Ethology teaches that all organisms are programmed to perceive the world in specific ways, to select and respond to *key stimuli* which possess special significance within the context of the organism's *Umwelt*. This highly specialized ability depends on the existence of central mechanisms for receiving and processing information so that all the stimuli bombarding the organism at any moment can be 'filtered', the significant stimuli eliciting attention while the rest are virtually ignored. In all species, stimuli capable of passing the filter possess the power to release certain specific patterns of behaviour in the organism perceiving them. It was to explain this process that Niko Tinbergen proposed the hypothesis of an innate releasing mechanism (IRM for short)". (From: A. Stevens, *Archetype*, p. 56.) Archetypes are innate patterns of behaviors and needs that relate to survival in response to environmental conditions. "Archetypal projection is not something one chooses to do: it happens to us, whether we like it or not. But there is evidently a natural tendency for the phenomenon to occur. Inherent in every archetype is the notion of unfulfilment: an inner awareness of need. Man needs woman, either as mother or mate, if he is to fulfil himself. The archetype ever seeks its own completion, and when activated reveals that which remains to be attained on the tortuous path forward to individuation." From: A. Stevens, *Archetype*, p. 68.

(22) That is to say, "viewed from the strictly biological standpoint, the archetype is an ancient, genetically determined releaser and inhibitor. From the psychological point of view it is, of course, a good deal more than that, since the survival of the species and the life of each member of the species, depends upon our capacity to 'know' situations, to recognize the essence of what we may find ourselves up against, and our ability to select from the vast repertoire of possible responses the behaviour and strategy most suited to the problem in hand". From: A. Stevens, *Archetype*, p. 54.

(23) Evolutionary functioning needs to be protected against left-brain censorship and a preoccupation with culturally conditioned responses to life.

(24) The history of this taboo shows the consistency of the bias against nature; it involves a rift that has reverberated through Western civilization in all its aspects. Judeo-Christian theology, throughout its history, has launched an attack to invalidate human evolution and to eradicate man's biological nature. Political philosophy has propagated the notion of a 'tabula rasa' to eliminate the evolutionary inheritance of man as a basis of political and social inequality. Behavioristic science has engaged its entire theoretical and laboratory arsenal to disprove the existence of the human unconscious. Favoring rationality and cognition, the scientific revolution has relegated psychic phenomena into the realm of the irrational and non-essential. The technological revolution, finally, has dissolved the mythic tradition that connected man to his archetypal nature. In its place, it has put the secular dogma of material values. "In fact, the whole history of the world since the Renaissance can be summed up in the neurological allegory of the ascent and apotheosis of the dominant hemisphere" (A. Stevens, *Archetype*, p. 278)—the left human brain. Western civilization comes with the prescription of a scientific reality and a homogenized behavioral culture.

(25) C. G. Jung, *Psychological Reflections: A New Anthology of His Writings*, 1905-1961, J. Jacobi, ed., Routledge & Kegan Paul, London, 1971, p. 76, quoted in: A. Stevens, *Archetype*, p. 270.

(26) C. G. Jung, *Psychological Reflections*, p. 76, quoted in: A. Stevens, *Archetype*, p. 270.

(27) The terms 'adaptation' and 'survival' are used in the biological, evolutionary sense.

(28) A. Stevens, *Archetype*, p. 263.

(29) The biological model of psychology which underlies adaptive therapy stresses the universal elements of life and personality preexistent in the genetic make-up of the human being. Jung's assertion and that of biological psychology in general "that all the essential psychic characteristics that distinguish us as human beings are determined by genetics and are with us from birth" (A. Stevens, *Archetype*, p. 16), the evidence of which is increasingly corroborated by modern neurophysiology, sociobiology and

human ethology, put psychology in a very different position. "These typically human attributes Jung called archetypes. He regarded archetypes as basic to all the usual phenomena of human life. While he shared Freud's view that personal experience was of critical significance for the development of each individual, he denied that this development was a process of accretion or absorption occurring in an unstructured personality. On the contrary, for Jung, the essential role of personal experience was *to develop what is already there*—to actualize the archetypal potential already present in the psychophysical organism, to activate what is latent or dormant in the very substance of the personality, to develop what is encoded in the genetic make-up of the individual, in a manner similar to that by which a photographer, through the addition of chemicals and the use of skill, brings out the image impregnated in a photographic plate." (A. Stevens, *Archetype*, p. 16). Jung's psychosomatic model of the human being and human life "proposes a phylogenetic structure, the interstices of which are filled out in the course of ontogenetic development. The phylogenetic structure is made up of archetypal units which possess the dynamic property of seeking their own actualization in the behavior and the developing personality of the individual as he lives out his life cycle within the context of his environmental circumstances". From: A. Stevens, *Archetype*, p. 64.

(30) See below for a detailed discussion of the methodology involved in adaptive therapy.

(31) The generic phylogenetic blueprint reappears in the ontogenetic development of the individual. See Chapter 2, pp. 56-57, for a description of the human brain.

(32) See for a detailed discussion of the formation and functioning of the human brain Chapters 2, 3, pp. 56-57, 89-90.

(33) N. Kazantzakis' book, *Zorba the Greek*, provides a wonderful illustration of the relationship between our internal faculties. This relationship and its components are embodied in the main characters of the book and their interactions. Zorba is the man of the south, the Latin, and the representative of instinct and intuition; the bookkeeper, the Englishman, is the man from the north, the cerebral world, and the representative of the intellect. "The universe for Zorba, as for the first men on earth, was a weighty, intense vision; the stars glided over him, the sea broke against his temples.

He lived the earth, the water, the animals and God, without the distorting intervention of reason." (N. Kazantzakis, *Zorba the Greek*, p. 140). Gradually, the Englishman comes to see the value of instinct and spirit in human life. In the end, he is convinced of their importance—as indicated in the last line of the book: "teach me how to dance". He now wants to go to Zorba's school. The story is partly about the integration of intellect with instinct and intuition; partly about the value of the natural intelligence of instinct and intuition—the unbroken vitality and unschooled wisdom of human nature.

(34) Our modern man-made world is a direct creation of the left cerebral hemisphere. It is an exact replica of the world within, based on the scientific, cultural and social values held by the intellect.

(35) A. Stevens, *Archetype*, p. 265.

(36) The particular strengths of the left brain lie in its logical, abstract and analytic abilities. It is responsible for rational and empirical thought. The propensity of the human intellect for "thinking, planning, using symbols to deputize for actions, are capacities of profound evolutionary significance" (A. Stevens, *Archetype*, p. 61). The left brain is action-oriented; it is "concerned with *doing*, with manipulating the environment" (A. Stevens, *Archetype*, p. 253). Left-hemispheric functioning, however, needs to be viewed with the caveat that it must not be allowed to thwart or usurp the adaptive process by dictating the realities, values and behaviors people should adopt. Left-brain functioning needs to be curtailed to its instrumental status in human adaptation and assigned its proper validity in that context. The adaptive functions of the right brain are equally remarkable. The right brain is basically "the strategic side of the brain" (See: B. B. Tregoe & J. W. Zimmerman, *Top Management Strategy: What It is and How to Make It Work*, Simon and Schuster, New York, 1980, pp. 102-4). It is responsible for synthetic and holistic perception and processes. It lets us see the whole picture, unconstrained by detail; and it makes it possible to transform experiences and thoughts into concepts and decisions. It works effectively without complete information and it enables us to incorporate change. While the left brain is prone to action and manipulation, the right brain "is concerned with monitoring events as they happen, with perceiving the world as it is rather than subjecting it to some purpose or design" (A. Stevens, *Archetype*, p. 253). And, finally, it

allows us to manage reality, a construct of individual and collective consciousness, giving us an internal frame of reference to differentiate between outside influences and stimulus conditions.

(37) A. Stevens, *Archetype*, p. 274. The biological approach to dreams and dreaming, stated by Jung, exemplifies the importance of the neurological connection between old and recent brain regions. Dreams, he believed, "are the means by which the psyche maintains its equilibrium . . . Night after night dreams put us in touch with our phylogenetic past, with the 'unitary soul of humanity', and it is in this extraordinary achievement that their therapeutic importance lies". (From: A. Stevens, *Archetype*, p. 270.) "The evolutionary stratification of the psyche is more clearly discernable in the dream than in the conscious mind . . . (through dreaming) the momentary life of consciousness can once more be brought into harmony with the law of nature from which it all too easily departs, and the patient can be lead back to the natural law of his being." From: C. G. Jung, *Collected Works 18*, para. 351; quoted in: A. Stevens, *Archetype*, p. 270.

(38) C. G. Jung, *Collected Works 13*, para. 2.

(39) The assumption is that the individual's consciousness is either not significant to his well-being, not relevant to therapeutic intervention, or not accessible to psychotherapy.

(40) C. G. Jung, *The Undiscovered Self*, Routledge & Kegan Paul, London, 1982, pp. 26-9.

(41) The religious archetype is the primary psychic function responsible for metabiological adaptation. Jung referred to it with the term 'religious' to indicate that religion usually and traditionally has provided the conceptual framework to deal with "uncontrollable and unpredictable forces" (C. G. Jung, *The Undiscovered Self*, p. 26). Generally speaking, however, the religious archetype enables mental adaptation for a whole spectrum of conceptual systems by providing the connection between experience and meaning.

(42) See: N. Tinbergen, *The Study of Instinct*, Oxford University Press, London, 1951.

(43) For a detailed discussion of ethics see Chapter 1, The Ethics of Biology, pp. 46-48; Chapter 3, The Evolution of Advanced Morality, pp. 97-98; Appendix/The Normative Foundations of Biological Behavior, pp. 349-52.

(44) See: L. Kohlberg, *The Psychology of Moral Development: Vol. II. Essays on Moral Development*, Harper & Row, New York, 1984; L. Kohlberg, *The Development of Moral Judgment and Moral Action*, in: L. Kohlberg et al., *Child Psychology and Childhood Education: A Cognitive-Developmental View*, Longman, New York and London, 1987, pp. 259-328.

(45) In addition to a protracted rearing period, which is longer than that of any other species, modern society has added an extended period of intellectual growth, psychosocial development and instrumental skill training before the young enter adulthood. Adolescence is a creation of modern society. While it is designed to prepare the young person through school and higher education for the ever-increasing intellectual, occupational, social and financial demands of the modern world, it simultaneously reinforces the very dependency it is designed to overcome. Tribal societies practice direct transition from childhood to adulthood. These societies do not have protracted dependency of the offspring. Rituals of initiation and transition establish clear roles and responsibilities at an early age, specifying adult status.

(46) Nature does not support anything that is not fit to survive. It eradicates weakness to secure health and viability of the species. The emphasis is on self-reliance and the ability to survive. Nature serves a somber lesson. It refers to the biological reality of life, where evolution and survival dictate the parameters of existence. Modern society, on the other hand, has for all practical purposes quasi-institutionalized dependency through its institutions and its way of life. The debilitating effects of this practice affect people individually and collectively. Prolonged or conditioned psychosocial dependency decreases self-reliance and survival ability, while increasing insecurity and anxiety.

(47) "The dynamics of personality is to a large extent governed by the necessity for gratifying one's needs by means of transactions with objects in the external world. The surrounding environment provides the hungry organism with food, the thirsty one with water. In addition to its role as the source of supplies, the external world plays another part in shaping the destiny of personality. The environment contains regions of danger and insecurity; it can threaten as well as satisfy. The environment has the power to produce pain and increase tension as well as to bring pleasure and reduce tension. It disturbs as well as comforts." From: C. S. Hall and

G. Lindzey, *Theories of Personality*, John Wiley & Sons, New York, 1970, p. 43.

(48) "Under the pressure of excessive anxiety, the ego is sometimes forced to take extreme measures to relieve the pressure. These measures are called defense mechanisms." From: C. S. Hall and G. Lindzey, *Theories of Personality*, p. 47.

(49) Except for mental disorders as a result of traumatization. In this context, also: some forms of mental disorder are beyond the reach of psychosocial intervention.

(50) The focus of traditional psychotherapy on the culturally conditioned psychology of the individual brings on its own inevitability. Conventional psychology's interest in the person's learned behavior and responses inevitably results in adjustment to society and the reinforcement of its behavioral prescriptions and values. As a descendant of rational Western tradition, socialized psychology is entrapped by its cultural bias of left-hemispheric functioning and its scientific, empirical premises, unable to transcend the confines of its own neurological model and unable to capture the existential essence of a person's life.

(51) The *instinctual* and *spiritual wounds*, incurred by the human psyche (see Chapter 1, The Effects of Human Civilization, pp. 44, 45), are the combined damage to our survival capability. The damage occurred in the relationship to the self, our inherent nature, and in our relationship with the world and the universe. The process of civilization and enculturation has damaged our innate, adaptive capability. Socialization overlays the innate features and abilities of the natural self like asphalt covers natural soil. The actual pathology is on the adaptive level. This wounded state is the focus of adaptive therapy. Healing the wounds of instinct and spirit recovers the adaptive capability of the individual. The adaptive deficit is reflective of Western civilization and the impact of its repressive policies on human nature.

(52) In conjunction with the brain stem, even though attitudinal and spiritual activities involve the right and left cerebral hemispheres.

(53) Freud's model of neurosis views anxiety as a psychological response to the anticipation of a failed or frustrated transaction with the environment for the purpose of need gratification. Anxiety is a culturally conditioned emotional response, indicating a neurological shift from the midbrain to

the neocortex. Adaptation to the environment requires activation of the survival behavior of the midbrain. It cannot be achieved on the level of the culturally conditioned psychology. Socialized psychology is not equipped to do it. Anxiety presents a shift in consciousness in our response to the world. Anxiety is a neocortical issue; fear, on the other hand, relates to midbrain functioning.

(54) Depression, of course, is a form of pain, too. It is, however, a learned and conditioned mental distress, which is self-induced through cognitive thought process (rumination, worry, etc.). Like depression and pain, anxiety and fear are conditioned and evolutionary polarities: one being a mental process of deducing or imagining possible difficulties and threats, the other being an organic response to a real situation of danger. A good recent example of how people learn how to feel is related to the schema of emotions, pertaining to death and dying, outlined in Kuebler-Ross' well-known book of the same title. The book outlines 5 stages of emotional experience (denial, anger, acceptance, etc.). On the basis of this emotional scale, people start to relate their own experiences to the model and to identify their feelings: "I feel x, y, z, therefore, I must be in 'denial'", etc. The issue of learned or conditioned emotion is, of course, much larger. It reflects the entire transformation from biology to culture imposed by modern man.

(55) Traditional psychotherapy potentially reinforces dysfunctional adaptation. It models the conditioned response. Survival is essentially an instinctive response. Adaptive therapy exemplifies functional, effective adaptation. It resorts to human nature and its powers, which are available in the evolutionary psyche and the genetically consolidated survival capability it contains. The evolutionary, biological response to life circumstances is always superior in that it relies on our natural life force and its innate resources. In contrast to traditional psychotherapeutic treatment, adaptive therapy involves the natural adaptive potential of the individual. By redefining the nature of pathology as a deficit in adaptive functioning and by resetting the focus of psychotherapy on the evolutionary psyche, adaptive therapy substantially alters the parameters of psychotherapy.

(56) See: H. Seyle, *The Stress of Life*, McGraw-Hill, New York, 1955. H. Seyle, *Stress Without Distress*, Lippincott, New York, 1974.

(57) The basic structure of the human psyche is preexistent as a result of evolutionary adaptation. This archetypal structure of the evolutionary psyche provides the essential adaptation of human life. However, "since the archetypes evolved to equip us for the hunter/gatherer existence in which our species has lived out 99 per cent of its existence, the archetypal programme equips us for a life which is not always in tune with the life of contemporary urban society" (A. Stevens, *Jung*, Oxford University Press, Oxford/New York, 1996, p. 44). The adaptation to the contemporary environment relative to personality, behavior and skills is mainly social and instrumental. This adaptation, which enables the interface with modern society, is driven by the 'social' or 'conformity' archetype (see: A. Stevens, *Jung*, p. 47). This process begins in childhood. It is motivated by the requirement to be able to function in modern society. Children are taught early on how to behave, how to relate, what they need to know, and what they must be able to do.

(58) Adaptive therapy has a strong developmental component, stressing maturation as the outcome of the personal evolution of the individual. It counteracts the compounding of dependency as a result of the socialization process. The resolution of dependency as the root cause of mental disorder is an issue and a goal that traditional therapy barely addresses or achieves.

(59) Ethological behavior goes back to the hunter/gatherer origins of our species where it constituted a vital element of 'an integrated biobehavior system' to secure human survival. The human survival instinct manifests in the hunting behavior pattern, which has established five particular adaptations: Goal-directedness, strategy-focus, field-independence, social organization, and empiricism. See: W. S. Laughlin, *Hunting, An Integrated Biobehavior System and Its Evolutionary Importance*; in: R. B. Lee & I. Devore, eds., *Man The Hunter*, Aldine Publishing Company, New York, 1982, pp. 304-320.

(60) Commenting on the effects of socialization on the psychology of the child, Eric Berne makes the following observation: "Childhood illusions have mainly to do with rewards for being good and punishments for being bad. Good means mainly not being angry ('Temper, temper!') or sexy ('Nasty, nasty!') but it is all right to be frightened or ashamed. That is, Jeder is not supposed to express either his 'instinct for self-preservation', whose expression can be quite satisfying, or his 'instinct for preservation

of the species', whose expression can be very pleasurable even at an early age; but he is allowed to have as many unsatisfying, unpleasant feelings as he wishes." (From: E. Berne, *What Do You Say After You Say Hello?: The Psychology of Human Destiny*, Grove Press, Inc., New York, (no date), p. 147.) At the very bottom, survival is an instinctual response. The human being possesses the same kind of biological energy and life force as bestowed on any living organism. This energy is the very essence of life itself. It powers the organism and generates vitality. It is the life instinct converted into energy. Instincts form the core behavior in human beings. The instincts involve a repertoire of responses, installed and validated by evolution, to ensure human survival. Therapy needs to reinforce that human survival rests on a powerful natural foundation. Our rudimentary nature is set up and wired for survival.

(61) J. Bowlby, *Attachment and Loss. Volume 1: Attachment*, Hogarth Press and the Institute of Psycho-Analysis, London, 1969, p. 45. Quoted in: A. Stevens, *Archetype*, p. 50.

(62) As a species "we are innately territorial, inclined to mate for life, potentially co-operative with allies and hostile to foes, prone to congregate in hierarchically organized communities, and so on, much in the same way as many other mammalian and primate species" (A. Stevens, *Archetype*, p. 7). We have done that as a species in the past and we are doing it today. The ethological parameters of hierarchy, territory, aggression, sexuality and xenophobia configure the survival reality of human organization and human behavior.

(63) People tend to act and react in evolutionary ways when situations involve survival issues. Such situations relate to archetypal needs and conditions. For instance, the protection of family and property, the performance of work roles, and the relationships in courtship, marriage and child-rearing call up evolutionary responses. Evolutionary principles determine and assist human adaptation.

(64) Ethological rehearsal represents a behavior reinforcement methodology not unlike the practices found in early hunting societies to enhance survival behavior and thus to ensure successful adaptation of individual and group. "Hunting is the master behavior pattern of the human species . . . The total biobehavioral configuration of hunting includes the ethological training of children to be skilled observers of animal

behavior, including other humans ... (Three indispensable parts of the hunting system are programmed into the child beginning early in life. These are the habit of observation, a systematic knowledge of animal behavior, and the interpretation and appropriate action for living with animals and for utilizing them for food and fabricational purposes) ... children are progressively trained to become active hunters ... In any community of hunters it is possible to find general exercises that prepare the child for active hunting ... (to impart) ethological knowledge ... (and) to instruct children in ethology." (W. S. Laughlin, *Hunting: An Integrating Biobehavior System and Its Evolutionary Importance*, in: R. B. Lee and I. Devore, eds., *Man the Hunter*, Aldine Publishing Company, New York, 1982, pp. 304-306.) Education and training in the evolutionary dimension of human life is indispensable for survival. Ethological training is about what works in the real world. It is about getting to know the living world and what to expect from it. Survival involves the evolutionary dimension of life. The instincts reflect the evolutionary reality of life. The instinctive system is central to our survival. Instinctive behavior helps us to adapt to external conditions. The instinctive system bonds us to the biological and psychic energy of the body, our life force. People who use their instincts can rely on an invaluable and inexhaustible fund of wisdom and vitality. Instincts have an uncanny quality of power about them—a personal charisma and crispness, coupled with confidence and certitude in action. Instincts represent an organic source of strength. People who remain separated from their instincts do not have the vigor, purposefulness, directness or sense of relevance and linearity necessary to meet vital life situations. Ethological rehearsal compensates for the impact of socialization on the individual and its subsequent repression of adaptive features. In many ways, it equates to taking a person through the rudimentary steps of self-preservation and survival.

(65) The adaptive teleology of ethological behavior lies in self-preservation. A system of natural inhibitions ensures that self-preservation does not jeopardize the preservation of the species; need gratification, therefore, is not pursued at the expense of others. Modern civilization has removed many of the natural inhibitory mechanisms of human nature, creating a condition that needs to be addressed by biological psychology. Furthermore,

ethological behavior must, therefore, not be confused with violence or destructive aggression with the intent to harm others. See also Chapter 1, The Ethics of Biology, pp. 47-48; Chapter 3, The Evolution of Advanced Morality, p. 97.

(66) Ethological power is crucial to human survival: it enables us to succeed in the competition for resources, to defend our interests and property, to sustain sexual potency, to protect our security, and to hold our own. Ethological power enables us to take a stand in the game of survival. Ultimately, ethological rehearsal intends to restore the behavioral confidence and the instinctive trust in our ability to fulfill our needs. Healing the *instinctual wound* in the psyche, it reverses the effects of 'domestication' on the human being and establishes a state of total confidence with regard to need gratification and the pursuit of our affairs in life.

(67) This program which is under the control of the human archetypes "provides for being parented, exploring the environment, distinguishing familiar figures from strange, learning the language or dialect of one's community, acquiring a knowledge of its values, rules, and beliefs, playing in the peer group, meeting the challenges of puberty and adolescence, being initiated into the adult group, accomplishing courtship and marriage, and child-rearing, contributing to the economy through gathering and hunting, participating in religious rituals and ceremonials, assuming the responsibilities of advanced maturity, old age, and preparation for death". Jung suggested that the "most profound influence of archetypes is in their regulation of the human life cycle". Both quotes from: A. Stevens, *Jung*, Oxford University Press, Oxford and New York, 1996, p. 44.

(68) The key to life lies in our nature. All the things we need to do in order to become fully human are already preformed in the archetypes of our species—the age-old, universal order of events, which takes us from birth to maturity and death. The human being, like any other living creature, needs to follow the design of its nature to find completion and fulfillment. In that sense, we have to be true to 'the nature of the animal we are'. Whether we know it or not, we live not only our own lives but also the life of our species. Our biology defines the basic cycle and needs of human life.

(69) Preexistent also is a pattern of human needs, which, to a large extent,

determines what is important in life. These are the archetypal needs, universal to our species and essential to human survival: the physical need for food, warmth and shelter; the need for security from enemies and predators; the need for community, initiation and identification; the need for language and communication; the need for home and belonging; the need for myth, religion, ritual, codes, values and rules; the economic need for hunting, gathering, and defense against warfare; and the need for a mate, children and family. Nature holds us to these needs, making it our task to satisfy its demands on our survival. It requires life to be on its terms. Nature holds us constantly accountable for any perpetration against its ways. It retaliates with restlessness, depression or disease. Adaptation that accommodates the requirements of human nature results in a life of health and inner peace. There is, of course, nothing new about the nature of human needs: what changes are the cultural circumstances that surround the satisfaction of these needs. Political and social trends, in the same way as economic conditions, tend to influence sentiments toward work, property, marriage, sexuality, family, religion, community, roles, rules, and so forth. Often, this revision of cultural attitudes leads us away from the importance of human nature and its demands on our lives. Also, cultural and social values often compete or conflict with the realization of our basic human needs. In fact, modern society has not only transformed social practice and institutions, it has revised the human life cycle altogether.

(70) "Since the archetypes evolved to equip us for the hunter/gatherer existence in which our species has lived out 99 per cent of its existence, the archetypal programme equips us for a life which is not always in tune with the life of contemporary urban society." From: A. Stevens, *Jung*, Oxford Press, Oxford and New York, 1996, p. 44.

(71) Our world has been described as "materially preoccupied, spiritually impoverished and technologically possessed" (A. Stevens, *Archetype*, p. 279) and quite disconnected from the biological foundations of human life. Most of us are dissociated from our ethological self.

(72) 'Sensation' is one of four psychological functions or types identified by Jung. See: C. G. Jung, *Collected Works 6*.

(73) The examples are many, such as, the transition from self-subsistence to

industrial employment; adolescence as an institutionalized form of delayed maturity; a general condition of heteronomy. Most of these conditions of increased dependence and dependency in modern society are the result of the technological, industrial revolutions and their effects on the sociology of human life.

(74) Biff's outcry that he cannot get a hold on life and hold his life together is symbolic for a civilization that has undercut the biological bearings of human functioning. See: A. Miller, *Death of a Salesman*.

(75) The world is the realm outside and beyond the womb—that place where security ends and reality begins. Womb and world are the cornerstones of the human experience, symbolic of the journey of life and the task of survival. Between them lies a force field of tension and temptation. Although we need to move on in life, it pulls us backwards as we try to "cling on to the comforting assurances of childhood, hoping thereby to halt the inexorable forward motion of the Self, and escape the ordeals of adult life" (A. Stevens, *Archetype*, p. 147). Or as Henry Miller puts it: "Every one, whether consciously or unconsciously, is trying to recover the luxurious, effortless sense of security which he knew in the womb. Those who are able to realize themselves do actually achieve this state; not by a blind, unconscious yearning for the uterine condition, but by transforming the world in which they live into a veritable womb". From: H. Miller, *The Cosmological Eye*, New Directions Publications, New York, 1961, p. 280.

(76) The form of anxiety identified by Freud as the basis of neurosis.

(77) Attitudinal reinforcement goes to the core of the dependency issue in modern society and culture, which developed almost in opposition to the principles of nature. Nature emphasizes self-reliance, the attitude that needs to be there to have a successful and peaceful life. In contrast, modern society tends to foster both dependence and dependency. This is where we have departed from nature at our own peril. Dependency affects individual functioning, both behaviorally and attitudinally, and creates significant adaptive deficits. It undercuts the biological connection with life. When it comes to survival, therefore, most people do not know how to act or how to relate to life. Adaptive therapy addresses the adaptive deficits and demands facing the individual in modern life.

(78) Jung referred to this genetic capability as the religious function or archetype and classified it as an 'instinctive attitude' and part of the evolutionary psyche. (From: C. G. Jung, *The Undiscovered Self*, Routledge & Kegan Paul, London, 1982, pp. 26-8.) This innate ability compensates for the fact that we are conscious beings, aware of our own existence and experiences. It also counterbalances the exposure to facts and forces, which are beyond our control. Without this inborn capacity to maintain psychological equilibrium in the face of unforeseen or uncontrollable events, such experiences would be psychologically unbearable and devastating.

(79) For a person to adapt mentally to difficult or changing conditions means to undergo an adaptive process which sets off a sequence of several steps: (a) first, the *impact* of the external event, followed by (b) the subjective or internal *reaction* to the event; once this experience has bottomed out the instinct ('religious function' or archetype) kicks in, activating the genetic capability 'to maintain the psychic balance' thus initiating (c) a *reversal* in the response process; the reversal leads (d) to *recovery* from the initial impact of the event and, finally, (e) to a coming to terms with the given situation and achieving *resolution* through problem solving, decision making and cognitive expansion by involving the content element of survival consciousness. In summary, the stages of mental adaptation are as follows: impact, reaction, reversal (genetic component), recovery, resolution (content component—cognitive, mental, spiritual). (See also Chapter 2, Psychic Function, pp. 82-83.) The changes and losses we incur in life require that we continuously resurrect ourselves. This is best done by reconnecting with the evolutionary psyche and, at the same time, by dissolving all remnants of history and conditioned psychology attached to these experiences. Recovery from any affliction or trauma needs to go through this process. The assurance that things will work out comes from our survival consciousness. It provides the tools to maintain psychic balance and to have trust in the future.

(80) A person who is insecure, anxious and immature most likely uses a survival concept to deal with difficult situations and conditions, which produces an immediate if superficial sense of security and control. A conceptual system like this would usually be quite rigid and constrictive. On the other hand, a person of substantial psychological maturity would typically

utilize a system of ideas, convictions and beliefs to explain existential events and experiences and to restore the coherence of her world that reflects an extended and profound life experience.

(81) Both educational reorientation and practice are designed to address the lack of awareness and the ensuing dormancy of adaptive capabilities as a result of the cultural repression of the natural self.

(82) The cure of modern man rests on his willingness and ability to make contact with the resources inherent in his own nature. Man has to reconnect with the biological foundations of his life and to reconcile himself with the "2 million year-old man that is in all of us" (C. G. Jung, *Psychological Reflections*, J. Jacobi, ed., Routledge & Kegan Paul, London, 1971, p. 76). Survival in the modern world is difficult. The heteronomy of modern life has created survival conditions that require strong and reliable measures (see: Rationale for Adaptive Therapy, below pp. 339-41). It requires us to reactivate and apply our biological capacity to survive and create our destiny. Evolution has established hunting as the 'master behavior pattern of our species'. Applying this pattern to our lives enables us to draw upon the resources of our own nature that we acquired during a long evolutionary history.

(83) Jung "asserted that all the essential psychic characteristics that distinguish us as human beings are determined by genetics and are with us from birth" (A. Stevens, *Archetype*, p. 16). Jung called these typically human attributes archetypes. The "archetypes are 'identical psychic structures common to all' (CW V, para. 224), which together constitute 'the archaic heritage of humanity' (CW V, para. 259)" (A. Stevens, *Jung*, Oxford University Press, Oxford/New York, 1996, p. 33). The "archetypal determinants of the phylogenetic psyche" (A. Stevens, *Archetype*, p. 58) form the *a priori structure* of human experience and determine the life cycle of the individual. Individual life evolves against the background of the evolutionary experience of the species: "the mental events experienced by every individual are determined not merely by his personal history, but by the collective history of the species as a whole (biologically encoded in the collective unconscious), reaching back into the primordial mists of evolutionary time". From: A. Stevens, *Archetype*, p. 39.

(84) Cultural evolution in the Western hemisphere was designed to dissociate our species from the course of biological evolution and history. As a

civilization, we have turned against nature. In rejecting nature as the salient aspect of our psychology and our world, we have refuted much of our own biological wisdom and the natural order of things—incurring the principal hubris that haunts modern civilization in the divorce and bankruptcy courts, psychiatric offices and confession booths, in the crime rates, poverty statistics, military budgets, ecological disasters and political conflicts, which make up the symptomatology of a world out of sync with itself.

(85) See: A. Stevens, *Archetype*, p. 37. "Believing as I do," wrote Darwin, "that man in the distant future will be a far more perfect creature than he now is, it is an intolerable thought that he and all other sentient beings are doomed to complete annihilation after such long continued slow progress." (Quoted in: A. Stevens, *Archetype*, p. 37). "Ultimately, the distinction between organic and inorganic matter is artificial, like the distinction between mind and body, a hypothetical construct developed to assist our comprehension of reality. Thus, the theory of evolution will not have been properly worked out until it has been carried back beyond the emergence of the simplest living organisms to encompass the changes occurring in the inorganic substance from which these organisms arose" (A. Stevens, *Archetype*, p. 71). This view of evolution acknowledges not only our biological past and our genetic endowment, but also our animal nature and the homologues of features with other species, especially mammalian. Archetypal structures are "fundamental to the existence of all living organisms" and are "continuous with structures controlling the behaviour of inorganic matter" (A. Stevens, *Archetype*, p. 71). In fact, Jung wrote: "The deeper 'layers' of the psyche lose their individual uniqueness as they retreat farther and farther into the darkness. 'Lower down', that is to say as they approach the autonomous functional systems, they become increasingly collective until they are universalized and extinguished in the body's materiality, i.e. in chemical substances. The body's carbon is simply carbon. Hence, 'at bottom' the psyche is simply 'world'". From: C. G. Jung, *Collected Works 9, Part I*, para. 291.

(86) Jung is given credit for building "a bridge between Darwin and God" in the sense that he "had reconciled the highest achievements of the human spirit with the base materials out of which that spirit had evolved" (A. Stevens, *Archetype*, p. 16). "Post-Darwinian biology, like the mythologies and religions of old, is capable of yielding a unified view of the origin and

nature of existence, a view capable of encompassing and reconciling the vast diversity of living forms and their behaviour, and establishing their fundamental continuity through the living protoplasmic thread of evolution. Without being anthropomorphic or sentimental, ethology enables us to comprehend the wonderful complexity of animal life, to place ourselves in relation to it, and, in the process, to re-establish the connection between ourselves and nature, thus healing the breach which opened up, to our spiritual impoverishment, at the beginning of the scientific revolution." From: A. Stevens, *Archetype*, p 36.

(87) Psychosomatic medicine, as well as, modern physics and sociobiology have shown us that the divisions between body and mind, life and nature, psyche and cosmos, between humans and the rest of creation, are artificial and hypothetical. The "human psyche, like the human body, has a definable structure which shares a phylogenetic continuity with the rest of the animal kingdom". From: A. Stevens, *Archetype*, p. 22.

(88) Modern quantum physics tells us that we are intelligent beings in an intelligent universe and that there is no separation between individual and universe. Also see: D. Chopra, *Quantum Healing: Exploring the Frontiers of Mind/Body Medicine*, Bantam Books, Doubleday Dell Publishing Group, Inc., New York, 1990; D. Chopra, *Creating Affluence: Wealth Consciousness in The Field of All Possibilities*, Amber-Allen Publishing, San Rafael, California, 1994.

(89) A. Stevens, *Archetype*, p. 38.

(90) A. Stevens, *Archetype*, p. 36.

Depression As a Case in Point

(1) A person's survival capacity is most commonly weakened by cultural conditioning; but adaptive response capability may also be impaired or inhibited as a result of traumatization.

(2) Mood disorders, respectively depressive episodes, usually include symptoms such as depressed mood, diminished interest or pleasure, significant weight loss, insomnia or hypersomnia, psychomotor agitation or retardation, fatigue or loss of energy, feelings of worthlessness, feelings of excessive or inappropriate guilt, diminished concentration, indecisiveness, recurrent thoughts of death. Source: *Diagnostic and Statistical Manual of Mental Disorders*, Forth Edition, published by the

American Psychiatric Association, Washington, D.C., 1994, pp. 317-391, specifically, p. 327.
(3) See: C. S. Hall and G. Lindzey, *Theories of Personality*, John Wiley & Sons, Inc., New York, 1970, pp. 43-47.
(4) The existential ground of anxiety lies in the 'instinctual wound'; see Chapter 1, The Effects of Human Civilization, p. 44.

The Normative Foundations of Biological Behavior

(1) These natural inhibitions of the human instincts depend on physical proximity. They involve body language, gestures, facial expressions. For a detailed discussion of the biological inhibitions of instinctual behavior, see: I. Eibl-Eibesfeldt, *Love and Hate*, pp. 90-105; also see pp. 106-28 and pp. 129-69.
(2) I. Eibl-Eibesfeldt, *Die Biologie des Menschlichen Verhaltens*, pp. 863-885.
(3) I. Eibl-Eibesfeldt, *Love and Hate*, p. 99.
(4) I. Eibl-Eibesfeldt, *Love and Hate*, p. 99.
(5) I. Eibl-Eibesfeldt, *Love and Hate*, p. 102.
(6) I. Eibl-Eibesfeldt, *Love and Hate*, p. 106.
(7) I. Eibl-Eibesfeldt, *Love and Hate*, p. 129.
(8) I. Eibl-Eibesfeldt, *Love and Hate*, pp. 106-211.
(9) See natural inhibitions of aggression, in: I. Eibl-Eibesfeldt, *Love and Hate*, pp. 95-102. The adaptive function of the instincts is remarkably resistant to modification. It takes extraordinary measures to corrupt the instinct and to convert its adaptive qualities into destructive deviance. But it can be done: "Among the military fraternities of Ancient Germany a young man, as part of his training to stifle inhibitions against killing, was required to strip naked; to dress himself in the hot, freshly flayed skin of a bear; to work himself into a 'bestial' rage: in other words, to go, quite literally, berserk. 'Bearskin' and 'berserk' are the same word. The helmets of the Royal Guards, on duty outside Buckingham Palace, are the descendants of this primitive battle costume." (From: B. Chatwin, *The Songlines*, Elisabeth Sifton Books, Viking Penguin Inc., New York, 1987, p. 217.) The biological reference to normative conduct is reiterated in mythology, the symbolic template of the archetypal life of the species:

"... whether myths are the coded messages of instinct, whose structures will reside in the central nervous system, or tales of instruction handed down from the Year Dot. One point cannot be emphasised too strongly. Seldom, if ever, in myth, is it desirable, morally, for a man to kill a man in cold blood". From: B. Chatwin, *Songlines*, p. 217.

(10) Statement by Arthur Koestler during a public lecture. Quoted in: B. Chatwin, *Songlines*, p. 211.
(11) I. Eibl-Eibesfeldt, *Love and Hate*, p. 101.
(12) I. Eibl-Eibesfeldt, *Love and Hate*, pp. 101-2. Also see: K. Lorenz, *Das sogenannte Boese*, Borotha-Schoeler, Wien, 1963.

Selected Bibliography

Attenborough, David, *Life on Earth: A Natural History*, Little, Brown and Company, Boston-Toronto, 1979.
Bronowski, Jacob, *The Ascent of Man*, Published by the British Broadcasting Corporation, London, 1980.
Campbell, Joseph, *The Hero With a Thousand Faces*, Bollingen Series, Princeton, New Jersey, 1973.
Campbell, Joseph, *Myths to Live By*, Bantam Books, The Viking Press, Inc., New York, 1980.
Campbell, Joseph, *The Portable Jung*, ed., Penguin Books Ltd, Harmondsworth, Middlesex, England, 1986.
Campbell Joseph with Bill Moyers, *The Power of Myth*, Doubleday, New York, 1988.
Eibl-Eibesfeldt, Irenaeus, *Die Biologie des menschlichen Verhaltens: Grundriss der Humanethologie*, Piper Verlag, Munich-Zurich, 1986.
Eibl-Eibesfeldt, Irenaeus, *Grundriss der vergleichenden Verhaltensforschung: Ethologie*, Piper Verlag, Munich-Zurich, 1987.
Eibl-Eibesfeldt, Irenaeus, *Love and Hate: The Natural History of Behavior Patterns*, Aldine de Gruyter, New York, 1996.
Jung, Carl G., *The Collected Works*, H. Read, et al., eds., Routledge & Kegan Paul, London, 1953-78.
Jung, Carl G., *Modern Man in Search of A Soul*, Ark Paperbacks, Routledge & Kegan Paul, London, Melbourne and Henley, 1984.
Jung, Carl G., *Man and His Symbols*, Doubleday & Company, New York, 1979.
Leakey, Louis S. B., *Adam's Ancestors: The Evolution of Man and His Culture*, Methuen and Company, London, 1934.
Lorenz, Konrad, *Ueber tierisches und menschliches Verhalten: Aus dem*

Werdegang der Verhaltenslehre, Band I und II, Piper Verlag, Munich-Zurich, 1981.

Lorenz, Konrad, *Das Wirkungsgefuege der Natur und das Schicksal des Menschen*, Piper Verlag, Munich-Zurich, 1983.

Stevens, Anthony, *Archetype: A Natural History of the Self*, Routledge & Kegan Paul, London and Henley, 1982.

Van der Post, Laurens, *Jung and The Story of Our Time*, Penguin Books Ltd., Harmondsworth, Middlesex, England, 1985.

Van der Post, Laurens, *The Heart of The Hunter*, Penguin Books Ltd., Harmondsworth, Middlesex, England, 1983.

Van der Post, Laurens, *A Walk With a White Bushman*, Penguin Books, published by the Penguin Book Group, London, 1986.

BVG